LANGUAGE LEARNING STRATEGIES

LANGUAGE LEARNING STRATEGIES

What Every Teacher Should Know

Rebecca L. Oxford

The University of Alabama

HEINLE & HEINLE PUBLISHERS
A Division of Wadsworth, Inc.
Boston, Massachusetts 02116

Director: Laurie E. Likoff
Production Coordinator: Cynthia Funkhouser
Cover Design: 20/20 Services, Inc.
Compositor: Crane Typesetting Service, Inc.

Language Learning Strategies: What Every Teacher Should Know

Library of Congress Cataloging in Publication Data

Oxford, Rebecca L.
Language learning strategies : what every teacher should know / by Rebecca L. Oxford.
p. cm.

1. Language and languages—Study and teaching. I. Title.
P51.094 1989
418′.0071—dc20 89-13109
CIP

63-26078 91 92 93 9 8 7 6 5 4

This book is dedicated to my family—David, Merry Lou, George, Tom, Ellie, and Mac—my most loving supporters.

It is also dedicated to the memory of Charles Meister, my favorite and best teacher, by whom I was first challenged to learn.

Foreword

In recent years there has been a shift in focus from the teacher to the learner—from exclusive focus on the improvement of teaching to an increased concern for how learners go about their learning tasks in a second or foreign language. It has become clearer that much of the responsibility for success at language learning rests with individual learners and with their ability to take full advantage of opportunities to learn. This being the case, books which train language learners directly and those which are intended to train teachers to train learners, such as this volume by Rebecca Oxford, are now clearly in vogue.

The appearance of Oxford's book marks a turning point in the treatment of learner strategies in foreign and second language learning. For the first time since learners and their strategies have begun to receive prime attention, there appears on the market a solo-authored volume that combines a solid theoretical basis and an astute mastery of the research literature with an impressive array of practical suggestions to teachers concerning how to train their students to be more successful language learners. The book presents, among other things, a new strategy classification system, suggested means for assessing students' learning strategies, and a model for strategy training accompanied by numerous strategy training exercises. The concept of strategy training is brought to life by a chapter describing a number of actual strategy training projects.

As a further testimonial to the value of the book, the volume underwent field testing and was received quite favorably by teachers, teacher trainees, and language learners. It was found, for example, that incorporating strategy training exercises into regular classroom activities, and treating learning strategies as a means of enhancing progress that students were already making, was more beneficial than having the exercises constitute a separate entity, disconnected from ongoing classroom work. This book was found to heighten an awareness of how to learn in general, not just how to learn languages.

It is most fortunate that the field of foreign and second language learning has a researcher, teacher trainer, and learner trainer as dedicated as Rebecca Oxford, and her book should serve the field well for many years to come.

Andrew D. Cohen
Jerusalem

Preface

A more practiced eye,
A more receptive ear,
A more fluent tongue,
A more involved heart,
A more responsive mind.

These are the characteristics we want to stimulate in students to enable them to become more proficient language learners. This book helps teachers encourage such qualities by means of *language learning strategies,* actions taken by second and foreign language learners to control and improve their own learning. Learning strategies are keys to greater autonomy and more meaningful learning. Although learning strategies are used by students themselves, teachers play an important role in helping students develop and use strategies in more effective ways.

A PERSONAL TALE

Language Learning Strategies: What Every Teacher Should Know is the result of years of struggling with issues of language learning and teaching. In my own school and university experience, most of the foreign language instruction was in the grammar-translation mode, consisting of memorized word lists, recited passages, verbatim translations scribbled in book margins, and no real interaction in the language. It was a painful shock to discover that most of my language teachers did not view communication as a priority, and the few who did care about communication knew little or nothing about how to help their students learn to communicate. Therefore, I spent many years making straight A's in my language courses but secretly feeling like a communicational failure.

Totally discouraged with language instruction as I experienced it, I began to take events into my own hands. Against what seemed to be insurmountable institutional odds, I started assuming some personal responsibility for my own language learning. I invented my own private strategies for learning new languages, techniques including making mental linkages, grouping and comparing words, and using pictures and colors. Eventually it dawned on me that new languages could be learned more readily through foreign travel, living abroad, and correspondence with foreign friends, and with great personal effort I began to use those techniques, too. Little did I know that these and other strategies had been potentially accessible the whole time, but that the instructional establishment had simply not understood the need to encourage learners to use such strategies.

By the time I became a language teacher, audiolingualism had arisen as a challenge to grammar-translation, and they both shared the stage as the primary language instructional methodologies. The language teaching profession was still not ready for much real communication. Nevertheless, I ventured to bring some homemade communicative instructional activities into the classroom. I also shared a few treasured learning strategies with my students, though I had no name for them; language learning strategies had not yet been "discovered."

Much has changed since that time. Communication at last seems to be a priority in many language classrooms. Communicative language instruction and its measurement-focused twin, proficiency-oriented instruction, have taken hold. Language learning strategies, based on the idea of learner self-direction, are beginning to command attention around the world. Now teachers require a practical and simple guidebook to help them in two ways: to understand learning strategies, and to train students in using better strategies in the context of a communicative approach to language learning. Born of my own grappling with language instruction, this book is intended to meet teachers' need for such a guidebook.

WHO CAN BENEFIT FROM THIS BOOK

This book is mainly for teachers of second or foreign languages at secondary, university, and adult levels, but language teachers in elementary schools are sure to find many useful ideas here as well. It will be especially useful for teachers seeking ways to help students become more active, self-directed, and effective learners. This book need not be used only by teachers in traditional academic settings; language trainers in international business settings, government agencies, and military institutions will also find it valuable. *Language Learning Strategies* can be used as a text for experienced teachers enrolled in advanced degree programs or in-service training workshops on learning strategies, communicative language instruction, proficiency-oriented instruction, or active learning of any kind. In addition, the book will be helpful as a course text for individuals who are training to become language teachers.

Because many learning strategies useful for languages are also applicable to other subject areas, teachers outside the language field may find a wealth of practical ideas within these covers. In this book, researchers are likely to uncover new areas of investigation, and language students may obtain useful strategy suggestions.

WHAT THIS BOOK OFFERS

Because the field of language learning strategies is so new, few books currently exist on the topic. This book is unlike other existing resources in that it

- Contains a clear, eight-step model for strategy training and a large number of ready-to-use-or-adapt strategy training exercises covering all four language skills.
- Presents useful surveys for assessing students' learning strategies with clear directions for administration and use, along with student profile sheets.
- Contains a new strategy system covering six main types of strategies in a coherent and consistent way, with visual and verbal cues throughout the book to help readers remember the system.
- Offers a networking chapter with real-life illustrations of learning strategies in action around the world.
- Is based on the latest language learning strategy research, which is interwoven in a practical, useful fashion throughout the text with detailed references in the chapter notes.
- Provides concrete examples of language learning strategies using different languages, such as English, French, German, Spanish, Russian, Italian, and Japanese, and different learning tasks and situations.
- Has been thoroughly field-tested with teachers in a variety of language learning settings.
- Makes extensive use of pictures and diagrams to highlight important material and spark interest.

ACKNOWLEDGMENTS

Thanks go especially to David Crookall of the University of Toulon, France (now at the University of Alabama). For almost two years he shared his rich instructional experience, computer skills, and affection as I wrote this book, thereby aiding me more than I can say. David also kindly provided some of his own student exercises for inclusion in this book.

I am deeply grateful to the five people who led the field test: H. Douglas Brown of San Francisco State University, San Francisco, California; W. Flint Smith and Joseph Wipf of Purdue University, West Lafayette, Indiana; Roberta Z. Lavine of the University of Maryland, College Park, Maryland; and Will Sutter of the Danish Refugee Council and the North Jutland Department of Adult Education, Aalborg, Denmark. Their comments were invaluable to me in making the final revisions, and their conclusions will be helpful to many readers. Flint was particularly adept and generous in helping me make key editorial decisions. Equally important was the support of my esteemed colleague and friend from the School of Education of the Hebrew University of Jerusalem, Andrew D. Cohen, whose constant letters gave me encouragement and excellent ideas.

To my "right arm" during the final draft stages, Haru Yamada, I give my loving gratitude. Mary Ann Zima and Melissa Eliason offered their expert editorial skills and gently assisted the book through labor and birth. Olivia Stockard, independent consultant and long-time friend, checked the sources of many favorite quotations. The editors at Newbury House Publishers, first Leslie Berriman and later Laurie Likoff, Director, facilitated my effort in several ways, most especially by suggesting the field test, the results of which increased the practical usefulness of the book. My dear friend and research colleague, Martha Nyikos of Indiana University, and her talented sister, Katalin Nyikos of Georgetown University, were helpful in modifying a previous version of the Strategy Inventory for Language Learning for use with learners of English. Another close friend and colleague, Madeline Ehrman of the Foreign Service Institute (FSI), has worked with me for almost four years on research studies and has been a catalyst for my thinking about learning styles and strategies.

For their strategy-related suggestions and material contributions, past or present, I am personally indebted to Judith Englert Brooks of the Army Research Institute for the Behavioral and Social Sciences (ARI), Anna Uhl Chamot of InterAmerica Research Associates, Kuan-Yi Rose Chang of the University of West Virginia, Donald Dansereau of Texas Christian University, Sally Hague of Duval County (Florida) Public Schools, Betty Leaver and John Lett of the Defense Language Institute Foreign Language Center, Anne Lomperis of Dade County Public Schools, Maria Matheidesz of the International House in Budapest (Hungary), Barbara McCombs of the Denver Research Institute, Douglas Morgenstern of the Massachusetts Institute of Technology, J. Michael O'Malley of Georgetown University, Joan Rubin of Joan Rubin Associates, Anna Smith of Project GRASP (England), and Anita Wenden of the City University of New York.

Finally, I am thankful to the more than one thousand language teachers who have attended my strategy workshops or have written or called to ask for information about strategies. Your enthusiasm underscores the value of language learning strategies. This book is chiefly directed to you and your teaching colleagues around the world. My challenge to all language teachers is to help students use better learning strategies, so that their eyes will be more practiced, their ears more receptive, their tongues more fluent, their hearts more involved, and their minds more responsive.

Rebecca L. Oxford
Tuscaloosa, Alabama

Contents

List of Tables

List of Figures

Chapter **1**

Looking at Language Learning Strategies

It takes better teachers to focus on the learner.
PETER STREVENS

PREVIEW QUESTIONS

1. Why are language learning strategies important?
2. How can this book best be used to understand learning strategies?
3. What terms are useful for understanding the learning strategy concept?
4. What are the most important features of language learning strategies?
5. How can language learning strategies be classified?

WHY LEARNING STRATEGIES ARE IMPORTANT

Learning strategies are steps taken by students to enhance their own learning. Strategies are especially important for language learning because they are tools for active, self-directed involvement, which is essential for developing communicative competence. Appropriate language learning strategies result in improved proficiency and greater self-confidence.

Although researchers have formally discovered and named language learning strategies only recently, such strategies have actually been used for thousands of years. One well-known example is the mnemonic or memory devices used in ancient times to help storytellers remember their lines. Throughout history, the best language students have used strategies, ranging from naturalistic language practice techniques to analytic, rule-based strategies.

Now, for the first time, learning strategies are becoming widely recognized throughout education in general. Under various names, such as learning skills, learning-to-learn skills, thinking skills, and problem-solving skills, learning strategies are the way students learn a wide range of subjects, from native language reading through electronics troubleshooting to new languages. Within the language instruction field, teachers are starting to discuss learning strategies among themselves. Learning strategy workshops are drawing big crowds at language teachers' conventions. Researchers are identifying, classifying, and evaluating language learning strategies, and these efforts are resulting in a steady stream of articles on the topic. Most encouraging of all, increasing numbers of language learners are beginning to recognize the power of their own strategies.

This chapter explains the organization and best use of this book, some important terms, key characteristics of language learning strategies, and a comprehensive classification system for language learning strategies.

ORGANIZATION AND BEST USE OF THIS BOOK

The major purpose of this book is to make learning strategies understandable to teachers of second and foreign languages, so they can enable students to become better learners. Others, too, may find useful ideas here [1]. To use the book most effectively, observe how its chapters are organized and notice their practical emphasis. Each chapter offers preview questions, a summary, activities to help you expand your understanding, and exercises to use with your students. In two "applications" chapters (3 and 5), the activities and exercises are intentionally as long as the chapter narrative, thus underscoring the hands-on nature of the book.

Appendices A through C present a useful strategy assessment survey. Appendix D lists sources of quotations used in this book. To make it easier for you to locate activities and exercises relevant to your own needs, *How to Find Activities for Readers* (Appendix E) and *How to Find Exercises to Use with Your Students* (Appendix F) are included. If you want to find all the strategies connected with a particular language skill, consult *Strategy Applications Listed According to Each of the Four Language Skills* (Appendix G).

The chapter you are now reading presents a general overview of the concept of language learning strategies. Chapter 2 examines three kinds of direct strategies for dealing with a new language, and Chapter 3 applies those strategies to the language skills of listening, reading, speaking, and writing. Chapter 4 explores three kinds of indirect strategies for managing learning, while Chapter 5 shows how these indirect strategies are used in developing all language skills. Chapter 6 describes techniques for assessing language learning strategies and presents a model for training with these strategies. Chapter 7 gives examples of learning strategy use around the world. Finally, the epilogue offers specific ideas about the next steps to take, and the notes provide crucial research data.

Guidelines for General Readers

Most readers of this book might be called general readers, who are interested equally in gaining a broad understanding of language learning strategies and in discovering a variety of applications. If you are one of these readers, you will want to read the chapters in the order in which they are given. By following this sequence, you will find out about language learning strategies in a step-by-step way, going from the overall strategy system to specific strategies, then moving to assessment and training applications and real-life examples.

To get the most from this book, read *actively* by using such strategies as purposeful reading and getting the idea quickly by using the preview questions (see Chapters 2 and 4 for definitions of these two strategies). Many of the reading strategies described in this book are as valuable for reading in one's own native language as they are for reading in a second or foreign language. Pay attention to the examples and illustrations. Do some or all of the readers' activities at the end of the chapters. With creative adaptation, almost all of the activities can be done in a variety of ways—alone, in a pair, or in a group.

Go beyond the readers' activities to the exercises you can use with your students. These are classroom exercises which make language learning strategies come alive for your own learners. Assess your students' learning strategies and give them information about their strategies. Ask them to focus on what they *do* in the process of learning the new language. Conduct learning strategy training with your students, making the training relevant to regular classroom language activities.

Apply the information in this book as much as you can. Reflect on it. Talk with your colleagues about it. Ask for help from others. Come back to the book for further guidance whenever you need it. Any book like this one, filled with ideas and suggestions, can be a valuable resource and a good friend to have around for a long time.

Guidelines for Readers Interested Mainly in Specific Strategy Assessment and Training Techniques

Some readers might have chosen this book primarily to find out about particular strategy assessment and training techniques. If you are such a reader, you might read this chapter to obtain an overview of the strategy system and then move immediately to Chapter 6, where strategy assessment and training are the focus. However, don't forget to return later to Chapters 2 through 5 in order to learn more about specific strategies and their applications, and don't miss the examples of strategies in action around the world as described in Chapter 7. Be sure to try out the activities and exercises. Strategy assessment and training are meaningful only if you understand particular strategies and how they can be used in real instances.

A WORD ABOUT TERMINOLOGY

Like any book, this book uses terms in certain ways, and it is helpful to understand these at the outset. The following are some important terms: *learning and acquisition, process orientation, four language skills, second language and foreign language, communication, communicative competence,* and *learning strategies.*

Learning and Acquisition

According to one well-known contrast, *learning* is conscious knowledge of language rules, does not typically lead to conversational fluency, and is derived from formal instruction. *Acquisition,* on the other hand, occurs unconsciously and spontaneously, does lead to conversational fluency, and arises from naturalistic language use [2]. Some specialists even suggest that learning cannot contribute to acquisition, i.e., that "conscious" gains in knowledge cannot influence "subconscious" development of language.

However, this distinction seems too rigid. It is likely that learning and acquisition are not mutually exclusive but are rather parts of a potentially integrated range of experience. "Our knowledge about what is conscious and what is subconscious is too vague for us to use the [learning-acquisition] distinction reliably," says one expert [3]; moreover, some elements of language use are at first conscious and then become unconscious or automatic through practice. Many language education experts [4] suggest that both aspects—acquisition and learning—are necessary for communicative competence, particularly at higher skill levels. For these reasons, a learning-acquisition continuum is more accurate than a dichotomy in describing how language abilities are developed [5]. In this book the term *learning* is used as a shorthand for the longer phrase *learning and acquisition.* The term *language learner* (or just *learner*) is used here in preference to more awkward terms, such as *language acquirer* or *language learner or acquirer.*

Language learning strategies contribute to all parts of the learning-acquisition continuum. For instance, analytic strategies are directly related to the learning end of the continuum, while strategies involving naturalistic practice facilitate the acquisition of language skills, and guessing and memory strategies are equally useful to both learning and acquisition. For ease of expression, the term *learning strategies* is used in this book to refer to strategies which enhance any part of the learning-acquisition continuum.

Process Orientation

Interest has been shifting from a limited focus on merely *what* students learn or acquire—the *product* or *outcome* of language learning and acquisition—to an expanded focus that also includes *how* students gain language—the *process* by which learning or acquisition occurs. This new emphasis involves looking at a variety of process factors: the development of an interlanguage (the learner's hybrid form of language use that ranges somewhere in between the first or native language and the actual new language being learned), the kinds of errors and mistakes the learner makes and the reasons for them, the learner's social and emotional adaptation to the new language and culture, the amount and kind of activities available to the learner inside and outside of class, and the learner's reactions to specific classroom techniques and methods and to out-of-class experiences with the language. Most relevant to this book, the process orientation also implies a strong concern for the learner's strategies for gaining language skills.

Interestingly, the process orientation (building on general systems theory, in which all phenomena are part of a dynamic system) forces us to consider not just the language learning process itself but also the *input* into this process. The general term *input* might include a variety of student and teacher characteristics, such as intelligence, sex, personality, general learning or teaching style, previous experience, motivation, attitudes, and so on. Input might also include many societal and institutional factors, such as unspoken and often inaccurate generalizations about particular students or about whole groups (e.g., simplistic expectations like "Girls must learn to be good wives and mothers, while boys must go out and conquer the world with their achievements," or overly stereotypical attitudes like "All Asian students are 'grinds' who study all the time"). It is important to identify the input factors in order to understand and interpret more clearly both the process and the outcome of language learning or acquisition.

Four Language Skills

Gaining a new language necessarily involves developing four modalities in varying degrees and combinations: listening, reading, speaking, and writing. Among language teachers, these modalities are known as the *four language skills*, or just the *four skills*. Culture and grammar are sometimes called skills, too, but they are somewhat different from the Big Four; both of these intersect and overlap with listening, reading, speaking, and writing in particular ways. The term *skill* simply means ability, expertness, or proficiency. Skills are gained incrementally during the language development process.

Second Language and Foreign Language

The *target language*, or language being learned, can be either a *second language* or a *foreign language*. Throughout this book the term *target language* is used as a generic phrase to cover the two circumstances, second language learning and foreign language learning. This "second versus foreign" distinction is often baffling to teachers, students, parents, and the general public. Nevertheless, it is important to understand the difference, since these terms appear so often in language instructional texts and sometimes galvanize competing camps of educators.

The difference between learning a second language and learning a foreign language is usually viewed in terms of where the language is learned and what social and communicative functions the language serves there. A *second language* has social and communicative functions within the community where it is learned. For example, in multilingual countries like Belgium or Canada, people need more than one language for social, economic, and professional reasons. Refugees or immigrants usually have to learn a second language in order to survive in their adopted country. In contrast, a *foreign language* does not have immediate social and communicative functions within the community where it is learned; it is employed mostly to communicate elsewhere. For instance, one might learn Russian in the USA, English in France, or German in Australia [6].

This book accepts that the differences between second language contexts and foreign language contexts are real, and that these differences occasionally have implications for language learning strategies. Some learning strategies might be easier to use in second language contexts than in foreign language settings, or vice versa. However, most learning strategies can be applied equally well to both situations. Therefore, in the rest of this book it is usually unnecessary to highlight the distinctions between second language learning strategies and foreign language learning strategies.

Communication, Communicative Competence, and Related Concepts

The word *communication* comes from a Latin word for "commonness," including the prefix *com-* which suggests togetherness, joining, cooperation, and mutuality. Therefore, communication is definable as "a mutual exchange between two or more individuals which enhances cooperation and establishes commonality" [7]. Communication is also seen as dynamic, not static, and as depending on the negotiation of meaning between two or more persons who share some knowledge of the language being used [8].

Communicative competence is, of course, competence or ability to communicate. It concerns both spoken or written language and all four language skills [9]. Some people mistakenly think of communication as occurring only through the medium of speech. In fact, even language learning experts have commonly used the term *communication strategies* to refer only to certain types of speaking strategies, thus unwittingly giving the false impression that the skills of reading, listening, and writing—and the language used via these modalities—are not really equal partners in communication [10].

One very useful model [11] provides a comprehensive, four-part definition of communicative competence:

1. *Grammatical competence* or *accuracy* is the degree to which the language user has mastered the linguistic code, including vocabulary, grammar, pronunciation, spelling, and word formation.
2. *Sociolinguistic competence* is the extent to which utterances can be used or understood appropriately in various social contexts. It includes knowledge of speech acts such as persuading, apologizing, and describing.
3. *Discourse competence* is the ability to combine ideas to achieve cohesion in form and coherence in thought, above the level of the single sentence [12].
4. *Strategic competence* is the ability to use strategies like gestures or "talking around" an unknown word in order to overcome limitations in language knowledge.

Ways in which language learning strategies contribute to the goal of communicative competence are described later in this chapter.

Learning Strategies

To understand learning strategies, let us go back to the basic term, *strategy*. This word comes from the ancient Greek term *strategia* meaning generalship or the art of war. More specifically, strategy involves the optimal management of troops, ships, or aircraft in a planned campaign. A different, but related, word is *tactics*, which are tools to achieve the success of strategies [13]. Many people use these two terms interchangeably. The two expressions share some basic implied characteristics: planning, competition, conscious manipulation, and movement toward a goal. In nonmilitary settings, the strategy concept has been applied to clearly non-adversarial situations, where it has come to mean a plan, step, or conscious action toward achievement of an objective [14].

The strategy concept, without its aggressive and competitive trappings, has become influential in education, where it has taken on a new meaning and has been transformed into *learning strategies* [15]. One commonly used technical definition says that learning strategies are operations employed by the learner to aid the acquisition, storage, retrieval, and use of information [16]. This definition, while helpful, does not fully convey the excitement or richness of learning strategies. It is useful to expand this definition by saying that learning strategies are specific actions taken by the learner to make learning easier, faster, more enjoyable, more self-directed, more effective, and more transferrable to new situations.

Important terms used in this book have just been presented, including some general definitions of the concept of language learning strategies. Now it is time to explain the central features of such strategies.

FEATURES OF LANGUAGE LEARNING STRATEGIES

Key features of language learning strategies are discussed below and summarized in Table 1.1 [17]. To illustrate some of these features, certain strategies or strategy groups are briefly mentioned here. Subsequent chapters offer complete strategy definitions and applications.

Communicative Competence as the Main Goal

All appropriate language learning strategies are oriented toward the broad goal of communicative competence. Development of communicative competence requires realistic interaction among learners using meaningful, contextualized language. Learning strategies help learners participate actively in such authentic communication. Such strategies operate in both general and specific ways to encourage the development of communicative competence.

It is easy to see how language learning strategies stimulate the growth of communicative competence *in general*. For instance, metacognitive ("beyond the cognitive") strategies help learners to regulate their own cognition and to focus, plan, and evaluate their progress as they move toward communicative competence. Affective strategies develop the self-confidence and perseverance needed for learners to involve themselves actively in language learning, a requirement for attaining communicative competence. Social strategies provide increased interaction and more empathetic understanding, two qualities necessary to reach communicative competence.

Table 1.1 FEATURES OF LANGUAGE LEARNING STRATEGIES

Language learning strategies:
1. Contribute to the main goal, communicative competence.
2. Allow learners to become more self-directed.
3. Expand the role of teachers.
4. Are problem-oriented.
5. Are specific actions taken by the learner.
6. Involve many aspects of the learner, not just the cognitive.
7. Support learning both directly and indirectly.
8. Are not always observable.
9. Are often conscious.
10. Can be taught.
11. Are flexible.
12. Are influenced by a variety of factors.

Source: Original.

Certain cognitive strategies, such as analyzing, and particular memory strategies, like the keyword technique, are highly useful for understanding and recalling new information—important functions in the process of becoming competent in using the new language. Compensation strategies aid learners in overcoming knowledge gaps and continuing to communicate authentically; thus, these strategies help communicative competence to blossom.

As the learner's competence grows, strategies can act in specific ways to foster *particular* aspects of that competence: grammatical, sociolinguistic, discourse, and strategic elements. For instance, memory strategies, such as using imagery and structured review, and cognitive strategies, such as reasoning deductively and using contrastive analysis, strengthen *grammatical accuracy*. Social strategies—asking questions, cooperating with native speakers, cooperating with peers, and becoming culturally aware—powerfully aid *sociolinguistic competence*. Strategies related to communication in a natural setting and with social involvement also foster the development of sociolinguistic competence. Many kinds of strategies—compensation strategies, including using contextual clues for guessing, social strategies, such as cooperating and asking questions, and cognitive strategies, like recombination and use of common routines—encourage greater amounts of authentic communication and thus enhance *discourse competence*. Compensation strategies—guessing when the meaning is not known, or using synonyms or gestures to express meaning of an unknown word or expression—are the heart of *strategic competence* [18].

Greater Self-Direction for Learners

Language learning strategies encourage greater overall self-direction for learners [19]. Self-direction is particularly important for language learners, because they will not always have the teacher around to guide them as they use the language outside the classroom. Moreover, self-direction is essential to the active development of ability in a new language.

Owing to conditioning by the culture and the educational system, however, many language students (even adults) are passive and accustomed to being spoon-fed [20]. They like to be told what to do, and they do only what is clearly essential to get a good grade—even if they fail to develop useful skills in the process. Attitudes and behaviors like these make learning more difficult and must be changed, or else any effort to train learners to rely more on themselves and use better strategies is bound to fail [21]. Just teaching new strategies to students will accomplish very little unless students begin to *want* greater responsibility for their own learning.

Learner self-direction is not an "all or nothing" concept; it is often a gradually increasing phenomenon, growing as learners become more comfortable with the idea of their own responsibility. Self-directed students gradually gain greater confidence, involvement, and proficiency.

New Roles for Teachers

Teachers traditionally expect to be viewed as authority figures, identified with roles like parent, instructor, director, manager, judge, leader, evaluator, controller, and even doctor, who must "cure" the ignorance of the students. As Gibson said, "You've got to make [students] toe the line all the time, you cannot assume that they'll come in, sit down and get on with the job." According to Harmer, "The teacher *instructs*. This is where [s]he explains exactly what the students should do" [22]. These familiar roles will stifle communication in any classroom, especially the language classroom, because they force all communication to go to and through the teacher.

The specter of role change may discomfort some teachers who feel that their status is being challenged. Others, however, welcome their new functions as facilitator, helper, guide, consultant, adviser, coordinator, idea person, diagnostician, and co-communicator. New teaching capacities also include identifying students' learning strategies, conducting training on learning strategies, and helping learners become more independent [23]. In this process, teachers do not necessarily forsake all their old managerial and instructional tasks, but these elements become much less dominant. These changes strengthen teachers' roles, making them more varied and more creative. Their status is no longer based on hierarchical authority, but on the quality and importance of their relationship with learners [24]. When students take more responsibility, more learning occurs, and both teachers and learners feel more successful.

Other Features

Other important features of language strategies are problem orientation, action basis, involvement beyond just cognition, ability to support learning directly or indirectly, degree of observability, level of consciousness, teachability, flexibility, and influences on strategy choice.

Problem Orientation Language learning strategies are tools. They are used because there is a problem to solve, a task to accomplish, an objective to meet, or a goal to attain. For example, a learner uses one of the reasoning or guessing strategies to better understand a foreign language reading passage. Memory strategies are used because there is something that must be remembered. Affective strategies are used to help the learner relax or gain greater confidence, so that more profitable learning can take place.

Action Basis Related to the problem orientation of language learning strategies is their action basis. Language learning strategies are specific actions or behaviors accomplished by students to enhance their learning. Examples are taking notes, planning for a language task, self-evaluating, and guessing intelligently. These actions are naturally influenced by the learners' more general characteristics or traits, such as learning style (broad, generalized approach to learning, problem solving, or understanding oneself or the situation), motivation, and aptitude, but they must not be confused with these wider characteristics.

Involvement Beyond Just Cognition Language learning strategies are not restricted to cognitive functions, such as those dealing with mental processing and manipulation of the new language. Strategies also include metacognitive functions like planning, evaluating, and arranging one's own learning; and emotional (affective), social, and other functions as well. Unfortunately, many language learning strategy experts have not paid enough attention to affective and social strategies in the past. It is likely that the emphasis will eventually become more balanced, because language learning is indisputably an emotional and interpersonal process as well as a cognitive and metacognitive affair.

Direct and Indirect Support of Learning Some learning strategies involve direct learning and use of the subject matter, in this case a new language.

These are known as *direct strategies*. Other strategies, including metacognitive, affective, and social strategies, contribute indirectly but powerfully to learning. These are known as *indirect strategies*. Direct and indirect strategies are equally important and serve to support each other in many ways.

Degree of Observability Language learning strategies are not always readily observable to the human eye. Many aspects of cooperating, a strategy in which the learner works with someone else to achieve a learning goal, can be observed, but the act of making mental associations, an important memory strategy, cannot be seen. It is often difficult for teachers to know about their students' learning strategies, because some strategies are hard to observe even with the help of videotape and closed-circuit television. Another problem with observing learning strategies is that many strategies are used (as they should be!) outside of the classroom in informal, naturalistic situations unobservable by the teacher.

Level of Consciousness The ancient Greek definition of strategies, given above, implies consciousness and intentionality. Many modern uses of learning strategies reflect conscious efforts by learners to take control of their learning, and some researchers seem to suggest that learning strategies are always conscious actions [25]. However, after a certain amount of practice and use, learning strategies, like any other skill or behavior, can become automatic. In fact, making *appropriate* learning strategies fully automatic—that is, unconscious—is often a very desirable thing, especially for language learning [26].

Perhaps paradoxically, the strategies some learners use—either appropriate or inappropriate ones—are already employed instinctively, unthinkingly, and uncritically. Strategy assessment and training might be necessary to help these learners become more aware of the strategies they are using and to evaluate the utility of those strategies.

Teachability Some aspects of the learner's makeup, like general learning style or personality traits, are very difficult to change. In contrast, learning strategies are easier to teach and modify. This can be done through strategy training, which is an essential part of language education [27]. Even the best learners can improve their strategy use through such training. Strategy training helps guide learners to become more conscious of strategy use and more adept at employing appropriate strategies.

Strategy training is most effective when students learn why and when specific strategies are important, how to use these strategies, and how to transfer them to new situations. Strategy training must also take into account learners' and teachers' attitudes toward learner self-direction, language learning, and the particular language and culture in question. As a strategy trainer, the language teacher helps each student to gain self-awareness of how he or she learns, as well as to develop the means to maximize all learning experiences, both inside and outside of the language area.

Flexibility Language learning strategies are flexible; that is, they are not always found in predictable sequences or in precise patterns. There is a great deal of individuality in the way learners choose, combine, and sequence strategies. The ways that learners do so is the subject of much current research (see the following discussion of factors influencing learners' choice of strategies).

However, sometimes learners *do* combine strategies in a predictable way. For instance, in reading a passage, learners often preview the material by skimming or scanning, then they read it more closely while using guessing to fill in any gaps, and finally they organize the material by taking notes or summarizing. In addition, some learning strategies contain within themselves an *internal* sequence of steps; for instance, deductive reasoning requires first considering a rule and then applying it to a new situation.

Factors Influencing Strategy Choice Many factors affect the choice of strategies: degree of awareness, stage of learning, task requirements, teacher expectations, age, sex, nationality/ethnicity, general learning style, personality traits, motivation level, and purpose for learning the language [28].

In a nutshell, learners who are more aware and more advanced seem to use better strategies. Task requirements help determine strategy choice; learners would not use the same strategies for writing a composition as for chatting in a cafe. Teacher expectations, expressed through classroom instructional and testing methods, strongly shape learners' strategies; for instance, classroom emphasis on discrete-point grammar-learning will result in development of learning strategies like analysis and reasoning, rather than more global strategies for communication.

Older learners may use somewhat different strategies than younger learners. Recent studies indicate that females may use a much wider, or at least a very different, range of strategies than males for language learning. Nationality or ethnicity influences strategy use; for example, Hispanics seem to use social strategies more than do some other ethnic groups. General learning style, such as field dependence-independence, analytic-global orientation, or the judging-perceiving mode, has a strong effect on the strategies that language learners use.

More highly motivated learners use a significantly greater range of appropriate strategies than do less motivated learners. Motivation is related to language learning purpose, which is another key to strategy use. For instance, individuals who want to learn a new language mainly for interpersonal communication will use different strategies than learners who want to learn a new language merely to fulfill a graduation requirement.

This review of the characteristics of language learning strategies is a useful background to the new strategy classification system, discussed next. Many elements of this system have already been touched upon, and they will be explained in greater detail now.

A NEW SYSTEM OF LANGUAGE LEARNING STRATEGIES

The strategy system [29] presented here differs in several ways from earlier attempts to classify strategies. It is more compehensive and detailed; it is more systematic in linking individual strategies, as well as strategy groups, with each of the four language skills (listening, reading, speaking, and writing); and it uses less technical terminology. Visual and verbal cues are used throughout this book for understanding and remembering the system.

Figure 1.1 presents a general overview of the system of language learning strategies. Strategies are divided into two major classes: direct and indirect. These two classes are subdivided into a total of six groups (memory, cognitive, and compensation under the direct class; metacognitive, affective, and social under the indirect class). This figure indicates that direct strategies and indirect strategies support each other, and that each strategy group is capable of connecting with and assisting every other strategy group. Figure 1.2 shows a different view of the same strategy system.

So far only general strategy definitions have been given. Complete strategy definitions are offered in Chapter 2 (for all the direct strategies) and Chapter 4 (for all the indirect strategies). Chapters 3 and 5 present detailed applications of direct and indirect strategies, respectively.

Mutual Support

What does it mean to say that direct and indirect strategies support each other, or that the six strategy groups (three direct and three indirect) interact with and help each other? To understand this, consider an analogy from the theater.

The first major class, direct strategies for dealing with the new language, is like the Performer in a stage play, working with the language itself in a variety of specific tasks and situations. The direct class is composed of memory strategies for remembering and retrieving new information, cognitive strategies for understanding and producing the language, and compensation strategies for using the language despite knowledge

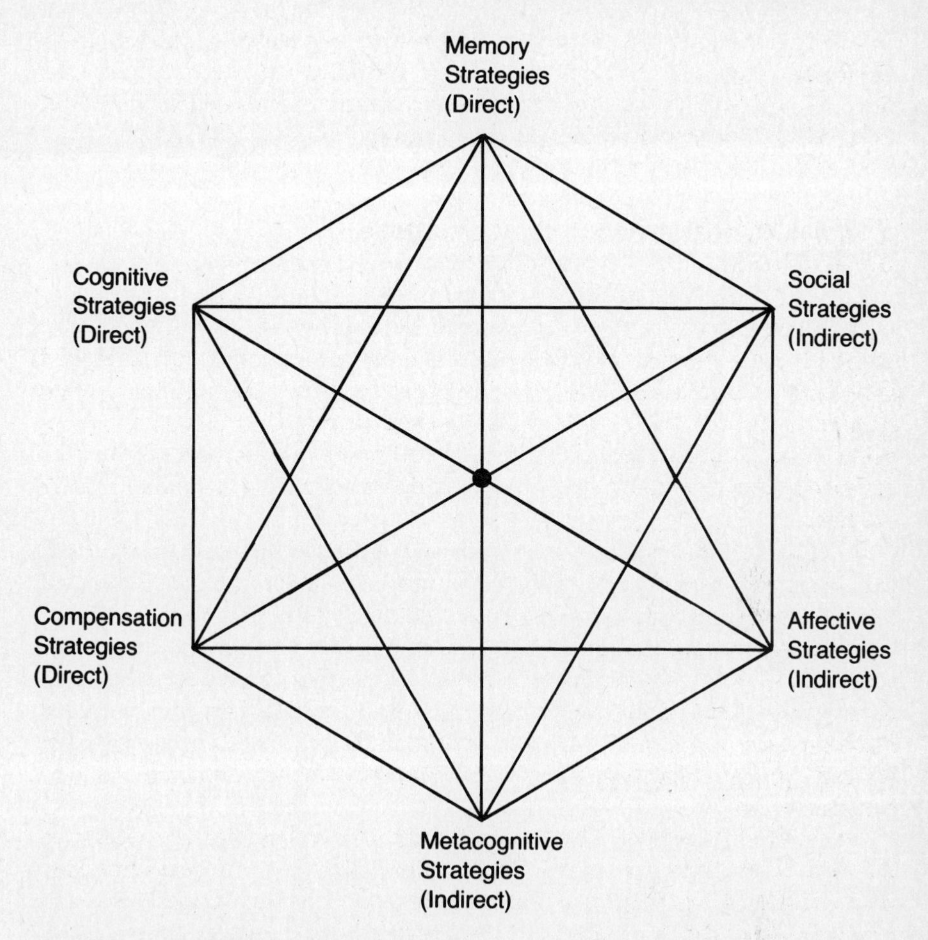

Figure 1.1 Interrelationships Between Direct and Indirect Strategies and Among the Six Strategy Groups. (*Source*: Original.)

gaps. The Performer works closely with the Director for the best possible outcome.

The second major strategy class—indirect strategies for general management of learning—can be likened to the Director of the play. This class is made up of metacognitive strategies for coordinating the learning process, affective strategies for regulating emotions, and social strategies for learning with others. The Director serves a host of functions, like focusing, organizing, guiding, checking, correcting, coaching, encouraging, and cheering the Performer, as well as ensuring that the Performer works cooperatively with other actors in the play. The Director is an *internal* guide

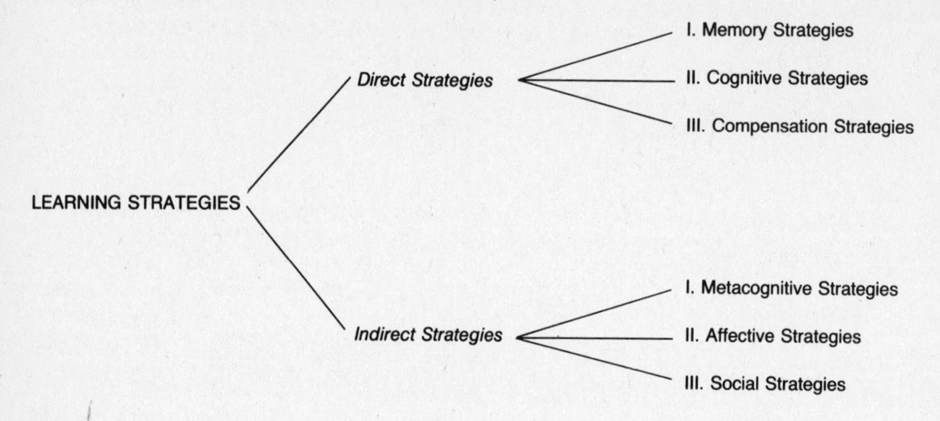

Figure 1.2 Diagram of the Strategy System: Overview. (*Source*: Original.)

and support to the Performer. The functions of both the Director and the Performer become part of the learner, as he or she accepts increased responsibility for learning.

The teacher allows and encourages the learner to take on more of the Director functions that might have earlier been reserved, at least overtly, for the teacher. In the past, teachers might have been the ones to correct learner errors and tell the learner exactly what to do when. Now learners do more of this for themselves, while teachers' functions become somewhat less directive and more facilitating, as described earlier in this chapter.

A large overlap naturally exists among the strategy groups in the system presented here. For instance, the metacognitive category helps students to regulate their own cognition by assessing how they are learning and by planning for future language tasks, but metacognitive self-assessment and planning often require reasoning, which is itself a cognitive strategy! Likewise, the compensation strategy of guessing, clearly used to make up for missing knowledge, also requires reasoning (which explains why some specialists call guessing a cognitive strategy), as well as involving sociocultural sensitivity typically gained through social strategies.

Figure 1.3 indicates how the six strategy groups are subdivided into a total of 19 strategy sets. Figure 1.4 shows the entire learning strategy system, including 62 strategies.

Cautions

It is important to remember that *any* current understanding of language learning strategies is necessarily in its infancy, and *any* existing system of strategies is only a proposal to be tested through practical classroom use

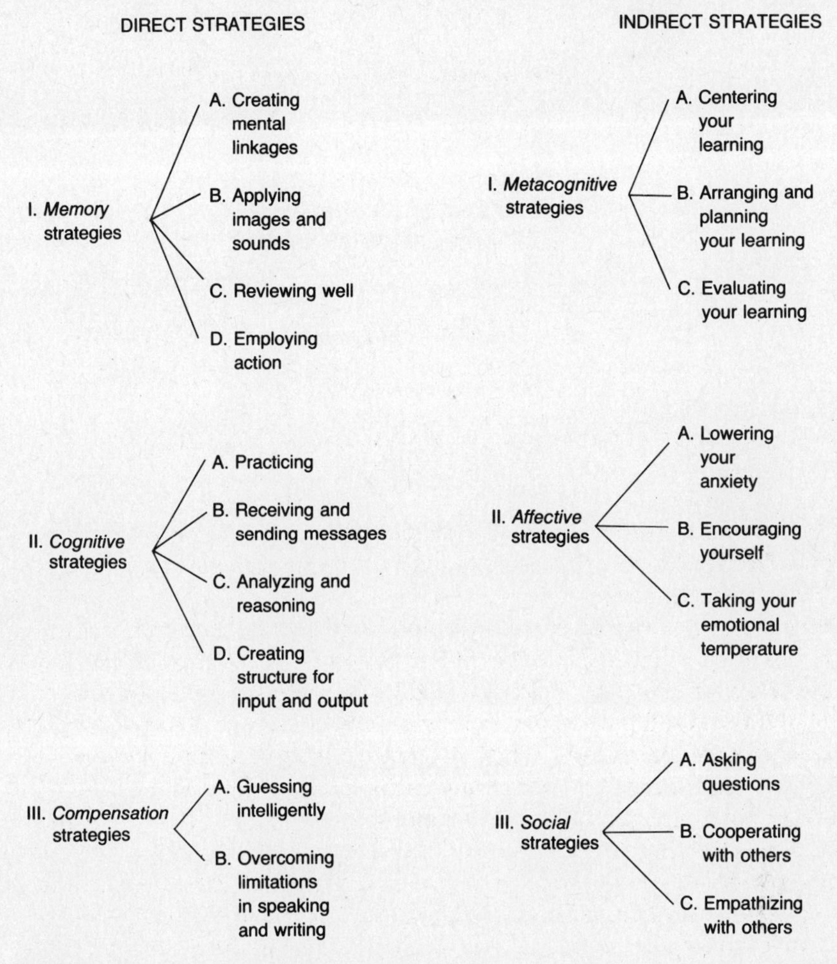

Figure 1.3 Diagram of the Strategy System Showing Two Classes, Six Groups, and 19 Sets. (*Source*: Original.)

and through research. At this stage in the short history of language learning strategy research, there is no complete agreement on exactly what strategies are; how many strategies exist; how they should be defined, demarcated, and categorized; and whether it is—or ever will be—possible to create a real, scientifically validated hierarchy of strategies. Some language learning strategies, such as naturalistic practice, are very broad, containing many possible activities, while others, like the keyword technique, are narrower, but breadth or narrowness cannot be the sole basis of a hierarchical structure for strategies.

Classification conflicts are inevitable. A given strategy, such as using synonyms if the exact word is not known to the learner, is classed by some

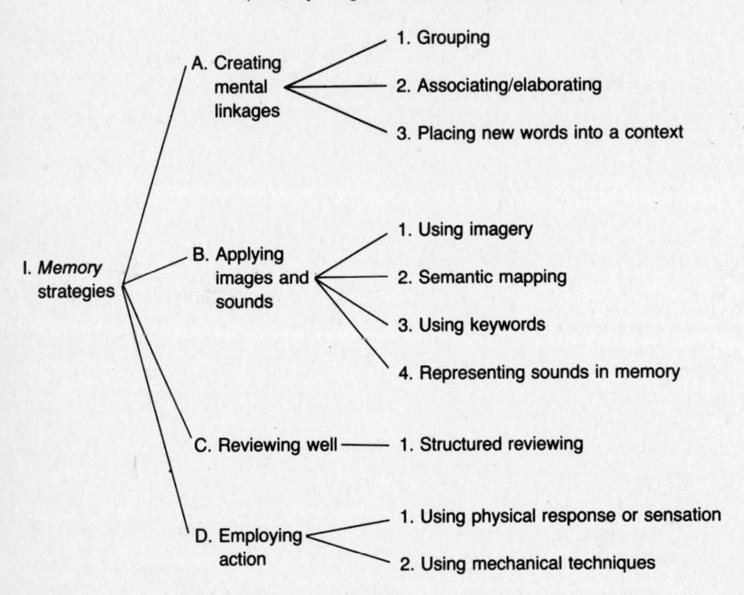

Figure 1.4 Diagram of the Strategy System Showing All the Strategies. (*Source*: Original.)

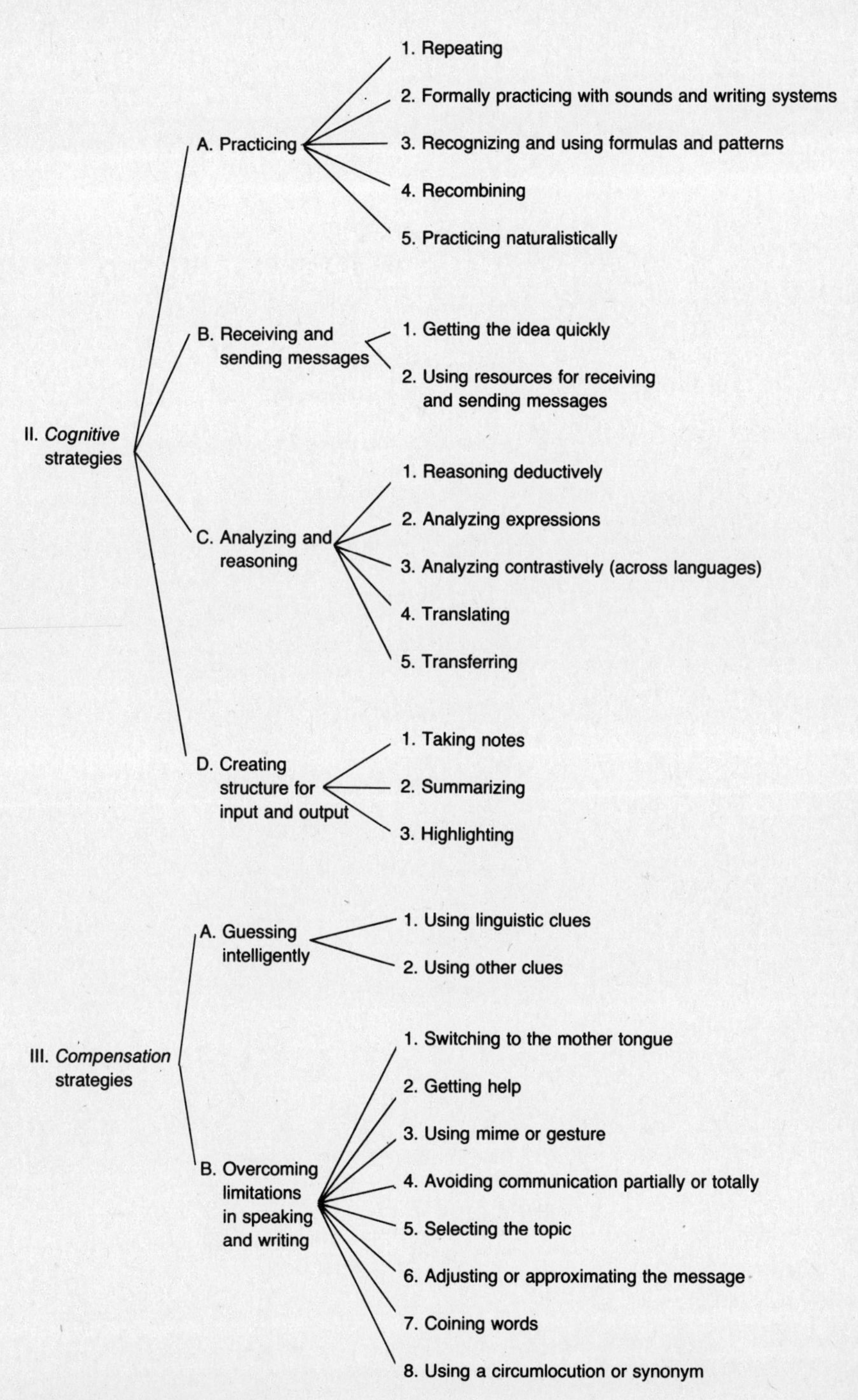

Figure 1.4 *(Continued)*

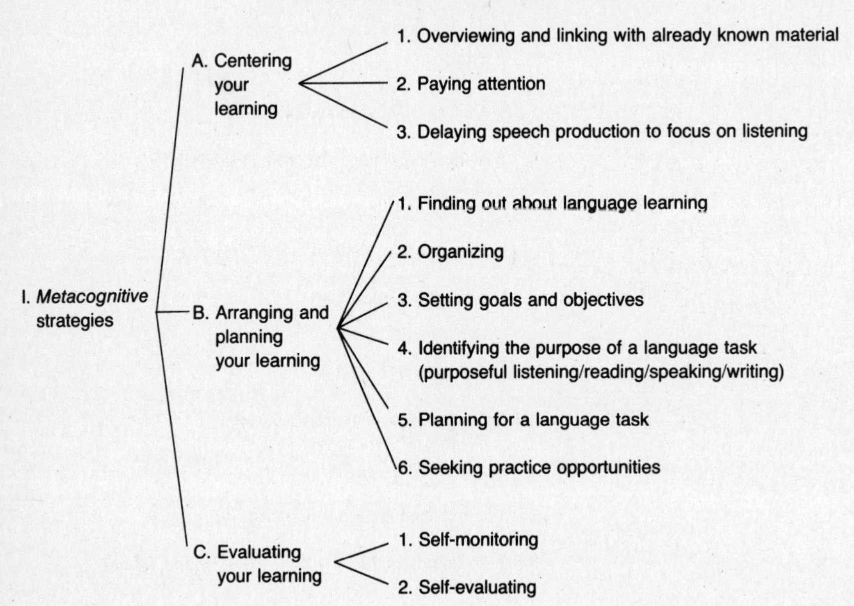

Figure 1.4 *(Continued)*

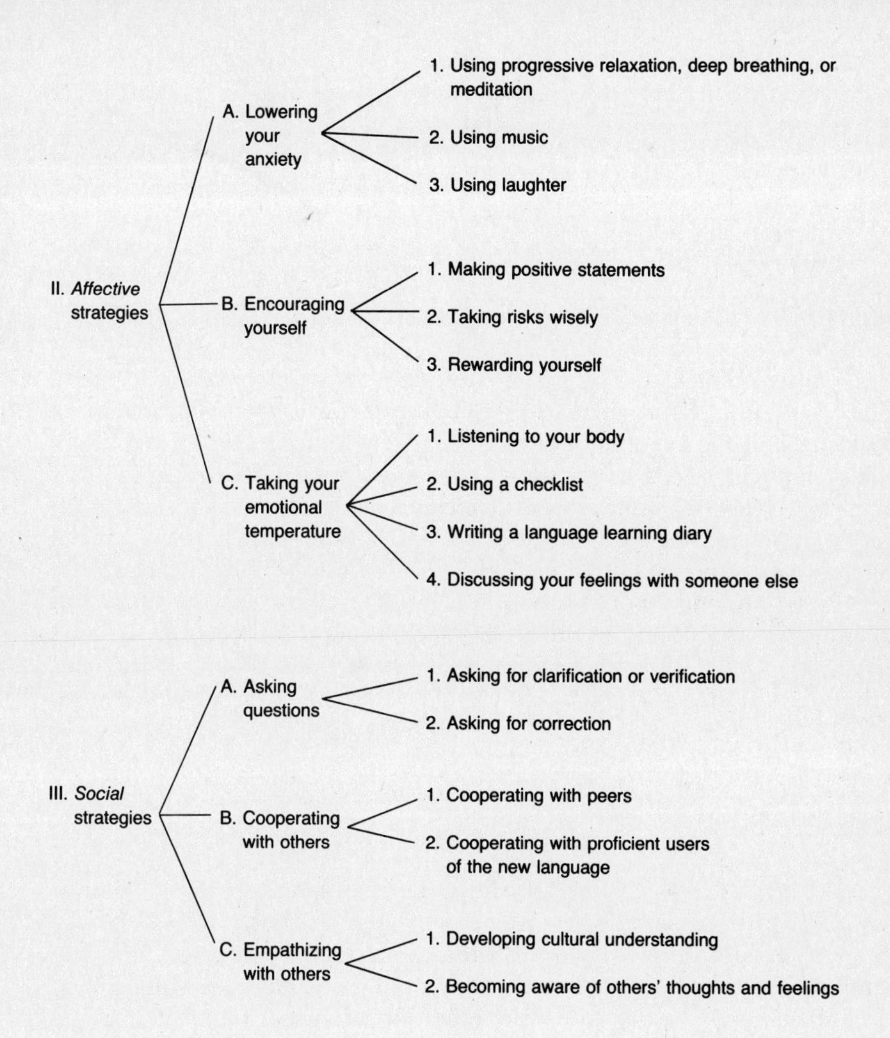

Figure 1.4 *(Continued)*

experts as a learning strategy (it is included here as such) but is unceremoniously thrown out of the learning strategy arena by other experts, who think it is merely a communication strategy which is not useful for learning. Also, there is confusion among some strategy specialists as to whether a particular strategy, like self-monitoring, should be called direct or indirect; this may be because researchers disagree on the basic definitions of the terms *direct* and *indirect*. Even individual researchers often classify a particular strategy differently at different times, in light of new insights. These difficulties are understandable, given the early stage of investigation concerning language learning strategies [30].

Despite problems in classifying strategies, research continues to prove that strategies help learners take control of their learning and become more proficient, and the experience of many teachers indicates that the strategy system shown above is a very useful way to examine such strategies. This system provides, albeit in imperfect form, a comprehensive structure for understanding strategies. It includes a wide variety of affective and social strategies which are not often enough considered by strategy researchers, teachers, or students. It unites the whole range of compensation strategies, so confusingly separated in other strategy classification schemes. Finally, it organizes well-known metacognitive, cognitive, and memory strategies so that you can access them easily.

SUMMARY

This chapter has explained the importance of language learning strategies and has discussed the best way you can use this book. In this chapter central terms are defined, key features of strategies explained, and the overall strategy classification system presented. Later chapters will provide more details on strategies and show how they are used to make language learning more effective.

ACTIVITIES FOR READERS

Activity 1.1. Brainstorm the Features of Learning Strategies

With others or by yourself, brainstorm all the characteristics of learning strategies that you can think of, listing them on a large sheet. Then organize them into categories, giving examples. How does your list compare with the one in this chapter?

Activity 1.2. Place Strategies on the Learning-Acquisition Continuum

Assume that learning and acquisition form a continuum. Draw this continuum on a flip-chart or backboard as follows:

ALL LEARNING	MAINLY LEARNING	BOTH EQUALLY	MAINLY ACQUISITION	ALL ACQUISITION

Take each of the six strategy groups (and the 19 strategy sets into which these groups are divided), as listed in this chapter. Place each one along the continuum in the spot where you think it belongs. Explain your reasoning.

Activity 1.3. Consider Degrees of Learner Responsibility

Henri Holec [31] advocates that language learners take charge of their learning in *all* respects, including determining the objectives, defining the content and progressions, selecting methods and techniques to be used, monitoring the procedures (rhythm, time, place, etc.), and evaluating what has been learned. Teachers can help learners take this responsibility, according to Holec, but the ultimate responsibility lies with the learners themselves.

What is your opinion about Holec's assertion that learners should take charge of their learning in all the respects listed above? Explain any reservations or agreements, and give examples.

Brainstorm specific ways learners might take responsibility for each of the language learning aspects cited by Holec.

Activity 1.4. Discuss Teacher Roles

Read the following list of classroom management behaviors, and then answer the questions.

Behaviors

1. Giving learners plenty of encouragement for their efforts.
2. Establishing a position of dominance over learners.
3. Ignoring disruptive behavior and praising appropriate behavior.
4. Giving pupils responsibility for their learning.
5. Learning the names of pupils quickly.
6. Keeping grading and attendance lists up to date.
7. Being warm, friendly, and open with the learners.

8. Establishing a daily and weekly routine.
9. Threatening with punishment learners who misbehave.
10. Setting learning tasks which are completed in total silence.

Questions

1. Which do you think are the most appropriate classroom management behaviors?
2. Which ones require the imposition of the teacher's power?
3. Which ones involve a lessening of social distance between teacher and students?
4. Which of these behaviors are task-oriented?
5. In what ways do these behaviors influence student motivation?
6. Which behaviors do your own learners expect? Which do their parents expect (if relevant)? Which does the administration expect?
7. How do these behaviors relate to the six groups of learning strategies included in this chapter?

Source Adapted from T. Wright (1987, pp. 52–53).

Activity 1.5. Consider Your Own Strategy Use

Think back to when you were learning a new language. Which of the six groups of strategies—memory, cognitive, compensation, metacognitive, affective, and social—did you use most often? Least often? Indicate any strategy groups you *never* used and discuss whether use of such strategies might have helped you.

Describe how you used language learning strategies, giving examples. Discuss how you used learning strategies in at least one other subject area and provide examples.

EXERCISES TO USE WITH YOUR STUDENTS

Exercise 1.1. Embedded Strategies Game

Purpose

This game helps participants to become acquainted with language learning strategies and can be used with either teachers or students as participants. Participants are asked to determine which language learning strategies (from the list in this chapter) are embedded in, or suggested by, certain language activities. The game is a process of matching a number of language activities with the names of the relevant strategies, and thus acquaints participants with the whole system of strategies.

Materials

Each participant gets a copy of the strategy system from this chapter (Figure 1.4) and a list of language activities (given below).

Time

This game, which takes 1 to 2 hours, can be spread over several class periods. Total time required depends on the number of language activities used.

Instructions

1. *Introduction* Give out the materials (strategy system in Figure 1.4 and list of language activities below). Explain that participants will be divided into small groups. Each small group will try to identify the language learning strategies embedded in, or suggested by, the series of language activities. Explain that all the language activities refer to the target language. Every language activity can be matched with *one or more language learning strategies.*

It is not necessary to consider the language activities in the order in which they are listed. Explain that participants must choose relevant strategies to match any given language activity on the list; but they must be able to justify or explain their selection of strategies! You might also tell participants they will not have access to complete definitions of the strategies; they will have only the strategy system, which lists the name of each strategy and shows how the strategies are grouped. The names are intentionally descriptive, so most participants will not have any trouble understanding the meaning of the strategies.

If you want to give a quick introduction to the strategy system itself, tell participants that some strategies deal directly with the target language, while other strategies do not deal with the language but instead support language learning indirectly through metacognitive, emotional, and social means. Do not give any more detail on the strategy system now; let the participants teach themselves to understand and use the system as they play the game.

Announce the time limit in advance. It does not really matter how many language activities a small group chooses to cover; the key is the number of relevant, justifiable strategies named. But encourage small groups to try to cover at least 15 language activities to get a general feeling for a variety of strategies.

NOTE: SCORING IS OPTIONAL. If you decide to score the game, explain how scoring works. Scoring: 1 point for each relevant strategy listed for any activity. The winning group is the one with the greatest number of *relevant* strategies matching the listed language activities within the time allowed. If you decide not to use scoring, Step 4 (below) can just be a whole-group explanation of the strategy choices, with each small group contributing its ideas but without counting points.

2. *Practice* Run through one or two examples with the whole group before breaking up into smaller groups. To do this, read a language activity description (for instance, the description for LISTENING IN—see list below) to the whole group, and get participants to call out any strategies that are suggested by the activity (e.g., practicing naturalistically, paying attention). Ask for a *very brief* (one sentence) explanation or justification for each strategy named. Make sure everyone understands how to play.

3. *Play* Divide everyone into groups of three to five people. Each small group now works through the list of activities (in any order), writing down on one or more large sheets of paper the strategies they consider relevant and useful for each activity and making sure they can explain or justify their choices.

4. *Explanation of strategy choices and determination of scores* Reconvene the whole group and ask each small group to post its list visibly at the front of the room. Now ask a spokesperson from each group to discuss the language activities covered by the group, and explain the strategies the group matched with each activity. (Other members of the small group can help the spokesperson, if needed, by adding explanations or justifications.) If the whole group generally agrees that the choice of a given strategy is a good one, the small group gets 1 point.

The easier and more obvious activity-and-strategy matchings can be explained or justified in just a sentence, but participants might want to discuss in a little more detail the more difficult or borderline cases. You need to keep this discussion condensed enough so that all small groups will have an equal chance to present their findings.

Note that the small groups presenting later may have a slight advantage over the small groups that present earlier, in that they have heard what the earlier groups have said. Urge the later-presenting groups not merely to repeat what has been said, but to add something new, if they can, to justify their strategy choices.

If you feel any small group's reasons for choosing a strategy are off course, ask questions to lead the group to understand, rather than just telling them the answer. Remember, there is often not just one solution to dealing with any given language activity; many strategies are often appropriate.

If you have decided to score the game, it is now time to let the small groups count up the number of points they have earned. Decide on a winning group—the one with the greatest number of relevant strategies (regardless of the number of language activities covered).

5. *Discussion* Be sure to leave at least 15 to 25 minutes for this discussion, which helps participants understand and consolidate what they have learned. Discuss what the participants learned about strategies, using the following questions as a guide. Were certain strategies relevant across

a number of language activities? Why might this be the case? Were there any *combinations of strategies* that recurred across language activities? Which strategies seem to go together? Which strategies seem to operate on their own? Which strategies do the participants tend to use themselves, when, and why? How can this game help participants in dealing with tasks in the foreign or second language?

List of Language Activities for the Embedded Strategies Game

ALL THE NEWS THAT FITS, WE PRINT—Read the newspaper in the target language to practice the language and keep up with events.

AS THE WORLD TURNS—Watch a soap opera every day to practice understanding the target language.

BRAINSTORM—Brainstorm with other language learners some possible topics for writing in the new language.

BREAK-DOWN—Break down into parts any long words and expressions in the new language that you find overwhelming.

CANNED TALK—Learn some common "canned" routines by heart in the new language so you can rattle them off easily when you need them in social conversation.

CHECK-UP—Check yourself to see the kinds of errors you make in the new language and then try figure out why.

CINEMA CITY—Go to a foreign film festival to get more exposure to the new language.

COLORS—Color-code your language notebook so you can find things easily.

CUISINE—Read and follow recipes in the target language.

DATING GAME—To meet a person of the opposite sex, read the computer dating company advertisement in the newspaper—in the new language, of course.

'FRAIDY CAT—Make positive statements to yourself in order to feel more confident and be more willing to take risks.

GETTING IT ALL TOGETHER—When preparing to give a talk in the new language, figure out the requirements, your own capabilities, and what else you will have to do in order to give a good talk.

GOOD OLD SHERLOCK—While reading the new language, constantly look for clues to the meaning.

GOSSIP—While a friend is telling you some juicy gossip in the new language, listen carefully so you can get it right when you tell it to someone else.

GUESS WHAT—While listening to a politician's TV speech in the new language, guess what the politician will say next.

HANDOUTS—Send off for free items advertised in target language magazines and newspapers.

HELP!—When you can't seem to find the word to say in the new language, ask for help from somebody else.

HELP, I NEED YOU—Look for native speakers who can help you practice speaking the new language or who can explain things to you about the new culture.

HOLY, HOLY, HOLY—Read a hymnbook, bible, prayerbook, etc., in the new language. See if there is anything similar to what you know from your own background. When you don't understand something, guess.

HOW AM I DOING?—Ask someone else for feedback on whether you have understood, said, or written something correctly in the new language.

HOW COME?—Try to figure out the reason for doing a certain language activity, so that you can prepare yourself better.

IT'S BEEN A HARD DAY—Schedule a break from language learning when you are tired.

KEEP QUIET—Try to just listen and understand the new language for a while because your speaking skills aren't so hot yet.

LISTENING IN—While the old lady ahead of you on the bus is chastising a young man in your new language, listen to their conversation to find out exactly what she's saying to him.

LOOKING AHEAD—Use preview questions or other ways to look ahead at the new target language reading material, so that you can orient yourself.

MARKERS—In reading the new language, look for markers in the text (headings, subheadings, topic sentences) to give you clues about the meaning.

MIND IMAGES—When learning a list of words in the new language, create a picture in your head of the words and the relationships among them.

MOUTHING—When trying to learn the sounds of the new language, pay attention to how a native speaker shapes his or her mouth when talking; then you do the same while looking at a mirror.

MUSIC TIME—Listen to song lyrics in the target language and try to sing along and learn the words.

NITPICKING—While reading or listening to the target language, look for specific new words, forms, or pieces of information.

PEERS WITHOUT TEARS—Stop competing with your fellow students and learn to work together in learning the new language.

PENPALS—Meet a native speaker visiting from another country and then keep in touch with that person by writing in the new language after the person returns home.

PHYSICAL TRAINING—In class, follow commands of your teacher, such as "Stand up. Go to the blackboard. Pick up the chalk. Write your name."

PICTURES ON THE WALL—Go to the art museum, get a target language brochure about the paintings, read about them, go to see the ones you are most interested in, and write your impressions.

REWARDS—Having done very well on a language test, reward yourself with a special treat.

SCRABBLE—While playing a game of Scrabble in the target language, use a dictionary but no other aids.

SECRETS—Keep a journal of your language learning progress and write down new words and expressions.

SHORT-HAIRED (OR LONG-HAIRED) DICTIONARY—Find a pal who is a native speaker of the target language, and get your pal to explain to you the meanings of new words in the target language.

SNOOP AROUND—Make it a point to look around at signs, billboards, names of streets and buildings, headlines, magazine covers, and all the visual symbols of the new language and culture.

SOUNDS OF THE CITY—Listen to city sounds (announcements, discussions, speeches, mumblings, commercials, arguments), trying to figure out what people are saying in the new language.

SPREAD 'EM OUT—Plan your sessions for reviewing new material in the target language so that the sessions are at first close together and then more widely spread out.

STEERING CLEAR—When the conversation in the new language gets onto topics for which you don't know the vocabulary, change the subject or just don't say anything.

TAKING THE PULSE—Stop to determine whether you are feeling especially nervous before you go into language class.

TALKING TO YOURSELF—Tell yourself that you really *can* learn this language; bad experiences you might have had before don't count anymore.

T-TIME—Take notes on what you hear or read in the new language by drawing a big T on the paper, writing the key idea or title at the top of the T, then listing details in the left column and examples in the right column.

WALKING AROUND TOWN—To take a walk around the foreign city, get a guidebook and map in the new language, mark the best places, wander a bit, stop at a cafe, and meet some interesting people.

WATERY WORLD—Go down to the bay or the river, count the ships, read their names written in the new language, and ask people where the ships come from and where they are going next.

WHAT'S THE BIG IDEA?—Find all sorts of ways to locate the main idea as you are reading a passage in the new language.

WRITER'S CRAMP—To combat your "mental block" against writing a report in the new language, try to calm down and relax by means of music and breathing exercises.

Source Original [32].

Exercise 1.2. Strategy Search Game

Purpose

This game helps participants, either teachers or students, to determine which language learning strategies are embedded in, or suggested by, certain language tasks/situations. These are a little more complicated than the language activities in the preceding Embedded Strategies Game (Exercise 1.1 above). The Strategy Search Game is a process of matching language tasks/situations with the names of relevant language learning strategies. Like the Embedded Strategies Game, this exercise acquaints participants with the whole range of strategies. It can follow the Embedded Strategies Game as a more in-depth look at strategies, or it can be used instead of Embedded Strategies if participants already know something about strategies and their use.

Materials

Each participant gets a copy of the strategy system from this chapter (Figure 1.4) and a list of language tasks/situations (given below).

Time

This game, which lasts 1 to 2½ hours, can be spread over several class periods. Total time required depends on the number of tasks/situations used.

Instructions

Follow the instructions for the Embedded Strategies Game (Exercise 1.1) above. However, in place of "language activity" substitute "language task or situation." A reminder: Again, leave plenty of time at the end for a discussion of what has been learned about language learning strategies!

Alternatives

1. Instead of giving each small group the *complete* list of *all* the tasks/situations from which to choose, let each small group pick a certain number of task/situation strips randomly from a well-shuffled set, so that no small group has the same task/situation strips as any other small group. Then each group must come up with all the relevant strategies for each of the task/situation strips it has randomly drawn. In Step 4 (explanation of strategy choices and determination of scores), small groups must read or describe each task/situation aloud to the whole group (so that everybody will know what the task or situation is). The explanation or justification operates as usual.

The rest of the game operates the same way as for the Embedded Strategies Game.

2. A small group makes up its own language tasks/situations, in addition to using the ones provided here within the time allowed. Strategies would be matched with the new tasks/situations in the same way as with the ones provided here.

3. Small groups act out their language tasks/situations. This works well with participants who are uninhibited or who know each other fairly well already.

Language Tasks/Situations for Strategy Search Game

(Cut into strips)

PRESENTING A PAPER: You are a Hungarian chemist in an industrial exchange program in the United States. Your task is to prepare a scientific paper to present orally to a group of your American colleagues. Your paper must be about 45 minutes long and must explain your research in some detail. Your oral English skills are not too good, but you know the technical vocabulary for your field and have a pretty fair grasp of English grammar. You are feeling nervous. Which language learning strategies do you need to use?

STRANGER: You are a 35-year-old refugee from Laos who has arrived in the United States. Your four children also escaped and are now with you. Your husband has died, and you are living on welfare funds. You are almost illiterate in your own language, as well as in English. You had a short course in English at the refugee processing camp, but all of your English skills are very poor. You need to learn enough English so that you can go shopping by yourself, deal with the social worker and the welfare office, take care of your family, and become adjusted to a totally new cultural situation. Which language learning strategies do you need to use?

ESPIONAGE: You are a spy. Your job deals with overhearing and understanding target language conversations in person, over the phone, and on tape. Your task is to track a covert group which has been conducting international sabotage and to uncover secrets about this group's activity. You have studied the language (called Unca) spoken by this group, but are not an expert; you need to work on your Unca listening skills—fast! Which language learning strategies do you need to use?

CARTOON: You are an English-speaking high school student learning Italian. You have a good sense of humor and enjoy jokes and cartoons. You decide to buy an Italian cartoon book. It is about 100 pages long, full of cartoons. You want to read the book, understand the cartoons, and explain some of the cartoons to your friends who do not know Italian at all. Which language learning strategies do you need to use?

TRAVEL AGENT: It is September. You are a British college student just starting a year's study in France. You want to go home for the Christmas holidays, and you've been told that you must book your tickets early or else you won't be able to get reservations. You have to take a train from Aix to Paris, another train from Paris to Cherbourg, and a ferry from Cherbourg to Plymouth, across the English Channel. You don't have much money, so you have to find the cheapest fare possible. Furthermore, you have some time constraints; you must return from England in time to see your girlfriend/boyfriend in France before the next semester starts. Your task is to talk to the travel agent, who does not understand English, and convey as much of this information as is relevant. Your French is rather limited, since you have not had much speaking practice yet. Which language learning strategies do you need to use?

ON TOUR: You are an Australian tourist in Greece. You have never been here before, and your study of Greek has been limited to skimming the Berlitz phrasebook. You managed to find your hotel with the help of a taxi driver. You went out for a walk on your own and got lost. Nobody around you seems to speak English. Your task is to find out where you are and get back to your hotel before it gets dark. You have 2 hours to do this. You are getting a little worried! Which language learning strategies do you need to use?

CHURCH: You are a visitor from the United States in Germany. It is Friday, and you want to prepare yourself to go to church on Sunday to worship, participate in the service, and possibly meet some German people afterwards. You had 2 years of German study, but that was a very long time ago. Which language learning strategies do you need to use?

NEWSWORTHY: You are a French student learning English in France. You try to read the *International Herald Tribune* regularly so you can practice English, but you keep getting stuck on unfamiliar words. You use a dictionary to find out the meaning of every word you don't know, but that slows you down too much, and not all the words are in the dictionary, anyway! It is very upsetting to have such difficulty, and you are about to give up. Which language learning strategies do you need to use?

VISITING GRANNY: You are in your 30s. Three months from now you will go to Warsaw to visit your grandmother, whom you have never met. You know from your parents that your grandmother speaks only a few words of English. You speak only a few words of Polish. You need to learn as much Polish as you can in the next 3 months, so you can find out all you can about your grandmother's life, the family history, and your Polish relatives when you get to Poland. Which language learning strategies do you need to use?

CHILD OF THE MIDLANDS: You are a Pakistani child in a medium-size city in the English midlands. You live in a Pakistani enclave. Your parents, brothers and sisters, and friends do not speak English at home or in the neighborhood. But in school there are children from 15 different language and cultural groups, and English is the primary language of communication across these groups. You need to learn English to get along with the other children and to get good grades in school. Which language learning strategies do you need to use?

DOWN IN TEXAS: You are a 13-year-old Mexican student. Your family has just moved to Texas from a small town in Mexico. You are in an English-as-a-second-language program at school with lots of other Mexicans. They call it a "transitional" program, because it is supposed to prepare you for regular classes. You feel annoyed and upset because you don't know much English, but you are highly motivated to learn. You want to be able to go to technical school or college after high school. You especially want to develop your language skills so that you will understand what your teacher says and so that you will be able to move more quickly into regular classes. Which language learning strategies do you need to use?

THE PLAY'S THE THING: You are an American high school student in your third year of French. Your task is to work with a small group to write and participate in a 30-minute play, all in French, about teenagers in France. You don't know much about teenagers in France, and you are terrified about speaking French in the play, but you are relieved that your friends are involved in it with you. Which language learning strategies do you need to use?

LEARNING RUSSIAN: You are a student of Russian in a university. You have not found any Russian natives in your town, except for your own professor. You realize that your speaking and listening skills are shaky, though you are doing OK in reading and writing (for instance, you can pick your way through a journal article or short story in Russian and can write a passable letter). Your task is to find ways to improve your speaking and listening skills so that you feel more confident. Which language learning strategies do you need to use?

FOREIGN POSTING: Your spouse has an offer of a high-level management post in a multinational firm that makes shoelaces in Costa Rica. You don't know Spanish. You studied a little bit of French and German in school many years ago, but that does not seem to help much. You are very interested in other cultures. Your task is to learn enough Spanish to be able to get along socially and to help you take care of daily needs once you get to Costa Rica. Which language learning strategies do you need to use?

TROPICS: You are a new Peace Corps volunteer in the Philippines. You have been studying the local dialect that you will need to speak when you are posted in the north. You have completed about half of the language training so far, but you don't feel much confidence in your skills. You know you will be working with village irrigation programs when you finish your language training, so you will need technical language about irrigation. But you also know that the Filipinos are very friendly and sociable, so you think it will be important to develop social language. Your task is to figure out whether to concentrate your language training on developing technical, job-related language skills and/or social, non-job-related language skills, and then to make the most of language training so that you will be able to get along in a new and unfamiliar situation. Which language learning strategies do you need to use?

NEWSPAPER: You are a foreign language student in your second year of study. With your classmates, you are writing and publishing a newspaper in the target language. Your task is to use written pieces of target language information given to you and then to transform that information into articles—news, features, editorials—and format them into a readable newspaper. Which language learning strategies do you need to use?

READING A CHAPTER: You are a graduate student in nuclear physics. One of the latest and best books on the subject is in Russian and has not yet been translated into your own language. You and your friends have decided to read this book together by having each of you read and summarize a chapter. You are looking at your chapter. You don't understand all of the text word for word, but you can see that it is fairly well organized and that it contains a lot of technical words you already know. Your task is to read and understand your chapter and provide a written summary of it to present to others. Which language learning strategies do you need to use?

TOOTHACHE: You are a student living in another country, whose language you speak only a little. One of your teeth fell out last night. It dropped on the floor, and you cannot find it. You don't like going to the dentist, but you know you have to. You have a dictionary and a phrasebook. You must learn how to ask about finding a dentist and how to get the telephone number and address. Then you must be able to call the dentist's office to explain the problem and set an appointment time. Once in the dentist's office, you need to be able to cooperate with the dentist in having the problem treated, and arrange for payment. Which language learning strategies do you need to use?

ERRANDS: You are a Canadian student who has just come to Austria to learn German. You must run the following errands in town. First you have to go to the market to get some fruit and vegetables, then to the pharmacy for bandages and toothpaste, then to the bakery for bread, and then to the post office for stamps. You don't yet have all the vocabulary you need for these errands, but you have about an hour to practice the language before you need to run the errands. Which language learning strategies do you need to use?

Source Original.

Chapter 2

Direct Strategies for Dealing with Language

Trying to learn to use words, and every attempt is . . . a raid on the inarticulate.

T. S. Eliot

PREVIEW QUESTIONS

1. What are direct strategies?
2. How do they differ from indirect strategies?
3. Why are direct strategies important for language learning?
4. What are the three groups of direct strategies?

INTRODUCTION TO DIRECT STRATEGIES

Language learning strategies that directly involve the target language are called *direct strategies.* All direct strategies require mental processing of the language, but the three groups of direct strategies (memory, cognitive, and compensation) do this processing differently and for different purposes. *Memory strategies,* such as grouping or using imagery, have a highly specific function: helping students store and retrieve new information. *Cognitive strategies,* such as summarizing or reasoning deductively, enable learners to understand and produce new language by many different means. *Compensation strategies,* like guessing or using synonyms, allow learners to use the language despite their often large gaps in knowledge. Figure 2.1 highlights these three groups of direct strategies.

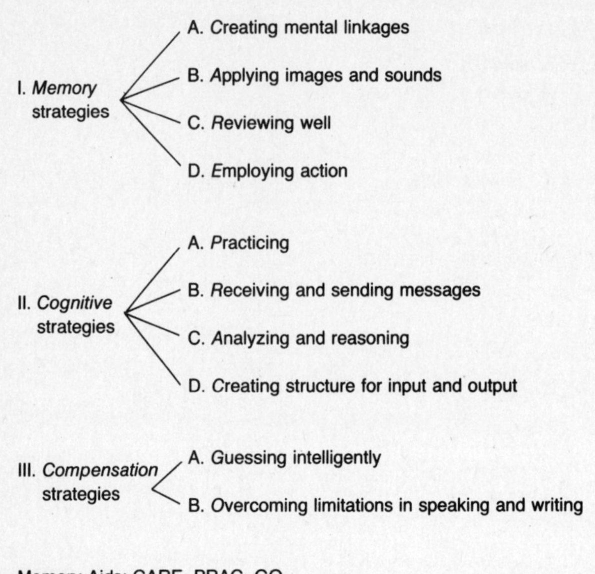

Figure 2.1 Diagram of the Direct Strategies: Overview. (*Source*: Original.)

MEMORY STRATEGIES

Memory strategies, sometimes called mnemonics, have been used for thousands of years. For example, orators in ancient times could remember a long speech by linking different parts of the speech with different rooms of a house or temple, and then "taking a walk" from room to room [1]. Before literacy became widespread, people used memory strategies to remember practical information about farming, weather, or when they were born. After literacy became commonplace, people forgot their previous reliance on memory strategies and disparaged those techniques as "gimmicks." Now memory strategies are regaining their prestige as powerful mental tools. The mind can store some 100 trillion bits of information, but only part of that potential can be used unless memory strategies come to the aid of the learner.

Memory strategies fall into four sets: *C*reating Mental Linkages, *A*pplying Images and Sounds, *R*eviewing Well, and *E*mploying Actions (see Figure 2.2). The first letters of each of these strategy sets spell CARE, an acronym that is itself a memory aid: "Take CARE of your memory and your memory will take CARE of you!" Memory strategies are clearly more effective when the learner simultaneously uses metacognitive strategies, like paying attention, and affective strategies, like reducing anxiety through deep breathing.

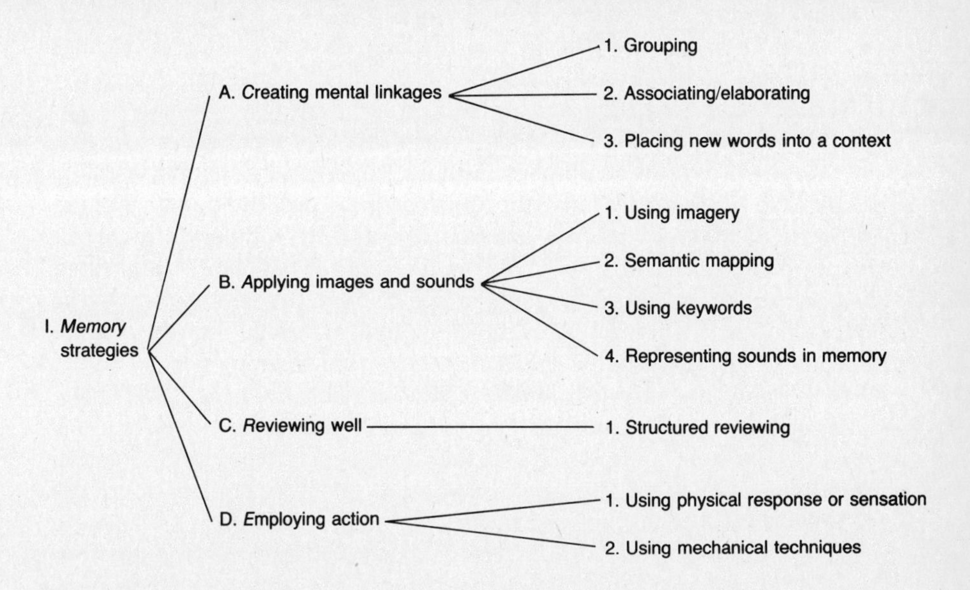

Memory Aid: CARE

"Take CARE of your memory, and
your memory will take CARE of you!"

The memory strengthens as you lay burdens upon it,
and becomes trustworthy as you trust it.

Thomas de Quincy

Figure 2.2 Diagram of the Memory Strategies. (*Source*: Original.)

Memory strategies reflect very simple principles, such as arranging things in order, making associations, and reviewing [2]. These principles all involve *meaning*. For the purpose of learning a new language, the arrangement and associations must be personally meaningful to the learner, and the material to be reviewed must have significance [3].

Though some teachers think vocabulary learning is easy, language learners have a serious problem remembering the large amounts of vocabulary necessary to achieve fluency. "Vocabulary is by far the most sizeable and unmanageable component in the learning of any language, whether a foreign or one's mother tongue" because of "tens of thousands of different meanings," according to Lord [4]. Memory strategies help language learners to cope with this difficulty. They enable learners to store verbal material and then retrieve it when needed for communication. In addition, the memory strategy of structured reviewing helps move information from the "fact level" to the "skill level," where knowledge is more procedural and automatic [5]. When information has reached the skill level, it is more easily retrieved and less easily lost after a period of disuse [6].

Memory strategies often involve pairing different types of material. In language learning, it is possible to give verbal labels to pictures, or to create visual images of words or phrases. Linking the verbal with the visual is very useful to language learning for four reasons. First, the mind's storage capacity for visual information exceeds its capacity for verbal material. Second, the most efficiently packaged chunks of information are transferred to long-term memory through visual images. Third, visual images may be the most potent device to aid recall of verbal material. Fourth, a large proportion of learners have a preference for visual learning [7].

While many language learners benefit from visual imagery, others have aural (sound-oriented), kinesthetic (motion-oriented) or tactile (touch-oriented) learning style preferences and therefore benefit from linking verbal material with sound, motion or touch. Certain memory strategies are designed to do this [8]. In memory strategies, as in other kinds of learning strategies, "different strokes for different folks" should be the cardinal rule.

Although memory strategies can be powerful contributors to language learning, some research shows that language students rarely report using these strategies [9]. It might be that students simply do not use memory strategies very much, especially beyond elementary levels of language learning. However, an alternative explanation might be that they are unaware of how often they actually *do* employ memory strategies. Below are the definitions of each memory strategy, as clustered into appropriate strategy sets.

Creating Mental Linkages

In this set are three strategies that form the cornerstone for the rest of the memory strategies: grouping, associating/elaborating, and using context.

1. Grouping

Classifying or reclassifying language material into meaningful units, either mentally or in writing, to make the material easier to remember by reducing the number of discrete elements. Groups can be based on type of word (e.g., all nouns or verbs), topic (e.g., words about weather), practical function (e.g., terms for things that make a car work), linguistic function (e.g., apology, request, demand), similarity (e.g., warm, hot, tepid, tropical), dissimilarity or opposition (e.g., friendly/unfriendly), the way one feels about something (e.g., like, dislike), and so on. The power of this strategy may be enhanced by labeling the groups, using acronyms to remember the groups, or using different colors to represent different groups.

2. Associating/Elaborating

Relating new language information to concepts already in memory, or relating one piece of information to another, to create associations in memory. These associations can be simple or complex, mundane or strange, but they must be meaningful to the learner. Associations can be between two things, such as bread and butter, or they can be in the form of a multipart "development," such as school–book–paper–tree–country–earth [10]. They can also be part of a network, such as a semantic map (see below).

3. Placing New Words into a Context

Placing a word or phrase in a meaningful sentence, conversation, or story in order to remember it. This strategy involves a form of associating/elaborating, in which the new information is linked with a context. This strategy is not the same as guessing intelligently, a set of compensation strategies (described later) which involve using all possible clues, including the context, to guess the meaning.

Applying Images and Sounds

Four strategies are included here: using imagery, using keywords, semantic mapping, and representing sounds in memory. These all involve remembering by means of visual images or sounds.

1. Using Imagery

Relating new language information to concepts in memory by means of meaningful visual imagery, either in the mind or in an actual drawing. The image can be a picture of an object, a set of locations for remembering a sequence of words or expressions, or a mental representation of the letters of a word. This strategy can be used to remember abstract words by associating such words with a visual symbol or a picture of a concrete object.

2. Semantic Mapping [11]

Making an arrangement of words into a picture, which has a key concept at the center or at the top, and related words and concepts linked with the key concept by means of lines or arrows. This strategy involves meaningful imagery, grouping, and associations; it visually shows how certain groups of words relate to each other.

3. Using Keywords [12]

Remembering a new word by using auditory and visual links. The first step is to identify a familiar word in one's own language that sounds like the new word—this is the "auditory link." The second step is to generate an image of some relationship between the new word and a familiar one—this is the "visual link." Both links must be meaningful to the learner. For example, to learn the new French word *potage* (soup), the English speaker associates it with a pot and then pictures a pot full of *potage*. To use a keyword to remember something abstract, such as a name, associate it with a picture of something concrete that sounds like the new word. For example, Minnesota can be remembered by the image of a *mini soda* [13].

4. Representing Sounds in Memory

Remembering new language information according to its sound. This is a broad strategy that can use any number of techniques, all of which create a meaningful, sound-based association between the new material and already known material. For instance, you can (a) link a target language word with any other word (in any language) that sounds like the target language word, such as Russian *brat* [брат] (brother) and English *brat* (annoying person), (b) use phonetic spelling and/or accent marks, or (c) use rhymes to remember a word.

Reviewing Well

This category contains just one strategy, structured reviewing. Looking at new target language information once is not enough; it must be reviewed in order to be remembered.

1. Structured Reviewing [14]

Reviewing in carefully spaced intervals, at first close together and then more widely spaced apart. This strategy might start, for example, with a review 10 minutes after the initial learning, then 20 minutes later, an hour or two later, a day later, 2 days later, a week later, and so on. This is sometimes called "spiraling," because the learner keeps spiraling back to what has already been learned at the same time that he or she is learning new information. The goal is "overlearning"—that is, being so familiar with the information that it becomes natural and automatic.

Employing Action

The two strategies in this set, using physical response or sensation and using mechanical tricks, both involve some kind of meaningful movement or action. These strategies will appeal to learners who enjoy the kinesthetic or tactile modes of learning.

1. Using Physical Response or Sensation [15]

Physically acting out a new expression (e.g., going to the door), or *meaningfully relating a new expression to a physical feeling or sensation* (e.g., warmth).

2. Using Mechanical Techniques

Using creative but tangible techniques, especially involving moving or changing something which is concrete, in order to remember new target language information. Examples are writing words on cards and moving cards from one stack to another when a word is learned, and putting different types of material in separate sections of a language learning notebook.

COGNITIVE STRATEGIES

Cognitive strategies are essential in learning a new language. Such strategies are a varied lot, ranging from repeating to analyzing expressions to summarizing. With all their variety, cognitive strategies are unified by a common function: manipulation or transformation of the target language by the learner [16]. Cognitive strategies are typically found to be the most popular strategies with language learners [17].

Four sets of cognitive strategies exist, as shown in Figure 2.3: *P*racticing, *R*eceiving and Sending Messages, *A*nalyzing and Reasoning, and *C*reating Structure for Input and Output. The first letters of each of these strategy sets combine to form the acronym PRAC, because "Cognitive strategies are PRACtical for language learning."

Strategies for practicing are among the most important cognitive strategies. Language learners do not always realize how essential practice is. During class, potential practice opportunities are often missed because one person recites while the others sit idle. Even when small group activities increase the amount of classroom practice, still more practice is usually needed to reach acceptable proficiency, a goal which requires hundreds or even thousands of hours of practice, depending on the difficulty of the language and other factors [18]. Given these facts, the practicing strategies—including repeating, formally practicing with sounds and writing systems, recognizing and using formulas and patterns, recombining, and practicing naturalistically—take on special value. Research has underscored the importance of naturalistic practice at all levels of language learning [19].

Strategies for receiving and sending messages are necessary tools. One such strategy, known as getting the idea quickly, helps learners locate the main idea through skimming or the key points of interest through scanning. This strategy implies that it is not necessary for learners to focus on every single word. Another strategy in this group, using resources, is useful for

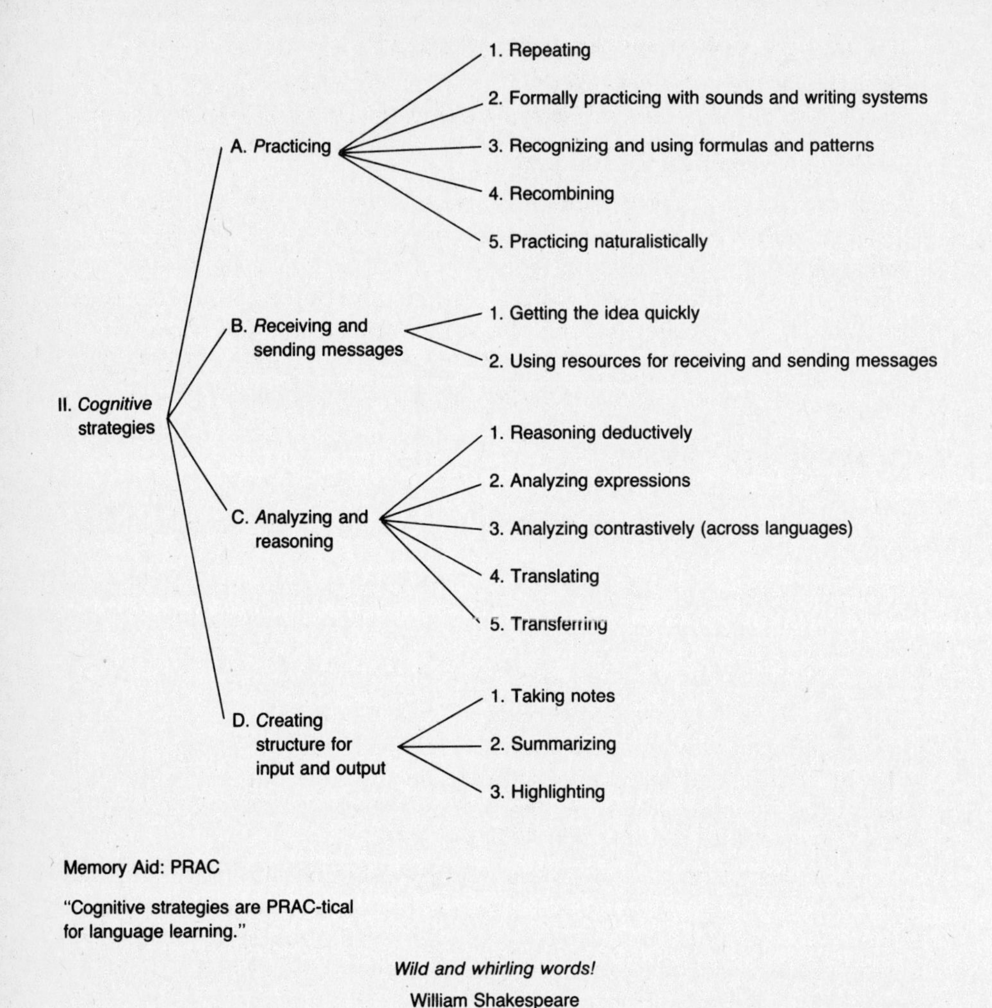

Figure 2.3 Diagram of the Cognitive Strategies. (*Source*: Original.)

both comprehension and production. It helps learners take advantage of a variety of resources, print or nonprint, to understand and produce messages in the new language.

Analyzing and reasoning strategies are commonly used by language learners. Many learners, especially adults [20], tend to "reason out" the new language. They construct a formal model in their minds based on analysis and comparison, create general rules, and revise those rules when new information is available. This process is extremely valuable. However, sometimes students make mistakes by unquestioningly generalizing the rules they've learned or transferring expressions from one language to another, typically from the mother tongue to the new language. Such mistakes characterize the "interlanguage," a hybrid form of language that lies somewhere between the native language and the target language [21]. Inappropriate use of literal translation also contributes to the interlanguage [22]. Interlanguage is a predictable, normal phase of language learning, but some language learners fail to leave that phase because they misuse or overuse some of the analyzing and reasoning strategies.

Language learners often feel besieged by "whirling words" from radio and TV programs, films, lectures, stories, articles, and conversations. To understand better, learners need to structure all this input into manageable chunks by using strategies such as taking notes, summarizing, and highlighting. Such structure-generating strategies are also helpful in preparing to use the language for speaking and writing.

Following are the definitions of important cognitive strategies.

Practicing

Of the five practicing strategies, probably the most significant one is practicing naturalistically.

1. Repeating

Saying or doing something over and over: listening to something several times; rehearsing; imitating a native speaker.

2. Formally Practicing with Sounds and Writing Systems

Practicing sounds (pronunciation, intonation, register, etc.) in a variety of ways, but not yet in naturalistic communicative practice; or *practicing the new writing system* of the target language.

3. Recognizing and Using Formulas and Patterns

Being aware of and/or using routine formulas (single, unanalyzed units), such as "Hello, how are you?"; *and unanalyzed patterns* (which have at least one slot to be filled), such as, "It's time to ———."

4. Recombining

Combining known elements in new ways to produce a longer sequence, as in linking one phrase with another in a whole sentence.

5. Practicing Naturalistically

Practicing the new language in natural, realistic settings, as in participating in a conversation, reading a book or article, listening to a lecture, or writing a letter in the new language.

Receiving and Sending Messages

Two strategies for receiving and sending messages are (a) getting the idea quickly and (b) using resources for receiving and sending messages. The former uses two specific techniques for extracting ideas, while the latter involves using a variety of resources for understanding or producing meaning.

1. Getting the Idea Quickly

Using skimming to determine the main ideas or scanning to find specific details of interest. This strategy helps learners understand rapidly what they hear or read in the new language. *Preview questions often assist.*

2. Using Resources for Receiving and Sending Messages

Using print or nonprint resources to understand incoming messages or produce outgoing messages.

Analyzing and Reasoning

This set of five strategies concerns logical analysis and reasoning as applied to various target language skills. Often learners can use these strategies to understand the meaning of a new expression or to create a new expression.

1. Reasoning Deductively

Using general rules and applying them to new target language situations. This is a top-down strategy leading from general to specific.

2. Analyzing Expressions

Determining the meaning of a new expression by breaking it down into parts; using the meanings of various parts to understand the meaning of the whole expression.

3. Analyzing Contrastively

Comparing elements (sounds, vocabulary, grammar) of the new language with elements of one's own language to determine similarities and differences.

4. Translating

Converting a target language expression into the native language (at various levels, from words and phrases all the way up to whole texts); *or converting the native language into the target language;* using one language as the basis for understanding or producing another.

5. Transferring

Directly applying knowledge of words, concepts, or structures from one language to another in order to understand or produce an expression in the new language.

Creating Structure for Input and Output

The following three strategies are ways to create structure, which is necessary for both comprehension and production in the new language.

1. Taking Notes

Writing down the main idea or specific points. This strategy can involve raw notes, or it can comprise a more systematic form of note-taking such as the shopping-list format, the T-formation, the semantic map, or the standard outline form.

2. Summarizing

Making a summary or abstract of a longer passage.

3. Highlighting

Using a variety of emphasis techniques (such as underlining, starring, or color-coding) to focus on important information in a passage.

COMPENSATION STRATEGIES

Compensation strategies enable learners to use the new language for either comprehension or production despite limitations in knowledge. Compensation strategies are intended to make up for an inadequate repertoire of grammar and, especially, of vocabulary. Ten compensation strategies exist, clustered into two sets: Guessing Intelligently in Listening and Reading, and Overcoming Limitations in Speaking and Writing (see Figure 2.4). These two sets can be remembered by the acronym GO, since "Language learners can GO far with compensation strategies."

Guessing strategies, sometimes called "inferencing," involve using a wide variety of clues—linguistic and nonlinguistic—to guess the meaning when the learner does not know all the words [23]. Good language learners, when confronted with unknown expressions, make educated guesses. On the other hand, less adept language learners often panic, tune out, or grab the dog-eared dictionary and try to look up every unfamiliar word—harmful responses which impede progress toward proficiency.

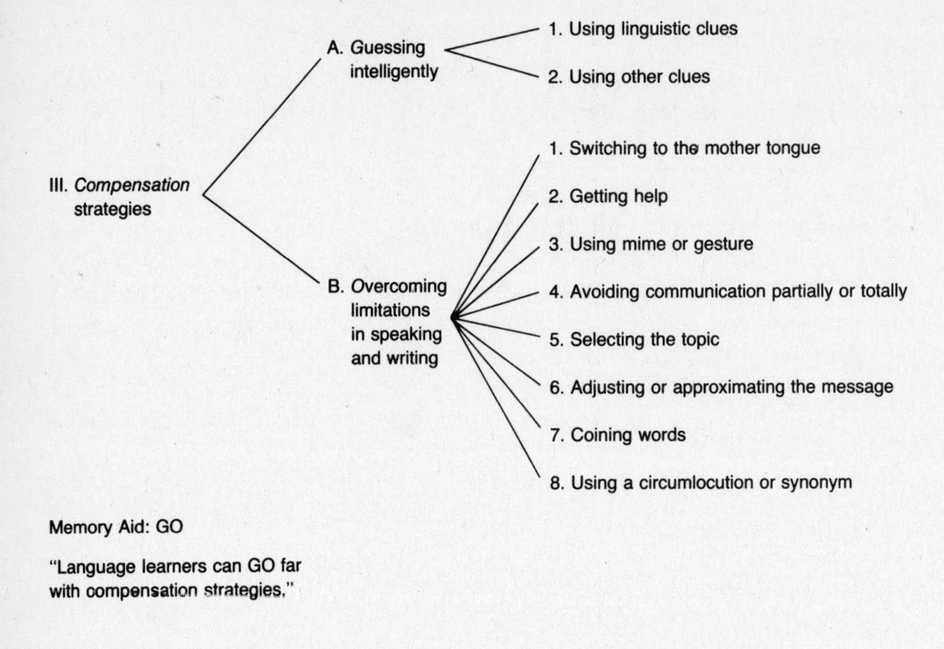

Figure 2.4 Diagram of the Compensation Strategies. (*Source*: Original.)

Beginners are not the only ones who employ guessing. Advanced learners and even native speakers use guessing when they haven't heard something well enough, when they don't know a new word, or when the meaning is hidden between the lines. Guessing is actually just a special case of the way people typically process new information—that is, interpreting the data by using the immediate context and their own life experience. "Meaning is in fact created by the receiver in light of the experience which [s]he already possesses," said MacBride [24]. It is this experience which provides the source of many intelligent guesses for both language experts and novices.

Compensation occurs not just in understanding the new language but also in producing it. Compensation strategies allow learners to produce spoken or written expression in the new language without complete knowledge. Researchers have typically paid attention only to compensation strategies for speaking [25]. It is true that certain compensation strategies, like using mime or gestures, are used in speaking. However, other compensation strategies—adjusting or approximating the message, coining words, using a circumlocution or synonym, or selecting the topic—can be used in informal writing as well as in speaking.

Many compensation strategies for production are used to compensate for a lack of appropriate vocabulary, but these strategies can also be used to make up for a lack of grammatical knowledge. For instance, if learners do not know how to express the subjunctive form of a verb, they might use a different form to get the message across.

Just as advanced learners and native speakers occasionally use guessing to help them understand, they sometimes use compensation strategies when experiencing a temporary breakdown in speaking or writing performance. Less proficient language learners need these compensatory production strategies even more, because they run into knowledge roadblocks more often than do individuals who are skilled in the language.

Compensation strategies for production help learners to keep on using the language, thus obtaining more practice. In addition, some of these strategies, such as adjusting or approximating the message, help learners become more fluent in what they already know. Still other compensation strategies, like getting help and coining words, may lead learners to gain new information about what is appropriate or permissible in the target language [26]. Learners skilled in such strategies sometimes communicate better than learners who know many more target language words and structures.

Here are definitions of some key compensation strategies.

Guessing Intelligently in Listening and Reading

The two strategies which contribute to guessing intelligently refer to two different kinds of clues: linguistic and nonlinguistic [27].

1. Using Linguistic Clues

Seeking and using language-based clues in order to guess the meaning of what is heard or read in the target language, in the absence of complete knowledge of vocabulary, grammar, or other target language elements. Language-based clues may come from aspects of the target language that the learner already knows, from the learners' own language, or from another language. For instance, if the learner does not know the expression *association sans but lucratif* ("nonprofit association," in French), previous knowledge of certain words in English (association, lucrative) and French (*sans* = without) would give clues to the meaning of the unknown word, *but* (aim, goal), and of the whole expression.

2. Using Other Clues

Seeking and using clues that are not language-based in order to guess the meaning of what is heard or read in the target language, in the absence of complete knowledge of vocabulary, grammar, or other target language elements. Nonlanguage clues may come from a wide variety of sources: knowledge of context, situation, text structure, personal relationships, topic, or "general world knowledge." For example, if the learner does not know what is meant by the words *vends* or *à vendre* in the French newspaper, noticing that these words are used in the context of classified ads, and that they are followed by a list of items and prices, provides clues suggesting that these terms probably refer to selling.

Overcoming Limitations in Speaking and Writing

Eight strategies are used for overcoming limitations in speaking and writing. Some of these are dedicated solely to speaking, but some can be used for writing, as well.

1. Switching to the Mother Tongue

Using the mother tongue for an expression without translating it, as in *Ich bin eine girl*. This strategy may also include adding word endings from the new language onto words from the mother tongue.

2. Getting Help

Asking someone for help by hesitating or explicitly asking for the person to provide the missing expression in the target language.

3. Using Mime or Gesture

Using physical motion, such as mime or gesture, in place of an expression to indicate the meaning.

4. Avoiding Communication Partially or Totally

Partially or totally avoiding communication when difficulties are anticipated. This strategy may involve avoiding communication in general, avoiding certain topics, avoiding specific expressions, or abandoning communication in mid-utterance.

5. Selecting the Topic

Choosing the topic of conversation in order to direct the communication to one's own interests and make sure the topic is one in which the learner has sufficient vocabulary and grammar to converse.

6. Adjusting or Approximating the Message

Altering the message by omitting some items of information, making ideas simpler or less precise, or saying something slightly different that means almost the same thing, such as saying *pencil* for *pen*.

7. Coining Words

Making up new words to communicate the desired idea, such as *paper-holder* for *notebook*.

8. Using a Circumlocution or Synonym

Getting the meaning across by describing the concept (circumlocution) or using a word that means the same thing (synonym); for example, "what you use to wash dishes with" as a description for *dishrag*.

SUMMARY

This chapter has explained direct strategies, which involve use of the new language, and has described these groups of direct strategies: memory, cognitive, and compensation. Definitions of a variety of specific strategies in each group were also given. In the next chapter, these strategies will be applied to the four language skills.

ACTIVITIES FOR READERS

Activity 2.1. Check Your Attitudes Toward Memory Strategies

Consider your attitudes toward memory strategies. Were you brought up to believe that memory strategies are just gimmicks or tricks that are not used by serious people? Or have you generally believed that memory strategies are valuable tools for improving mental power? Explain how your attitude toward memory strategies has or has not changed through reading this chapter.

List at least eight new ideas about memory strategies you gained from this chapter. Put one star beside each of the ideas which might benefit you personally. Put two stars beside each of those which might help your students as well.

Activity 2.2. Examine Memory Strategies in Different Settings

Brainstorm the ways that memory strategies might be used in two different settings: the language classroom and a naturalistic language setting outside of the classroom (for example, a local cultural event where the language is used). Be as specific as possible.

Activity 2.3. Think About Language Loss

Have you or your students experienced loss of language skills through nonuse? If so, under what circumstances? What kinds of memory strategies might have helped prevent this loss?

Activity 2.4. Consider the Nature of Practicing

Draw a continuum ranging from more realistic to less realistic. Now classify the five practicing strategies on that continuum. List the differences between the more realistic practicing strategies and the less realistic ones. Indicate when each would be useful.

Activity 2.5. Work with Skimming and Scanning

The next time you read the newspaper in your own language, pay attention to how you read. Notice whether you use skimming or scanning to get the idea quickly, or whether you try to comprehend every word. Consider how you can help your students develop and practice their own skimming and scanning skills in the target language.

Activity 2.6. Find Resources

Make a list of the resources that students might use to understand, say, or write something in the new language. Indicate where those resources might be found. Consider how you can help your students know about these resources.

Activity 2.7. List the Pros and Cons of Analyzing/Reasoning

List all the ways that analyzing and reasoning can assist language learning. Now list all the ways that analyzing and reasoning can inhibit progress toward language proficiency. Discuss how teachers can help their students avoid traps such as overgeneralization.

Activity 2.8. Consider the Need for Structure

List ways in which people might use structuring strategies such as note-taking, summarizing, and highlighting in everyday life. Now discuss how these strategies can be used in learning a new language.

Activity 2.9. Notice Students' Compensatory Speaking Strategies

Notice your students' compensation strategies as they speak with each other and with you in the target language. Make a list of these strategies.

Indicate which of the strategies occur most often and least often. Note whether this depends on the student, with some students using certain compensation strategies more than others.

Activity 2.10. Consider Learning and Communication

Do you feel that the saying "Learning takes place *through* communication" is accurate in regard to your students? Explain.

EXERCISES TO USE WITH YOUR STUDENTS

Exercise 2.1. Ask Students to Identify Their Memory Strategies

Purpose

This exercise helps students consider the kinds of memory strategies they use and introduces them to new ones.

Materials

Large sheets of paper for the list.

Time

This exercise, lasting 20 minutes or more, can be done periodically in order to add to the list.

Instructions

Ask your students to identify their own memory strategies. It is not necessary to try to classify those strategies according to the list in this chapter. Just let students come up with their own strategy descriptions and share them with each other. Add to the list as time goes by, on the basis of classroom activities involving vocabulary learning. Encourage students to keep sharing their memory strategies.

Source Original.

Exercise 2.2. Get the Message

Purpose

This exercise helps students practice a variety of strategies for understanding an oral message.

Materials

Film, cartoon, or news program; equipment to play it.

Time

It takes 30 minutes to 1 hour, depending on the length of the material.

Instructions

Get hold of a short suspense film, cartoon, or TV news program in the target language. Play it for your students, asking them in advance to pay attention to the ways they receive the message. Afterwards, have them brainstorm the ways they used skimming, scanning, guessing, or other strategies to understand.

Alternatively, run the show *twice*—the first time without the sound but with the visual input, and the second time with both sound and visual input. After each run, ask your students to explain (a) what they understood and (b) the clues they used to help them understand.

Source Original.

Exercise 2.3. Play Twenty Questions

Purpose

This exercise gives practice in guessing using a familiar game.

Materials

None.

Time

The exercise takes 20 to 45 minutes.

Instructions

Play the game Twenty Questions, first in the native language and then in the target language. To play the game, one person thinks of an expression, such as "hiking in the mountains." Then that person provides clues about the expression to the other participants, so they can guess what the expression is. They can ask only 20 questions, which must be answerable by either "yes" or "no." Permissible extra clues include whether the expression refers to something animal, vegetable, or mineral; the number of words in the expression; and whether the expression contains the definite article (*the*) or the indefinite article (*a, an*), for those languages which have such articles. After one round is over, switch roles so that a different participant thinks of an expression, and the others guess. Use this game as a springboard to a discussion of the uses of guessing strategies.

Source Traditional parlor game.

Exercise 2.4. Hold a Conversation

Purpose

This exercise enables students to consider the kinds of strategies they use in a conversation and how often they use them.

Materials

Paper for a list.

Time

Lasts 30 to 45 minutes.

Instructions

Ask your students to hold a 5-minute conversation in the new language, on any topic, with a classmate. Ask them to list the strategies they used either to understand what was said or to produce expressions when they did not know the precise words. Ask them to make a rough estimate of the number of times each strategy was used by each person in the conversation. Now ask them how they felt when they used these strategies (happy to keep on in the conversation, ignorant because unable to think of the right word, pleased to be understood, etc.).

Source Original.

Chapter 3

Applying Direct Strategies to the Four Language Skills

It is better to see once than to hear a hundred times.
RUSSIAN PROVERB

PREVIEW QUESTIONS

1. How can the direct strategies be applied to the four language skills?
2. How are these strategies applied differently to the four skills?
3. Are any direct strategies especially useful to the development of a particular skill?

INTRODUCTION TO APPLYING THE DIRECT STRATEGIES

This chapter discusses how the three groups of direct strategies—memory, cognitive, and compensation strategies (see Figure 3.1)—are used to develop each of the four language skills: listening, reading, speaking, and writing. These direct strategies work best when supported by indirect strategies, which are described in detail in Chapter 4.

Underlying the discussion are two assumptions. First, all four language skills are important and deserve special attention and action [1]. Second, learning strategies help students to develop each of the skills. In this chapter, the language skills related to each strategy are noted, following the section title, like this: Ⓛ (listening), Ⓡ (reading), Ⓢ (speaking), Ⓦ (writing), Ⓐ (all skills).

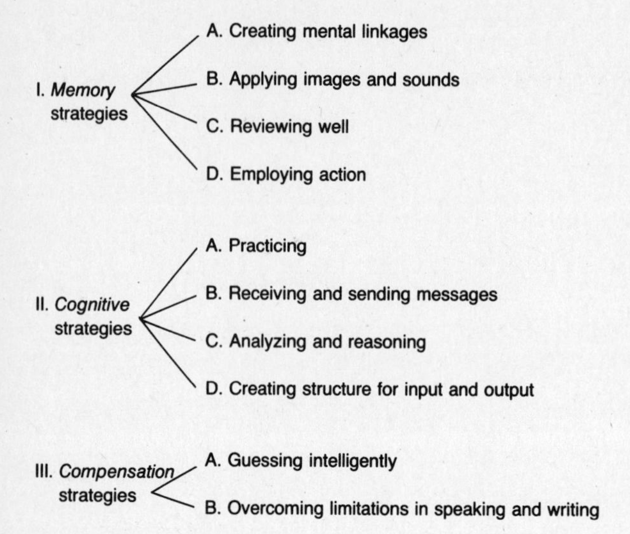

Figure 3.1 Diagram of the Direct Strategies to Be Applied to the Four Language Skills. (*Source*: Original.)

APPLYING MEMORY STRATEGIES TO THE FOUR LANGUAGE SKILLS

Storage and retrieval of new information are the two key functions of memory strategies. These strategies, as shown in Figure 3.2, help learners *store* in memory the important things they hear or read in the new language, thus enlarging their knowledge base. These strategies also enable learners to *retrieve* information from memory when they need to use it for comprehension or production. Descriptions of memory strategies below focus mostly on the storage function, because that is the initial key to learning, but some general comments are included about the retrieval function as well.

Creating Mental Linkages

Three kinds of strategies are useful for making mental linkages: grouping, associating/elaborating, and placing new words into a context. These are the most basic memory strategies and the foundation of more complex memory strategies.

Grouping Ⓛ Ⓡ Grouping involves classifying or reclassifying what is heard or read into meaningful groups, thus reducing the number of unrelated elements. It sometimes involves labeling the groups, as well. Notice

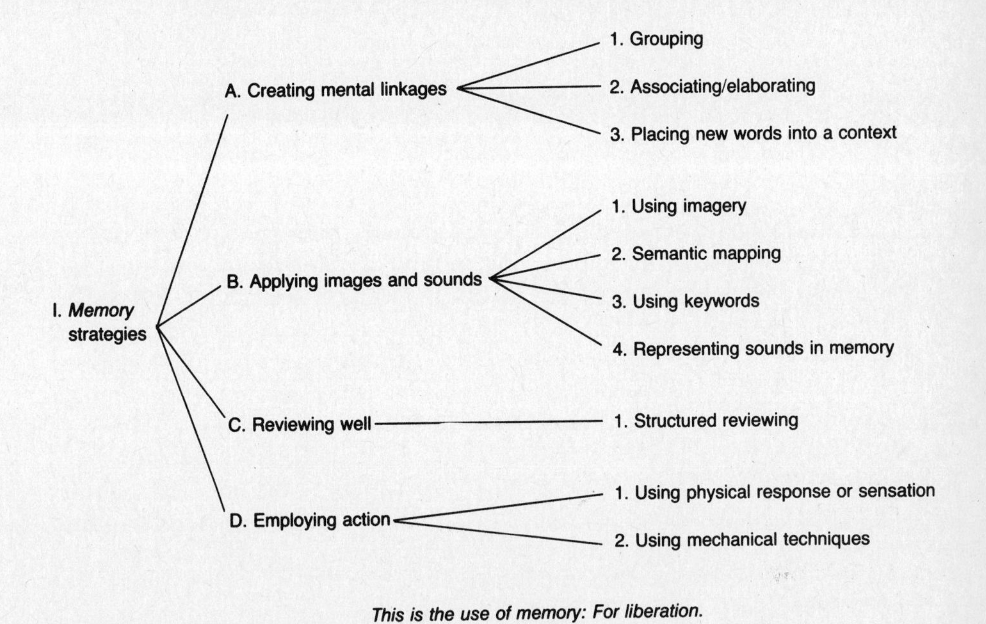

Figure 3.2 Diagram of the Memory Strategies to Be Applied to the Four Language Skills. (*Source*: Original.)

that some of the examples below involve other strategies, too, such as paying attention or taking notes.

The following examples show ways to group material that has been heard in the new language [2]. First, Norberto, who is learning English, writes down in his notebook new words when he hears them, and he categorizes them grammatically: for example, *you, he, she, they, someone; hard, easy, kind, soft; quickly, heatedly, markedly, completely*. Then he labels these categories: pronouns, adjectives, and adverbs. Second, Jennie, a student of French, is listening to a talk about computers. She writes down the important words, such as *l'informatique* (computer science), *l'ordinateur* (computer), *le moniteur* (monitor), *l'écran* (screen), *le clavier* (keyboard), *la puce* (chip, literally flea!), *l'unité centrale* (central processing unit), and *les touches* (the keys). Then she groups these words according to whether they are masculine or feminine.

Here are some examples of grouping of written material that has been read. First, Lucien, a French speaker learning English, groups new words that he reads by conceptual similarities (e.g., *hot, warm, fire*), and in reading he actively looks for the opposites, such as *cold, cool, ice*. Second, while Stephanie is reading, she jots down new Russian verbs that she encounters, putting them into various categories, such as motion verbs and nonmotion verbs. Third, Donny makes a column for each of the important French prefixes (e.g., *e-*, *en-/m*, *entre-*, *para-*, *sou-*) and each of the suffixes (e.g., *-able*, *-age*, *-ier*, *-oir*, *-eux*). Then, as he reads French, Donny writes down interesting examples of words he encounters which use these prefixes and suffixes.

Associating/Elaborating Ⓛ Ⓡ This memory strategy involves associating new language information with familiar concepts already in memory. Naturally, these associations are likely to strengthen comprehension, as well as making the material easier to remember. Below are some real instances of associating/elaborating that are personally significant to the learners involved. Any association must have *meaning* to the learner, even though it might not make a geat deal of sense to someone else.

Here are some examples of associating/elaborating in the listening area. First, Mike wants to remember the name of Solange, the university librarian, who has just been introduced in French. He associates the name Solange with something else about her by saying "*So long*, library, I'm leaving!" or "Solange's face is *so long*." Second, Corazon, a learner of English, hears the word *billboard*. She associates it with a previously learned word, *board*, used for displaying; therefore she understands and remembers *billboard* more effectively.

Following are some examples of associating/elaborating in reading. First, Benjamin reads a German story that contains the word *Wissenschaft* (knowledge). He associates this word with the English words *wise* and *shaft* and remembers the German word by thinking of knowledge as a *shaft of wisdom*. Second, Glennys reads the Russian word *soyuz* [союз] (union); to remember this word, she associates it with her friend Susie.

Placing New Words into a Context Ⓐ This strategy involves placing new words or expressions that have been heard or read into a meaningful context, such as a spoken or written sentence, as a way of remembering it. As an example in listening, Michel has heard the names of the Great Lakes in the United States and wants to remember them. To do so, he uses the acronym *HOMES* (standing for Huron, Ontario, Michigan, Erie, and Superior) and puts it in the context of the spoken sentence, "My *HOME'S* on the Great Lakes."

Written selections often present new words in a meaningful context. However, students sometimes encounter written lists of words or phrases they must learn with no supporting or explanatory context. In such cases, it helps for learners to create their own context. For example, Katya, a learner of English, encounters a list of words and expressions related to sewing, such as *hook, eye, seam, zipper, button, snap, thread, needle, baste, hem*, and *stitch*. She writes a little story to put these words into a meaningful context. And Keith, while reading his German language book, finds a list of verbs that are unrelated in meaning, though they have some grammatical similarities (e.g., *ankommen*, to arrive, *aufstehen*, to get up, *ausgehen*, to go out, *fortfahren*, to go on, *einsteigen*, to get in, *wegnehmen*, to take away, *abreisen*, to set out, *zumachen*, to shut). He creates a funny tale that contains all these verbs.

Applying Images and Sounds

The four strategies for applying images and sounds are useful for remembering new expressions that have been heard or read. These strategies include using imagery, semantic mapping, using keywords, and representing sounds in memory. One of these strategies, semantic mapping, is immediately helpful for comprehension, too.

Using Imagery Ⓛ Ⓡ A good way to remember what has been heard or read in the new language is to create a mental image of it. Here are some illustrations. First, Adel, a Spanish bank manager learning English, tries to remember the American phrase *tax shelter*, which he has just heard [3]. He uses a mental image of a small house protecting or sheltering a pile of money inside. Second, Quang remembers a whole set of verbs related to household chores (e.g., *cooking, cleaning, washing, cutting, buying*) by making a mental image of the situation in which he first heard these words during an English class in the refugee camp. Third, Helen has just read the phrase *les mouettes blancs* (French for the white seagulls), and she mentally pictures white seagulls flying in the sky. Fourth, Jeff has read the Russian sentence *Ya hochu pisat' pis'mo* [Я хочу писать письмо] (I want to write a letter), and he pictures these Russian words in his mind.

One kind of imaging has special value in reading. It involves remembering a written item by picturing the place where it is located. For instance, Mariette remembers new English verbs by imagining the place where they are on the page. Jill remembers the expression *Cédez le passage* (yield) by picturing the road sign where she first read it.

The imagery used to remember expressions does not have to be purely mental. Drawings can make mental images (of objects like *house* or *tree*, or descriptive adjectives like *wide* or *tall*) more concrete. Even abstract words like *evil* or *truth* can be turned into symbols on a piece of paper for the purpose of remembering. For many prepositions, such as the equivalent of *above, over, under, among, between, below*, or *into*, learners can draw diagrams with arrows to illustrate meanings. These visual products do not need to be artistic. Just about anyone can draw stick figures, sketches, or diagrams to communicate a concept worth remembering.

Semantic Mapping Ⓛ Ⓡ This strategy involves arranging concepts and relationships on paper to create a semantic map, a diagram in which the key concepts (stated in words) are highlighted and are linked with related concepts via arrows or lines. Such a diagram visually shows how ideas fit together. This strategy incorporates a variety of other memory strategies: grouping, using imagery, and associating/elaborating. This strategy is valuable for improving both memory and comprehension of new expressions. It can be used for prelistening or prereading activities designed to help learners understand and remember vocabulary that will be heard or read. It can also be used as the basis for an entire listening or reading activity by giving the main concept or expression and asking students to listen and fill in the rest. Semantic mapping also provides a good note-taking format. Of course, in an exercise based on semantic mapping, there is no single "right answer," because different students will have different approaches to clustering ideas—unless a particular formula is taught (not a useful practice if the purpose is for learners to make their *own* associational linkages) [4].

Three examples of semantic mapping appear in Figures 3.3, 3.4, and 3.5. In the first illustration (Figure 3.3), *la corrida de toros* (the bullfight) is the key concept, and sets of related vocabulary are listed around this central theme and linked with it by means of lines. The next two figures (3.4 and 3.5) show a different example, in which the concept *hair* is mapped with its related concepts. Figure 3.4 is a simple version, mainly using words connected with lines. Figure 3.5 enhances the meaning of the words by using abundant pictures of objects. On their own, learners can make semantic maps like this to cluster or group related concepts visually, thus making the concepts easier to remember.

Using Keywords Ⓛ Ⓡ This strategy combines sounds and images so that learners can more easily remember what they hear or read in the new language. The strategy has two steps. First, identify a familiar word in one's own language or another language that sounds like the new word. Second, generate a visual image of the new word and the familiar one interacting in some way. Notice that the target language word does not have to sound exactly like the familiar word. (Additional pronunciation practice may be needed via the strategy of formally practicing with sounds and writing systems.)

Here are some examples of keywords for remembering what is heard or read. Brian links the new French word *froid* (cold) with a familiar word, *Freud*, then imagines Freud standing outside in the cold. *Sobor* [собор] is the Russian word for council, so Alice links this new word with *so bored*, picturing a bunch of councillors "so bored" with their meeting. Howard links the new Spanish word *sombrero* (hat with a large brim) with *somber*, and imagines a somber man wearing a sombrero. Fourth, in Italian the word for fly is *mosca*, so Bernie pictures flies invading Moscow. Julianne reads the new Spanish word for waitress, *camarera*, relates it to a *camera*, then imagines a waitress with a camera slung around her neck. Jeremy

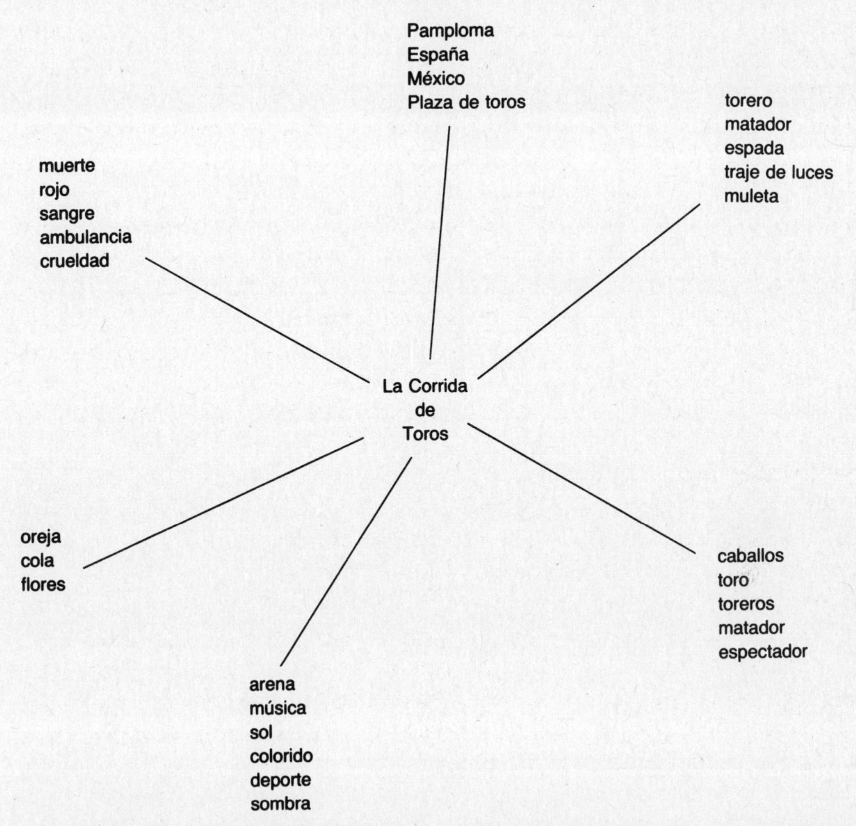

Figure 3.3 Example of a Semantic Map for "Bullfight" (*La Corrida de Toros*) Using Related Words. (*Source*: Hague (1987, p. 222).)

reads a new French word, *grève* (strike), and links it with a familiar English word that sounds similar, *grievance*, picturing a group of strikers taking a list of grievances to their employer. Yolande, a French speaker, reads the English word *pool*. To remember it, she thinks of the French word *poulet* (chicken, also slang for policeman) and imagines a chicken (or a policeman!) with sunglasses sitting by a pool.

Representing Sounds in Memory Ⓛ Ⓡ Ⓢ This strategy helps learners remember what they hear by making auditory rather than visual representations of sounds. This involves linking the new word with familiar words or sounds from any language: the new language, one's own language, or any other.

Rhymes are a well-known example of representing sounds in memory. Most English speakers know the helpful spelling rhyme "*I* before *E* except

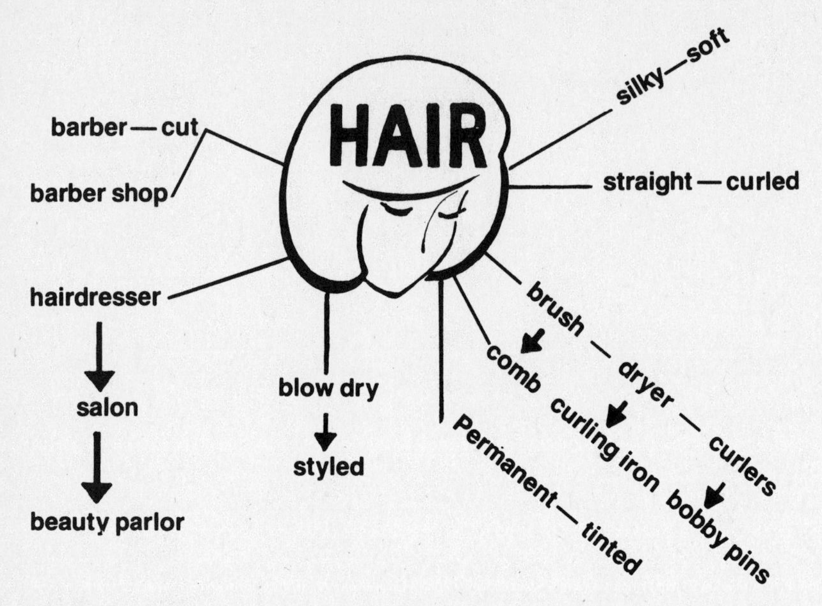

Figure 3.4 Example of a Semantic Map for "Hair" Using Related Words. (*Source*: Brown-Azarowicz, Stannard, and Goldin (1986, p. 32).)

after *C*." Learners can use rhymes, especially in context (see the strategy of placing new words into a context), to remember new vocabulary they have heard. Here are three examples. Rollande uses rhyme to learn the sounds of English words, such as *goat, coat, boat, float, moat, dote,* and she makes up nonsense rhymes using these words. Antonio creates the nonsense rhyme "I hit a parrot with my carrot. The parrot said I am dead!" Rudy associates the new French word *poubelle* (trash can) with a similar-sounding French phrase, *plus belle* (more beautiful), and he puts these into humorous rhyme by saying, *la plus belle poubelle* (the prettiest trash can).

Rhymes are not the only way to represent sounds mentally. Consider these other ways. Kelley links the new Russian word *gazyeta* [газета] with the English word *gazette,* which has a similar sound and meaning. Carlos links the new word *cart* with the familiar Spanish word *carta* because of similar sounds, though the words have different meanings. Gerard, a learner of Russian, encounters the word *moloka* [молока] (milk) in a story. He sounds out the new word in his mind and associates it with an English word that sounds similar (milk) and means the same thing. Kiri is reading an article and finds the new English word *familiar*. It sounds like a word she knows, *family*, so she can remember the new word by the auditory link.

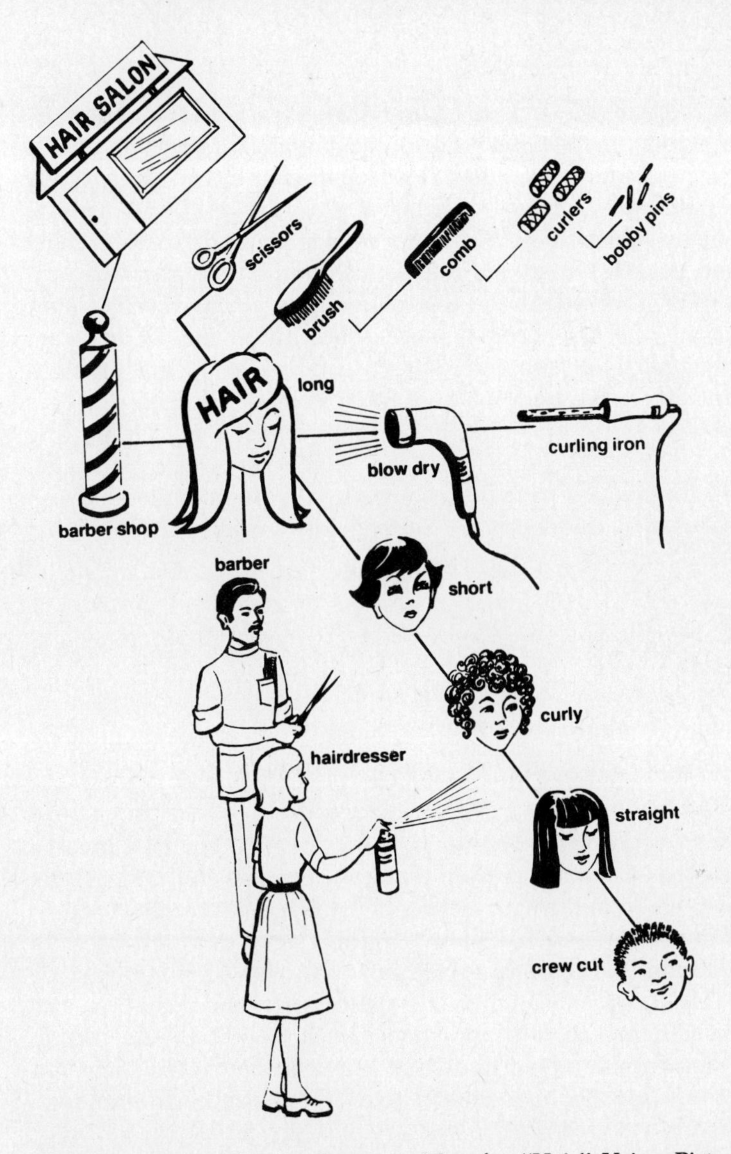

Figure 3.5 Example of a Semantic Map for "Hair" Using Pictures and Words. (*Source*: Brown-Azarowicz, Stannard, and Goldin (1986, p. 33).)

Reviewing Well Ⓐ

The sole strategy in this set is structured reviewing, which is especially useful for remembering new material in the target language. It entails reviewing at different intervals, at first close together and then increasingly far apart. For instance, Misha is learning a set of vocabulary words in English. He practices them immediately, waits 15 minutes before practicing them again, and practices them an hour later, three hours later, the next day, two days later, four days later, the following week, two weeks later, and so on until the material becomes more or less automatic. In this way, he keeps spiraling back to these particular vocabulary words, even though he might be encountering more material in class. Each time he practices these vocabulary words, Misha does it in a meaningful way, like putting them into a context or recombining them to make new sentences. Naturally, the amount of time needed to make new material automatic depends on the kind of material involved. Figure 3.6 provides an illustration of one way to approach structured reviewing.

Employing Action

The two memory strategies under employing action are using physical response or sensation and using mechanical techniques.

Using Physical Response or Sensation Ⓛ Ⓡ This strategy may involve physically acting out a new expression that has been heard. The teaching technique known as Total Physical Response [5] is based on this strategy; students listen to a command and then physically act it out (and later are able to give commands to other people). For example, Akram is told by the teacher, "Take the pencil, go to the pencil sharpener, sharpen the pencil, write your name with it, and then give it to Maria." As Akram carries out these instructions, he finds that physical movement helps engrave the new information in memory. A different use of the strategy involves associating the heard expression with a physical sensation. For instance, Jack trains himself to get a feeling of physical heat whenever he hears a new feminine noun in German, a feeling of cold for masculine noun, and a feeling of moderate temperature for a neuter noun; this helps him to remember the gender of the new nouns he hears.

The strategy of using physical response or sensation can also be applied for remembering written material. Learners can act out what they read, or associate physical sensations with specific words found in reading passages.

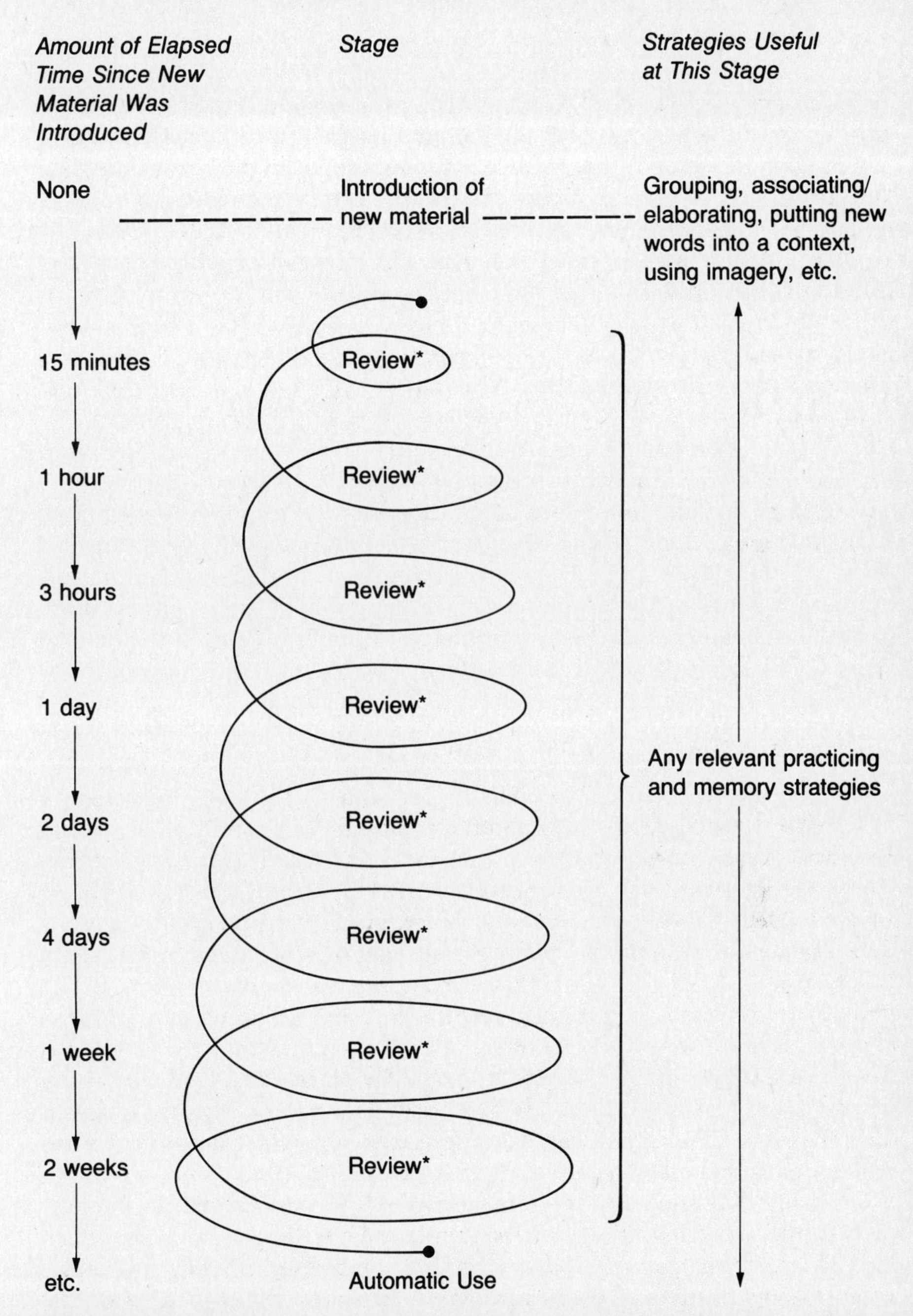

Figure 3.6 An Illustration of Structured Review (Spiraling). (*)*Review as needed* in increasingly separated intervals until the stage of automatic use is reached. Goal is to retain the material in long-term memory and to retrieve it easily and automatically when required. (*Source*: Original.)

Using Mechanical Techniques Ⓛ Ⓡ Ⓦ To remember what has been heard or read, mechanical techniques are sometimes helpful. For instance, flashcards, with the new word written on one side and the definition written on the other, are both familiar and useful. To contextualize a new expression and get writing practice, learners can write the new expression in a full sentence on a flashcard. Flashcards can be moved from one pile to another depending on how well the learner knows them. Separate sections of the language learning notebook can be used for words that have been learned and words that have not.

Using Memory Strategies for Retrieval Ⓐ

Learners can use memory strategies to retrieve target language information quickly, so that this information can be employed for communication involving any of the four language skills. The same mechanism that was initially used for getting the information into memory (for instance, a mental association) can be used later on for recalling the information. Just thinking of the learner's original image, sound-and-image combination, action, sensation, association, or grouping can rapidly retrieve the needed information, particularly if the learner has taken the time to review the material in a structured way after the initial encounter.

Here are some examples of retrieving information through memory strategies. Bud, a student of French, initially learned the 17 *être* verbs (i.e., verbs that take *être* instead of *avoir* in the perfect tense) by using the acronym *DR. MRS. VANDERTRAMPP*, another example of the strategy of placing new words into a context. This acronym stands for *devenir, revenir, monter, rester, sortir, venir, aller, naître, descendre, entrer, rentrer, tomber, retourner, arriver, mourir, passer*, and *partir* [6]. Later, whenever Bud has to use one of these verbs in the perfect tense in speaking or writing, he immediately thinks of *DR. MRS. VANDERTRAMPP* and knows the right form.

Mathilde wants to remember the Italian word for drawer (*cassetto*), so she can write a note to her Italian friend explaining that the important papers are in the drawer. Mathilde originally learned the word by using the keyword strategy, which involved making a mental picture of herself keeping *cassettes* in a drawer. In writing the note, Mathilde recalls this picture and remembers the required word, *cassetto*.

Finally, Lih originally used the acronym *BAGS*, a form of placing new words into a context, along with a mental image of bags, to learn which French adjectives come before nouns (pronominal adjectives), unlike the majority of adjectives: *B* for beauty words like *beau, joli*; *A* for age words, like *jeune, vieux, nouveau*; *G* for goodness words, like *bon, mauvais, vrai*; and *S* for size words, like *petit, grand, gros, long*. When Lih has to use any adjective in speaking or writing, she just remembers *BAGS* and knows where to put the adjective.

As just discussed, memory strategies are valuable for storing and retrieving new information in the target language. In addition, a variety of cognitive strategies—the second group of direct strategies—can be used for learning a new language.

APPLYING COGNITIVE STRATEGIES TO THE FOUR LANGUAGE SKILLS

Four sets of cognitive strategies (see Figure 3.7) are practicing, receiving and sending messages, analyzing and reasoning, and creating structure for input and output. All these bring benefits to language learners.

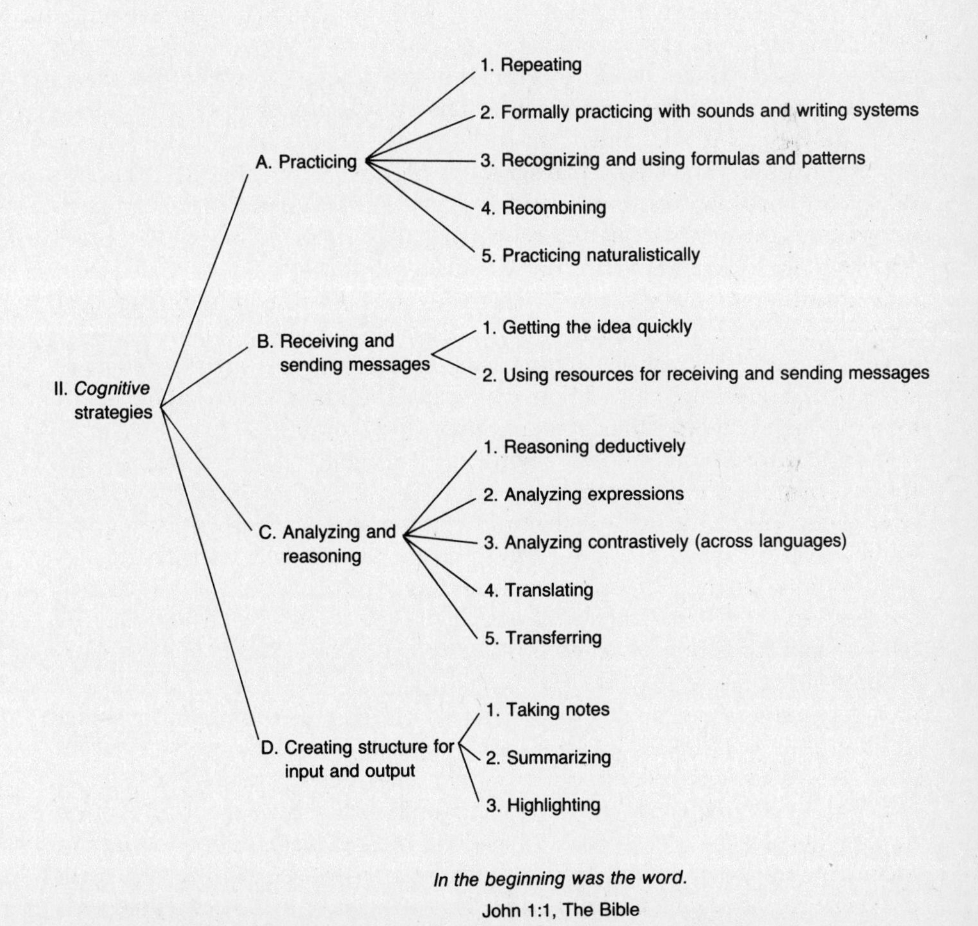

Figure 3.7 Diagram of the Cognitive Strategies to Be Applied to the Four Language Skills. (*Source*: Original.)

Practicing

The first and perhaps most important set of cognitive strategies, practicing, contains five strategies: repeating, formally practicing with sounds and writing systems, recognizing and using formulas and patterns, recombining, and practicing naturalistically.

Repeating Ⓐ Although the strategy of repeating might not at first sound particularly creative, important, or meaningful, it can be used in highly innovative ways, is actually essential for all four language skills, and virtually always includes some degree of meaningful understanding [7].

One use of this strategy is repeatedly listening to native speakers of the new language on a tape or record, with or without silent rehearsal (repeating the words to oneself mentally). Here are some examples. Milton listens to the weather report in French every day while eating breakfast. He is now very familiar with weather-related terms such as *le soleil* (sun), *chaud* (hot), *froid* (cold), and *il fait beau* (the weather is fine). Lyle, who is learning Russian, repeatedly plays a song, *Moskovskiye Vechera* [Московские Вечера] ("Moscow Evenings") and listens to the Russian words, trying to understand them while silently rehearsing them.

The strategy of repeating might mean reading a passage more than once to understand it more completely. A profitable technique is to read a passage several times, each time for different purposes: for example, to get the general drift or the main ideas, to predict, to read for detail, to write down questions, and so on. The learner might also take notes about a reading passage and then review them several times.

Repetition might involve saying or writing the same thing several times. For instance, Lori repeats orally or in writing the item in the *same* way each time, as a way of making it automatic. Yacoub, on the other hand, says or writes a single expression or passage in *different* ways. A well-known language teaching method, Suggestopedia, asks teachers and students to repeat the same oral passage several times, each time saying the passage at a different speed by matching it to the cadence of a different kind of music being played.

Repeating something in different ways can be a means of emphasizing it, as in the "tell 'em" rule often used in speaking and writing: "Tell 'em what you're *going* to tell 'em, then *tell* 'em, and then tell 'em what you *told* 'em." This rule, which works well for certain kinds of oral or written reports in many languages and cultures, means there is an introduction laying out the main points, followed by the body of the text explaining the main points in greater detail, and finally a brief summary of these points phrased somewhat differently. A related but different principle involving repeating is called the "lead paragraph" rule, which is widely used in written and oral journalism. This principle involves putting into the lead paragraph (that is, the first or leading paragraph) all the salient details of who, what, when, where, why, and how—the essence of the entire story in a few hard-hitting introductory sentences. The paragraphs following the lead paragraph flesh out this skeleton, giving more information and background details, usually in order of decreasing importance. Sometimes there is a real conclusion or summary at the end, and sometimes not [8].

Imitation of native users of the language is another repeating technique used for both speaking and writing. Mindless or meaningless imitation is generally not worthwhile [9]. In imitating native speakers, learners can improve their pronunciation and their use of structures, vocabulary, idioms, intonation, gestures, and style. Help your students by providing varied examples of target language speech and writing for them to imitate. Consider the following examples of imitation of native users of the language. Marian, learning German, imitates aloud the intonation patterns and word order used by her German friend Heidi, as in *Wir haben Tennis gespielt* (we have played tennis). Adrienne imitates a word or phrase (along with the appropriate gestures) used by her Italian-speaking friend Giovanni, who takes this as a sign that Adrienne is truly involved and interested in the conversation. Steve, an advanced student of Russian, imitates the writing he finds in *Pravda* [Правда], while Maya, an intermediate Russian student, imitates the composition style she finds in simplified, vocabulary-controlled Russian texts. Elisabeth, a French speaker studying English, imitates the tone and format of business letters written in English.

In writing, still another use of the repeating strategy is revising, that is, going through a written draft in detail (usually more than once) in order to correct or amend it. Nothing ever rolls off the pen or the keyboard perfectly the first time, so revising is almost always necessary. Writers revise in different ways. For instance, some treat writing and revision as distinct phases, while others revise as they write in a continuous, ongoing process. Also, not every detail is always covered in any single revising effort. Sometimes writers concentrate on specific things for one revision (for instance, expressing the main themes clearly) and other things for another revision (e.g., checking punctuation). Help your students learn the best way to revise their writing, and help them avoid becoming bogged down in a premature and fruitless quest for perfection.

Formally Practicing with Sounds and Writing Systems Ⓛ Ⓢ Ⓦ In listening, this strategy is often focused on perception of sounds (pronunciation and intonation) rather than on comprehension of meaning [10]. In listening *perception* exercises (as opposed to listening *comprehension* exercises), it is essential to keep visual and contextual clues to a minimum; therefore, recordings, not live speech, are recommended for listening perception [11].

Here are some instances of formally practicing with sounds. Leni marks the stress in the English sentence "I'm terribly tired; I think I'll go and have a rest" (I'm /terribly /tired; I /think I'll /go and /have a /rest). Haruko, a learner of English, listens to different words containing the letters *ough*, a combination that sounds different in various words: *through, though, tough*, and *trough*. She creates her own phonetic spelling of these words (*throo, thow, tuff*, and *troff*) to understand them better. Parker listens to the French vowel sounds of *eu, e, a*, and so on. He does a listening exercise with a tape, checking off the vowel sounds that he hears.

This strategy can be extended to include not just listening but also speaking. Tapes or records assist this strategy well. Some tape arrangements allow learners to record themselves so they can hear and compare their own voices with a native speaker's voice. Lisha, who is learning French, practices the many sounds of *ille* [12] by taping her speech, comparing it with that of a native speaker, and looking in the mirror so she can see herself when saying these sounds.

This strategy also centers on learning new writing systems necessary for using the target language. Of course, language learners do not always have to learn a new writing system, but many languages have alphabets, syllabaries, or idiographic systems that differ from the learners' own writing system. With a language such as Russian, Arabic, or Hebrew, the alphabet might be different from the learners' own. Some languages, like Thai, do not have alphabets but instead rely on syllabaries—nonalphabetic characters that represent sounds of whole syllables. In contrast, Chinese has thousands of idiographs—pictures representing ideas or objects. Japanese uses Chinese idiographs but also has two distinct syllabaries. Korean is moving from an idiographic system to a syllabary-based system. Formal practice with writing systems can include copying letters, copying words, comparing similar-sounding words in the native and target languages in terms of their written representation, using visual imagery and humor to remember new symbols, and putting symbols into meaningful verbal contexts [13].

Recognizing and Using Formulas and Patterns Ⓐ Recognizing and using routine formulas and patterns in the target language greatly enhance the learner's comprehension and production. *Formulas* are unanalyzed expressions, while *patterns* have at least one slot that can be filled with an alternative word. Teach students such expressions as whole chunks early in their language learning process. These routines will help build self-confidence, increase understanding, and enhance fluency.

Here are some examples of common formulas:

Hello.

Good-bye.

How are you?

The weather's nice, isn't it?

D'accord. (*OK,* as a sign of agreement in French)

Spasibo [Спасиво]. (*thanks* in Russian)

Ça va? and *Ça va.* (*Hello,* literally *How's it going?* and *OK* in French)

Wie geht's dir? or *Wie geht es Ihnen?* (*How are you?* in German)

¿Habla usted inglés? (*Do you speak English?* in Spanish)

A demain. (*until tomorrow* in French)

Bis später. (*until later* in German)

Jaa ne. (*see you later* in Japanese)

A tout à l'heure! (*see you later* in French)

Es geht mir gut. (*I like it* in German)

Spokoinoi nochi [Спокойной ночи]. (*good-night* in Russian)

Chotto matte. (*just a minute* in Japanese)

Perdóneme. (*pardon me* in Spanish)

Tout à fait. (*completely* in French)

Dommage or *Tant pis.* (*too bad* in French)

Some formulas are most often used for the express purpose of managing conversations. Teach learners to recognize these formulas as used by native speakers, and to say these formulas to continue in a conversation or show interest. Conversation management formulas include target language equivalents of expressions like this:

Yes, that's right.

And what happened then?

That's not so bad.

Hey, that's great!

Tell me more.

This is a funny story.

I know what you mean.

That's interesting.

In addition to all the formulas above, many useful patterns exist in every language. Help your students to understand these patterns when they hear or read them, and to say or write them when appropriate. Examples include the following:

I don't know how to . . .

I would like to . . .

U menya [У меня] . . . (*I have* . . . in Russian)

Hajimemashite . . . to moshimasu. (*My name is* . . . in Japanese)

Per piacere, dov'è . . . (*Please, where is* . . .? in Italian)

Il y a . . . (*There is* . . . in French)

Qu'est-ce que c'est que . . . (*What is* . . .? in French)

Mieux vaux . . . (*It's best to* . . . in French)

Recombining Ⓢ Ⓦ The strategy of recombining involves constructing a meaningful sentence or longer expression by putting together known elements in new ways. The result might be serious or silly, but it always provides useful practice. For instance, Sam, a learner of German, knows the expression *Ich bin so gut wie Sie* (I am as good as you), *Sie sind gut* (you are good), and *sie ist besser* (she is better). He strings them together in new ways, using connecting words to say: *Sie sind gut, und ich bin so gut wie Sie, aber sie ist besser* (You are good, and I am as good as you, but she is better). Rosine knows the three expressions *weather's fine, I think I'd like* . . ., and *take a walk.* In practicing her spoken English, she creates the following new sentence from these three expressions with some additional words: *The weather's fine today, so I think I'd like to take a walk.*

The recombining strategy can be used in writing as well as in speaking. One way to use it is to string together two or more known expressions into a written story. For example, Ferenc, who is learning English, knows some terms for everyday tasks, such as *going to the store, going to the laundromat, washing clothes, getting some gas,* and *going to the library.* He writes a little story about a man who does all these things in the same afternoon.

But the recombining strategy does not always imply stringing together items in this way; it might involve using known forms, such as *going to the concert,* with different pronouns, such as *he, she, we, they, you.* For instance, Natalya writes, *He's going to the concert, but she's not. We're going to the concert, too. I hope you'll go with us!*

Practicing Naturalistically Ⓐ This strategy, of course, centers on using the language for actual communication. Any of the four skills, or a combination, might be involved. Because you as a teacher often have a great influence on the availability of practice opportunities, the following discussion details certain *instructional or teaching strategies* that you can use to make it easier for your students to exercise the *learning strategy* of practicing naturalistically.

As applied to listening, this learning strategy involves understanding the meaning of the spoken language in as naturalistic a context as possible. Help your students feel they are learning a language they can use, and give them confidence in their ability to succeed in listening tasks. To do this, use live speech for listening comprehension exercises as much as possible. Speech need not be completely authentic for listening exercises; in fact, it is often better to use an approximation to authentic speech, somewhat modified to take into account the learners' proficiency level. Employ semiscripts or notes rather than reading from a fixed script. If unedited authentic listening materials are used, these should be short segments of recorded broadcasts or live or taped interviews with native speakers on familiar topics [14].

Construct listening comprehension exercises around a specific task, in which students are required to do something in response to what they hear. For example, they might be required to express agreement or disagreement, take notes, mark a picture or diagram according to instructions, or answer questions. This requirement gives learners a purpose for listening. Learners should respond throughout the task, not just at the very end. Choose listening tasks that demand some kind of judgment or thinking and that are geared to the learners' level. Listening exercises should not include tasks that require a lot of reading (such as answering multiple-choice questions) or writing (such as extensive or detailed note-taking), unless the intention is to develop several skills jointly. Base the task on easily grasped visual materials (diagrams, pictures, grids, maps) and quick, simple responses (physical movement, checking off responses, or writing one-word answers). Students can also practice listening to directions for a task that they need to do. For instance, describe a picture while they draw it, or ask students to act out a pantomime as you tell them a story, or give directions for a physical action or sequence of actions. Help your students in class to practice using the telephone in role-plays with each other; this makes the telephone less intimidating. Tell students the correct answers immediately after the exercise, so they can check their own performance, then explain in more detail the reasons why certain responses are preferred. This encourages learners to use strategies such as self-monitoring and self-evaluating, which are powerful motivators and enhancers of understanding [15].

Technology offers many opportunities for naturalistic listening practice inside or outside of the classroom. Learners can use tapes and records to practice on their own. Learners can even make their own tapes of recorded material from radio or records. Audiocassette decks are useful for listening practice. International shortwave radio stations offer a huge variety of programs in many languages at various proficiency levels [16].

The addition of a visual image often provides learners with an invaluable context to which they may relate the spoken form. Realia, drawings, and homemade videos are very basic visual tools to enhance listening practice. Films are a wonderful sound-and-image resource. Towns and cities with large foreign populations often show films in other languages. It is also possible to borrow films from public libraries, boards of education, regional educational centers, universities, national film boards, and even aerospace centers. Television provides other sound-and-image possibilities. Local TV does not usually carry much in the way of multilingual programming, but there are some notable exceptions, such as Spanish programs in many parts of the United States, bilingual (English-Japanese) news and movies on Japanese TV, and multilingual TV channels in frontier regions of Europe. For second language learners who are in the midst of the target language community, TV is a great resource for listening practice. TV soap operas provide excellent listening practice and an interesting slant on the culture. Alternatives to film and TV for listening practice are the videocassette and direct broadcasting by satellite (DBS) [17].

Practicing naturalistically also means using the language in an authentic way for reading comprehension. The most common medium for reading material is, of course, print. Print material in just about any target language is easy to come by and comparatively inexpensive. Target language newspapers and magazines are often available at newsstands, or readers can subscribe. In addition, books in other languages are obtainable in libraries and shops or by mail order. Readily available menus, advertisements, brochures, pamphlets, department store catalogues, comic books, university catalogues, travel brochures, and timetables all provide cultural information as well as practice in reading the language. Spend some class time having students write letters to request some of these materials. Also encourage students to collect and share print material in the new language (from any source) as a basis for reading exercises. Help your students practice their reading by giving them active and interesting reading tasks. Use simulations in which learners are required to read the instructions or the main documents (such as scenarios) in the new language. Do jigsaw reading exercises to involve readers in cooperatively sharing and rearranging information that they gain from reading. Find out what your students' main interests are, and provide reading materials and activities that address those interests. Encourage students to read in the new language outside of class. Consider giving them credit for out-of-class reading. Develop and provide a lending library of materials in the new language so that learners can check out books and magazines for home reading. Provide information on where and how they can obtain other reading materials on their own.

In the speaking area, practicing naturalistically involves practice in speaking the language for realistic communication. Speaking with other people in natural settings provides interactive, rapid, personal communication. Being in the country or community where the target language is spoken natively, either as a permanent resident or a temporary visitor, is the best way to find opportunities for practice in speaking. Living in a place where the language is normally spoken is an informal immersion in the language and culture. In such a situation, the learner generally has no choice but to communicate and to understand how the language is used in its wider social context. Subtleties of gestures, facial expressions, and tone of voice become much clearer and more understandable in the cultural setting where the language is spoken natively. However, even without traveling to the country where the language is spoken, it is often possible to converse with native speakers right in the learners' home community. Making friends with native speakers of the target language is possible, usually by seeking them out individually or by finding an association, such as an international friendship club, where there are numerous native speakers. Casual chatting with friends in the target language—either abroad or at home—is a fine way to improve communication skills. For most language learners, making friends with target language speakers is one of the most important reasons for language learning [18]. Help your students find these opportunities for using the language conversationally.

The classroom itself can provide practice that combines listening and speaking and thus approaches natural language use. Role-plays, drama activities, games, simulations, and structured communication exercises offer practice that takes learners' attention away from language learning and directs it toward the communication of meaning. In doing these activities, learners sometimes become so engrossed in communicating that they forget they are trying to use a new language! Such activities can increase learners' confidence in their oral communication skill. Greater confidence leads to better attitudes and increased motivation to continue using the new language. In addition to providing interesting and challenging communication activities, you can also change the classroom environment to facilitate naturalistic practice. Transform the room into a place where communication can occur normally and easily. Move the chairs so they are not in straight rows. Put students into small groups or pairs to converse. Let the classroom come alive with talk. Banish the teacher-centered mode in which all communication occurs between the teacher and one student at a time, with everyone else sitting, waiting, and daydreaming. Encourage learners to express their own personality and needs. Bring in native speakers whenever possible. Invite learners to hold communication sessions on their own without your being present. Occasionally go out of the room for short periods during normal classes, so that learners realize they don't need you to tell them to speak. Give them materials to help them organize themselves while you are gone, if necessary. (Note that the other two language skills, reading and writing, can often be integrated with listening and speaking by means of role-plays, simulations, games, and other activities.)

Practicing naturalistically is very important for developing writing skill [19]. It can involve many different activities, such as creation of separate products by individuals, individual contributions to multipart products, coauthorship of a single piece by multiple writers, or exchanges of written messages between individuals or teams. In all of these activities, real readers are involved. Often students read the writings of their peers. Therefore reading and writing skills can be jointly developed.

The first of the naturalistic writing modes is creation of separate products by individuals. Individual writing efforts might include all sorts of formats: autobiographical sketches, interviews of family or friends, factual reports, stories, poems, diary entries in the target language, and so on. The length can vary from a sentence or paragraph to 20 or more pages, depending on the language proficiency of the learners.

The second naturalistic writing mode is joint writing projects composed of individual contributions. Examples include newspapers, newsletters, literary magazines, sports digests, scrapbooks, or scripts for simulated radio and TV programs, in which each person contributes his or her own different items to a written product. Excellent simulations exist for producing radio scripts, such as RADIO COVINGHAM, and news bulletins and newspapers, like NEWSIM [20]. These provide the experience of writing with a real purpose for a defined audience, as well as working together to create a product. Another suggestion for joint writing practice is to have learners interview each other using a semistructured format, and then turn the interviews into feature articles which are, after revisions, published in a class magazine. Student-created literary magazines containing poetry, stories, pictures, and other items are sometimes very popular.

The third naturalistic writing mode is coauthorship of a single product. Two or more learners can work together to write one piece—a single article, short story, play—as is often done in "real life" outside of the classroom. Because they are equally invested in a single, integrated product, writing partners provide constant encouragement and feedback to each other. A more playful way to use coauthorship is jigsaw writing. Learners are given unrelated target language story fragments, a sentence or two each, and are required to write a story that weaves all the story lines together into a reasonably coherent whole, transitions and all. The results are entertaining and often comical, and the process gives learners practice in finding (or making) interesting linkages.

The last naturalistic writing mode involves exchanges of written messages between individuals or teams. This includes journal exchanges, letter writing, and computer interaction. Dialogue journals are one way of making writing a more interactive process, in which learners exchange messages with their teachers. Language students write anything they want in their dialogue journals and share these journals with the teacher, who responds with comments—not in a threatening, red-ink, corrective mode but in a supportive, nonjudgmental, idea-evoking way. The process continues, back and forth, with both sides learning from each other as students get increasing practice with writing. Dialogue journals are very effective and highly motivating for language learning [21]. Letter writing to penfriends or for business purposes is another kind of written exchange between individuals, but not just between teachers and students. In correspondence, learners know their writing is meaningful and important to someone else, they get practice using the language for both writing and reading, they learn all sorts of things about new cultures and their own culture as well, and they begin to view writing as part of a rewarding social process.

Exchanges between individual writers or teams of writers are also stimulated by computer interaction. Computers don't have to be used just for drill and practice; they can be a medium of real communication in the target language, including composing and exchanging messages with other students in the classroom or around the world [22]. Language teachers are helping their students at all proficiency levels set up local, regional, national, and international networks for the exchange of student-created messages with other students, who may be either native speakers or learners of the target language. An outstanding example of such an information exchange is the Computer Chronicles Newswire operating from San Diego, California. A month-long, computerized international simulation, ICONS, has teams of students writing messages in various languages and sending them to teams representing other countries around the globe [23]. In addition to student-oriented computer interactions, established computerized information networks not originally designed for educational purposes sometimes encourage useful written exchanges. In any computerized exchange, communication is both meaningful and urgent. Because on-line cost is a factor, it is necessary to write quickly, so learners must also think quickly and appropriately in the new language. In addition, learners use the target language for a practical purpose and cease to focus on the language as a mere object of study. Of course, the computer does not guarantee the instant development of writing skill. However, it does allow collaborative exchanges which dramatically increase students' motivation to write, and it also provides potentially large amounts of interactive writing practice.

It is possible to publish or disseminate material that your students have written for their language class. For instance, the BBC World Service reads aloud original stories on its "Short Story" program, and these are occasionally written by students [24]. Newsletters, specialty publications (such as magazines about refugee resettlement or Hispanic issues), local newspapers, language teaching journals, and other outlets might be willing to publish your students' materials. Hearing their work broadcast or seeing it in print is an incredibly motivating experience for students.

The foregoing discussion has concerned the strategy of practicing naturalistically. A good deal of attention was devoted to this strategy and its instructional manifestations, since this is one of the most essential learning strategies. Now we will turn to some highly specific and useful strategies for receiving and sending messages.

Receiving and Sending Messages

This set consists of two strategies: getting the idea quickly and using resources for receiving and sending messages.

Getting the Idea Quickly Ⓛ Ⓡ This strategy is used for listening and reading. It helps learners home in on exactly what they need or want to understand, and it allows them to disregard the rest or use it as background information only. Two techniques constituting this strategy are skimming and scanning. *Skimming* involves searching for the main ideas the speaker wants to get across, while *scanning* means searching for specific details of interest to the learner.

Preview questions help learners to skim and scan more easily. For beginning learners of the target language, preview questions often provide many clues and require simple "true/false," "yes/no" responses or a choice from a set of answers. With more proficient learners, fewer clues are given by preview questions. Provide preview questions to help learners skim; for instance, "What are the three key ideas in this reading passage?" or "What is the theme of this passage?" Ask skimming questions in the learners' native language or in the new language, depending on the skill level of the learners. Preview questions for scanning, on the other hand, focus readers not so much on the main ideas but rather on specific facts, like "Who is the man in the dark hat? Where does he come from? What does he want from the old woman?" There are advantages and disadvantages to asking scanning questions in the target language. Using the target language gives hints about the vocabulary the readers should look for, but readers might be tempted to search for those expressions and answer without fully understanding.

Charts to complete, lists to write, diagrams to fill out, and other mechanisms also provide clues about what kind of general points or specific details the learners need to pick up in a listening or reading passage. These help learners get the idea quickly and efficiently. In the beginning, these charts, lists, and diagrams may provide a lot of clues about what to listen or read for, and later, as the learners progress, fewer clues might be given. Another useful tip: Skimming and scanning in the classroom setting are often enhanced by another strategy, taking notes.

Two instances of skimming are as follows. Jean-Claude is listening to get the main ideas of the talk on American architecture given at the international social club. Monica is trying to get the gist of a front-page article in the Chinese newspaper. Here are some examples of scanning. Rowena has agreed to listen for certain details in Spanish, such as the names, ages, professions, and general background of three visitors from South America, while Jim will scan for other information, such as how long the visitors will stay, what they want to do on their visit, or whom they want to meet.

Waiting in the Köln train station, Pascual (a learner of German) is worried about his late train, and therefore he listens closely for an announcement of its estimated arrival time and scans the schedule board periodically.

Remember that not all listening or reading involves getting the idea quickly. For instance, the techniques of skimming and scanning might not be too useful for listening to a radio play or for reading poems or stories. Irony, suspense, and humor can sometimes be ruined by too much skimming and scanning. Thus, the efficiency of skimming and scanning, while often useful, is not the only approach to listening or reading.

Using Resources for Receiving and Sending Messages Ⓐ This strategy involves using resources to find out the meaning of what is heard or read in the new language, or to produce messages in the new language. To better understand what is heard or read, printed resources such as dictionaries, word lists, grammar books, and phrase books may be valuable. Encyclopedias, travel guides, magazines, and general books on culture and history can provide useful background information so that learners can better understand the spoken or written language. Printed resources on just about any topic can be found in the target language. Nonprint resources include tapes, TV, videocassettes, radio, museums, and exhibitions, among others. These cannot easily be used during speaking, but they can help learners prepare for speaking activities. Printed resources like thesauruses, target language dictionaries, and bilingual dictionaries are especially helpful for writing.

Here are some examples of using resources to understand a spoken or written message. Rusty, a beginning learner of Spanish, uses a Spanish/English dictionary to look up the definitions of new words he has written down in his language learning notebook. Sandrine, who is more advanced in Spanish, uses an all-Spanish dictionary to look up definitions and variations of new words. Susan, a learner of French, has heard many similar phrases in the new language, but she does not always understand the differences, so she uses reference resources. For instance, she uses a phrase book to look up the meaning of *Fais gaffe!* (be careful). She wants to know how this phrase relates to different-sounding expressions with similar meanings, such as *Attention!* and *Fais attention!*, and to similar-sounding expressions with entirely different meanings, such as *faire une gaffe* (make a mistake). Pablo, who is learning German, uses the German grammar book to look up information on separable prefixes, since he has had a hard time understanding them on the German tape. Marc, a learner of Spanish, is reading a Spanish short story filled with modern slang terms. Most of the time he succeeds in grasping the meaning from the context, but when totally baffled he finds it necessary to use a dictionary of Spanish slang.

Following are some examples of using resources to produce the target language in speaking or writing. Akira uses a dictionary and a grammar book in composing an English-language talk about a favorite hobby, sailing. Ellen looks up a few useful social phrases in her German phrase book before she goes to the cafe to meet her German acquaintances. Louisa uses all the background material she can find—articles, books, and TV news shows—to gather information about the terrorist movement in Spain in preparation for writing a report in Spanish on the subject.

Analyzing and Reasoning

The five strategies in this set help learners to use logical thinking to understand and use the grammar rules and vocabulary of the new language. These strategies are valuable, but they can cause problems if overused.

Reasoning Deductively Ⓐ This strategy involves deriving hypotheses about the meaning of what is heard by means of general rules the learner already knows. Reasoning deductively is a common and very useful type of logical thinking. Here are examples of successful use of this strategy for the four skills. First, Julio, who is learning English, hears his friend say, "Would you like to go to the library with me at five o'clock?" Julio correctly understands that he is being asked a question to which he must respond, because he recognizes that part of the verb comes before the subject (a general rule he has learned). Second, Roberta is reading a Russian story involving a character named Elisavyeta Ivanovna. Roberta has not encountered this name before, but she knows that *-ovna* means "daughter of," so she understands immediately that the person must be Elizabeth, Ivan's daughter. Third, Marcie, who is learning French, knows the general rule that the future tense is not used for things that will happen very soon, and that the *futur proche* (near future) tense or even the present tense would be better. So, when she wants to say in French the equivalent of "I'm leaving soon," Marcie applies the general rule and says *Je vais bientôt partir* or *Je pars bientôt*, not *Je partirai bientôt*. Fourth, in writing, Marianne applies the general rule that an article (definite or indefinite) is ordinarily used in front of a French or German noun.

Sometimes the strategy of reasoning deductively results in overgeneralization errors, as in the following examples. Spanish-speaking Lugo knows that the past tense in English uses *-ed*, so he applies this rule to say *bringed* and *goed*. The perfectly good English questions "What is it?" and "Where are they?" are overapplied by Josef in the sentence *I don't know what is it* and by Marcello in *Find out where are they*. Sometimes an expression is overgeneralized to a situation where its semantic limitations become painfully obvious, as when Gabriele says, "He is pretty." Miko, a Japanese speaker, knows the general rule that the English plural is formed by adding

-s or *-es;* this works very well with *house/houses*, but not so well with *mouse/ mouses*. Cesar, learning English, overuses the progressive, as in *We are not knowing the rules. Who can Angela sees?* is an example produced by Mario, another learner of English, who applies the rule for forming the third-person-singular verb ending when it should not be used.

Analyzing Expressions Ⓛ Ⓡ To understand something spoken in the new language, it is often helpful to break down a new word, phrase, sentence, or even paragraph into its component parts. This strategy is known as analyzing expressions [25]. If the learner is in the midst of a conversation there may not be enough time to analyze the new expression, but it is sometimes possible to jot down the expression (phonetically if need be) and analyze it later. Analysis is a good strategy for learners of Welsh, who encounter very long words—such as the longest place name in the UK, *Llanfairpwllgwyngyllgogerychwyrndrobwllllantysyliogogogoch*. (This means St. Mary's church in a hollow by the white hazel, close to the rapid whirlpool, by the red cave of St. Tysilio.) Just think of trying to grasp this word if you heard it in a casual conversation! Admittedly, Welsh provides some of the most exciting and extreme instances of the need for analyzing expressions, but any language with compound words can benefit from this strategy. Though analyzing expressions is helpful for listening, it is even more useful for reading, because readers have more time to go back and analyze complicated expressions when reading than when listening.

Here are some helpful examples of analyzing expressions. First, Martina is learning English. She does not immediately understand the phrase *premeditated crime*, which she hears in a TV news broadcast. She breaks down this phrase into parts that she does understand: *crime* (bad act), *meditate* (think about), and *pre-* (before). Thus, she figures out the meaning of the whole phrase: an evil act that is planned in advance. Second, Lloyd, a learner of French, hears the French phrase *le génie inépuisable*, in a radio program about the German composer Wagner. He knows that Wagner was a brilliant person, a genius. Using analysis, he divides the unknown word, *inépuisable*, into parts to understand it: *in* (not), *épuis* (from *épuiser*, meaning to exhaust), and *-able* (able). Putting these back together, Lloyd knows that the phrase must mean that Wagner was an inexhaustible genius. Third, Marijane reads a new German word, *Deutschlehrerverband*. She divides it into *Deutsch* + *lehrer* + *verband* (capitalization would differ if these were really being used as separate words, of course) to understand the meaning, *German teachers' association*. Fourth, David understands the meaning of *parapluie* (umbrella) by breaking it into *para* (for) and *pluie* (rain).

Analyzing Contrastively Ⓛ Ⓡ This strategy is a fairly easy one that most learners use naturally. It involves analyzing elements (sounds, words, syntax) of the new language to determine likenesses and differences in comparison with one's own native language. It is very commonly used at the early stages of language learning to understand the meaning of what is heard or read. Here are some examples of analyzing contrastively in listening and reading. Stanley recognizes through contrastive analysis that the German word *Katze* sounds like the English word *cat*. Nora recognizes the similarities between *chair* in English and *chaise* in French. In reading an English passage, Luis immediately understands the word *cream*, which corresponds to the French word *crème* and the Spanish word *crema*. Rita, an English speaker, is fascinated by the similarities in a number of words she finds in reading other languages, such as *sister* (English), *syestra* [сестра] (Russian), *Schwester* (German), and *soeur* (French). She figures out that the English word *sorority* is related to the others. John is interested in the different ways his own name is expressed in other languages: *Jean* (French), *Joan* (Portuguese), *Juan* (Spanish), and *Johann* (German). A beginner in Japanese, Reba finds that many current Japanese words are simply English words with a Japanese phonetic veneer: *orengi* (orange), *remon* (lemon), *chokoreto* (chocolate), *pankeiki* (pancakes), *hamueggu* (ham and eggs), *soseji* (sausage), *sarada* (salad), *sandowitchi* (sandwich), *aisukurimu* (ice cream), *appurupai* (apple pie), *puddingu* (pudding), *jusu* (juice), *supu* (soup), *resutoran* (restaurant), *basu* (bus), *tenisu* (tennis), *takushi* (taxi), and *chekku* (check) for example.

However, remind your students to beware of "false friends," sometimes called by their French name, *faux amis*. These are the target language words that sound or look like words in the learners' own language, but whose meaning is very different. French is full of false friends for English users, as Lillian learns from the following examples. *Actuellement* does not mean *actually*; it means right now. *Assister* has nothing to do with *assisting*; it means to attend. And *attendre* is not the same as attend; it means to wait. Imagine the misunderstandings caused by these words!

Some of the most significant and embarrassing "false friends" to warn your students about are those with sexual overtones. For instance, in some countries *preservatives* are used to keep food fresh, but Brooke discovers to her chagrin that *preservatif* in France means a male contraceptive. Ron learns that the Japanese word *guramaa* is originally borrowed from the English word *glamorous*, but it now implies that the *guramaa* woman has big breasts. Richard, an American visitor to Madrid, tries to apologize for a Spanish error, saying *¡Estoy embaražada!*—and when he finds out his intended apology means *I'm pregnant*, then he is truly embarrassed.

Translating Ⓐ Translating can be a helpful strategy early in language learning, as long as it is used with care. It allows learners to use their own language as the basis for understanding what they hear or read in the new language. It also helps learners produce the new language in speech or writing. However, word-for-word (verbatim) translation, though a frequent occurrence among beginners, can become a crutch or provide the wrong interpretation of target language material. Furthermore, translating can sometimes slow learners down considerably, forcing them to go back and forth constantly between languages.

The following examples show how translating can be used, and misused, for understanding what is heard or read in the new language. In a conversation when the Russian speaker says, *Ya chitayu zhurnal* [Я читаю журнал], Billie mentally translates this to mean "I'm reading the newspaper," the English equivalent. In this case a straight translation is correct. Herb, a learner of German, hears his German friend say, *Du hast Recht*. He doesn't understand; the sentence cannot be translated directly into English. He discovers later that the friend was saying, "You're right." Lauren finds it impossible to understand in English the literally translated meaning of the French phrase, *il y a . . .* (roughly meaning *there is/are . . .*). Elton reads the words *beau-frère* and *belle-soeur* in French. He tries to understand them through literal translation, but they just come out as "handsome brother" and "beautiful sister"! Later he discovers that they mean brother-in-law and sister-in-law.

Beginning speakers and writers often rely on the strategy of translating to produce messages in the target language. For instance, in Spanish it is correct for Amado to say or write *No comprendo*, but translating this directly into English produces *No understand*, a rather primitive expression in English. And there's no single verbatim translation of *I've got to go* in French; Martha learns to say one of the following, all of which have slightly different connotations: *Il faut que j'y aille, Je dois partir, Il faut que je parte, Il faut que je m'en aille, Je dois aller, On m'attend*, and so on.

Transferring Ⓐ The last of the analyzing and reasoning strategies is transferring, which means directly applying previous knowledge to facilitate new knowledge in the target language. This strategy relates to all four skills. Transferring can involve applying linguistic knowledge from the learner's own language to the new language, linguistic knowledge from one aspect of the new language to another aspect of the new language, or conceptual knowledge from one field to another. Transferring works well as long as the language elements or concepts are directly parallel, but most of the time they are not! It can lead to inaccuracy if learners transfer irrelevant knowledge across languages.

The following are some correct examples of transferring. When Dwight hears the expression *weekend* in French, he correctly knows through transfer that it means the same as in English, and that *bon weekend* means "Have a good weekend." Reading German, Erwin finds that it is easy to understand through transfer from English the German names for most of the months of the year.

Here are some less appropriate instances of transferring. Mildred is reading a French article about a scandal involving a *notaire*. An American notary is a clerk who has certain official rights such as stamping and sealing legal papers. On the basis of incorrect transfer, Mildred thinks that a French *notaire* is the same thing, but she finds out later that a *notaire* is a trained lawyer with a much higher level of education and professional status than a typical American notary. Jana is writing a letter in French. She discovers that transferring the word *possibly* into *possiblement* doesn't work, because the latter does not exist in French; *peut-être* (meaning perhaps) is correct. Transfer errors frequently occur in word order, as illustrated by Fritz, a German speaker learning English, who says, *Donald always fools so much around*, with *around* incorrectly placed at the end of the clause like a German separable prefix [26].

Like translating, transferring has its perils. Learners cannot expect that all the varied hues of meaning will be the same for words and concepts across two languages; sometimes there is just no equivalent from one language to the other. In addition, grammatical differences are sometimes very great.

Creating Structure for Input and Output

This is another set of strategies that aids all four skills. The three strategies in this group—taking notes, summarizing, and highlighting—help learners sort and organize the target language information that comes their way. In addition, these strategies allow students to demonstrate their understanding tangibly and prepare for using the language for speaking and writing.

Taking Notes Ⓛ Ⓡ Ⓦ This is a very important strategy for listening and reading, but learners generally are not taught to use it well, if at all. The focus of taking notes should be on understanding, not writing. Note-taking is often thought of as an advanced tool, to be used at high levels of proficiency—such as when listening to lectures. However, developing note-taking skills can begin at very early stages of learning. Key points can be written in the learners' own language at first. Depending on the purpose, later note-taking can be in the target language, thus involving writing practice. Or you can also allow a mixture of the target language and the learners' own language, with known vocabulary words written in the target language and the rest in the native language.

There are many different ways to take notes, the simplest and most common form being that of raw notes, which are unstructured and untransformed [27]. For raw notes to become useful, learners need to go back immediately (before they forget what was said) and organize the notes using a different system. A better way is to use the "shopping list" or T-formation as the very first step, omitting the raw notes. The advantage of using one of these formats initially is that they help learners organize what they hear while they are hearing it, thus increasing the original understanding and the ability to integrate new information with old.

If your students ordinarily take notes word for word, as in a dictation exercise, give them practice in listening for and taking notes on only the key points of information. After they are able to note the main points, help them to develop their skill in noting details. Use graphics and visuals wherever possible to highlight the main ideas as your students take notes. Teach your students to use various kinds of note-taking formats and then to choose the ones they like the best.

The shopping list format is extremely simple, but it does impose some sort of order and organization on the spoken material. It involves writing down information in clusters or sets that have some internal consistency or meaning. An example of the shopping list format is shown in Figure 3.8.

The T-formation is shown in Figure 3.9 using the same language material as for the shopping list. This format is similar in intent to the shopping list format, but it allows learners to use the space on the paper in a more effective way. First draw a large T on a piece of paper, taking up the whole sheet. Then write the main theme or title on the top line (the crossbar of the T). On the left side of the vertical line, write the basic categories or topics that have been discussed; on the right side of the vertical line, write details, specific examples, follow-up questions, or comments.

A semantic map is also a useful note-taking format, requiring learners to indicate the main word or idea and to link this with clusters of related words or ideas by means of lines or arrows; see examples of this format under memory strategies earlier in this chapter. Another useful form for notes is the tree diagram, sometimes transformed into a flow chart by means of arrows, diamonds, circles, and so forth. Examples of the tree diagram format are found throughout this book [28]. In addition, the standard outline form (using Roman numerals, letters, etc.) deserves special mention as a note-taking format. This outline structure, shown in Figure 3.10, can be extended to as many levels of detail as learners might ever

Banana Cake Ingredients	lemon juice	baking powder	milk
	walnuts	sugar	butter
	bananas	cream cheese	vanilla
	eggs	confectioner's sugar	
Equipment Needed	large bowl	measuring cup	fork
	greased pan	spoon	

Figure 3.8 Shopping List Note Form. (*Source*: Hamp-Lyons (1983, p. 112).)

Banana Cake

ingredients needed	lemon juice milk sugar bananas vanilla eggs (etc.)
equipment needed	large bowl measuring cup fork greased pan spoon

Figure 3.9 T-Formation Note Form. (*Source*: Hamp-Lyons (1983, p. 118).)

need. Just add more symbols, such as (a), (b), (i), (ii), or (iii), as needed. An alternative numbering system involves decimals (e.g., 1, 1.1). Well-structured reading passages lend themselves to the standard outline form, one version of which is shown in Figure 3.10.

Provide exercises that require your students to take notes on their listening and reading (including the instructions you give them in class). Allow students to take notes either in their own language or the target language at first, but encourage them to move toward taking notes mostly or solely in the target language if possible.

Note-taking techniques can be integrated with regular language activities and materials as a natural element in language learning. A metacognitive strategy closely associated with note-taking is organizing, which includes keeping a notebook for gathering new language information and for tracking progress (see Chapters 4 and 5). Any notes should be kept neatly and organized in some fashion; a loose-leaf notebook is perhaps the best way. For students who are writing substantial pieces in the target language, it is helpful to jot down ideas as soon as they pop into the head. Therefore, the notebook should be kept close at hand at all times.

Summarizing Ⓛ Ⓡ Ⓦ Another strategy that helps learners structure new input and show they understand is summarizing—that is, making a condensed, shorter version of the original passage. Writing a summary can be more challenging (and sometimes more useful) than taking notes, because it often requires greater condensation of thought.

At the early stages of language learning, summarizing can be as simple as just giving a title to what has been heard or read; the title functions as a kind of summary of the story or passage. Another easy way to summarize

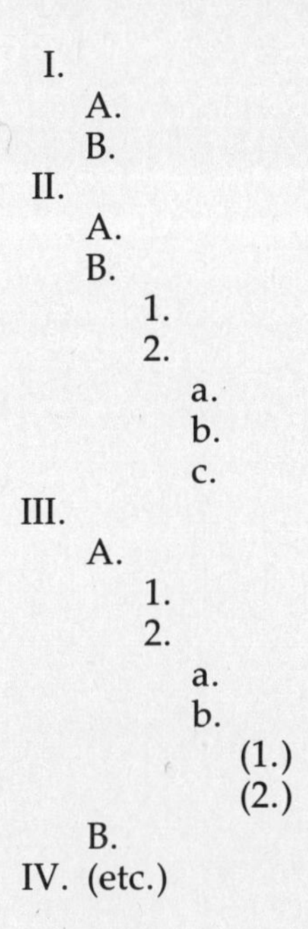

Figure 3.10 Standard Outline Structure. (*Source*: Original.)

is to place pictures which depict a series of events in the order in which they occur in the story. This is a very useful exercise, especially for beginners, because it links the verbal with the visual.

As students advance in their knowledge of the language, their summaries can be made in the target language, thus allowing more writing practice. The summaries they construct can also become more complex; for example, learners can write complete sentences or paragraphs (called a "précis" or an "abstract") summarizing what they have heard or read.

Highlighting Ⓛ Ⓡ Ⓦ Learners sometimes benefit by supplementing notes and summaries with another strategy, highlighting. This strategy emphasizes the major points in a dramatic way, through color, underlining, CAPITAL LETTERS, Initial Capitals, **BIG WRITING**, **bold writing**, ★ stars ★, boxes, circles and so on. The sky's the limit in thinking of ways to highlight.

The three structuring strategies are often, but not always, used together. For instance, Monte uses the shopping list note form for his initial class notes, and later the same day he cleans up his notes, underlines the important points, and makes a short written summary. Eli is preparing to give an oral report on irrigation problems in a Central American country. He takes notes on the subject, summarizes the problems involved, and highlights the main issues. Gilberto, learning Russian, uses different colors to highlight different types of information (vocabulary, grammar points, cultural concepts) in his Russian textbook, and he outlines these in his language learning notebook.

A new twist in using these strategies is to have learners take notes on, summarize, or highlight *each other's* speaking or writing when it has reached a fairly well-developed stage. This procedure has two benefits. First, it allows learners to know what it is like to have a real audience trying to get the gist of their message. Second, the notes, summaries, and highlightings will tell learners whether or not they have succeeded in getting their main points across clearly. If you try this procedure in your classes, be sure to review the techniques of taking notes, summarizing, and highlighting so that everyone knows how. Otherwise, the benefits of this activity will be lost.

The cognitive strategies, a large and varied group, have been discussed. Now it is time to examine applications of compensation strategies, the last group of direct strategies.

APPLYING COMPENSATION STRATEGIES TO THE FOUR LANGUAGE SKILLS

The compensation strategies, displayed in Figure 3.11, help learners to overcome knowledge limitations in all four skills. For beginning and intermediate language learners, these strategies may be among the most important. Compensation strategies are also useful for more expert language users, who occasionally do not know an expression, who fail to hear something clearly, or who are faced with a situation in which the meaning is only implicit or intentionally vague.

Guessing Intelligently in Listening and Reading

Guessing is essential for listening and reading. It helps learners let go of the belief that they have to recognize and understand every single word before they can comprehend the overall meaning. Learners can actually understand a lot of language through systematic guessing, without necessarily comprehending all the details. Two compensation strategies relevant to listening and reading involve using linguistic clues and other clues.

Using Linguistic Clues Ⓛ Ⓡ Previously gained knowledge of the target language, the learners' own language, or some other language can provide linguistic clues to the meaning of what is heard or read. Suffixes, prefixes, and word order are useful linguistic clues for guessing meanings. Here are

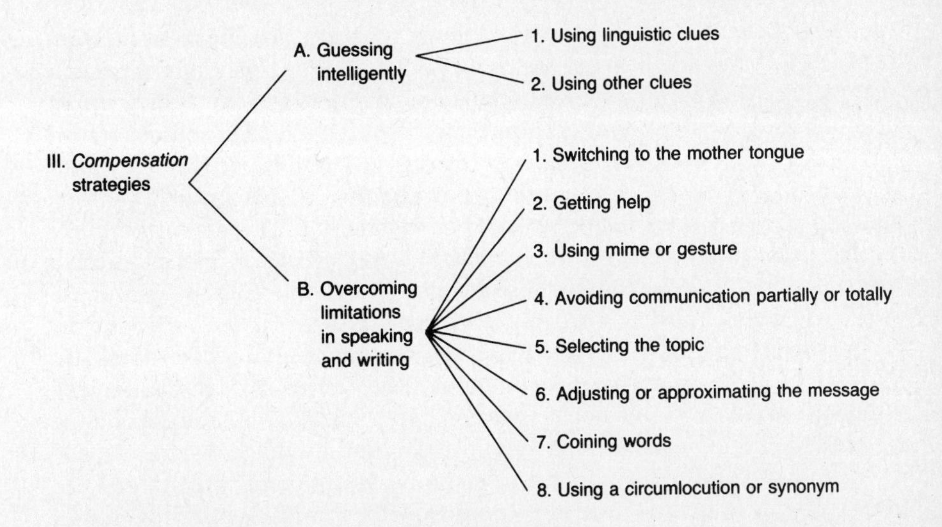

Language grows out of life, out of its needs and experiences. . . . Language *and* knowledge *are indissolubly connected; they are interdependent. Good work in language presupposes and depends on a real knowledge of things.*

Annie Sullivan

Figure 3.11 Diagram of the Compensation Strategies to Be Applied to the Four Language Skills. (*Source*: Original.)

some examples of guessing based on partial knowledge of the target language. Andrey recognizes the English words *shovel*, *grass*, *mower*, and *lawn*, so he knows that the conversation is about gardening. Wladislaw hears the sentence "*Jim* rejected the offer." The primary stress in this sentence is on Jim, so Wladislaw, alert to the significance of stress patterns in English, figures that Jim is being contrasted with someone else; the meaning would be different if the stress were on "offer" or some other word in the sentence.

Knowledge of the learner's own language provides still more clues for understanding material heard in the new language. For instance, Frank might be able to guess, given his knowledge of English, that *J'arrive!* means *I'm coming!* Sally realizes that every language has polite greetings, so when someone says *Zdravstvuitye* [Здравствуйте] in Russian, she guesses that this is a way of greeting her.

Linguistic clues are the bedrock of many correct guesses about the meaning of written passages [29]. For example, Vivian knows that *le lavabo* (sink) and *la toilette* (toilet) relate to *la salle de bains* (bathroom); so when she encounters *le robinet* (tap, faucet) and *le carrelage* (tiling) in the same advertisement, she figures that these are accessories or parts of the bathroom.

Using Other Clues Ⓛ Ⓡ In addition to clues coming purely from knowledge of language, there are clues from other sources. Some clues are related to language but go beyond (such as forms of address which imply social relationships), and others come from a variety of other sources which are not related to language [30].

Forms of address, such as titles or nicknames, help learners guess the meaning of what they hear or read. For instance, the terms *my pet, dear husband, mein Liebchen* (my little love), and *chère amie* (dear friend) imply a close relationship between two characters. Use of the formal *vous* or *Ihr* (you) signifies distance or respect. Titles such as *Herr Doktor Professor* (Mr. Dr. Professor) and *P.D.G.* (Président Directeur Général) indicate status. To the learner, all these are aids for understanding the rest of the passage.

Close observation of nonverbal behavior, such as the speaker's tone of voice, facial expression, emphasis, and body language (gestures, distance, posture, and relaxation versus tension), helps learners to understand what is being said. For instance, Broderick, the English-speaking learner of French, does not know the meaning of the word *Salaud!* but is aware of the speaker's angry tone and menacing body language. He uses this nonverbal information to guess that the speaker is saying something insulting or angry.

Knowing what has already been said frequently gives important information for getting the meaning of what is currently being said and for anticipating what will be said. Simone, listening to a dialogue about a policeman questioning a suspect, hears the sentence, "He gave him a real grilling." On the basis of what has been said already in the dialogue, Simone guesses that the word *grilling* in this context has nothing to do with cooking but has something to do with questioning. Molly asks herself questions, such as "What will happen now?" and "What might the author want to say next?" She then answers these questions in light of what has already been said, and checks to see whether her guesses are correct. Given even a hazy understanding of what the writer has said so far in a Brazilian newspaper editorial (maybe aided by background knowledge of the paper's political leanings), Andrew can guess what the writer will say next, even if he doesn't understand all the Portuguese words.

In listening, perceptual clues concerning the situation aid the listener's understanding. These clues can be audible (e.g., background noise) or visual (e.g., the number of people involved, what they appear to be doing). For instance, Miguel, a learner of English, is watching TV. He hears one of the TV characters say to his buddy, "Quick! Let's get out of here!" and at the same time he sees both TV characters start running out the door. Using the situational context, Miguel infers that the phrase means something about leaving. Ismael is listening to the radio. He hears a lot of noise from a crowd and some fast, excited speech, of which he catches a few words; he figures out from these signals that this must be a broadcast of a basketball game. Lisette is watching TV. A woman is reading something from a piece of paper, slowly, deliberately, and with a sense of rhythm, so Lisette immediately understands these clues to indicate that this is a poetry reading.

In listening or reading, an important source of clues to meaning is the text structure—that is, introductions, summaries, conclusions, titles, transitions, and ways of dividing the text. It is possible to obtain many clues by noticing the speaker's or author's structural, organizational use of words, phrases, numbers, and letters that indicate importance or priority; for instance, *first . . ., second . . ., third . . .; the most important idea is . . .;* or *the two main points are. . . .* Structural clues are often given, like *By way of introduction, We will now turn to . . ., So far we have covered . . .,* and *In conclusion . . . .* Proper names may be used over and over to indicate importance. Graphs, pictures, tables, and appendices can help readers get an idea of the meaning.

Descriptions of people in oral or written stories can also give clues about the meaning of the rest of the passage. For instance, if a character is described as sinister or mean, learners will expect the person to behave in a particular way later in the story, and even if they don't know all the words, they can guess the general kinds of things the character might do. Recognizing, even in very general terms, how the people in the listening or reading passage treat each other (kindly, subserviently, cruelly, respectfully) can help readers guess the events and the main message of the story. Identification of the situation described in the passage—a trip by train, a horse race, or a classroom scene—helps provide still more clues.

General background knowledge (including knowledge of the target culture, knowledge of the topic under discussion, and general world knowledge of current affairs, art, politics, and literature) helps language learners to make guesses about what they hear or read. A recent study [31] indicates that associating newly heard information with prior knowledge (see the strategy of associating/elaborating, as described earlier) is a powerful and very frequently used way to guess the meaning of a listening passage. All listeners make mental associations with prior knowledge, but when compared with ineffective listeners, good listeners make many more of these associations, make them more personally meaningful, and intentionally use them for guessing. The same undoubtedly holds true for reading. Here are some examples of using clues from background knowledge to guess meanings. Millicent, who is learning Russian, hears the word *apparatchik* [аппаратчик] used in a discussion of Soviet government. On the basis of her general knowledge of the way governments work, she guesses that the word must refer to the government employee, who is part of the *apparatus* of government. The rest of the discussion confirms her guesses. Knowing about the culture where the language is spoken gives many clues; for instance, in reading Spanish, Hilde might expect to encounter a passage about *la corrida de toros* (the bullfight), but Robert would probably be surprised to encounter such a passage in German.

However, learners do not all have the same kind of knowledge upon which to draw. For instance, an English-as-a-second-language class may be composed of people representing many different languages and nationalities and many kinds of life experiences, some including severe hardship and deprivation. For some learners, such differences are a real handicap to understanding the target language. One solution to this problem is to use a variety of listening and reading materials covering as many different topics as possible. Another solution is to try to anticipate the kinds of materials and topics your students, as a group or individually, will have trouble with and the ones they will find easier. Focus on the easier ones at first, in order to build the students' confidence and give them the sense that they can listen and read (and guess!) in the target language. Move into more difficult topics and formats gradually.

How to Promote Guessing

Build guessing skills systematically by leading students step by step through different stages of guessing. Start with global comprehension. To stimulate guessing, ask students some preview questions before they start reading or listening, or interrupt a story in the middle to ask for predictions about what will happen, or give just the ending and ask for guesses about the beginning. Ask which picture corresponds to what they are hearing or reading. Alternatively, give students a sentence in the new language and ask them to complete it [32]. Whenever you use activities like these, be sure to give students feedback immediately (or soon) about the correctness or appropriateness of their answers. Discuss the source of the guesses, so that students can learn from each other and so you can know whether learners are using all possible sources of clues.

The guessing strategies relate to listening and reading. The next group of compensation strategies is tailored for speaking and writing.

Overcoming Limitations in Speaking and Writing

All the compensation strategies for speaking and writing contribute to learning by allowing learners to stay in conversations or keep writing long enough to get sustained practice. Some of these strategies also provide new knowledge in a more obvious way (e.g., getting help).

Switching to the Mother Tongue Ⓢ This strategy, sometimes technically called "code switching," is used for speaking and involves using the mother tongue for an expression without translating it. Here are some examples of this strategy. Geraldo, a Spanish speaker learning English, uses *balón* for *balloon*, and *tirtil* for *caterpillar*. Trudy, an English-speaking student of French, says, *Je suis dans la wrong maison* (I'm in the wrong house), inserting "wrong" when the French word is unknown. Leslie, an English speaker learning French, states, *Je ne pas go to school*, thus switching back to English in midstream. June, another learner of French, uses the expression *le livre de Paul's* (Paul's book), including the non-French word *Paul's*. And Henri, a French speaker learning English, declares, *I want a couteau*, a knife.

Creatively using this strategy, Norman adds word endings from the target language onto words from the mother tongue, as in *Wir sind Soldieren* (We are soldiers, using the English word *soldier* with the German *-en* tacked on). An English speaker, Nicki, wants to describe a clock over the fireplace, but says instead *Il y a une cloche sur la cheminée* (there's a bell over the fireplace). Of course, these two examples might be misunderstood by native speakers of the new language.

Getting Help Ⓢ This strategy involves asking someone for help in a conversation by hesitating or explicitly asking for the missing expression. This strategy is somewhat similar to the strategy of asking for clarification or verification; the difference is that in getting help, the learner wants the other person to simply *provide* what the learner does not know, not to explain or clarify. For example, Clive, a learner of Spanish, signals a desire for help by saying only the first part of the sentence, as in *El quiere . . .?* (He wants . . .?), and Hector, a native Spanish speaker, finishes the sentence with *qué te vayas* (the whole sentence means, "He wants you to go"). Edna, a learner of French, asks in English, *How do you say "staple" in French?* Terry, another learner of French, says, *Je veux, uh, how do you say it?* (I want . . .). Often this strategy is combined with the next one, using mime or gesture, in order to ask for help.

Using Mime or Gesture Ⓢ In this strategy, the learner uses physical motion, such as mime or gesture, in place of an expression during a conversation to indicate the meaning. Following are some examples. Kirsten does not know the expression for a large wooden desk with drawers, so she makes gestures indicating the size of the desk, the hardness of the wood, and the way the drawers pull out. Not able to say, "I am afraid," Jaime instead mimes the emotion of fear by crouching with his arms crossed over his head. Aviva does not yet know how to say, "Put it over there, please," and instead points to the place, hoping the other person will catch the meaning and put the object down in the right spot. Not knowing how to express approval verbally, Tonio claps loudly to indicate approval, then nods in an exaggerated fashion while saying "yes."

Avoiding Communication Partially or Totally Ⓢ This strategy involves avoiding communication when difficulties are anticipated or encountered.

It includes a total avoidance in certain situations, as when required to use persuasive skills or to compete with others for a turn to speak. It also includes avoiding certain topics for which the learner does not know the words, concepts, or grammatical structures in the new language. This strategy goes against the aim of speaking as much and as often as possible, but it does have an advantage of keeping the learner emotionally protected and possibly more able to speak about other things later in the conversation. The avoidance of a specific expression is illustrated by Constanze, a learner of English, who avoids saying *air pollution* (or any description or synonym for this expression) and says instead, *It's hard to breathe*; this might also be used as an example of the strategy of adjusting or approximating the message. The abandonment of communication midway is exemplified when Miki says, *If I only had a . . .* but then fails to finish the sentence.

Selecting the Topic Ⓢ Ⓦ When using this strategy, the learner chooses the topic of conversation. The reasons for this are obvious. Learners want to make sure that the topic is one in which they are interested and for which they possess the needed vocabulary and structures. For example, Rashid, a learner of English, is interested in football and knows a lot about it, including useful terms, so he often directs conversation to this theme. Marcelle is more comfortable discussing subjects like family, school, and weather and thus frequently attempts to move the conversation toward these topics. Learners using this strategy must be careful not to be overly domineering. They should allow the other person to guide the conversation, too.

Writers in any language sometimes use this strategy, but it is particularly valuable to writers in a language other than their own. Of course, circumstances sometimes force language learners to deal with topics they don't want to write about, but whenever possible learners should select a topic that interests them. The only caveat is that learners, when choosing a topic for writing, need to be aware of their audience's interests, needs, and level of understanding.

Adjusting or Approximating the Message Ⓢ Ⓦ This strategy is used to alter the message by omitting some items of information, make the ideas simpler or less precise, or say something slightly different that has similar meaning [33]. Here are some examples. Omitting details that the learner cannot yet say is illustrated when Vanya, asked about his family, says he has two children but does not indicate that they are now fully grown adults; another learner, Nina, says she has to leave now, but does not indicate that she has an appointment at the dentist's in 20 minutes. Using less precise expressions to substitute for more precise but unknown ones, Carmelita might say *pipe* for *waterpipe*. Using a French word that has a similar meaning to the intended French word, Laura says *bureau* (office) to mean shop, as in *un bureau pour cosmetics et perfume*. Franny, a learner of Spanish, uses "presidente" to mean principal, as in *Señor Smith es el presidente de la escuela* (Mr. Smith is the president of the school).

Writers often resort to this strategy when they simply cannot come up with the right or most desirable expression. For instance, instead of writing the more difficult sentence "I would have liked to have visited Australia, but I could not go because I lacked the necessary funds," Nubia writes "I did not go to Australia, because I did not have money."

Coining Words Ⓢ Ⓦ This simple strategy means making up new words to communicate a concept for which the learner does not have the right vocabulary. For instance, Zoltan might say *airball* to mean *balloon*. A German learner of English, Gottfried, does not know the expression *bedside table* and therefore coins the expression *night table*, a direct translation of the German *Nachttisch*. (Note the use of the strategy of translating in the service of coining words during a conversation.) Lucille, an English-speaking learner of German, does not know how to say *dishwasher* in German and consequently makes up the word *Abwaschmaschine*, a combination of *abwaschen* (to wash up) and *Maschine* (machine). Finally, Omar, a learner of English, is not familar with the word *bucket* and therefore coins *water-holder*.

When there is no time to look up the correct word, or when the dictionary fails them, writers sometimes make up their own words to get the meaning across. For example, Stavros uses the term *tooth doctor* instead of *dentist* when writing a note to indicate where he is going this afternoon.

Using a Circumlocution or Synonym Ⓢ Ⓦ In this strategy the learner uses a circumlocution (a roundabout expression involving several words to describe or explain a single concept) or a synonym (a word having exactly the same meaning as another word in the same language) to convey the intended meaning. Examples of circumlocution are as follows. Renato, a learner of English, does not know *car seatbelt* and therefore says, "I'd better tie myself in." Liz, a learner of French who does not know the word for *stool* (*tabouret*), describes it instead: *une petite chaise de bois, pour reposer les jambes quand on est fatigué, elle n'a pas de dos* (a little wooden chair for resting the legs when one is tired, it doesn't have a back). Osmin, a learner of English, cannot come up with the right word and therefore ambles around the topic: "She is, uh, smoking something. I don't know what's its name. That's, uh, Persian, and we use in Turkey, a lot of." Heinrich does not know how to say *towel* in English, so he says, "a thing you dry your hands on." Domenico uses the close synonym *sofa* or *couch* to mean the specific piece of furniture, *divan*. Frequently learners use high-coverage terms that are very close to (but not quite) synonyms; for instance, *pen* instead of *ballpoint pen*, *fruit* for *strawberry*, or *meat* instead of *ham*.

Synonyms or circumlocutions are sometimes used in informal writing. For instance, Siu cannot think of the word *briefcase*, so he writes, "I lost my leather package that holds papers," a circumlocution that gets the point across.

SUMMARY

The focus of this chapter has been use of direct strategies—memory, cognitive, and compensation strategies—to enhance performance in the four language skills. This chapter has shown how certain direct strategies, like taking notes, work across all four skills, while other direct strategies, like getting the idea quickly, are useful for only a subset of these skills. A huge range of applications of direct strategies has been covered here. However, these strategies, to be used most effectively, require their allies, the indirect strategies, which are detailed in Chapters 4 and 5. Before moving on to those chapters, do some of the following activities and exercises to solidify your understanding and stimulate your students' interest in and comprehension of direct strategies.

ACTIVITIES FOR READERS

Activity 3.1. You Can Quote Me on That!

In the left-hand column below is a list of quotations [34] relating to the four language skills: listening, reading, speaking, and writing. Identify the skill or skills mentioned or implied in the quotation, by writing L, R, S, or W in the middle column next to the quotation. Then in the right-hand column, for *each* quotation list *at least three* direct strategies which would strongly enhance development of *each of the skills* mentioned.

QUOTATION	SKILL(S) (L,R,S,W)	STRATEGIES
The time has come, the Walrus said, to talk of many things. Lewis Carroll		
To read without reflecting is like eating without digesting. Edmund Burke		
There can be no fairer ambition than to excel in talk. Robert Louis Stevenson		
Prick up your ears. Movie title		

QUOTATION	SKILL(S) (L,R,S,W)	STRATEGIES
True ease in writing comes from art, not chance, as those move easiest who have learned to dance. Alexander Pope		
Reading is a psycholinguistic guessing game. June Phillips, quoting Frank Smith		
Lend me your ears. William Shakespeare		
Speak out: What is it thou hast heard, or seen? Lord Tennyson		
Polonius: What are you reading? Hamlet: Words, words, words. William Shakespeare		
Genius is one percent inspiration and ninety-nine percent perspiration. Thomas A. Edison		
I took a course in speed reading, learning to read straight down the middle of the page, and was able to read *War and Peace* in twenty minutes. It's about Russia. Woody Allen		
Dear authors! Suit your topic to your strength, And ponder well your subject And its length. Lord Byron		
A good listener is a good talker with a sore throat. Katherine Whitehorn		
To write simply is as difficult as to be good. Somerset Maugham		

Activity 3.2. Remark on Remembering

This chapter shows how memory strategies are used to *store* new information that is heard or read, and to *recall* or *retrieve* the information later when needed in a situation involving any of the four skills. Give your own examples of these two functions of memory strategies as applied to each of the four language skills.

Activity 3.3. Cogitate About Cognitive Strategies

List all the cognitive strategies that you have observed your students using. Now, next to each strategy, list the language skills (listening, reading, speaking, writing, or some combination) that your students have developed by using the strategy.

Activity 3.4. Accentuate the Positive

Brainstorm all the ways compensation strategies might be useful for listening, reading, speaking, and writing. Give your own examples. How do these strategies help to "accentuate the positive"? What are the reasons why you might place guessing strategies (useful in listening and reading) alongside strategies like circumlocution (useful in speaking and writing)?

Activity 3.5. Stalk the Strategies

Carefully study the exercises below. In the margin or on another sheet, indicate all the strategies that are called for by each of the exercises. Do not be limited by the strategy information in the descriptions of "purpose" at the top of each exercise. List *all* the strategies that *you* think are involved.

EXERCISES TO USE WITH YOUR STUDENTS

Note: The exercises here focus primarily on *direct* strategies—memory, cognitive, and compensation—but in many cases *indirect* strategies—metacognitive, affective, and social—are also necessary to do these tasks. As mentioned earlier, direct and indirect strategies work together for optimal learning.

Exercise 3.1. Memory Practice

Purpose

This exercise helps learners to distribute or space their memory practice with new vocabulary words, using structured review and other memory strategies.

Materials

Large sheet of paper for the list.

Time

Although the exercise takes 30 to 50 minutes, you might also hold short sessions periodically to add to the list later.

Instructions

Ask your students to brainstorm about all the memory strategies they now use, or have used, to learn a language. Make the list as long as possible. Then ask the students to tell which of these were useful and which were not, and have them explain why. Put a star (*) beside those which students describe as effective. Add to the list periodically. (If students cannot think of the memory strategies they use, do a few language learning tasks in class, then ask your students to list all the memory strategies they used for those tasks and to indicate which ones they felt were the most helpful.)

Then explain some of the principles of remembering. For instance, describe in your own words the need for *structured reviewing at increasing intervals*, and give or show them a copy of Figure 3.6. Ask them to learn specific vocabulary for an upcoming lesson by using this strategy. Ask them to report back to the class on the effects.

During a vocabulary learning task in class, give your students practice in making *associations*, using *imagery*, and putting new words into the *context* of a sentence. To do this, ask students to work in small groups and share their associations, images, or contexts (sentences) aloud as they work on learning new expressions.

Source Original.

Exercise 3.2. Grouping and Labeling

Purpose

These tasks help learners see the value of grouping and labeling. Learners get practice with both of these as they learn vocabulary.

Materials

Word lists.

Time

The exercise takes 20 to 30 minutes.

Instructions

Tell your students the following in your own words: Grouping information helps you remember it. Putting a label on the groups you have made can also help you recall it later. Both of these techniques are really organizational functions, which help you sort information and reduce it to smaller, more cohesive units.

Let's show how grouping helps you. First, try to memorize List A after reading through it a few times. (Give learners the list.)

LIST A

cocoa	Indian	bed	soda
post office	hello	soap	what
able	that	registration	personality
rigidity	loop	disk	yellow

Now put the list away and then try to write down as many of the words in the list as you can remember. Then count the number of words you have recalled. (Take a few minutes here to do an informal survey of how many of the 16 words were recalled; get a rough average for the group.) These are your results when you do *not* use any special kind of grouping—that is, when the information in a list is completely unorganized.

Now let's try another experiment. Try to memorize List B. Read through it a few times now. (Give learners the list.)

LIST B
Office Supplies and Equipment

Desk-related:	pens pencils rubber bands paper clips tape stapler desk
Computer-related:	paper ribbon hard disk floppy disk VDT
Telephone-related:	telephone notepad phone book answering machine

Now put the list away and again write down as many of the listed words as you remember. Count the number of words you have written down. (Take time to survey the students again and obtain an average of the number of words. It is likely that students remembered more from List B than they did earlier from List A.) This is how you perform when the information is more organized—that is, grouped and labeled so that it is easier to remember.

We will now try List A again, but this time you'll organize the words and use any labels you want to use. (Give students time, say 3 to 5 minutes, to organize the words from List A into groups of their own making.) Be sure to write down the words as you group them and then put labels on the groups. Put away the list now. Try to write down as many of the words as you remember, and then count the number of words you recall from your "organized List A." (Check how many words have been recalled; it will probably be far more than students remembered the first time they dealt with List A, partly due to grouping and partly due to having a second encounter with the material.)

Though List B was already grouped, you might find it useful to regroup and relabel the words in List B in a way that suits you better personally. Take a few minutes to think of a different grouping system. Jot the words down in their new groups, and give each group a name. Now remember the words. (Do another survey about the words remembered from List B, and see if the average is any better than it was with the original List B.)

Now let's discuss grouping and labeling. How does grouping help you remember? What functions does it serve? What does labeling do for you? Is it better to create labels before or after the groups are formed? Is it better to generate your own groups and labels, or have the groups and labels given to you, or does it make any difference? What role does structured review play, and what role does grouping play? (Let students have time to discuss these questions, possibly in small groups or pairs, reporting to the larger group at the end.)

Source Original.

Exercise 3.3. Make Your Own Groups

Purpose

This exercise gives learners the opportunity to create their own groups of words and consider the best criteria for doing so, as a way of remembering vocabulary.

Materials

Word cards.

Time

This lasts 45 minutes.

Instructions

Give your students 50 to 100 small cards containing vocabulary words in the new language. Let them work in pairs to group the cards and then label their groups. To do this, they should lay the cards out on a table, putting them into as many groups as necessary and then devising labels for each group. Suggest that they transfer this information onto a large sheet and then draw lines between any groups of words that might have some relationship to each other, thus creating a *semantic map*. You might show them an example of a semantic map from this chapter. Students should be able to find relationships, either direct or far-fetched, among many groups!

Then ask the pairs to compare notes with other pairs about their resulting groups, labels, and semantic maps. Ask them to consider what criteria they used for grouping, labeling, and figuring out relations between groups. Ask them to consider which ways of grouping, labeling, and finding relationships helped them remember better.

Alternative

For advanced students, all the discussion could take place in the new language.

Source Original.

Exercise 3.4. Find the Odd Word

Purpose

This activity is an extension of the grouping exercises. It requires learners to find the word that does *not* fit into the groups. This provides more complex grouping practice, helps in discrimination skills, and helps in remembering new words.

Materials

Word lists, instruction sheet.

Time

The exercise takes 15 minutes, more if alternatives are used.

Instructions

Give your students the word lists and instructions below.

Which word does not belong in each of the four lists below? Circle the "odd" word in the cluster and explain why you chose it.

LIST 1	LIST 2
der Regen (rain)	der Friseur (hairdresser)
das Gewitter (thunderstorm)	der Vetter (cousin, masc.)
das Unglück (misfortune)	der Großvater (grandfather)
der Donner (thunder)	die Kusine (cousin, fem.)

LIST 3	LIST 4
das Theater (theater)	breit (broad)
das Gebäude (building)	weit (wide)
die Kirche (church)	eng (narrow)
der Käfig (cage)	weich (soft)

Alternatives

1. Some highly creative students always seem to find relationships among almost any set of words, and they are able to give logical reasons, too! If you are dealing with such students, run the exercise as above. Then run it a second time, this time asking learners to think of reasons why the four words in each group *do* fit together.

2. If learners are more advanced, they can do the exercise, including all discussion, entirely in the target language.

Source Omaggio (1981, p. 27) for basic exercise. Alternatives are original.

Exercise 3.5. Yes/No Game

Purpose

This exercise helps learners to improve their perception and discrimination of sounds in the new language. The exercise involves the strategy of formally practicing with sounds.

Materials

None.

Time

It takes 5 to 10 minutes.

Instructions

Call out two words to the students. Tell them to indicate if the words are the *same* (if so, write YES) or *not the same* (if they are not the same, write NO). Each pair of words will have a number, and YES or NO will be written next to the appropriate number. Give students an example on the board, like this:

WORD PAIR NUMBER	YES (the same) or NO (not the same)?
1. (book/look)	NO
2.	
3.	
4.	
5.	

Alternatives

Call out a series of several words and ask students to indicate which, if any, is not the same as the others. For the set FAR, BAR, FAR, FAR, learners would write down 2 to show that the second word in the series is not like the others.

OR

Give students a page with sets of words listed, two to four at a time. Ask students to circle the words that they hear you read aloud from each set.

Source Original; however, these sound discrimination exercises are fairly standard in any listening comprehension textbook.

Exercise 3.6. Finding Your Way

Purpose

This exercise is a listening comprehension task involving students in marking a route on a map according to spoken directions. It requires a combination of many strategies, such as direct strategies like practicing naturalistically, guessing, and using imagery and indirect strategies like paying attention.

Materials

Map photocopied for each student.

Time

This will take 20 minutes.

Instructions

Get a clear road map of an interesting area (see examples in Figures 3.12 and 3.13). Make copies for all students and yourself. On your own copy, sketch the route you want students to go. Then, without showing your copy to the students, describe in words where to go, adding comments on the scenery and landmarks, discussing the kinds of people you will meet (e.g., the butcher, the minister, the teacher), and mentioning reasons for visiting certain places. These hints will help students as they mark on their map the route you are describing.

Source Original instructions; however, such activities are typically found in good listening comprehension books, such as Ur (1984).

Exercise 3.7. Physical Response

Purpose

This exercise has learners listen carefully for directions about how they should perform physical movement, a useful memory strategy.

Materials

None.

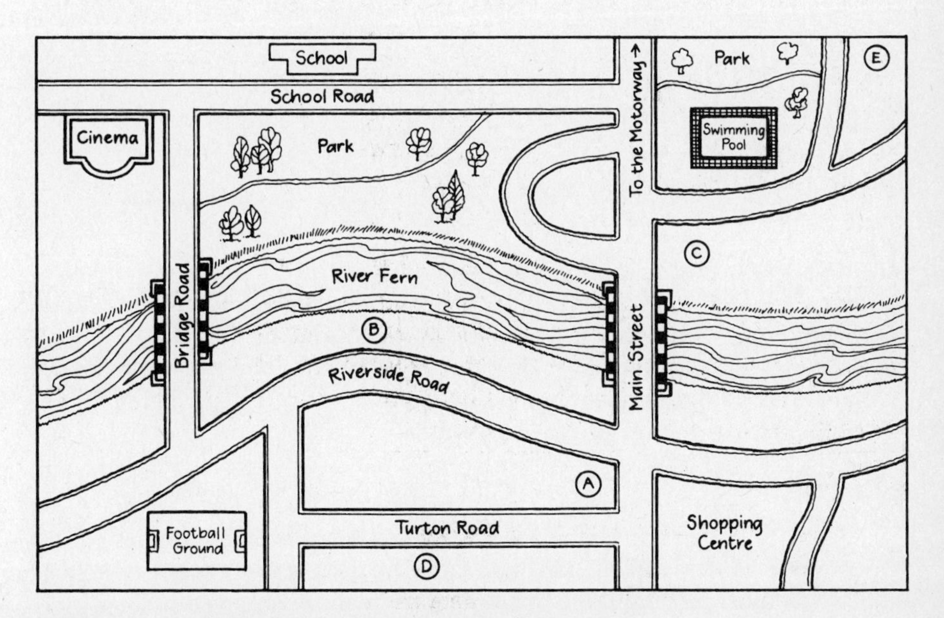

Figure 3.12 English Road Map. (*Source*: Ur (1984, p. 61).)

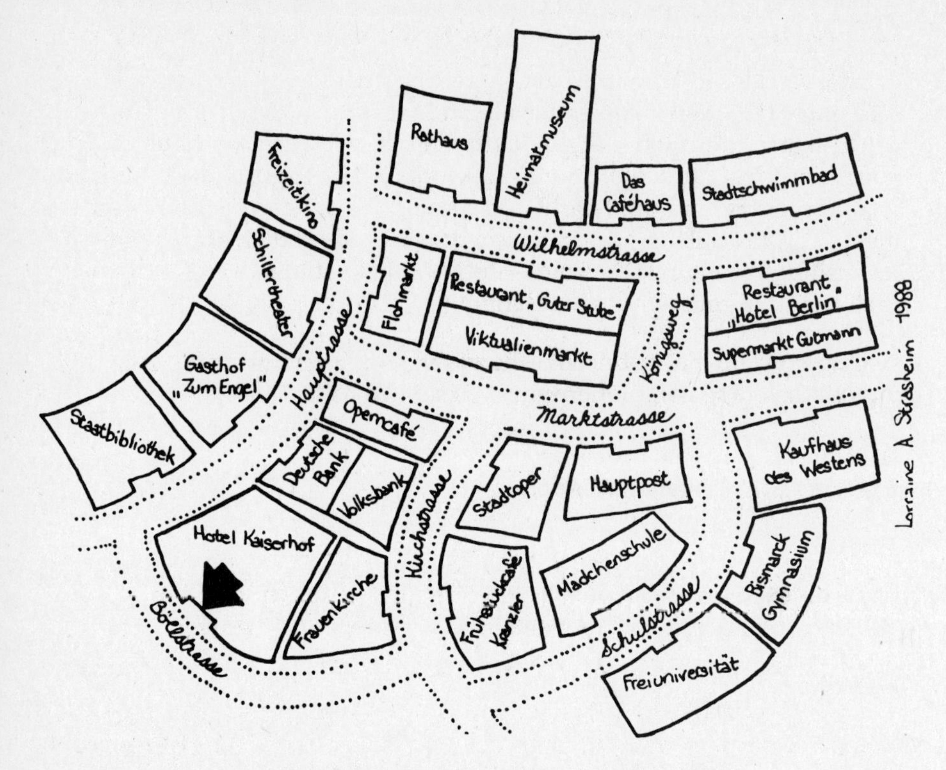

Figure 3.13 German Road Map. (*Source*: Strasheim (1988, p. 3).)

Time

Variable.

Instructions

Using physical response is usually a lot of fun for students and provides excellent practice in both listening comprehension and memory. Give your students commands as to what to do: stand up, sit down, touch (something), close (something); or for more advanced students, make longer commands by linking several together. Commands can also include telling students to take certain physical positions, sometimes funny ones.

Alternative

Ur (1984) suggests giving students commands but demonstrating *different* movements yourself. This will force learners to pay attention to what you are actually saying! You might also try having your students pair up and give each other commands.

Source Original instructions, but these are typical of many Total Physical Response exercises.

Exercise 3.8. Jigsaw Listening

Purpose

This exercise allows students to listen to different extracts from a text and then collate their information in order to get a complete understanding of the situation. It involves direct strategies like practicing naturalistically, guessing, and note-taking, as well as indirect strategies like paying attention and cooperating.

Materials

Tapes containing extracts of a narrative.

Time

Depends on narrative length and proficiency level.

Instructions

Ask your students to fill out a grid (see Table 3.1) by listening to extracts of a narrative on tape, and then pooling information from their extracts. The purpose of the grid is to describe characters in the narrative by name, profession, address, age, and appearance. One-third of the students would have Extract 1, another third Extract 2, and the last third Extract 3.

Table 3.1 PERSONAL CHARACTERISTICS GRID FOR JIGSAW LISTENING

Name				
Profession				
Address				
Age				
Appearance				

Source: Ur (1984), p. 153.

Here are some sample extracts taken from Ur (1984). Note that these are only brief extracts! The real narrative would need to be longer and more detailed.

Extract 1

PAT: Do you know those four people over there by chance?

JON: I know the old man with the beard, Mr. Sutton. He's headmaster of the local school and lives here in Cheston. I think the younger man's also a teacher in the school. I've seen him around, the one that's talking to the doctor.

Extract 2

JASON: Do introduce me to that attractive girl talking to old Mr. Sutton—who is she?

ELSA: No luck, Jason, she's married, that's her husband, the tall man next to her. Name of Smith.

JASON: She looks too young to be married.

ELSA: Rose? She's twenty-two, we were at school together. She works as a secretary in her husband's school—they live quite near here.

Extract 3

GRANDMA: Thelma, do go and ask that nice Dr. Thorndike if she'd come and talk to me for a while.

THELMA: All right, Grandma, which one is she?

GRANDMA: She's that middle-aged, very well dressed lady standing over there talking to Mr. Smith. She lives in London and doesn't come down here very often, so I'd love to have a chat with her.

Note Jigsaw listening tasks such as this one are entertaining and very useful for listening comprehension. However, there are drawbacks: the need for the right number of recordings and machines, and the need to have each group listen to its own extract without being overly distracted by others. See Ur for details and other suggestions for jigsaw listening.

Source Ur (1984, pp. 152–154).

Exercise 3.9. Guessing the Meaning of Reading Passages

Purpose

This exercise helps learners to guess the meaning of a reading passage and explain how they made those guesses.

Materials

Sheet with reading passages.

Time

This takes 30 to 50 minutes, depending on amount of discussion.

Instructions

Explain to your students that they will be practicing their guessing skills in various languages. Give them a sheet containing the following instructions and reading passages (or others of your own selection). Keep the number of passages down to four or five, or whatever you think your students can handle profitably.

Read the following passages and try to guess the general meaning, even if you do not know all the words! You will be answering some questions about these passages at the end.

1. . . . It was really a very nice appetizing bit of pischa they'd laid out on the tray—two or three lomticks of like hot roast beef with mashed kartoffel and vedge, then there was also ice-cream and a nice hot chasha of chai. And there was even a cancer to smoke and a matchbox with one match in it. (Burgess, 1963, p. 99)
2. Dr. Lightfoot, who guffled my aunt's flumps, is a fine surgeon. (Mendelsohn, 1984, p. 70)
3. URSS: LE PLUS ANCIEN DES "REFUSNIKS" VLADIMIR SLEPAK A QUITTÉ MOSCOU POUR ISRAEL. M. Vladimir Slepak, l'un des principaux dissidents juifs soviétiques, est arrivé le dimanche 25 octobre à Vienne, en provenance d'Union Soviétique et à destination d'Israel.

   A leur arrivée dans la capitale autrichienne, le "refusnik" et sa femme Maria ont été accueillis par leur fils Alexandre, qui avait emigré aux Etats-Unis il y a dix ans. Celui-ci a dit espérer que la liberation de ses parents annonçait un tournant dans la politique soviétique à l'égard des juifs.

   En revanche, son père a declaré: "Selon moi, [ma liberation] est un geste en direction de l'Occident parce que les autorités soviétiques ont besoin d'aide et de crédit (. . .) Ce sont des tyrans". (URSS . . ., *Le Monde*, 1987)
4. Selected Items from Menu from Al-Ikhwa Hotel, Taiz, Y.A.R.: Coloured Soop, Fish with Potatoes & Latic, Fish with Eggs & Potatoes Beas, Rost Meat with Potatoes Beans, Stick Meat with Potatoes & Beas, Kutlet Meat, Small Meat, Dry Meat Shab, Stick with Eggs & Potatoes, Kari Meat & Rice, Kari Hans with Rice, Hans with Potatoes & Beas, Hurts with Eggs & Patatoes Beas, Mukroni with Eggs Meat Bakred, Sandwish Colured, Sweat Boding, Lce and Tea, Lce with Coffee and Milk, Turkey Coffee, Vimto, Franch Lemon, Lec-Cream . . . (Private Eye, 1979, p. 54)

Now answer the following questions, working with another person:

1. Summarize the meaning of each passage in one sentence.
2. How well did you understand the meaning of each of the passages above? Which passages gave you the most trouble, and why?
3. If you did not understand certain words, which ones were they?
4. Did you try to guess the meaning of unknown or unclear words? If so, how often? What are some examples of unknown words you were able to guess? What information did you use to make your guesses?
5. What other information sources might you have used to guess the meanings? List as many sources as you can think of.
6. Did you need to know (or guess) the meanings of all the words in a passage in order to know (or guess) the overall meaning of the *whole* passage? In other words, do you need to get the details in order to get the general idea?

Source Original.

Exercise 3.10. Guessing with Pictures

Purpose

This exercise helps learners practice their guessing strategies using pictures.

Materials

Cartoons without words (as in Figure 3.14).

Time

It will take 10 to 30 minutes, depending on the number of cartoons.

Instructions

Give students cartoons without any words at all, as in Figure 3.14. Ask them to fill in the missing captions with their own words in the target language. Remind them to use all the clues they find in the pictures in order to create appropriate captions.

Source Moran (1984).

Exercise 3.11. Scanning a Reading Passage for Personal Facts

Purpose

This exercise helps learners to scan a reading passage for personal facts.

Figure 3.14 Guessing with Pictures. Use your imagination—and your new language—to fill in the missing captions! (*Source*: Moran (1984).)

Materials

Sheet with reading passages and instructions.

Time

Variable, depending on proficiency level and passage length; you should limit the time for scanning.

Instructions

Tell your students the following in your own words: Below are the names of four characters in the reading passage. (Teacher provides these names from a reading passage the students have not yet read.) For each of the characters listed here, you are to give information from the reading passage about the person's

1. nationality
2. age
3. occupation
4. future plans
5. main traits

(Learners receive the passage and do the task here.)

Here are the correct answers. Check yours against these to see whether you are right. If you made any errors, how might you have been confused by the passage?

Alternatives

Adapt this for use with a listening passage. Or have learners scan a passage for actions, new words, or any other details. See Phillips (1984) for ideas.

Source Adapted from Phillips (1984, p. 291).

Exercise 3.12. Skimming a Reading Passage for the Main Idea

Purpose

This exercise helps learners to skim a reading passage for the main idea.

Materials

Sheet with reading passages, instructions, and headlines.

Time

Variable, depending on proficiency level and length of the passages; you should limit the time for skimming.

Instructions

Tell your students the following in your own words: You will be given a series of short news articles with three possible headlines for each. Read as quickly as you can and choose the most appropriate headline for each article.

(Provide students with articles and possible headlines.) Now that you have finished the task, compare notes with someone else.

Alternatives

An alternative with news or magazine articles has students skim the lead paragraph and decide in which section of the index or table of contents it belongs, such as national news, life-style, sports. Or adapt this for use with a listening passage. Or read a passage and provide a one-word or one-sentence summary of the passage. Or read a passage and provide a one-word summary of each paragraph.

Source Adapted from Phillips (1984, p. 290). For additional skimming exercises, see Phillips (1984).

Exercise 3.13. Inventions

Purpose

This exercise helps readers practice naturalistically, search for meaning, and use information to complete a diagram. This exercise could easily be adapted for any set of chronological facts from any culture or subject area.

Materials

Invention list (below), incomplete diagram (Figure 3.15).

Time

Takes 45 minutes.

Instructions

Give your students the following instructions orally and in writing: The diagram in Figure 3.15 plots the time between the date of conception

```
1880   90   1900   10   20   30   40   50   60   1970
  .     .     :     .    .    .    .    .    .     .
                                                         Invention
                    10             40
A       .     :     *  ----30----  *    .    .     A ____________________
                              38     45
B       .     :     .    .    . *-- 7 --*.   .     B ____________________
             01               34
C       .     :*-----33 -----*      .    .    .     C ____________________
                 08        23
D       .     :  * -- 15 --*   .    .    .    .     D ____________________
1880   90   1900   10   20   30   40   50   60   1970
                             28                 60
E       .     :     .    .   *-----/ 32 ----    *   E ____________________
                  04                41
F       .     :   *----- 37- ----   *    .    .     F ____________________
                                  34      56
G       .     :     .    .    .   * -- 22 --*  .    G ____________________
                                    45    48
H       .     :     .    .    .     : -3 - *   .    H ____________________
1880   90   1900   10   20   30   40   50   60   1970
                         19                        65
I       .     :     .    *---------46 -------*
                                                    I ____________________
                             27  39
J       .     :     .    .   *-12-*        .    .   J ____________________
                 04              39
K       .     :  *----- 35 -----*          .    .   K ____________________
       90               14
L      *---- 24 ----*   .    .    .    .    .    .   L ____________________
1880   90   1900   10   20   30   40   50   60   1970
                                       48    55
M       .     :     .    .    .    . *-- 7 --*.    M ____________________
                     09    20
N *  ------------63 -------------*.    .           N ____________________
                                    40      56
O       .     :     .    .    .     *-- 16 --*.    O ____________________
1880   90   1900   10   20   30   40   50   60   1970
                                          50 56
P       .     :     .    .    .    .      *-6-*.    P ____________________
                                  35     50
Q       .     :     .    .    .   * - 15 - *   .    Q ____________________
      83                13
R    *---- 30 ----*          .    .    .    .       R ____________________
                          .
1880   90   1900   10   20   30   40   50   60   1970
```

Figure 3.15 Inventions. (*Source*: Crookall (1984, p. 25).)

and the date of realization for 19 different inventions (A to S). For example, invention A was first thought of in 1910 and did not become a concrete reality until 1940, a time lapse of 30 years; invention M was conceived in 1948 and took 7 years before it was realized in 1955.

Your task is to use the information in the sentences given here to label each invention on the diagram in Figure 3.15. In other words, you have to decide which inventions (mentioned in the sentences) go with which lines in the diagram. The problem is to find out which invention took the least time between its conception date and its realization date.

- The zipper was thought of just one year before the television.
- Both nylon and radar were developed in the same year, but the latter was conceived at the turn of the century, in the same year as the helicopter was thought of.
- The long-playing record took less than half the time, from conception to realization, than the roll-on deodorant.
- Antibiotics took the same time as the zipper to be made, while the heart pacemaker and fluorescent lighting took, respectively, 2 and 3 years longer.
- Instant coffee was thought of in the same year as fluorescent lighting was produced, and the same relationship holds for the transistor and antibiotics.
- The invention which took the most time between its conception and its realization was the television.
- The VTR (video tape recorder) took only half as long as nylon to be made, and one-quarter the time that radio took.
- The Xerox copier and frozen foods each took as much time to produce as the combined time it took for the ballpoint pen and the VTR (video tape recorder), and each took half as long as the zipper.
- The television took 17 years longer to become a reality than did nuclear power.
- The roll-on deodorant took just a little longer to come into being than did the VTR (video tape recorder), and both were conceived and produced more or less concurrently.

Source Adapted from Crookall (1984a, pp. 24–25).

Exercise 3.14. Jigsaw Reading

Purpose

This exercise asks learners to put together two or more pieces of a written text that have been separated, thus requiring that learners guess by using text structure and content clues. Other strategies, such as a range of cognitive strategies, are involved.

Materials

Books, articles, advertisements, or stories cut up (see below).

Time

Variable, depending on the materials used.

Instructions

Jigsaw reading involves cutting up a text and asking the students to put it back together. This exercise can take many forms: (a) matching headlines with the relevant newspaper articles, (b) matching pictures with the stories, advertisements, or articles from which they came, (c) matching cartoons with their captions, (d) matching two parts of an interview, i.e., the interviewer's questions with the interviewee's answers, (e) putting together in the proper sequence all the questions and answers from an interview, (f) matching pictures, captions, and text that have been split and putting them all into the right order, and so on.

You can make up your own variations, and you can make them as simple or complex as you want. Simple matching of one thing with another, e.g., cartoons with their captions, is interesting, fun, and easy. See Figures 3.16 and 3.17 for examples.

More challenging but also exhilarating for students is the matching of various elements (captions, split-up text, pictures) and putting them all *in the right order*. Note that some texts (e.g., advertisements that contain lists of testimonials) do not always have a particular order. However, most texts do have an order based on meaning, and learners can gain a great deal by having to search for the meaning for the purpose of putting the material into the right order.

It is best to have students work in pairs for the more complicated jigsaw reading tasks, but they may work individually for the easier ones. After the task is done, the pair (or individual) compares results with other pairs (or other individuals). For beginning and intermediate learners, the discussion will likely lapse into the mother tongue, but since the focus is on the meaning of the reading passage, this may be all right. For more advanced learners, the discussion should be in the target language if possible.

Note For an excellent combination of jigsaw reading with a writing task (writing a memo), see Withrow (1987), p. 54. For details on the conceptual skills involved in jigsaw reading, and various aspects of this activity, see Crookall and Watson (1985).

Figure 3.16 Match the Captions with the Pictures for Hobbies. To use this with your students, remove the captions and list them in random order on another sheet. Ask students to match the captions with the pictures of various hobbies (*Freizeitbeschäftigungen*). (*Source*: Picture is from *Kinder Monatszeitschrift*, VIII (3), 1986.)

Figure 3.17 Match the Captions with the "Peanuts" Cartoon. To use this with your students, remove the captions and list them in random order on another sheet. Ask students to match the captions with the "Peanuts" cartoon. (*Source*: Picture is from *Kinder Monatszeitschrift*, VIII (6), 1986.)

Source Original description of Jigsaw Reading. *Kinder Monatszeitschrift* VIII (3) (1986) for Figure 3.16 and VIII (6) (1986) for Figure 3.17.

Exercise 3.15. Alibi

Purpose

This exercise is an adaptation of the parlor game Alibi. It aims to get students communicating authentically, putting together information, and guessing meanings in a suspenseful situation.

Materials

None.

Time

This exercise takes 1 hour.

Instructions

In the original Alibi game, two people go out of the room and make up a story about what they did together during a given period, say between 6:00 P.M. and 9:00 P.M. the previous day. The first person comes back in, tells his or her version of the story, and is questioned for detail by the jury—that is, the rest of the people. The second person then comes in, tells his or her version of the story, and is cross-examined. These two people are suspected of committing a crime during the given period, so they must have an "alibi," a reasonable story that proves they are not guilty, and their two versions of the story must be consistent with each other.

This game has been adapted for use in the language classroom, so that the two people are interrogated at the *same time* by different juries (different sets of classmates), so that more time is spent in actual communication in the target language. Some participants have to defend themselves and refute accusations, while others act as their juries. They all become totally involved in the activity and engaged in heated communication in the new language.

It is important that for every variation of the game, each jury must consist of *two to five students*.

Variation 1 (Class Size: 6–12; 2 Suspects and 2 Juries)

Stage A—Story Creation and Interrogations The two suspects, A and B, go out and make up their story. The class is split into two juries, 1 and 2.

When the suspects return, jury 1 interrogates suspect A, and jury 2 questions suspect B. After a while the two suspects change over for a second round of interrogations: Jury 1 now has suspect B, and jury 2 has A.

Stage B—Further Cross-Examination (and Optional Preparation) For this stage, there are at least three possible procedures: (1) The whole class comes together and the two juries can now cross-examine the suspects further to cover anything so far missed. Suspect A is not allowed to intervene if the question is directed at B, and vice versa. The juries must enforce this rule, which itself involves meaningful language use. (2) Alternatively, the suspects go back to their original juries for further cross-examination. (3) Instead of, or following, (1) or (2), the suspects come together again and prepare their final defense, which occurs in Stage C. To do this they will have to find out what discrepancies have emerged during their separate interrogations. At the same time, juries will meet together and discuss their strategies.

Stage C—Final Defense With the whole class together, each jury now presents the contradictions it has found in the suspects' alibi stories. This time the suspects are allowed to interrupt and respond freely. They must explain any discrepancies, refute accusations, make excuses, etc.

Variation 2 (Class Size: 9–18; 3 Suspects and 3 Juries)

Stage A—Story Creation and Interrogations For the first round of interrogations, suspect A goes to jury 1, suspect B to jury 2, C to 3. For the second round, suspects move to the next jury (A to 2, B to 3, C to 1). The decision to have a third round will depend on length of previous rounds, students' level, and complexity of the alibi.

Stage B—Further Cross-Examination (and Optional Preparation) Might be useful, but not really necessary if a third round of interrogations has taken place in Stage A.

Stage C—Final Defense Same as Stage C under Variation 1.

Variation 3 (Class Size: 19–24; 4 Suspects and 4 Juries)

Variation 3 uses the same stages as Variation 2.

Source Adapted from Crookall (1979).

Exercise 3.16. What We Have in Common

Purpose

This exercise allows learners to work in pairs to communicate naturalistically about things of personal significance. Can be used as an ice-breaker.

Materials

None.

Time

Takes 20 minutes.

Instructions

1. Split the class up into groups of about eight. Within these groups, ask people to pair off and find five things they have in common with their partner and five things they don't have in common. Tell them to note these down.

2. Once the questioning in pairs is over, ask the students to report to their group of eight. The reports in the groups go on simultaneously. If the students are elementary level give them structures to help the reporting, for example:

We both like . . .	S/he lives in . . . but I . . .
We are both wearing . . .	I prefer . . . , but s/he prefers . . .

Note In using this exercise as an ice-breaker, don't prescribe structures for the paired questioning. Listening to how they go about this unguided will prove a golden diagnostic opportunity for you.

Source Frank and Rinvolucri (1983, p. 17).

Exercise 3.17. What's My Line?

Purpose

This exercise allows development of guessing and naturalistic practice skills in an entertaining format.

Materials

None.

Time

Takes 20 to 30 minutes, depending on number of rounds.

Instructions

Tell your students the following in your own words: One person will take the role of a "secret person" who has a certain occupation ("line"). The other student(s) will ask questions that can be answered by either yes or no; their task is to find out what the occupation of the person is. The "secret person" can be famous (e.g., Napoleon) or not famous (e.g., a bricklayer).

Alternative

You can make up many variations of this game. One variation is to ask students to select only a famous person as their "secret person." This gets into all sorts of interesting historical and cultural information. If students figure out that the secret person is dead, they can use the past tense; if the secret person is alive, they can use the present tense.

Source Old American TV show, "What's My Line?"

Exercise 3.18. Picture Stories

Purpose

This exercise gives students a chance to create a new story; use memory strategies, particularly imagery, to remember sequences; practice naturalistically; and compensate for missing information.

Materials

Pictures on small cards, about 80 in all (reusable).

Time

Takes 30 minutes.

Instructions

First you create the cards, one picture per card. These can be cut out of magazines, travel brochures, advertisements, mail order catalogues, etc., and should be clear, interesting, colorful, and varied. (You can get your students to bring in picture materials and help you make the cards! It will take much less time and will be fun for them.) On the back of each card, write the vocabulary related to the picture (e.g., "tennis/have a game of tennis/play tennis/racket/court"). Now you are ready to have your students play the game.

Stage 1—Story Construction Split the class into four groups (preferably equal in size). Each group sits at four different tables, A through D. Explain to the students that they will each be dealt a number of cards, say three or four, to use for constructing a story. The first student in each group starts the game by placing one of his or her cards on the table and making up a sentence related to the picture. The second student then chooses a card from his or her set, places it next to the first card, and says a sentence related to that picture and linking the story with what the previous person said. The third person does likewise, continuing the story. Encourage students to create real linkages, no matter how improbable; the result should be a story, not a set of discrete sentences. Also let students know that they are not allowed to write down their story; they need to remember it, using the pictures as cues. Continue the process until the group runs out of cards, or until you stop the proceedings. If a group runs out of cards before the other groups, give them a few more cards and let them continue their story-making. While all this is going on, you go from table to table and give each person a number, 1 to 4; tell the students to remember their numbers because they will need them later.

When a group has about 15 or 20 cards down on the table, take up the unused cards. Explain to the group that it should now go over the story so as to remember it well, since in a moment they will have to tell it to another group. Go around to each group and explain the same thing. Students may be surprised, and they usually respond with a noticeable increase in concentration. (Slower groups may not have a chance to go completely through their story again, but that is all right.)

Stage 2—Telling the Stories Students are told that some will move and that some will stay where they are, but that they shouldn't move until they all know where to go. All students who have the number 1 stay where they are. All the other students (numbers 2, 3, and 4) will move to the next table; that is, students 2, 3, and 4 at table A go to table B; students 2, 3, and 4 at table B go to C; C to D, and D to A. Then they move. The task now of student 1 is to tell the story to the "new" students who have just arrived at the table.

Stage 3—Retelling the Stories Here all students who have number 2 are told that they have to stay where they are (i.e., with the new story they have just been told). Students 1, 3, and 4 at table A move to B, and B to C, etc. They move, and it is now the turn of student 2 to tell the story to the other three who've just sat down. This time the story is being told not by one of its creators but by someone to whom it has just been told. Since no one who made up the story is present, there is now a tendency for students to comment on the story.

Stage 4—Retelling the Stories Same as previous two stages, except that it is now the turn of student 3 to tell the story.

Stage 5—Checking the Original This is the last stage of the game. Students are told that they must listen carefully because they will not move in exactly the same way as they've done before. Student 4 does stay where he or she is, but the others (1, 2, and 3) go back to their original tables, to the tables of the story they made up at the beginning of the game. Once in their places, student 4 has to tell the story and the others see what changes have been made to their original story, noticing in what ways it has been deformed over the various "tellings." Sometimes very little will have changed, while in some cases important details and even whole chunks will have been completely left out, new things put in, and so on. These changes can provoke some interesting discussion and even heated debate.

Alternatives

1. The game as described above is for 16 students. For classes of more or fewer than 16, here are some possible alternatives: 9 students = 3 groups, 3 students/group, 4 stages; 25 students = 5 groups, 5 students/group, 6 stages; 18 students = as for 9 students, but 2 separate games; 10 students = as for 9 students, but 2 of the 9 students work as 1. Other figures are given in Crookall (1983b). You will need more than 80 cards for classes of greater than 16. NOTE THAT IN EVERY CASE, THE NUMBER OF PEOPLE IN A GROUP MUST BE EQUAL TO, OR LARGER THAN, THE NUMBER OF GROUPS.
2. It is possible to follow this with a writing assignment in which students write up the stories.

Source Adapted from Crookall (1983b). More details on this game are found there.

Exercise 3.19. Crystal Ball

Purpose

This exercise allows students to develop prediction/guessing skills, which are often required for understanding a reading passage.

Materials

Reading passage.

Time

Variable, depending on amount of discussion.

Instructions

1. You and the students silently read a specified portion of the selection. In the beginning, this should be no more than a few lines or a short paragraph.

2. With your book closed, invite the students to ask you as many questions as they can about the portion that was read. The students may refer to the text during this phase, and all speaking is done in the new language.

3. When the students have exhausted their questions, they must close their books, and you ask them questions about the same portion of the text.

4. Repeat steps 1, 2, and 3 several times.

5. At a predetermined point, stop the reciprocal questioning routine and ask the students to predict the outcome of the story or selection. Their predictions are written on the board.

6. Then you and the students silently read the remainder of the story.

7. Discuss the outcome of the story with the students, comparing the predictions with the actual ending.

Alternatives

1. Work with only the ending of a story, and make predictions about the beginning; then read the beginning and find out whether the predictions were correct.

2. Adapt this procedure for use with a listening passage.

Source The ReQuest procedure developed by Manzo (1969) as described by Hague (1986a).

Exercise 3.20. Protest

Purpose

To make guesses from context and to write meaningfully and authentically.

Materials

Newspaper article (one copy per student).

Time

Variable, depending on amount of discussion.

Instructions

Tell your students in your own words: Read the newspaper article I will give you. Then, working with a partner, write what you think each person said. Here is a copy of the article:

"Protest Gets Nasty—41 Arrested" by Birney Jarvis

About 200 anti-war demonstrators went wild yesterday, invading stores, knocking down pedestrians, and breaking windows before police moved in to arrest them.

The problem began when a small group of punk rockers, "skinheads," admitted anarchists, and students ran into one of the department stores at Post and Powell streets at 6 p.m. pushing and shoving customers. Some were knocked down, witnesses said.

Within seconds, several squads of police in riot gear and 30 motorcycle officers and mounted police moved in. A total of 41 people were arrested.

The Police Commander, Ray Canepa, said ____________________

____

____

____

______________. A store owner on Powell Street said ______________

____

____

____

____________________. One of the protesters, a high school student at Concord High, said ____

____

____

____

______________, and one of the customers who was pushed around by the rioters said ____

____

____

____

____________________________. The mayor, who came down to the scene

of the riot, said ____

____

____

____

____.

Now that you have finished this part, discuss the following questions with your partner:

1. How do you feel about demonstrations? Do they help a cause? How?
2. Can a demonstration hurt a cause? How?
3. Do you think the demonstration in the article helped the anti-war cause? Why or why not?

Source Jones and Kimbrough (1987, pp. 60–61).

Exercise 3.21. Interviews

Purpose

This exercise stimulates meaningful spoken and written communication, is personally meaningful to learners, and encourages group solidarity. It involves direct strategies like using resources, practicing naturalistically, taking notes, summarizing, and guessing, along with various indirect strategies.

Materials

Reference books (e.g., dictionaries, grammar books).

Time

Variable, depending on proficiency level and your own intention for how to use this multiphase project.

Instructions

1. *List Interview Questions.* Ask your students as a group to call out questions that would be good to use in interviewing each other. Make a list in the new language. Post it on the board or give everyone a copy. Tell the students they do not have to use all these questions, and they can make up additional ones.

2. *Conduct Interviews.* Ask the students to find a partner to interview. One student in the pair interviews the other one, finding out interesting details about that person's life. Then they switch roles, with the second person interviewing the first. You should put a realistic time limit on the interviews and inform the students of this in advance. (They can meet at another time on their own if they want to continue.)

3. *Write Articles, Get Feedback, and Revise.* Now each student uses the information from the interview to write an article about the interviewee. The writer checks what he or she has written with the interviewee to make sure that the facts are all correct and that the person is willing to have those facts in print! In addition, the partners help each other with style, tone, organization, and language. Then each pair meets with another pair to swap articles and get further feedback on content, style, tone, organization, and language.

4. *Publish Articles.* When the articles are as good as they can be on the basis of this feedback, they are posted on the bulletin board, or else put together in a class magazine.

Note You may have to help students with vocabulary and grammar from time to time, but restrain yourself from "red-inking" all the errors. The point is to get the message across, even if it is not perfect. Provide plenty of printed resources in accessible places so students can help themselves to improve their writing after the interview phase is over.

Source Original.

Exercise 3.22. Sending a Telegram

Purpose

This exercise gives learners a chance to express themselves in writing in an important and personally meaningful situation, just as in real life. Many cognitive and compensation strategies are required to do this task.

Materials

Telegram forms (see Figure 3.18 for an example in Russian).

ф· ТГ-1

В начале телеграммы перед текстом пишется: категория (срочная), особый вид (уведомление телеграфом, вручить лично, ответ и др.), куда, кому.

Слов	Плата	
	руб.	коп.
Итого		
Принял ______		

МИНИСТЕРСТВО СВЯЗИ СССР

ТЕЛЕГРАММА

Из ______

№ ______

______ сл. ______ го ______ час. ______ мин.

ПЕРЕДАЧА

______ го ______ час. ______ мин.

№ связи ______

Передал: ______

Служебн. отметки

Категория и отметки особого вида:

Куда, кому ______

Фамилия отправителя и его адрес (в счет слов не входят, не оплачиваются и по телеграфу не передаются).

Тип «Ставр. правда», 1971 г. 911 13.900.00.

Figure 3.18 Russian Telegram Form. (*Source*: Culhane (1986, p. 20.)

Time

Variable.

Instructions

Give your students the following instructions, *modified to fit the language and culture:* You will work in pairs. Person 1 is due to go from Leningrad to Moscow by plane. Person 1 discovers that Pulkovo Airport in Leningrad is closed and will not be open for another 4 days. Person 1 will have to send a telegram to Person 2 saying that Person 1 will be coming by train instead of plane, arriving in Moscow at 10:00 a.m. on Wednesday, August 8. Person 2 needs to respond to that telegram with another telegram, telling Person 1 that Person 2 got the message and indicating exactly where Person 2 will meet Person 1 at the Moscow train station (by the magazine racks, at the information desk, etc.).

Source Adapted from Culhane (1986, pp. 115 and 120).

Exercise 3.23. Doctor's Appointment

Purpose

This exercise gives learners practice in planning an upcoming language task and then demonstrating comprehension and production. A range of direct strategies is necessary, such as taking notes, practicing naturalistically, recombining, guessing, and using synonyms—along with indirect strategies of various types.

Materials

(Optional) Teacher-prepared audiotapes and scripts of conversations relevant to the task.

Time

The exercise is divided into three 1-hour segments.

Instructions

Tell students the following in your own words: You need to make a doctor's appointment for yourself over the telephone.

1. Identify the situation. The task, making a doctor's appointment over the telephone, requires that you have to speak with the receptionist, explain the symptoms, and arrange a convenient time. (What are your

symptoms? Define them. If the symptoms are acute, you'll need an immediate appointment! If not, the appointment is not so urgent.)

2. Consider the general functions required by the task. You will probably need greetings, requests, giving biographical information, describing symptoms, getting directions, thanking, and leave-taking.

3. Check your own resources. This means considering whether you are able to do all the functions—that is, whether you have all the vocabulary and forms needed.

4. Decide what else is needed and work on it. For instance, if you cannot yet describe symptoms in the target language, this is what you will need to work on.

5. Now listen to several samples of relevant conversations provided by the teacher on audiotape, and analyze scripts of the conversation by identifying expressions that accomplish the necessary functions (e.g., greetings, requests). Take notes of the key expressions.

6. If audiotapes of the situation are not available, work with others in a small group and discuss possible expressions that would accomplish the necessary functions (e.g., greetings, requests). Possibly ask for help from a native speaker. Take notes of the key expressions.

7. With other people, think of problems or issues that might arise, and expressions that would be necessary to handle them. Take notes.

8. Rehearse the key expressions, putting them together in a reasonable sequence, as for a real telephone conversation.

9. Now that you are ready, role-play the telephone call to the doctor's office, with one person playing the sick person and the other playing the receptionist. It is possible to do this in fours, with two people playing the sick person and coaching each other (helping by adding information that may have been forgotten) and two people playing the receptionist in the same way.

10. Now evaluate the results—what was understood and what was not, and reasons why. Make notes of specific problems: word order, sounds, politeness expressions. Decide why these problems might have occurred and what to do next time.

Alternative

You, rather than a student, might play the doctor's receptionist in the role-play if desired. It might be less tense if learners played both roles, however.

Source Adapted from Stewner-Manzanares, Chamot, O'Malley, Kupper, and Russo (1985, p. 33).

Chapter **4**

Indirect Strategies for General Management of Learning

They know enough who know how to learn.
HENRY ADAMS

PREVIEW QUESTIONS

1. What are indirect strategies?
2. How do they differ from direct strategies?
3. Why are indirect strategies important for language learning?
4. What are the three groups of indirect strategies?

INTRODUCTION TO INDIRECT STRATEGIES

This chapter discusses the indirect strategies that underpin the business of language learning. Indirect strategies are divided into metacognitive, affective, and social (see Figure 4.1). Metacognitive strategies allow learners to control their own cognition—that is, to coordinate the learning process by using functions such as centering, arranging, planning, and evaluating. Affective strategies help to regulate emotions, motivations, and attitudes. Social strategies help students learn through interaction with others. All these strategies are called "indirect" because they support and manage language learning without (in many instances) directly involving the target language. The indirect strategies explained here work in tandem with the direct strategies described earlier. Indirect strategies are useful in virtually all language learning situations and are applicable to all four language skills: listening, reading, speaking, and writing.

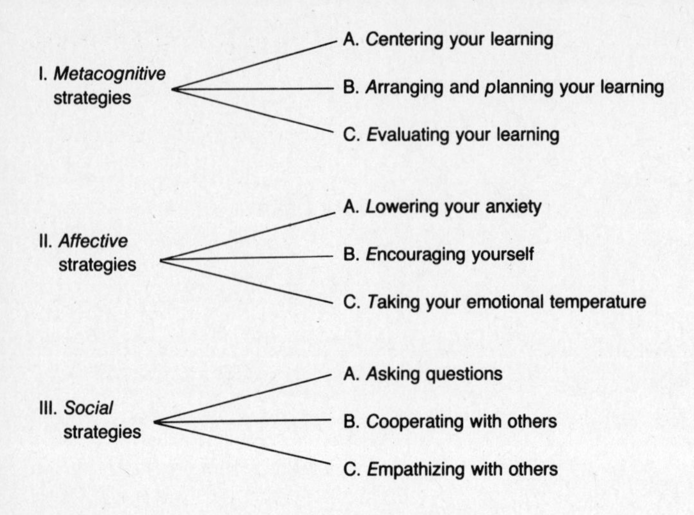

Figure 4.1 Diagram of the Indirect Strategies: Overview. (*Source*: Original.)

METACOGNITIVE STRATEGIES

"Metacognitive" means beyond, beside, or with the cognitive. Therefore, metacognitive strategies are actions which go beyond purely cognitive devices, and which provide a way for learners to coordinate their own learning process. Metacognitive strategies include three strategy sets: Centering Your Learning, *A*rranging and *P*lanning Your Learning, and *E*valuating Your Learning. Ten strategies form these three groups, the acronym for which is CAPE (see Figure 4.2). Remember these strategy sets by saying, "Metacognitive strategies make language learners more CAPE-able."

Metacognitive strategies are essential for successful language learning. Language learners are often overwhelmed by too much "newness"—unfamiliar vocabulary, confusing rules, different writing systems, seemingly inexplicable social customs, and (in enlightened language classes) nontraditional instructional approaches. With all this novelty, many learners lose their focus, which can only be regained by the conscious use of metacognitive strategies such as paying attention and overviewing/linking with already familiar material.

Other metacognitive strategies, like organizing, setting goals and objectives, considering the purpose, and planning for a language task, help learners to arrange and plan their language learning in an efficient, effective way. The metacognitive strategy of seeking practice opportunities is especially important. Learners who are seriously interested in learning a new

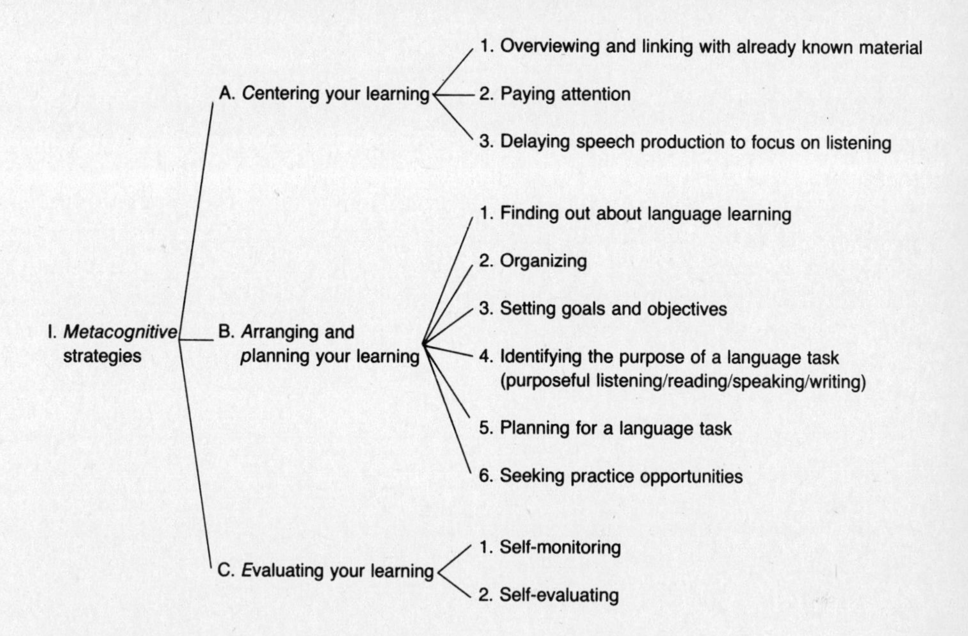

Memory Aid: CAPE

"Metacognitive strategies make language learners more CAPE-able."

A mighty maze! But not without a plan.
Alexander Pope

Figure 4.2 Diagram of the Metacognitive Strategies. (*Source*: Original.)

language must take responsibility to seek as many practice opportunities as possible, usually outside of the classroom. Even in a second language situation, ripe with opportunities for practice, learners must actively search for, and take advantage of, these possibilities.

Sometimes language learners have problems in realistically monitoring their errors. Students may become traumatized when they make errors, thus failing to realize that they will undoubtedly make them and should therefore try to learn from them. Students may also underrate or overrate their proficiency. Confusion about overall progress is made worse by the academic grading system, which generally rewards discrete-point rule-learning rather than communicative competence. These problems—unrealistic monitoring of errors and inadequate evaluation of progress—can be ameliorated by using the metacognitive strategies of self-monitoring and self-evaluating [1].

Though metacognitive strategies are extremely important, research shows that learners use these strategies sporadically and without much sense of their importance. In several studies of second and foreign language learning [2], students used metacognitive strategies less often than cognitive strategies and were limited in their range of metacognitive strategies, with planning strategies most frequently employed and with little self-evaluation or self-monitoring. Likewise, university and military foreign language students in other studies [3] reported using certain metacognitive strategies, such as being prepared and using time well, but they failed to employ other crucial metacognitive strategies, like accurately evaluating their progress or seeking practice opportunities. Obviously, learners need to learn much more about the essential metacognitive strategies. Detailed definitions of these strategies are given below.

Centering Your Learning

This set of three strategies helps learners to converge their attention and energies on certain language tasks, activities, skills, or materials. Use of these strategies provides a focus for language learning.

1. Overviewing and Linking with Already Known Material

Overviewing comprehensively a key concept, principle, or set of materials in an upcoming language activity and associating it with what is already known. This strategy can be accomplished in many different ways, but it is often helpful to follow three steps: learning why the activity is being done, building the needed vocabulary, and making the associations [4].

2. Paying Attention

Deciding in advance to pay attention in general to a language learning task and to ignore distractors (by *directed attention*), and/or *to pay attention to specific aspects* of the language or to situational details (by *selective attention*).

3. Delaying Speech Production to Focus on Listening

Deciding in advance to delay speech production in the new language either totally or partially, until listening comprehension skills are better developed. Some language theorists encourage a "silent period" of delayed speech as part of the curriculum, but there is debate as to whether all students require this [5].

Arranging and Planning Your Learning

This set contains six strategies, all of which help learners to organize and plan so as to get the most out of language learning. These strategies touch many areas: finding out about language learning, organizing the schedule and the environment, setting goals and objectives, considering task purposes, planning for tasks, and seeking chances to practice the language.

1. Finding Out About Language Learning

Making efforts to find out how language learning works by reading books and talking with other people, and then using this information to help improve one's own language learning.

2. Organizing

Understanding and using conditions related to optimal learning of the new language; organizing one's schedule, physical environment (e.g., space, temperature, sound, lighting), and language learning notebook.

3. Setting Goals and Objectives

Setting aims for language learning, including long-term goals (such as being able to use the language for informal conversation by the end of the year) or short-term objectives (such as finishing reading a short story by Friday).

4. Identifying the Purpose of a Language Task

Deciding the purpose of a particular language task involving listening, reading, speaking, or writing. For example, listening to the radio to get the latest news on the stock exchange, reading a play for enjoyment, speaking to the cashier to buy a train ticket, writing a letter to persuade a friend not to do something rash. (This is sometimes known as *Purposeful Listening/Speaking/Reading/Writing.*)

5. Planning for a Language Task

Planning for the language elements and functions necessary for an anticipated language task or situation. This strategy includes four steps: describing the task or situation, determining its requirements, checking one's own linguistic resources, and determining additional language elements or functions necessary for the task or situation.

6. Seeking Practice Opportunities

Seeking out or creating opportunities to practice the new language in naturalistic situations, such as going to a second/foreign language cinema, attending a party where the language will be spoken, or joining an international social club. Consciously thinking in the new language also provides practice opportunities.

Evaluating Your Learning

In this set are two related strategies, both aiding learners in checking their language performance. One strategy involves noticing and learning from errors, and the other concerns evaluating overall progress.

1. Self-Monitoring

Identifying errors in understanding or producing the new language, determining which ones are important (those that cause serious confusion or offense), tracking the source of important errors, and trying to eliminate such errors.

2. Self-Evaluating

Evaluating one's own progress in the new language, for instance, by checking to see whether one is reading faster and understanding more than 1 month or 6 months ago, or whether one is understanding a greater percentage of each conversation.

AFFECTIVE STRATEGIES

The term *affective* refers to emotions, attitudes, motivations, and values. It is impossible to overstate the importance of the affective factors influencing language learning. Language learners can gain control over these factors through affective strategies. As shown in Figure 4.3, three main sets of affective strategies exist: *L*owering Your Anxiety, *E*ncouraging Yourself, and *T*aking Your Emotional Temperature (10 strategies in all). The acronym LET comes from the first letter of each one of these strategy sets—"affective strategies help language learners LET their hair down!"

"The affective domain is impossible to describe within definable limits," according to H. Douglas Brown [6]. It spreads out like a fine-spun net, encompassing such concepts as self-esteem, attitudes, motivation, anxiety, culture shock, inhibition, risk taking, and tolerance for ambiguity [7]. The affective side of the learner is probably one of the very biggest influences on language learning success or failure. Good language learners are often those who know how to control their emotions and attitudes about learning [8]. Negative feelings can stunt progress, even for the rare learner who fully understands all the technical aspects of how to learn a new language. On the other hand, positive emotions and attitudes can make language learning far more effective and enjoyable. Teachers can exert a tremendous influence over the emotional atmosphere of the classroom in three different ways: by changing the social structure of the classroom to give students more responsibility, by providing increased amounts

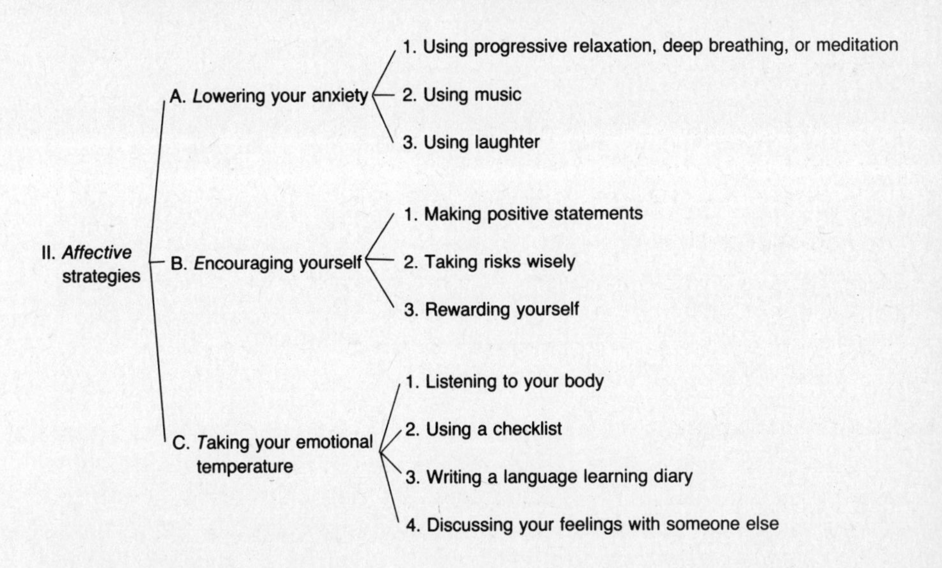

Figure 4.3 Diagram of the Affective Strategies. (*Source*: Original.)

of naturalistic communication, and by teaching learners to use affective strategies.

Self-esteem is one of the primary affective elements. It is a self-judgment of worth or value, based on a feeling of efficacy—a sense of interacting effectively with one's own environment [9]. Low self-esteem can be detected through negative self-talk, like "Boy, am I a blockhead! I embarrassed myself again in front of the class." The three affective strategies related to self-encouragement help learners to counter such negativity.

The sense of efficacy that underlies self-esteem is reflected in attitudes (mental dispositions, beliefs, or opinions), which influence the learner's motivation to keep on trying to learn [10]. Attitudes are strong predictors of motivation in any area of life, and especially in language learning [11]. Just as attitudes affect motivation, attitudes and motivation work together to influence language learning performance itself—including both global language proficiency and proficiency in specific language skills, such as listening comprehension, reading comprehension, and oral production [12]. In addition, research findings suggest that the combined attitude/motivation factor strongly influences whether the learner loses or maintains language skills after language training is over [13]. Self-encouragement strategies are powerful ways to improve attitudes and, thus, motivation [14].

A certain amount of anxiety sometimes helps learners to reach their peak performance levels, but too much anxiety blocks language learning. Harmful anxiety presents itself in many guises: worry, self-doubt, frustration, helplessness, insecurity, fear, and physical symptoms. Even the ordinary language classroom can create high anxiety, because learners are frequently forced to perform in a state of ignorance and dependence in front of their peers and teacher [15]. When learners attempt to practice outside of the language classroom, anxiety may mount still further. Anxiety becomes most pronounced during culture shock, which has even been called a form of temporary mental illness [16]. Anxiety-reducing strategies like laughter and deep breathing are therefore necessary. However, strategies directly targeted at anxiety reduction are not the only ones that help learners to calm down. Self-encouragement via positive statements can change one's feelings and attitudes and can indirectly reduce performance anxiety, including the tension which surrounds test taking [17]. In addition, the self-assessment strategies listed under Taking Your Emotional Temperature help learners realize when they are anxious. Listening to bodily signals is an especially helpful strategy for discovering and controlling anxiety.

The language learner who is overly anxious, either in a typical language classroom or in a more serious culture shock situation, is likely to be inhibited and unwilling to take even moderate risks. Successful language learning necessitates overcoming inhibitions and learning to take reasonable risks, as in guessing meanings or speaking up despite the possibility of making a mistake [18]. Inhibited learners are paralyzed by actual or anticipated criticism from other people and from themselves, so they try to ensure that there are as few "chinks in their armor" as possible [19]. Self-encouragement and anxiety-reducing strategies can help learners lower their inhibitions and take appropriate risks [20].

Tolerance of ambiguity—that is, the acceptance of confusing situations—may be related to willingness to take risks (and also reduction of both inhibition and anxiety). Moderate tolerance for ambiguity, like moderate risk taking, is probably the most desirable situation. Learners who are moderately tolerant of ambiguity tend to be open-minded in dealing with confusing facts and events, which are part of learning a new language. In contrast, low ambiguity-tolerant learners, wanting to categorize and compartmentalize too soon, have a hard time dealing with unclear facts and events. One study [21] discovered that tolerance for ambiguity was one of the two factors that predicted success in foreign language learning. Other studies have found that language learners who are tolerant of ambiguity are more successful in certain language tasks [22] and may use somewhat more effective learning strategies than learners who are less tolerant of ambiguity and who need to seek rapid closure [23].

Again, self-encouragement and anxiety-reducing strategies help learners cope with ambiguity in language learning.

Few studies have examined the frequency of use of affective strategies, but those which have done so reveal that these strategies are woefully underused—reported by about 1 in every 20 language learners [24]. This situation is distressing, given the power of affective strategies. These strategies are useful for the vast majority of language learners who have ordinary hang-ups and difficulties. However, these strategies are not intended as a substitute for psychotherapy or a mechanism for solving deep psychological problems, nor can they single-handedly change general traits, such as low global self-esteem [25]. With this in mind, consider the following affective strategies and their definitions.

Lowering Your Anxiety

Three anxiety-reducing strategies are listed here. Each has a physical component and a mental component.

1. Using Progressive Relaxation, Deep Breathing, or Meditation

Using the technique of *alternately tensing and relaxing* all of the major muscle groups in the body, as well as the muscles in the neck and face, in order to relax; or the technique of *breathing deeply* from the diaphragm; or the technique of *meditating by focusing* on a mental image or sound.

2. Using Music

Listening to soothing music, such as a classical concert, as a way to relax.

3. Using Laughter

Using laughter to relax by watching a funny movie, reading a humorous book, listening to jokes, and so on.

Encouraging Yourself

This set of three strategies is often forgotten by language learners, especially those who expect encouragement mainly from other people and do not realize they can provide their own. However, the most potent encouragement—and the *only* available encouragement in many independent language learning situations—may come from inside the learner. Self-encouragement includes saying supportive things, prodding oneself to take risks wisely, and providing rewards.

1. Making Positive Statements

Saying or writing positive statements to oneself in order to feel more confident in learning the new language.

2. Taking Risks Wisely

Pushing oneself to take risks in a language learning situation, even though there is a chance of making a mistake or looking foolish. Risks must be tempered with good judgment.

3. Rewarding Yourself

Giving oneself a valuable reward for a particularly good performance in the new language.

Taking Your Emotional Temperature

The four strategies in this set help learners to assess their feelings, motivations, and attitudes and, in many cases, to relate them to language tasks. Unless learners know how they are feeling and why they are feeling that way, they are less able to control their affective side. The strategies in this set are particularly helpful for discerning negative attitudes and emotions that impede language learning progress.

1. Listening to Your Body

Paying attention to signals given by the body. These signals may be negative, reflecting stress, tension, worry, fear, and anger; or they may be positive, indicating happiness, interest, calmness, and pleasure.

2. Using a Checklist

Using a checklist to discover feelings, attitudes, and motivations concerning language learning in general, as well as concerning specific language tasks.

3. Writing a Language Learning Diary

Writing a diary or journal to keep track of events and feelings in the process of learning a new language.

4. Discussing Your Feelings with Someone Else

Talking with another person (teacher, friend, relative) to discover and express feelings about language learning.

SOCIAL STRATEGIES

Language is a form of social behavior; it is communication, and communication occurs between and among people. Learning a language thus involves other people, and appropriate social strategies are very important in this process. Three sets of social strategies, each set comprising two specific strategies (see Figure 4.4), are included here: *A*sking Questions, *C*ooperating with Others, and *E*mpathizing with Others. These can be remembered by using their acronym, ACE: "ACE language learners use social strategies!"

One of the most basic social interactions is asking questions, an action from which learners gain great benefit. Asking questions helps learners get closer to the intended meaning and thus aids their understanding. It also helps learners encourage their conversation partners to provide larger quantities of "input" in the target language and indicates interest and involvement. Moreover, the conversation partner's response to the learner's question indicates whether the question itself was understood, thus providing indirect feedback about the learner's production skills. The content of questions is important, of course. One social strategy concerns asking questions for clarification (when something is not understood) or verification (when the learner wants to check whether something is correct). A related social strategy involves asking for correction, which is especially useful in the classroom. The classroom setting provides much more overt correction than do natural, informal social settings.

In addition to asking questions, cooperating in general—with peers and with more proficient users of the target language—is imperative for language learners. Cooperation implies the absence of competition and the presence of group spirit. It involves a cooperative task structure or a cooperative reward structure [26], either of which can encourage "positive

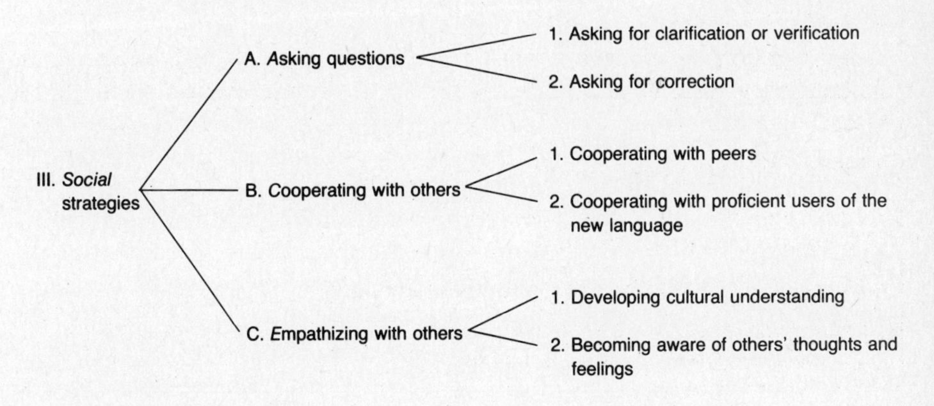

Memory Aid: ACE

"ACE language learners use social strategies!"

Probably no greater need exists than to learn how to participate effectively. . . . Humans are, and always have been, social animals.

James Botkin

Figure 4.4 Diagram of the Social Strategies. (*Source*: Original.)

interdependence" and mutual support [27]. Many studies outside of the language learning field have strongly demonstrated the utility of cooperative learning strategies [28]. Cooperative learning consistently shows the following significant effects: higher self-esteem; increased confidence and enjoyment; greater and more rapid achievement; more respect for the teacher, the school, and the subject; use of higher-level cognitive strategies; decreased prejudice; and increased altruism and mutual concern [29]. In the area of language learning, cooperative strategies have accrued the same benefits, as well as the following additional advantages: better student and teacher satisfaction, stronger language learning motivation, more language practice opportunities, more feedback about language errors, and greater use of different language functions [30].

However, cooperative strategies might not be second nature to all language learners. Research shows that on their own, with no special training or encouragement, language learners do *not* typically report a natural preference for cooperative strategies [31]. Competition is strongly reinforced by the educational establishment, with schools often pitting students against each other in competition for approval, attention, and grades in all subject areas, including language learning [32]. Although competition might sometimes result in a positive desire to improve and do better than other people, more often it results in debilitating anxiety, inadequacy, guilt, hostility, withdrawal, fear of failure, and desire for approval [33]. To promote cooperative language learning strategies, either inside or outside the classroom, it might be necessary to help learners confront—and possibly modify—their culturally defined attitudes toward cooperation and competition.

Empathy is the ability to "put yourself in someone else's shoes" in order to better understand that person's perspective. Empathy is essential to successful communication in *any* language; it is especially necessary, although sometimes difficult to achieve, in learning another language. People differ in their natural ability to feel and demonstrate empathy. However, social strategies can help all learners increase their ability to emphathize by developing cultural understanding and becoming aware of others' thoughts and feelings. Following is a list of social strategies and their definitions.

Asking Questions

This set of strategies involves asking someone, possibly a teacher or native speaker or even a more proficient fellow learner, for clarification, verification, or correction.

1. Asking for Clarification or Verification

Asking the speaker to repeat, paraphrase, explain, slow down, or give examples; asking if a specific utterance is correct or if a rule fits a particular case;

paraphrasing or repeating to get feedback on whether something is correct.

2. Asking for Correction

Asking someone for correction in a conversation. This strategy most often occurs in conversation but may also be applied to writing.

Cooperating with Others

This set of two strategies involves interacting with one or more people to improve language skills. These strategies are the basis of cooperative language learning, which not only increases learners' language performance but also enhances self-worth and social acceptance.

1. Cooperating with Peers

Working with other language learners to improve language skills. This strategy can involve a regular learning partner or a temporary pair or small group. This strategy frequently involves controlling impulses toward competitiveness and rivalry.

2. Cooperating with Proficient Users of the New Language

Working with native speakers or other proficient users of the new language, usually outside of the language classroom. This strategy involves particular attention to the conversational roles each person takes.

Empathizing with Others

Empathy can be developed more easily when language learners use these two strategies.

1. Developing Cultural Understanding

Trying to empathize with another person through learning about the culture, and trying to understand the other person's relation to that culture.

2. Becoming Aware of Others' Thoughts and Feelings

Observing the behaviors of others as a possible expression of their thoughts and feelings; and when appropriate, asking about thoughts and feelings of others.

SUMMARY

This chapter described the significance of three groups of indirect strategies: metacognitive, affective, and social. For each of these groups, specific strategies were identified and defined. Indirect strategies are an essential counterpart to direct strategies, which were described in Chapters 2 and 3.

ACTIVITIES FOR READERS

Activity 4.1. Consider a Difficult Subject

Although you might be a teacher, consider your previous experience as a student. This will help you understand what students face as they cope with a new subject.

1. Write down three examples of times when a new subject seemed overwhelming to you owing to its novelty, complexity, difficulty, or scope.
2. Then choose the single most interesting example and discuss what made that subject so difficult to you.
3. Now list your affective (emotional and attitudinal) responses to that subject and explain what strategies you used to cope with those responses.
4. Consider your metacognitive control over the subject. For instance, describe how you tried to focus your efforts and organize your environment, schedule, and materials. Explain what you did about setting goals and finding practice opportunities. Cite any efforts to evaluate your own progress.

Activity 4.2. Experiment with Metacognitive and Affective Strategies

Metacognitive and affective strategies are useful for any area of learning or work. This week try out at least one metacognitive strategy and one affective strategy you do not ordinarily use. Write down the effects of your experiment and discuss them with other people. What did you do that was most effective? What did you do that was least effective?

Activity 4.3. Ask Questions

Consider your questioning style by trying the following:

1. When you are talking with native speakers of a language that is not your own, observe how often you ask questions for clarification, verification, or correction.
2. Do you tend to use questioning techniques more often with some people than with others? Why or why not?

3. Observe your own behavior in your native language. Do you ask questions for clarification, verification, or correction in your own native language? If so, under what circumstances, and with whom? Do you use questioning in the same way in your native language as in the target language?

Activity 4.4. Judge Your Empathy

How much empathy do you have for others? Do you think you identify well with others or not? How do you feel this influences your ability to learn languages? To get along with other people? Give specific examples to back up your statements. How can the strategies listed under Empathizing with Others help you increase your empathy? How can you help others, especially your students, strengthen their empathy?

Activity 4.5. Weigh Competitiveness and Cooperation

In a small group or by yourself, answer the following questions:

1. Do you agree with the statements in this chapter about the effects of competitiveness and cooperation in language learning? Why or why not?
2. Have you ever felt competitive in a language learning experience? If yes, what were the circumstances? What aspects of the situation, or of yourself, might have encouraged you to feel competitive? Is this a typical learning mode for you?
3. In what ways have you exercised cooperation in language learning? Was this in a classroom setting or in a naturalistic language situation? What differences in types of cooperation exist between these two kinds of environments?

EXERCISES TO USE WITH YOUR STUDENTS

Exercise 4.1. Listen to Self-Talk

Ask your students how often they say positive things to themselves about language learning. Ask them to list all the positive things they say and to explain how these statements make them feel about themselves and about continuing their language learning.

Now request that your students list all the negative things they say to themselves, and ask how these negative statements affect their self-esteem as language learners.

Exercise 4.2. Let Students Consider Cooperation and Competition

Run a cooperative learning activity—one which has either a cooperative task or a cooperative reward or both, and which therefore encourages cooperative learning strategies. Afterwards, discuss with your students how they felt about that activity and about learning cooperatively in general. Ask them how they have reacted to cooperative learning experiences in other classes, and encourage them to give specific examples.

Now ask students about their feelings of competition with their peers, both in the language class and in other classes. Find out whether they are more comfortable with competition than with cooperation. Discuss with your students what they would need to increase their use of cooperative strategies in the language class.

Exercise 4.3. Try Out Indirect Strategies

In order to stimulate greater use of a range of indirect strategies, ask students to do any or all of the following activities listed above for readers of this book: Activities 4.1, 4.2, 4.3, or 4.4. Assess results. You might need to modify some of the directions slightly for use with students. Make sure there is time to discuss the results.

Chapter 5

Applying Indirect Strategies to the Four Language Skills

Order is the shape on which beauty depends.
PEARL BUCK

PREVIEW QUESTIONS

1. How can the indirect strategies be applied to the four language skills?
2. How are these strategies applied differently to the four skills?
3. Are any indirect strategies especially useful to development of a particular skill?

INTRODUCTION TO APPLYING THE INDIRECT STRATEGIES

This chapter shows how learners can apply the indirect strategies—metacognitive, affective, and social—to each of the four language skills. These powerful strategies are shown in Figure 5.1. As in Chapter 3, examples of applications of strategies to the different skills are indicated after the section title, like this: Ⓛ (listening), Ⓡ (reading), Ⓢ (speaking), Ⓦ (writing), Ⓐ (all skills). Although this chapter focuses on applications of indirect strategies, remember that indirect strategies work best when used in combination with direct strategies. By definition, *direct strategies* involve the new language directly, whereas *indirect strategies* provide indirect support for language learning through focusing, planning, evaluating, seeking opportunities, controlling anxiety, increasing cooperation and empathy, and other means.

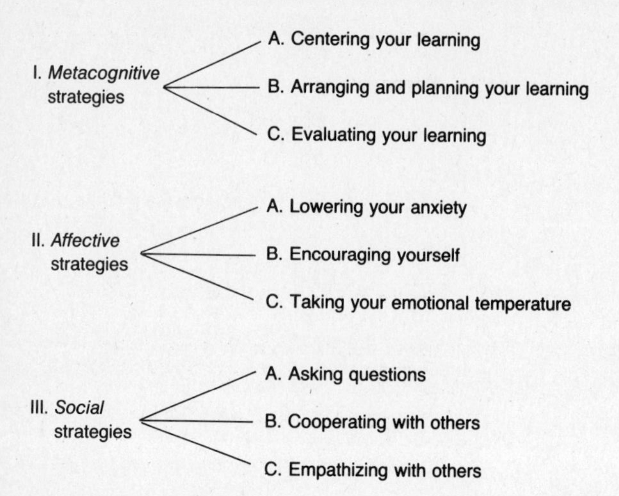

Figure 5.1 Diagram of the Indirect Strategies to Be Applied to the Four Language Skills. (*Source*: Original.)

APPLYING METACOGNITIVE STRATEGIES TO THE FOUR SKILLS

The three sets of metacognitive strategies displayed in Figure 5.2 (Centering Your Learning, Arranging and Planning Your Learning, and Evaluating Your Learning) are useful in developing all the language skills.

Centering Your Learning

Finding a focus or center for learning is important no matter what the language skill. Without appropriate strategies for centering, language learners face merely confusion and noise.

Overviewing and Linking with Already Known Material Ⓐ This strategy involves previewing the basic principles and/or material (including new vocabulary) for an upcoming language activity, and linking these with what the learners already know. Exactly how this strategy is used depends in part on the skill level of the learners. With higher-level students, you can be less directive in helping them learn to use this strategy. Regardless of the students' level, let students express their own linkages between new material and what they already know, rather than pointing out all the associations yourself. Following are examples of the overviewing/linking strategy applied to each of the four language skills. Although the target

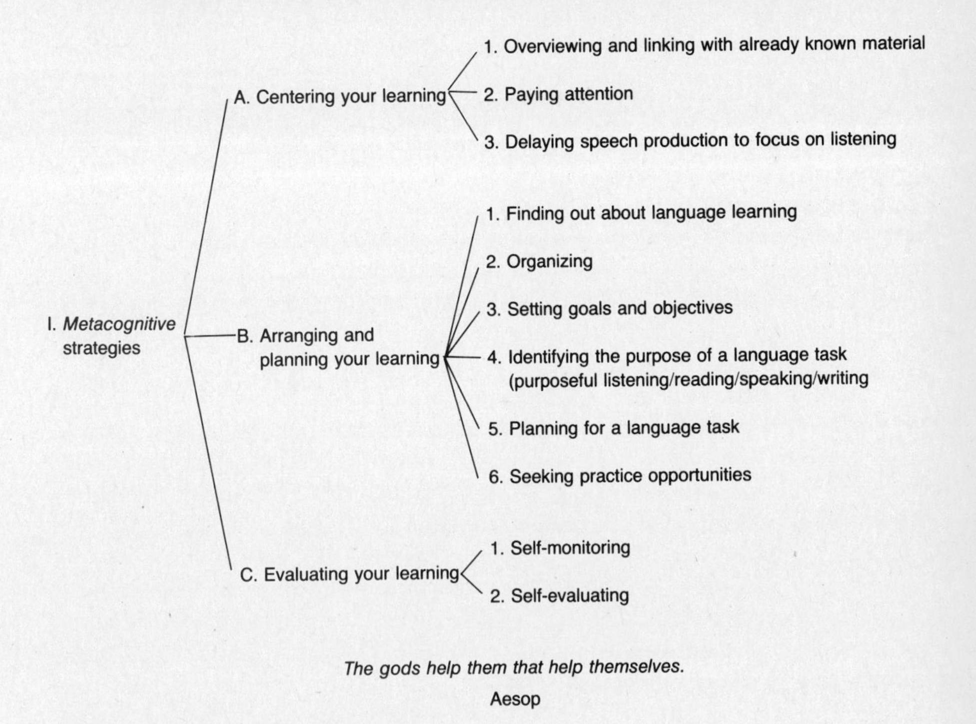

Figure 5.2 Diagram of the Metacognitive Strategies to Be Applied to the Four Language Skills. (*Source*: Original.)

language is sometimes shown in these examples, the main focus is on the act of overviewing/linking, not on how the language is used in that act.

Preparing for a listening exercise, Ricky and his classmates preview French vocabulary about irritation and exasperation, like *C'est insupportable, inadmissable, inacceptable, révoltant, dégoûtant, incroyable!, Ça m'énerve,* and so on, because they know their upcoming task will be to check off these phrases as they hear them on the tape. As they preview, Ricky and his friends demonstrate each expression in the context of a sentence, add some other relevant French expressions they already know, and finally compare the French expressions for irritation with those in their own language.

Anh, a refugee learning English, sees that the next story to be read is about workers in a big city. She overviews the material and considers how the troubles of the workers in the story relate to her own struggles to get a good job. Mac overviews the upcoming Russian lesson in the grammar book concerning seasons and times of day. He rapidly sees that the handling of seasons and times is different in Russian and English, as in the contracted Russian expressions *lyetom* [летом] (in the summer), *utrom* [утром] (in the morning), among others.

In preparing for an Italian role-play about a family going to Naples on vacation, Katalin and her small group create role descriptions of each of the family members. Then they discuss their best and worst family vacations and identify ways in which an Italian vacation might be different from their own experiences.

Getting ready to do a writing assignment, Saskia does 10 minutes of "nonstop writing," a kind of written brainstorming in which ideas are not censored [1]. At other times, Saskia brainstorms out loud with a small group or participates in debates to generate ideas for writing [2]. Such activities help her bring out her own existing ideas and start expanding them as preparation for the future writing task.

In any of the skill areas, vocabulary building can be an important part of the overviewing/linking strategy. Students can help each other create and expand lists of relevant vocabulary for an upcoming language task, putting those expressions into context and considering similar (or contrasting) expressions in the native language.

Paying Attention Ⓐ The strategy of paying attention is necessary for all of the language skills. This strategy involves two modes, *directed attention* and *selective attention.* Directed attention (almost equivalent to "concentration") means deciding *generally or globally* to pay attention to the task and avoid irrelevant distractors. In contrast, selective attention involves deciding in advance to notice *particular* details. Encourage directed attention by providing interesting activities and materials, reducing classroom distractions, reminding students to focus, and rewarding them when they do so. Facilitate selective attention by giving learners an incomplete chart to fill out, a table or checklist on which to mark details, or some other activity which requires attention to specifics.

Both of these attention modes, directed and selective, are important for listening. For instance, Murray's mind begins to wander when he is listening to someone talk in the new language, so he consciously directs his attention to the conversation. In a Spanish-language simulation about catching a plane at the airport, Reinhardt quickly learns that he must notice the announcements about times of arrival and departure for his plane. Janos selectively notes expressions as he hears them, using a checklist provided by the teacher.

In reading, Emily decides to pay close attention to the way characters in her German short story bring conversations to a close and how they use polite phrases. In reading a Tolstoy novel in Russian, Chloë focuses on the names and tries to remember who's who—sometimes a tall order! Bertolt decides to focus on ways in which the French past tense forms are used in front-page articles in *Le Monde.*

Full participation in spoken communication demands directing attention to the general context and content. Learners can also pay selective attention to particular elements of the speech act, such as pronunciation, register, style, physical distance from other speakers, grammar, and vocabulary. For instance, Lorraine, a student of Russian, decides to engage herself fully in the conversation with her Russian friends, and in the conversation she intends to pay special attention to using the correct forms of nouns and pronouns after prepositions. In his oral report in German, Alain concentrates on making his spoken argument as logical as possible. Rifka tries to set a melancholy mood as she tells her story in English.

Writing in the new language, like writing in the native language, requires directed attention. For instance, Sangeeta determines she will concentrate wholeheartedly on writing a letter in her new language, Chinese, blocking out noise and interruptions until she is finished. For writing, selective attention may mean deciding in advance which aspects of the writing to focus on at any given time, like structure, content, tone, sentence construction, vocabulary, punctuation, or audience needs. Especially for beginners, it is hard to pay attention to all these elements at once. Here are some examples of selective attention applied to writing. In writing his French paper Karl keeps constantly in mind the informational needs of the reader and tries to structure the paper to address those needs. Marijke decides to focus on phraseology in writing her article in Spanish. Juan, fresh from a small group discussion, wants to make sure his English essay includes all of the key points from the discussion. These three students are focusing attention on specific aspects of their writing.

Delaying Speech Production to Focus on Listening Ⓛ Ⓢ This strategy relates to listening and speaking rather than reading and writing. You do not have to teach or encourage this strategy, because many learners do it automatically by postponing their speaking in the target language for hours, days, weeks, or possibly even months. This phenomenon is often viewed as a way of focusing on listening comprehension before students feel comfortable enough to speak. The speech delay may be total (no target language speech) or partial (for instance, saying only stock phrases but no creative sentences). The delay occurs because listening is more rapidly developed than speaking, and because speaking seems more threatening to many students. Some instructional theorists have stressed the importance of allowing a "silent period" for all learners, and various language teaching methods reflect this emphasis, but research evidence concerning the significance and optimal length of the silent period is mixed [3]. Help build solid listening comprehension skills, and encourage students to speak as soon as they are ready, without any externally imposed delay.

Here are some examples of delaying speech production. Judy lets others speak in her German class, while she repeats silently to herself, because she does not yet feel confident enough to speak. Aleta, a learner of Russian, says routine phrases such as *dobry den'* [добрый день] (good day), and *do svidaynia* [до свидания] (good-bye), but she does not yet say anything more than these standard phrases. Jon, a traveler in Israel, decides he is ready to try pronouncing the names of the items on the menu, but he feels unable to speak the language in normal conversations with Israelis.

Arranging and Planning Your Learning

The six strategies for arranging and planning are helpful in developing all language skills. These concern discovering the nature of language learning, organizing to learn, establishing aims, considering task purposes, planning for tasks, and looking for chances to practice.

Finding Out About Language Learning Ⓐ This strategy means uncovering what is involved in language learning. Learners often do not know much about the mechanics of language learning, although such knowledge would make them more effective learners. Books about language learning are a good source of information [4]. Help your students by allowing them to talk about their language learning problems, ask questions, and share ideas with each other about effective strategies they have tried. Taking class time to talk about the learning process will reap rewards for the students [5]. All four skills are aided by this strategy, especially if time is allotted to talk about special problems in each of the skills.

Organizing Ⓐ This strategy includes a variety of tools, such as creating the best possible physical environment, scheduling well, and keeping a language learning notebook. First, having the right physical environment is important for every language skill. Listening and reading especially require a comfortable, peaceful setting without too much background noise. Help establish a good classroom environment, and encourage your students to create an appropriate setting for learning at home.

Second, assist your students in developing practical weekly schedules for language learning, with plenty of time devoted to outside-of-class practice in the language skills which are most needed. Note that certain skills like reading and writing are, for many students, best developed with unbroken stretches of time. Relaxation time should be built into the schedule, too, because students can become exhausted with too much work, leading to lowered performance.

Finally, a language learning notebook is an excellent organizational aid to learners. The notebook is useful for writing down new target language expressions or structures and the contexts in which they were encountered, class assignments, goals and objectives, strategies which work well, things to remember, and so on. Encourage your students to obtain a language learning notebook and organize it for the best use.

Setting Goals and Objectives Ⓐ Goals and objectives are expressions of students' aims for language learning. Students without aims are like boats without rudders; they do not know where they are going, so they might never get there! Goals and objectives should be noted in the language learning notebook, along with deadlines for accomplishing them and an indication as to whether those deadlines were met. *Goals* are generally considered to be long-range aims referring to the outcome of many months or even years. *Objectives* are short-term aims for hours, days, or weeks. Aid your students in determining goals and objectives in each of the skill areas, realizing that different students will have different aims. In the examples below, some of the aims reflect full-blown communicative competence, while others reflect relatively minimal skill development.

Some possible goals for listening might be to attain an advanced listening proficiency rating, to be an effective listener in occasional conversations with native speakers, to understand the language well enough for foreign travel, or to be able to hold a job that depends on skilled, in-depth listening. Examples of listening objectives might be as follows. Betty will tune in to the Spanish-language news this evening and will try to understand at least half of it. Bill will visit his French-speaking uncle twice this week and work to improve his listening comprehension. Alden plans to listen to a Chinese tape on the way to work daily for the next 3 weeks.

Reading goals might be to become proficient enough to read professional materials in a technical area, to read magazines or newspapers for pleasure, to read short stories with ease, to understand signposts in the foreign country, to reach a superior reading proficiency level, or to pass the reading exam required for graduate school entrance. Reading objectives might look like these. Johann decides to master the Cyrillic alphabet by Friday, so he can proceed with learning simple Russian words. Kathleen wants to learn a set of vocabulary words this afternoon, so it will be easier for her to read the Italian story tonight. Muriel, who is learning French, plans to finish the Camus novel by the end of the month.

Speaking goals might be to develop sufficient speaking skill to survive in a second language environment, to communicate occasionally with acquaintances who speak the target language, to get a job requiring daily spoken communication in the language, to negotiate foreign travel arrangements, and the like. Sample speaking objectives might be as follows. Sonya decides to master the common German greetings before the next class meets. Manning plans to practice the Russian past tense verb endings this week until he can say them perfectly. Alfonso will speak English for half an hour with his teacher and will apply some of the new conversation management techniques he has just learned.

Goals for writing might include developing enough writing skill to maintain correspondence with foreign friends, to succeed in school or university courses conducted entirely in the target language, to write acceptable business letters, to write scientific articles publishable in international journals, or to pass the language course. Writing objectives might be like the following. Marianne wants to finish her essay within the next few days. Helmuth wants to share the first draft of his autobiography with Wilhelm by the following Tuesday. Edward hopes to meet his early and intermediate writing deadlines, so that he can avoid a "crash" writing effort at the end.

Identifying the Purpose of a Language Task Ⓐ This strategy involves determining the task purpose—an act useful for all language skills. (However, *carrying out* that purpose is the subject of various direct strategies, such as analyzing expressions, guessing, and practicing.) The strategy of considering the purpose is an important one, because knowing the purpose for doing something enables learners to channel their energy in the right direction. Help your students understand the purpose by allowing them to discuss the purpose before doing the task itself.

Figuring out the purpose for listening or speaking is made easier by understanding the kind of speech being used—for instance, casual speech, deliberate speech, reading aloud from a written text, and speaking from a memorized script [6]. Here are some examples of considering the purposes of listening and speaking tasks. When he meets his Italian-speaking friends for a casual lunch on Tuesday, Pierre's chief communication purposes are to have fun, find out how his friends are, and tell them what he has been doing. Juana, who has a job interview in English, has more serious purposes in mind. Her listening purpose is to understand key questions, and her speaking purpose is to respond appropriately and convince the interviewer that she is qualified for the job. In listening to a lecture in Polish, Michael has as his main purpose to understand and take notes on the most salient ideas. Going to a German-language suspense film, Leonida and Pasha have the purpose of using the visuals to help them enhance their understanding of the language and the plot. Meredith's purpose is to ask for information about Nice-to-Paris train schedules and about overnight sleeping accommodations, and to understand that information well enough to purchase an appropriate ticket. Classroom listening and speaking exercises need to become more like these authentic communication tasks, so that task purposes are clear and realistic.

Reading activities are also enhanced by having a clear purpose. Teach your students to look for the purpose in light of the situation and the type of material. Various formats suggest different purposes for reading: looking quickly through the piece to get the main idea or gist (skimming), searching rapidly for a particular piece of information (scanning), reading a longer text for pleasure (extensive reading), and reading a shorter text carefully and in detail (intensive reading) [7]. Following are some examples of reading with a purpose. Myra races through the news article to understand the key idea. Caroline pages rapidly through the German telephone book to find the phone number of the cinema. Sandor relishes the English novel as he reads slowly for pleasure. Bridget reads a Spanish editorial carefully and in detail, trying to separate the assumptions and opinions from the facts.

The purpose of a writing task is related to the type of written format and the needs of the potential audience. Language learners will have a great advantage if they know some possible purposes for writing, such as providing factual information, convincing the audience of the validity of a point, persuading someone to act or think in a certain way, entertaining the audience, making the reader feel an emotion deeply, or evoking a certain mood (light, happy, serious, somber, tense, fearful). Here are some examples of writing with a purpose. Writing a letter to her American pen-pal, Danni, Sibella includes a long list of things that Danni might do in Germany when she comes to visit; the purpose is to make a clear, factual list that will enable her friend to choose among alternatives. Walt wants to write a funny story in Spanish to entertain his classmates. Karen's purpose is to write a serious report in Japanese about the influence of Japanese investments in North America. Gert, a German speaker, is making a written list of duties in English for his summer assistant from Britain, who has just arrived in Munich and does not yet know much German.

Planning for a Language Task Ⓐ Regardless of the language skill(s) involved, this strategy always involves identifying the general nature of the task, the specific requirements of the task, the resources available within the learner, and the need for further aids. These four steps can be illustrated for each of the language skills.

Felicia, a student of Russian, wants to listen to the Radio Moscow news. In planning for this task she first identifies the nature of the task—that is, listening to a news program that is likely to be mainly political and economic. Then she figures out the probable elements, like nuclear arms, diplomatic talks, warships, American and Soviet attitudes, economic change. Next she checks her own internal resources and decides she knows most of the political words but not the economic terminology. Therefore, she looks up terms which she might need but does not yet know. Of course, she cannot determine everything in advance, but she can anticipate and prepare for many of the topics and thus become better prepared for the listening activity.

The same steps are used for a reading task. Janette decides to read an article about fashion in the German women's magazine *Burda*. She figures this task will require her to recognize and understand a variety of words related to women's attire, such as clothing items, styles, and colors. She considers whether she has the needed vocabulary, realizes she knows a few fashion-related words, and assumes she can guess many more expressions from the pictures and the text. To help her if she gets completely stumped, Janette decides to keep a dictionary handy.

Here is an example of preparing for a spoken presentation in the target language. In the first step, describing the nature and purpose, Christoph decides to talk in Spanish about Mexican education in the year 2000. The next step is identifying the language elements needed—for instance, the future tense, comparatives, and vocabulary for primary and secondary schools, universities, vocational schools, education ministries, and so on. Christoph then checks whether he has the necessary knowledge and finally works to develop any missing elements.

In using this strategy for a writing task, Livia realizes first that she wants to write a letter to a friend overseas. Next she decides her letter will require a range of specific language functions (like asking questions, describing, and explaining), a number of structures (such as past, present, future, and conditional), and vocabulary that is adequate to talk about personal things to her friend. After considering whether she has the necessary knowledge, she seeks additional resources by asking a native speaker for help with certain colloquial expressions. (In a longer piece of writing, the planning steps would occur repeatedly, with plans made and remade as ideas evolve.)

Seeking Practice Opportunities Ⓐ Language learners must seek out—or create—opportunities to practice any and all of the four language skills. If students want to reach moderate to high proficiency, classroom time cannot usually provide adequate practice opportunities. Therefore, students will need to find additional chances to practice the language and must realize it is *up to them* to search for these occasions. This strategy underscores students' responsibility to generate their own opportunities to practice. Challenge your students to look for such chances whenever and wherever possible. For ideas about practice possibilities, read the discussion of the strategy of practicing naturalistically in Chapter 3.

Here are some examples of seeking practice opportunities. Viva, who is learning Spanish, decides to practice her listening comprehension skills by listening to popular songs on the radio. Sachi actively seeks out new American friends to talk with at the local community club. Bob decides to submit his name and address to the German magazine's pen-pal list so that he can begin a correspondence in German. Eva takes out a subscription to *Le Monde* as a way of pushing herself to practice reading French every day. Each of these examples involves a conscious decision to look for or create new chances to practice the target language.

Evaluating Your Learning

The two strategies in this set relate to monitoring one's own errors and evaluating one's overall progress. Both are useful in all the skill areas.

Self-Monitoring Ⓐ This strategy does not center as much on using the language as it does on students' conscious decision to monitor—that is, notice and correct—their own errors in any of the language skills. Encourage your students to write down their most significant difficulties in their language learning notebooks and try to eliminate them. In considering a particular *faux pas*, learners can often benefit from trying to determine the reason why it was made. Tracking the cause of the problem, such as overgeneralization from a native language rule, or inappropriate verbatim translation, helps learners understand more about the new language or about their own use of learning strategies [8]. However, error analysis—even this positive kind—must not be too strongly emphasized, or else learners will become overly self-conscious about their performance.

Although monitoring one's own errors is often thought to be used mainly in speaking and writing, it is frequently used for listening and reading as well. One study [9] reported that self-monitoring is extensively used by effective listeners, who check whether they correctly understand the meaning of whole chunks of the message, monitor any confusion they encounter, and correct inaccurate guesses. A similar process occurs in reading. Readers often skim or scan, make guesses about what will come next, and correct any misinterpretations as they move ahead. Here are some specific cases of self-monitoring for listening and reading. Lyla is talking with Uwe in German, and she misinterprets what he says about the age of his nephews. Later she corrects her understanding of their ages as Uwe continues to talk about the nephews' school activities. Briggi is reading a detective novel in English. She guesses whenever she does not fully understand the details of the plot, like who is where at what time, but she subsequently corrects her understanding as she gets more facts.

Self-monitoring is important for speaking, but students should not become obsessed with correcting every speech difficulty, because this would kill communication. Without expecting to be perfect, learners should notice and rectify their important speech problems, such as those which are socially offensive or which cause confusion. Here are some examples of self-monitoring of speech. Phyllis notices that the French school director is offended when she uses just a single-word response instead of saying the more polite expression, *Oui, Madame la Directrice,* so Phyllis quickly corrects herself. Hans, a German learning English, transfers *am Telefon* directly into English, as in the incorrect statement, *I promised it to you at the telephone* [10]. Carlos, a Spanish speaker, makes English speech errors like *I want to explain you the problem.* The difficulties of Hans and Carlos are not serious or offensive at the beginning stage of language learning, so they might not need immediate correction—although more experienced language learners should know and use the correct forms. Encourage your students to keep track of and correct their important speech problems.

For writing, avoid teachers' frequent practices of appropriating the whole error-monitoring function and splashing fountains of red ink over students' compositions. These practices can lead to a sense of defeat for both you and your students [11]. Learners can help each other monitor their writing difficulties without your constant intervention. If the classroom climate is sufficiently nonthreatening, peers can read and comment on each others' written drafts. Mark the most important writing problems, or certain kinds of problems, and then ask students to figure out the correct forms with help from their friends and from reference books. Encourage students to use published checklists to monitor their own errors in spelling, punctuation, vocabulary, organization, content, and tone [12]. Here is an example of self-monitoring in writing. Alberto, an Italian student of English, is writing a letter to Beth, his English-speaking friend, in order to make plans for a trip. Alberto mistakenly uses an Italian *pensare*-type construction when he writes, "We think to come by car." In rereading the letter, he realizes this is an inappropriate construction and changes it to: "We are thinking of coming by car."

Self-Evaluating Ⓐ This strategy involves gauging either general language progress or progress in any of the four skills. Global impressions are often faulty, and the more specific the learner is in self-evaluating, the more accurate the evaluation [13]. Of course, any self-evaluation must take into consideration the difficulty of the situation or the language. Checklists, diaries, or journals can help learners evaluate their progress, at the same time as getting in touch with feelings. For instance, an advanced ESL student wrote in his journal, "My research paper has turned out decently. . . . I definitely failed to make the topic enchanting but I hope I described it satisfactorily and showed my point of view. . . . Life is blossoming again" [14]. See the exercises at the end of this chapter for applications of checklists and diaries for self-evaluation. Following are some ideas about how to evaluate progress in each of the four skills.

Listeners can check with the speaker to determine whether what they understood is really accurate. They can estimate what percentage of a conversation has been understood (for instance, less than half, more than half, almost all). They can assess whether they are at the stage of listening comprehension they expected or wanted to be at this time. Students can consider whether their listening has improved since last week or last month, based on what they understand.

As applied to reading, self-evaluating might consist of learners' assessing their proficiency in a variety of ways. For instance, learners might consider whether their speed or comprehension is acceptable at this point. They might estimate whether their reading skills have improved since the last check. They might consider what proportion of a reading passage they understand, and whether this represents any sign of progress.

In speaking, there are many ways to self-evaluate. Learners may record their own speech on a tape recorder and then listen to the recording to find out how they sound compared with native speakers. During a face-to-face interaction or a telephone conversation, they can make a rough count of the number of times they are asked to repeat something. Learners can also pay attention to the responses of native-speaking listeners when they speak: Do they appear confused or comprehending, upset or calm, alienated or involved? Learners can ask themselves whether, given such signs, their speaking seems to have improved since last month or last year.

Finally, learners can learn to use self-evaluating effectively for writing. They can review samples of their own work, note the style and content of the writing, and assess progress over time. They can compare their writing with the writing of more proficient language users and with that of their peers. Some important criteria are sentence length, complexity of thought, power of arguments, written organization, accuracy, and social appropriateness.

APPLYING AFFECTIVE STRATEGIES TO THE FOUR SKILLS

The three sets of affective strategies are highlighted in Figure 5.3 and explained below as they apply to various language skills.

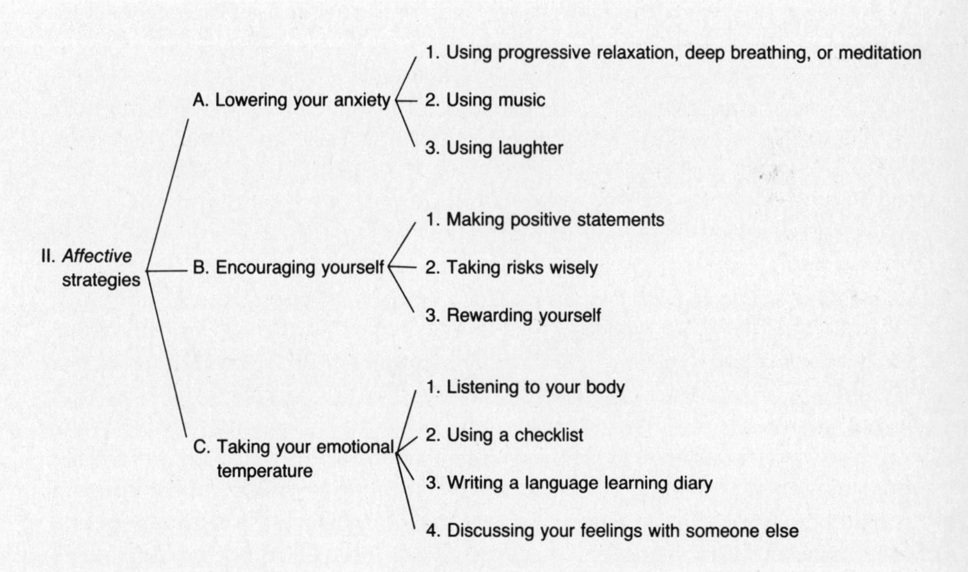

Figure 5.3 Diagram of the Affective Strategies to Be Applied to the Four Language Skills. (*Source*: Original.)

Lowering Your Anxiety

In any of the four skills, anxiety can play a strong role, short-circuiting potential learning. Speaking the new language often causes the greatest anxiety of all, but some learners also experience tremendous anxiety when listening, reading, or writing the new language. The following strategies help learners to lower their anxiety, no matter which skill or combination of skills is involved.

Using Progressive Relaxation, Deep Breathing, or Meditation Ⓐ These techniques are all effective anxiety reducers, according to scientific biofeedback research. Progressive relaxation involves alternately tensing and relaxing all the major muscle groups, one at a time. Deep breathing is often an accompaniment to progressive relaxation. It involves breathing low from the diaphragm, not just from the lungs. The simple act of deep breathing brings greater calmness almost immediately. Meditation means focusing on a mental image or sound to center one's thoughts, and it, too, helps to reduce the anxiety that often dogs language learners. All of these techniques can be used in the classroom or just about anywhere else. Learners do not need to lie down or assume yoga poses to benefit from any of these techniques. A few minutes of relaxation in the classroom or at home using progressive relaxation, deep breathing, or meditation will help learners accomplish their learning tasks more peacefully and more efficiently. Train your students to use these techniques.

Specific examples of this strategy are as follows. Daniela, who is learning German, is frightened by the prospect of the upcoming Goethe Institute examinations, which are known to be tough but fair. She relaxes by using deep breathing techniques before entering the testing room. Libby, a student of Spanish, uses progressive relaxation and meditation for a few minutes before giving a talk in Spanish.

Using Music Ⓐ This strategy is useful before any stressful language task. Five or 10 minutes of soothing music can calm learners and put them in a more positive mood for learning. The language teaching method known as Suggestopedia is based partly on the use of baroque music to alter students' moods and mental states. The powerfully relaxing capabilities of music cannot be denied in the language learning context. As an illustration of using music to relax, Flint listens to his favorite, most upbeat country music before practicing Russian. Sara relaxes with classical music before her German study sessions.

Using Laughter Ⓐ Laughter is the best medicine, as the saying goes. The use of laughter is potentially able to cause important biochemical changes to enhance the immune system, so many hospitals are now using "laughter therapy" to help patients relax [15]. Language learners, too, can benefit from laughter's anxiety-reducing powers. Laughter brings pleasure to the classroom. Laughter is not just the result of teacher-centered joke-telling or Rassias-type dramatics; it can be stimulated by many kinds of classroom activities, such as role-plays, games, and active exercises in which learners are allowed to play as they learn. Laughter is part of a general atmosphere of enjoyment for students of all ages. As an example, Marguerita reads comic books in French for relief, relaxation, and language practice. Ingmar tells jokes and laughs with his friends, so that he can unwind and study more effectively. Grace enjoys doing comical role-plays in class.

Encouraging Yourself

Teaching students some self-encouragement strategies will pay off in all of the skill areas. Language learners often need to find ways to keep their spirits up and persevere as they try to understand or produce the new language.

Making Positive Statements Ⓐ The strategy of making positive statements can improve each of the four language skills. Demonstrate the kinds of positive statements your students can privately make to themselves. Urge them to say those statements regularly, especially before a potentially difficult language activity. Here are some examples:

I understand a lot more of what is said to me now.

I'm a good listener (reader, speaker, writer).

I pay attention well.

I enjoy understanding the new language.

I can get the general meaning without knowing every word.

I'm reading faster than I was a month ago.

People understand me better now.

I had a very successful conversation today.

I can tell my fluency is increasing.

I enjoy writing in the new language.

Writing helps me discover what's on my mind.

I don't have to know everything I'm going to write before I start.

I'm confident and secure about my progress.

I'm taking risks and doing well.

It's OK if I make mistakes.

Everybody makes mistakes; I can learn from mine!

When used before or during a language activity, positive statements are for *self-encouragement*. For example, before presenting a talk in Japanese, Rose says to herself, "I'm sure I can get my point across, even if I make errors." When used after a very good performance, such statements also take on a *self-reward* function (see the strategy of rewarding yourself, described below). For instance, Udo says, "I really did a good job this time!"

Taking Risks Wisely Ⓐ This strategy involves a conscious decision to take reasonable risks regardless of the possibility (or probability) of making mistakes or encountering difficulties. It also suggests the need to carry out this decision in action—that is, employing direct strategies to use the language despite fear of failure. This strategy does not imply wild, unnecessary risks, like guessing at random or saying anything at all regardless of its degree of relevance. Risk taking must therefore be tempered by good judgment. Deciding to be a wise risk taker may require the supportive use of other affective strategies, such as making positive statements or rewarding yourself.

For example, Grigori decides to prod himself to speak in his beginning English class, though he is afraid of sounding like a fool, but he intends to say something sensible and not just blurt out something irrelevant. Mohammad decides to guess at meanings in the article he is reading, even though his guesses might not always be right.

Rewarding Yourself Ⓐ Learners often expect to be rewarded only by external sources, such as praise from the teacher, a good grade on a test, or a certificate of accomplishment. However, learners need more reward than they can get externally. They also need it more regularly and more often. Some of the most potent and useful rewards come from within the learners themselves. Therefore, learners need to discover how to reward themselves for good work in language learning. Naturally, self-reward relates to all four language skills. Rewards differ from one person to another and must be personally meaningful to the individual.

Rewards need not be tangible or visible. They can also come from the very act of doing a good job. Students can learn to relish their own good performance. For instance, they can begin to value more highly a well-crafted composition in the new language, or a conversation in which the learner participates fully and communicates as well as possible. Positive statements, when used after a particularly good performance on the part of the learner, can become a form of self-reward, as seen above.

Here are some examples of more tangible rewards. Hildegarde rewards herself for good work by watching a favorite TV show. Elgard eats a big pizza. Lindsay goes out shopping. Lois calls up a friend for a long chat. Frederick goes to hear a beautiful opera. Ernie takes his family out for a drive by the lake. These are potent rewards for the individuals involved.

Taking Your Emotional Temperature

This set of strategies for affective self-assessment involves getting in touch with feelings, attitudes, and motivations through a variety of means. Language learners need to be in touch with these affective aspects, so that they can begin to exert some control over them. The strategies described here enable learners to notice their emotions, avert negative ones, and make the most of positive ones.

Listening to Your Body Ⓐ One of the simplest but most often ignored strategies for emotional self-assessment is paying attention to what the body says. Performance in all four language skills is affected by the learner's physical state. Negative feelings like tension, anxiety, fear, and outrage tighten the muscles and affect all the organs of the body. Positive feelings like happiness, pleasure, contentment, and excitement can have either a stimulating or a calming effect, but certainly an effect that is discernibly different from the effect of negative feelings. Language learners need to learn to pay attention to these physical sensations frequently. "Tuning in" to the body can be a first step toward greater emotional self-understanding and control. For example, Regina feels her stomach knotting up and her legs going weak just before she has to talk with a native speaker of Thai, so she knows she is nervous and decides to do something about it. Pardee, a learner of German, has a headache, realizes that it is coming from tension about performing in German, and determines that he will relax a bit more every day.

Using a Checklist Ⓐ A checklist helps learners in a more structured way to ask themselves questions about their own emotional state, both in general and in regard to specific language tasks and skills. Learners can use a checklist every day or every few days to assess their feelings and attitudes about language learning. Encourage students to complete checklists periodically at home, or else give students 10 or 15 minutes of class time on a regular basis to do checklists. Use checklists to stir up class discussions of feelings about language learning. Here are examples of this strategy in action. Liselotte uses a checklist each night to note her changing attitudes about her intensive Chinese course, her teacher, and her own progress in learning Chinese. Alton's teacher asks the members of the class to complete a checklist every Monday morning, then Alton discusses the checklist responses with his language partner. Zaria realizes through using a checklist that she feels more at ease and less scared about learning English than she felt before.

Writing a Language Learning Diary Ⓐ Language learning diaries or journals are narratives describing the learners' feelings, attitudes, and perceptions about the language learning process. They can also include specific information about strategies which learners find effective or ineffective for each of the four language skills. You can either give guidelines for your students' diaries or allow those diaries to be freewheeling [16].

Some learners like to share their diaries or journals with other people. In Vladimir's English class, students use diaries to understand and keep track of their thoughts, attitudes, and language learning strategies, and if they feel comfortable enough, they share their diary entries during group discussion in class once or twice a week. Lorelei, a student of Spanish, gets a new perspective by sharing her language learning diary with her sister, who is not studying Spanish.

Other learners prefer to keep their diaries or journals private. For example, while writing in her diary, Bea admits she is bored in her Polish class and does not like the Polish textbook. This realization, which she does not share with her Polish teacher or classmates, makes Bea decide to inject more energy and variety into the learning situation.

Discussing Your Feelings with Someone Else Ⓐ Language learning is difficult, and learners often need to discuss this process with other people. As noted above, written checklists and diaries can be used as input to oral discussions about feelings and needs related to any of the language skills. Learners can benefit from discussing these topics with peers—and with you! Amazing transformations of classroom activity and atmosphere can occur because of these discussions; anxieties and inhibitions diminish, and learners feel they have more control over their own fate. Discussions of feelings can also take place outside of class with a friend, a parent, a counselor, or a native speaker of the language. Encourage students to express their feelings about the language learning process and discover what they need to be better learners. Examples of discussions with other people inside and outside the language classroom have already been given for Alton, Vladimir, and Lorelei (see above).

APPLYING SOCIAL STRATEGIES TO THE FOUR SKILLS

Sometimes people mistakenly think that social strategies (see Figure 5.4) are used only for listening and speaking, but social strategies are helpful and indeed essential to all four language skills.

Asking Questions

This set of strategies includes both asking for clarification or verification and asking for correction. These two strategies are used differently in the

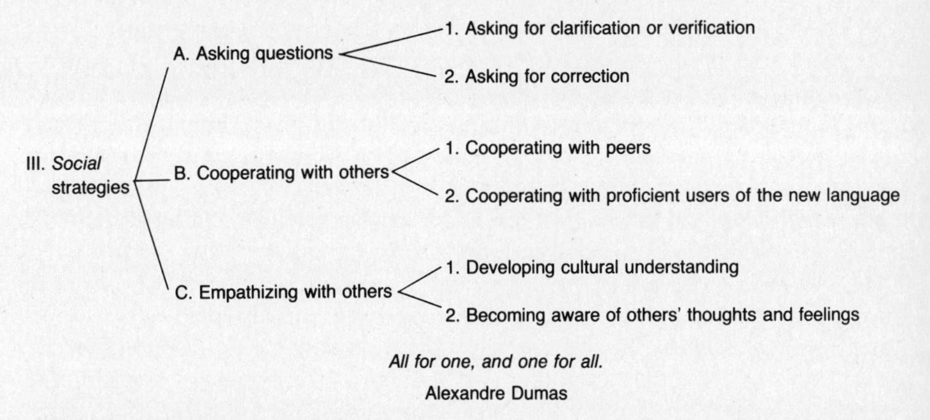

Figure 5.4 Diagram of the Social Strategies to Be Applied to the Four Language Skills. (*Source*: Original.)

four skill areas. In listening and reading, asking questions for clarification or verification is used more often than asking for correction. In speaking and writing, asking for correction is more prevalent.

Asking for Clarification or Verification Ⓛ Ⓡ Asking for clarification in listening involves asking the more proficient speaker to slow down, paraphrase, repeat, explain, or otherwise clarify what he or she has said. Asking for verification in listening means checking to make sure that something has been rightly understood. Learners need to learn acceptable ways to ask for clarification or verification, since it is done differently in different cultures and different languages. Help your students learn appropriate conversational questions like the following:

Would you repeat that, please?
Please speak more slowly.
I'm sorry, I don't understand.
Pardon me.
What was that again?
Did you say———?
What does ______ mean?

Learners who are reading in the new language may also use the strategy of asking for clarification or verification. Usually they ask someone more proficient in the target language, although students at the same proficiency level can often provide clarifying or verifying information. In jigsaw listening or reading exercises, or in other activities involving these two skills, this strategy is commonly used.

Here are some instances of asking for clarification or verification for listening and reading. Marina, who is learning English, does not understand when Rae says, "Wadja wanna do?" Marina asks Rae to slow down and repeat, and Rae clarifies by saying more distinctly, "What do you want to do?" Vicki, reading a French passage, does not comprehend the meaning of the phrase *à toute allure*, confusing it with *à tout à l'heure*. She asks Helene for clarification and is told that the first expression means "at great speed" and the second means "see you very soon."

Asking for Correction Ⓢ Ⓦ This strategy is mostly used in speaking and writing, because errors which are most obvious to other people occur in producing the new language. It is related to the strategy of self-monitoring, in which students notice and correct their own difficulties.

In a spoken conversation, learners can ask the other person for correction of important problems—that is, those which cause confusion or offense. However, the other person cannot be expected to correct all errors made by the learner, because this would intimidate the learner, halt the conversation, and turn the conversation partner into a "speech cop."

Language learners should ask for correction of some writing difficulties, but the kind and amount of correction depends on the level of the learner and the purpose of the writing. Heavy-handed correction, especially in the beginning stages of language learning, can have two possible negative effects: students' morale plummets, or students simply ignore the corrections. If advanced learners are expected to create a polished written product, they might ask for a greater amount of correction, or at least a noting of problems which they themselves can correct.

Following are specific examples of asking for correction. Paige is sure that she has made an error when her Spanish friend looks surprised at what she says, so she asks to be corrected. Aurelius wants to improve his writing, so he asks the teacher to mark his most serious difficulties, for which he then tries to find the correct form on his own. Felix asks his Russian teacher for correction of the written phrase representing "date of birth, 16th of April, 1959" (*data rozhdyeniya, 16oye apryelya 1959 goda* [дата рождения, 16ое апреля 1959 года]). The teacher says that no correction is needed.

Cooperating with Others

Because language in all its aspects is a social act, cooperating with other people is essential. This cooperation requires that the learner interact well with both peers and more proficient language users. Some of the actions mentioned here under cooperating are similar to those in Chapter 3 under the cognitive strategy of practicing naturalistically.

Cooperating with Peers Ⓐ This strategy involves a concerted effort to work together with other learners on an activity with a common goal or reward. Games, simulations, and other active exercises challenge students to develop their ability to cooperate with peers while using a variety of language skills.

Here are some examples of cooperating with peers in listening and speaking. Agnes's small group is working on French jigsaw listening activities, which require individual language learners to listen to different pieces of a story and then figure out the whole story by putting the pieces together in the right order. In another kind of listening exercise, Johanna and José listen to the same passage in English, and Johanna summarizes it in English, with José asking questions and prompting. Then, while listening to a different passage, they reverse their roles. Barbro and Stefan, regular language learning partners at the advanced level of English, have daily telephone conversations with each other, thus receiving listening and speaking practice in the company of a friend.

Reading, though usually considered an independent activity, can be a cooperative enterprise as well. For example, Wally works with his small group on a Russian-language jigsaw reading activity. Each group member has part of the story to read, and together they have to figure out the entire story through a process of negotiating, questioning, and cooperating. At first they do this in English. Later, when they are more advanced, they do it in Russian; when this happens, listening and speaking skills enter the reading act. No matter how it is done, jigsaw reading encourages cooperation with peers.

Writers in any language are often viewed as lonely figures, cloistered in some dim and drafty nook, scribbling silently or pounding the keys of their word processor or typewriter. Though such views might have more than just a grain of truth, writing can also be a social, cooperative activity. For instance, Manolo writes a journal and shares it with his English-language classmate, who responds with comments. Beate participates in brainstorming activities to generate ideas for writing. Daniel takes notes on his friend Max's writing and shares comments with him. Charlene writes in Portuguese to a pen-pal in Lisbon. Before sending a letter, Charlene shows it to her language partner, Sue, to obtain feedback.

Cooperating with Proficient Users of the New Language Ⓐ This strategy applies to all four skills. When used for listening and speaking, this strategy involves taking specific steps to enhance communication with a proficient user of the new language. For example, Lynda reminds herself to keep Rudolph, her German-speaking friend, informed of her own listening needs (e.g., slowing down, repeating). She knows she must listen actively, ask questions, and observe natural feedback, like gestures, facial expressions, and body distance.

In reading and writing the target language, students often need to cooperate with proficient language users. This frequently happens when language learners encounter proficient language users on the job, in the classroom, or on a trip. For instance, Sean needs to get help from Jean-Louis in order to understand some highly technical written instructions while on the job. Diana seeks advice from her Danish friends as she writes reports in Danish. Belinda cooperates with Germans, who help her understand the German tour book.

Empathizing with Others

Understanding and producing the new language involves empathy with other people, especially with individuals from the target culture.

Developing Cultural Understanding Ⓐ Background knowledge of the new culture often helps learners understand better what is heard or read in the new language. Such knowledge also helps learners know what is culturally appropriate to say aloud or in writing. Help students sharpen their cultural understanding by injecting short cultural discussions into classroom activities, and by comparing and contrasting behavior in the students' native culture and the target culture. Turn the language classroom into a cultural laboratory. In second language classes, where many nationalities may be represented and where students are learning the language of the immediate community, learners can bring in materials from their own cultural group to share and can discuss how their background differs from that of the culture in their new homeland. In foreign language classes, where learners are learning a language from a distant country and are generally from a homogeneous cultural background, students can bring in cultural artifacts from traveling abroad or from visiting any ethnic enclaves that exist in their own community.

Outside of the classroom, encourage students to find out all they can about the target culture through reading, going to lectures, or watching films in the target language. All these activities develop greater cultural awareness, which is necessary for achieving proficiency in the new language.

Here are some instances of developing cultural understanding. Paco, who is studying in England, listens to the BBC to try to get a flavor of the culture. Clem and his classmates sign up for a trip to Central America so they can learn about the culture in person as they speak the Spanish language. Lucretia looks at department store catalogs from France to understand more about French culture.

Becoming Aware of Others' Thoughts and Feelings Ⓐ Learners can purposefully become aware of fluctuations in the thoughts and feelings of particular people who use the new language. Such awareness brings learners closer to the people they encounter, helps them understand more clearly what is communicated, and suggests what to say and do.

Observing the behavior of others during face-to-face communication often sharpens this awareness. Listening carefully to what is said, and what is left unsaid, enables learners to become more aware of the mindset of other people. For instance, Rosalee carefully listens to the tone and expression of the mother in the Italian "host family," so that she can be more sensitive to the mother's feelings. Ramon observes the physical signals and speech of his teacher, so he can be more aware of the teacher's mood and thoughts. With this knowledge, Rosalee and Ramon both understand better what they themselves should say.

In addition, learners can become aware of the feelings of others as expressed in writing. Students can sense the feelings of people with whom they communicate informally through letters, notes, or memos. Formal writing like novels, stories, and articles can be understood more easily when learners consciously try to "get inside the skin" of the writer to understand the writer's point of view. For informal or formal writing, this awareness might mean reading on two levels: the literal, verbatim level and the covert, between-the-lines level. The literal meaning might be perfectly sensible in many instances, but sometimes meanings are expressed in both explicit and subtle ways, and learners need to read for both types of meanings. For example, Mickey reads the letter from his Asian friend on both levels to determine what is directly expressed and what is implied. This helps Mickey know how to respond in the next letter he writes to his friend. Sandy reads the Tredyakovsky poem in Russian, being aware of both possible levels of meaning.

SUMMARY

This chapter presented information on how the three kinds of indirect strategies—metacognitive, affective, and social—can be applied to the four language skills. These strategies provide a rich and powerful support to any language learning effort. They work in concert with direct strategies, which were presented earlier in Chapters 2 and 3. The following activities and exercises are geared toward applications of indirect strategies.

ACTIVITIES FOR READERS

Activity 5.1. Examine Indirect Strategies in the Four Skills

On a large sheet write five columns and give them the following labels: *strategy* in Column 1, and the four skills, *listening, reading, speaking,* and *writing,* in Columns 2–5, as in Table 5.1. In the strategy column, list all the indirect strategies shown earlier in this chapter in Figures 5.2, 5.3, and 5.4. Now consider how strongly each of these indirect strategies enhances learners' growth in each of the four skills. Put one check in the skill box if a particular strategy supports development of the skill to a moderate level, and two checks in the skill box if a particular strategy strongly facilitates skill development. Leave the box blank if you feel the strategy is totally irrelevant to the skill. (This will rarely be the case!) Discuss your results with someone else. Note differences and similarities.

Table 5.1 INDIRECT STRATEGIES AS RELATED TO THE FOUR SKILLS

	Four skills			
Strategy	**Listening**	**Reading**	**Speaking**	**Writing**

Source: Original.

Activity 5.2. Consider Your Use of the Indirect Strategies

Think back to when you were a language learner yourself. Which of the indirect strategies did you use often? sometimes? rarely or not at all? Which ones do you wish you had known about and tried? Explain your answers.

Activity 5.3. Ponder the Purposes of Writing and Speaking

In one column on a large sheet of paper, list all the kinds of writing formats you can think of (e.g., reports, stories, letters, memos, personal notes, lists, catalogs, plays). List at least 20. Now, in another column, list the purposes for which the author might be using this format (for instance, convincing, entertaining, challenging the reader). Next, do the same thing for speaking: List a variety of formats, and then note the purposes for using each format. Then put a star (*) by the formats and purposes that might be useful for your students as they learn a new language. Finally, brainstorm ways you could help learners consider the multiple purposes for speaking and writing.

EXERCISES TO USE WITH YOUR STUDENTS

Exercise 5.1. Make a Weekly Schedule

Purpose

This exercise produces a generalized, weekly schedule for language learning. Learners can then add details and make changes week by week.

Materials

Anything necessary to make a schedule (paper, ruler, pen).

Time

Takes 20 minutes for general schedule, 20 minutes a week thereafter.

Instructions

Tell the students the following in your own words: Make a schedule of your typical week, including classes, independent study, time for practicing the language with others, job (paid or unpaid), sleeping, eating, and so on. Block out your major time slots. Pay special attention to the amount of time you have available for language learning. Also note any time conflicts you have that need to be worked out. Leave plenty of time for relaxing and taking breaks, since "time off" increases your efficiency. Keep in mind that shorter, more frequent study sessions are better than longer, less frequent ones.

Also consider the basic principles of structured reviewing. You should review a lesson or piece of information frequently at first, and then less frequently (for example, at first once every 30 minutes, then once an hour, then at gradually greater intervals), coming back to it periodically even after you have moved on to new material.

Table 5.2 **WEEKLY SCHEDULE**

	Morning	Midday	Afternoon	Evening
Sun.				
Mon.				
Tues.				
Wed.				
Thurs.				
Fri.				
Sat.				

Source: Original.

If you want, you can reproduce this schedule and use it in a more detailed way each week to organize your language learning. Week by week, write down your plans for learning the language. List times you will do language assignments, times you plan to meet with native speakers or your regular language partner, special events in the target language, and so on. Table 5.2 provides a possible model for the schedule.

Source Original.

Exercise 5.2. Create a Language Learning Notebook

Purpose

This exercise helps learners create a notebook that will help them throughout their language learning.

Materials

Notebook, dividers.

Time

It will take 1 hour to consider contents and make divisions. Time needed for using the notebook is up to the learner!

Instructions

Tell your students the following in your own words: If you don't already have one, create a language learning notebook. This will help you organize your language learning. Your notebook can be used for any of the following purposes, or other purposes that you might think of:

To record your goals and objectives for learning the language

To write down assignments given by the instructor

To keep a list of new words or expressions you have learned or want to learn

To write down words you have heard or read that you want to ask someone about or look up in the dictionary

To write down grammar rules you have learned or figured out in some way

To keep notes about conversations you have had in the language

To summarize what you read in the new language

To keep a record of errors you want to work on, and your hunches about why you might have made those errors

To comment on strategies you have used successfully or unsuccessfully

To record the amount of time you spend each week studying or using the target language

Make your notebook as simple or detailed as you want. The structure of your notebook depends on your learning style, your personality, and your purposes for using the notebook. If you want to color-code the sections of the notebook, go ahead. Write in your language learning notebook every day or as often as possible. Use it as a good friend in the language learning process. It is one of the best ways to get organized and to manage your learning.

Source Original.

Exercise 5.3. Set Your Goals and Objectives

Purpose

This exercise helps learners set their goals and objectives.

Materials

Copy of questionnaire below, additional paper.

Time

Setting long-term goals: 15 minutes to 1 hour. Setting short-term objectives: should be done periodically; amount of time varies.

Instructions

Tell your students the following in your own words: Let's work on setting goals and objectives for language learning. Your goals and objectives may differ from those of your friends in the class, but that is not important. What is important is that you become clear about why you are learning the language and what you want to get from language learning. To do this, answer the questions in Table 5.3.

Alternative

Learners can work in pairs on this. Or they can work individually and then compare their goals and objectives with those of others.

Source Original.

Table 5.3 QUESTIONNAIRE FOR DETERMINING LANGUAGE LEARNING GOALS AND OBJECTIVES

1. *Setting long-term goals* First set some long-term goals for yourself. To do this, answer the following questions:

a. Why are you learning this language? (check one or more)

_____ For advancement

_____ For good grades

_____ For a new or better job

_____ For travel

_____ Because the language is required for graduation

_____ To get to know people from the new culture

_____ Because it's fun

_____ Other (list) ________________________________

b. Which skills are the most important to you? Given the purposes you have identified, decide which skills are the most important and how you need to spend your learning time. Indicate below the importance of each skill area (1 = least important, 5 = most important). Then indicate how proficient you want to become in each of these skills (low, medium, high).

Skill	**Importance** (list 1 to 5)	**Desired proficiency** (list Low, Med, High)
Listening	_____	_______________
Speaking	_____	_______________
Reading	_____	_______________
Writing	_____	_______________

c. On the basis of your purposes for learning the language and of your skills priorities, what are your long-term goals for learning the new language for the next months or years? Sample goals: being able to hold a long social conversation in the new language; reaching a certain overall proficiency level; being able to give instructions in the new language without constantly using a dictionary. Goals should be realistic.

____

____

____

____

____

Now go back and write down a date for each goal—a time by which you expect to reach the goal. Setting such a date will enable you to check your progress toward meeting your goals.

Table 5.3 Continued

2. *Setting your objectives* After you have set long-term goals, set yourself some short-term objectives, too. These are aims for the next few hours, days, or weeks. Sample short-term objectives include memorizing a set of vocabulary words; mastering the past tense of regular verbs; reading a specific text or complete a particular assignment. Some of these objectives might take only a few hours, while others might take several weeks. Again, set a deadline for yourself for achieving these objectives so you can check your progress. (Repeat this process as needed.)

   ____

   ____

   ____

   ____

   ____

3. Now put this questionnaire in your language learning notebook to remind you of your goals and objectives. Review periodically so that you will remember them and gear your learning toward them. Revise them as needed.

Source: Original.

Exercise 5.4. Opportunity Knocks!

Purpose

This exercise helps learners to consider the possibilities that exist for practicing the new language.

Materials

Paper, pen, instruction sheet.

Time

Takes 30 minutes.

Instructions

Provide your students with an instruction sheet with the following details:

On a sheet of paper, mark off two columns, numbering them Column 1 and Column 2, as shown in Table 5.4.

In Column 1, list *all* the opportunities that you can think of for practicing the new language *in any of the four language skills: listening, reading, speaking, and writing*. These can be existing opportunities or opportunities that you might create. (You don't have to be taking advantage of these opportunities now.) Be specific! Example: reading a newspaper in the new language every day. Now count up the number of ideas you have listed in Column 1, and write down this number where Table 5.4 says "Total number of opportunities."

In Column 2, next to each opportunity you have just listed (see Column 1), indicate whether or not you are now taking advantage of that opportunity. If yes, write 1; if no, write 0. For example, if you are already reading a target language newspaper regularly, put a 1; if not, put a 0. Now add up the points in this column, and write down this number where Table 5.4 says "Total points."

In Column 3 multiply the number of ideas (Column 1) by the number of points (Column 2), and write down the result where Table 5.4 says "Grand total."

Finally, evaluate your results using the scale in Table 5.4.

Source Original.

Table 5.4 OPPORTUNITY KNOCKS!

Column 1	Column 2	Column 3
List opportunities	Now taking advantage? Yes = 1, No = 0	Multiply total number of opportunities by total points
a.		
b.		
c.		
d.		
e.		
f.		
g.		
h.		
i.		
j.		
etc.		
Total number of opportunities _____	Total points _____	Grand total _____

Evaluating Your Results

If you have 15 or more points—GREAT!
If you have 11–14 points—WELL DONE!
If you have between 7–10 points—OK!
If you have between 3–6 points—BETTER LUCK NEXT TIME!
If you have 0–2 points—GOSH!?!

Source: Original.

Exercise 5.5. Gauge Your Skill Progress

Purpose

This exercise helps learners to assess their own progress in language learning skill by skill.

Materials

Paper, pen.

Time

Up to the students.

Instructions

Tell your students the following in your own words: As you learn the new language, you need to measure how well you are progressing—not according to what the teacher says but according to your own criteria of what is important for you. Sometimes learners tend to be too hard or too lenient on themselves. This is because they do not know how to evaluate their efforts. Rate yourself on your progress on each skill and then overall, using Table 5.5.

If you rated yourself as a 3 in any of the skill areas or overall, what can you do about it? What strategies might you use to improve your performance? If you want to keep your ratings private, that is OK, but you might get some benefit out of discussing them with another student or with the teacher.

Source Original.

Table 5.5 SELF-EVALUATION QUESTIONNAIRE

Listening

1. What percentage of a typical conversation with a native speaker do you understand (less than half, more than half, all of it)? ________
2. What percentage of a typical listening comprehension exercise in class do you understand (less than half, more than half, all of it)? ________
3. Has your listening comprehension improved since last month, i.e., do you understand more now than you did then? ______
4. Are you generally able to guess the meanings of what you hear? ______

On the basis of these questions, give yourself a rating on *listening* (circle one):

1. Doing just fine, about where I should be
2. Not too bad, nothing to worry about
3. Serious problems

Table 5.5 Continued

Reading

1. How much do you understand of a typical reading passage in a magazine or newspaper in the new language (less than half, more than half, all of it)? ________
2. How much do you understand of a typical classroom reading passage (less than half, more than half, all of it)? ________
3. Has your reading comprehension improved since last month? _____
4. Are you generally able to guess the meanings of what you read? _____

On the basis of these questions, give yourself a rating on *reading* (circle one):

1. Doing just fine, about where I should be
2. Not too bad, nothing to worry about
3. Serious problems

Speaking

1. When you speak to native speakers of the new language, do they seem to understand you most of the time, without your being asked to repeat? ____
2. In class do your classmates generally understand what you say in the new language? _____
3. Has your speaking improved since last month in terms of quality and quantity? _____
4. Do you find ways to express yourself orally even if you don't know all the words? _____

On the basis of these questions, give yourself a rating on *speaking* (circle one):

1. Doing just fine, about where I should be
2. Not too bad, nothing to worry about
3. Serious problems

Writing

1. When you write in the new language outside of class, do people generally understand your meaning? _____
2. When you write in the new language in class, do people generally understand your meaning? _____
3. Has your writing improved since last month in terms of quality and quantity? _____
4. Do you find ways to express yourself in writing even if you don't know all the words? _____

On the basis of these questions, give yourself a rating on *writing* (circle one):

1. Doing just fine, about where I should be
2. Not too bad, nothing to worry about
3. Serious problems

Now, on the basis of these evaluations of each skill, give yourself an *overall rating* for your general language progress so far (circle one):

1. Doing just fine, about where I should be
2. Not too bad, nothing to worry about
3. Serious problems

Source: Original.

Exercise 5.6. Relaxing

Purpose

This exercise helps learners to relax so that they are able to deal more effectively with language learning.

Materials

None.

Time

This might take 10 to 15 minutes each time (can be more or less, depending on the learner).

Instructions

Tell your students the following in your own words: Tension and anxiety get in the way of language learning. You can learn how to relax. This will help you in language learning and in many other aspects of your life. First, tighten up your lower arm muscles as much as you can, and hold this position for 20 or 30 seconds. It probably hurts a little. Now let go and see how much better it feels. Many of us go around most of the time—especially in times when we have to use the new language—all tensed up, when we could relax instead.

Now let's relax all over by using progressive relaxation. Loosen your clothes a bit around the neck and waist. If you can, lie down; if not, sit in a comfortable position. Tense your feet, and then relax them. Now move up to the ankles, and do the same. Move up to the thighs, then the hips, then the lower back, and on up all the way to your shoulders, tensing and relaxing each major group of muscles. Do the same to your neck muscles and your face muscles, where a lot of tension is stored. By now you should feel really comfortable and relaxed. To maintain this feeling, for a few minutes imagine a lovely, relaxing scene, like a beach or a forest. Center your thoughts on this beautiful spot, meditating on it gently as you breathe deeply. This is a scene you can return to as often as you want, to help you relax.

Source Original.

Exercise 5.7. Calm Down Through Meditation and Music

Purpose

This exercise helps learners to focus and become calm, so that language learning does not feel so stressful.

Materials

None.

Time

Takes 10 to 20 minutes a day (can be more or less, depending on the learner).

Instructions

Tell your students the following in your own words: You can meditate for a few minutes at a time, several times a day. You will be surprised at how focused and calm this can make you, and how much readier you will feel to deal with the new language.

All you have to do is to sit comfortably in a quiet place and think of one thing: an object, a word, a syllable, or a pretty place. Your mind will wander at first, but bring it back to the thing you are thinking about. As you meditate, breathe slowly and deeply from your abdomen, not from your chest. That's the basic idea. If it helps you, you might also play some peaceful background music while you meditate. Try this now in class, and repeat it in the morning and the evening at home. Do it any time you feel tension as a way of relaxing your body and centering your mind.

Source Original.

Exercise 5.8. Praise Be!

Purpose

In this exercise, learners praise themselves for good work and encourage themselves to keep on learning.

Materials

Small cards (optional).

Time

The exercise takes 5 to 10 minutes each day.

Instructions

Tell the students the following in your own words: Pay attention to your *specific* accomplishments and successes in learning, and make positive comments (sometimes called "affirmations") to yourself about your work. Such comments might include things like:

I understood almost everything the teacher said today.

I'm reading much faster now in Spanish than I was a month ago.

I was able to understand and write down the telephone number in French when the caller left a message.

I didn't get paralyzed when I made an error today; I just kept right on going.

I took a risk in using that new expression today, and I'm glad I did it.

It was hard for me to talk in English class today, but I tried.

I held a very successful conversation in German today.

I met with my language partner today, and I can tell that my Russian fluency is increasing.

Make statements that are relevant to you and what you have specifically accomplished. These statements help you change negative attitudes about yourself as a language learner, and they can speed up the process of learning by convincing you that you will succeed. Say positive statements to yourself at least three to five times a day, more if possible.

You can also make more *general* statements that will help you feel more confident. These might include:

I am a good language learner.

I am confident and secure in language learning.

I am progressing well in my language learning.

I can learn from my errors and do not have to be afraid of them.

It's OK if I take risks in language learning.

I don't have to understand everything all at once.

I can tolerate a bit of confusion.

My warm personality helps me in language learning.

Make up your own favorite (and most relevant) general statements to encourage yourself. You might write these statements on little cards and look at them in the morning and at night—or more frequently during the day—as a psychological suggestion to yourself. Gradually you might memorize them, and you might not have to look at the cards anymore. Saying general statements to yourself several times a day helps you internalize these concepts and believe them at a deeper level. You'll be surprised at the power these simple statements can have! If you have a language learning partner whom you trust, you might share your positive statements with that person, and vice versa.

Make positive statements several times a day for a week. (If you miss one time, don't give up. Go back to the schedule and keep on encouraging yourself!) After the first week, check on the success of your efforts. Are you feeling more confident? Better able to help yourself and manage your emotions? More committed to learning the language? Write down your evaluative comments in your language learning diary or notebook.

Source Original.

Exercise 5.9. Assess Your Emotions

Purpose

This exercise helps learners use a checklist to assess their emotional state regularly and often, and to link their emotional state with the events of their language learning and other aspects of their lives.

Materials

Checklist.

Time

Takes 5 minutes each day.

Instructions

Tell your students the following in your own words: Use the checklist in Table 5.6 to keep tabs on your feelings. The checklist is simple to use, requires little time, gives you a record for comparison from time to time, is private, and helps you link your feelings with the language tasks and events in which you are involved. If you decide to use this checklist, you should do so at least once a week, but you could use it every single day. This checklist is not a complicated psychological profile that tells deep secrets about you! It is an easy way for you to keep in touch with yourself in a private, personal, and regular way, so that you can better handle the demands of language learning.

Source Original.

Table 5.6 TAKING YOUR EMOTIONAL TEMPERATURE: A CHECKLIST FOR LANGUAGE LEARNERS

Part A

Date: ____________ Language studied: ____________

Period covered (check one):

_____ Day _____ Week _____ Other (specify): ____________

Part B List language tasks or events in which you have just been involved, for example, giving an oral report, writing a letter, doing drills, holding a conversation. (Give whatever details are useful to you, including, if you want, the other people involved. Don't skip this; it shows you how certain tasks/events trigger particular feelings!)

____

____

____

____

____

Part C Describe how you're feeling now, especially in relation to the learning tasks or events above. (Check the one descriptor per line that *best describes you*. Realize that nothing is either black or white, and that any single descriptor is not necessarily better than its opposite.)

_____ happy	_____ unhappy
_____ proud	_____ ashamed
_____ confident	_____ unconfident
_____ peaceful	_____ anxious
_____ unafraid	_____ afraid
_____ risk-taking	_____ cautious
_____ clear-thinking	_____ confused
_____ friendly	_____ unfriendly
_____ interested	_____ bored
_____ calm	_____ angry
_____ strong	_____ weak
_____ energetic	_____ tired
_____ outgoing	_____ shy

Table 5.6 Continued

_____ accepting	_____ critical
_____ able to tolerate contradictions	_____ unable to tolerate contradictions
_____ want to learn the language	_____ don't want to learn the language
_____ want to know the culture	_____ don't want to know the culture

Source: Original.

Exercise 5.10. Stress Check

Purpose

This exercise helps learners to assess their stress level, which directly influences language learning.

Materials

Checklist.

Time

Variable, depending on students' needs.

Instructions

Provide students with the stress checklist in Table 5.7, and give them oral instructions as well as printed ones.

Here is what you can say to students, in your own words, of course: You might be feeling under a little or a lot of pressure lately. You might not yet know what is causing the problem. If you are feeling stressed, think about what the cause might be. Don't just mask the stress with alcohol, drugs, TV, or something else; think about what's causing you to worry. Are you worried about how you are doing in your studies? About money? About roommate or family problems? About a friend or lover—or the lack of one?

The first thing to do is to identify, if you can, what it is that is bothering you most about the problem or situation. Is there anything you can do about it? What steps might you take to solve the problem or address the main issue? What would your best friend or a respected adviser do about the problem if faced with it?

Try to look for someone to talk to about the problem. Get new ideas about how you might deal with it. If the problem is truly serious, seek professional help from a teacher, counselor, or other person.

It is also useful to consider the worst thing that might happen if the problem does not get resolved. Paint the "worst case scenario" in your mind, and consider what it feels like. Is there any way that you might be able to accept such a situation and learn to live with it? How could you minimize your discomfort under those circumstances?

Can you take your mind off the problem a bit by doing something else that is interesting and positive? Is there anything in your life that feels really good just now? Make a list of the good things that exist, and read the list to yourself a couple of times each day. In this way you might be able to develop some perspective about the difficulties you face.

Source Original.

Table 5.7 STRESS CHECKLIST

Circle each of the signs of stress that you have noticed in yourself lately.		
Anger	Inability to think, concentrate, or make decisions	Tight muscles
Isolation	Depression	Headaches
Exhaustion	Anxiety	Sleeping too much or too little
Pickiness	Fear	Eating too much or too little
Irritability	Worry	Reliance on alcohol or drugs

Source: Original.

Exercise 5.11. Keep a Diary

Purpose

The purpose of a language learning diary is to record feelings about the language learning process.

Materials

Diary.

Time

Variable.

Instructions

Tell your students the following in your own words: Use a diary or journal to express your feelings about learning the new language. Feel free to write whatever you want, but write something every day. The diary describes *how you are learning the language and how you feel about it*. Diary entries do not have to be long and involved. In fact, a few lines or a few paragraphs a day might be enough. When you want to explore a particular problem or a happy event in more detail, you can write more than usual. The diary is for you, and you can use it any way you want: to describe emotions, desires, issues, difficulties, achievements, other people, learning strategies, conversations, how you spent your time. You will probably want to use the diary to evaluate the general progress (or lack of it) that you feel you are making.

Unless the diary is used as a class assignment, you don't have to show it to anyone else. You can decide what you want to write and can be completely honest and open. You won't hurt anyone else by writing down your feelings, even the angry ones, and you will open the door to an important new world inside yourself.

In addition to providing a record of emotions, writing a diary is actually a form of therapy in itself. Diaries are useful for "letting off steam," helping you sort through conflicting feelings, and sometimes coming to new conclusions about how to feel, think, and act. Diaries can help you think through your learning problems and identify your accomplishments.

Source Original.

Chapter 6

Language Learning Strategy Assessment and Training

We cannot teach another person directly; we can only facilitate his [or her] learning.
CARL ROGERS

PREVIEW QUESTIONS

1. What techniques exist for finding out what language learning strategies students use?
2. When are various techniques appropriate?
3. Which of these techniques might be useful to you?
4. Is it possible to help someone learn how to learn?
5. If so, what methods can be used most effectively?

INTRODUCTION TO STRATEGY ASSESSMENT AND TRAINING

Now that you know how language learning strategies can be applied to the four language skills, you are ready to put strategies into action. The first step involves identifying and diagnosing your students' strategies so that the training program you devise will be effective. The second step is conducting the training.

STRATEGY ASSESSMENT

Some of the most important strategy assessment techniques include observations, interviews, "think-aloud" procedures, note-taking, diaries or journals, and self-report surveys.

Observations

Many language learning strategies take place mentally and cannot be observed by the teacher. For instance, associating/elaborating, using imagery, and guessing intelligently are "invisible" or "mentalistic" strategies in terms of standard observation schemes. However, cooperating with peers, asking for clarification or verification, and overcoming limitations in speaking through gesture or mime are activities that are directly observable and can yield information on how your students currently go about learning languages.

Keeping in mind that any observation scale will miss many of the mentalistic strategies, you can choose a good scale from several that have been published and are readily available [1]. Or you can devise your *own* observation form by making a list of the strategies you think are important and which you wish to observe. On this observation form you can record the strategies in several ways:

- By taking impressionistic or structured notes.
- By checking off the strategies you see in a certain period of time, such as during one class period.
- By combining these two approaches.

Also, consider the level of detail you plan to observe. If you have the time, and perhaps another colleague to help out, you can observe and record detailed information about the context in which strategies are used.

In addition, consider the focus of your observations. You can (perhaps very roughly) observe the strategies typically used by the whole group, you can track the strategies of one small group of students, or you can observe the strategies of one student, including this student's interactions with others. You also need to decide whether you will observe for brief intervals or for a long session, and whether you will repeat your observations. Think about how to select or sample the observation times so they will reflect typical situations.

Videotaping of observation sessions can be valuable. It provides a permanent record of the sessions, so you can replay them for detail. The videotape medium will lose some peripheral information—activity that takes place outside the frame of the picture—but it will also capture details that you might not notice on first viewing.

Observations are just one way to gather strategy data. Other ways include interviews and think-aloud procedures.

Interviews and Think-Aloud Procedures

These techniques can be used together or separately. Totally unstructured interviews, in which there is no particular questioning technique or no data coding form, are difficult to use because they require you to create all your categories for analyzing and interpreting *after* the interview. Slightly more structured techniques are easier to handle.

A Model for Interviewing The Cohen-Hosenfeld interview model [2] helps you gather data on unobservable mental processes. In this model, the three dimensions of activity, time, and content can be applied to language learning strategies.

Activity: Thinking aloud and self-observation are two ways to observe learning strategies. By *thinking aloud*, the student lets his or her thoughts flow verbally in a stream-of-consciousness fashion without trying to control, direct, or observe them. In *self-observation*, the subject consciously "watches" and analyzes his or her own thoughts to some degree.

Time: Varying amounts of time can elapse between the use of a learning strategy and its verbalization. Think-aloud data must reflect the present time (within a few seconds of the thought). Students "think aloud" as they learn. In contrast, self-observation can take place later, not just when the learning is under way [3].

Content: Thoughts may be focused on a topic, such as a particular language learning task, especially if guided by a researcher [4].

A Guide for Think-Aloud Interviews The Interviewer Guide developed by Carol Hosenfeld and her colleagues [5] is valuable for assessing reading strategies. Originally, the guide (see Table 6.1) was used for preliminary diagnosis of strategies before training, and then to assess changes in strategy use after training.

To use this guide, ask a student to perform a language task and to think aloud, describing what he or she is doing to accomplish the task. Record the learner's general behavior while the learner says out loud what he or she is doing. In just a few minutes per student, you can check the first 13 strategies. If you have more time, you can assess all 20. The guide is a useful and concise format for think-aloud interviews, except that more space will be needed for comments. You might want to adapt the Interviewer Guide to include the strategies found in this book for any of the four skill areas [6].

Of course, not all interviews actually involve performing a task and simultaneously thinking aloud about the strategies employed. The next technique describes a way to obtain interview information on what students *usually* do, without having them perform the task during the interview.

Interviews Involving Self-Observation J. Michael O'Malley, Anna Uhl Chamot, and their colleagues developed a useful Student Interview Guide [7] which asks learners to think about what they generally do when faced with familiar language tasks, such as pronunciation, oral grammar exercises, vocabulary learning, following directions, communicating in a social

Table 6.1 INTERVIEWER GUIDE FOR READING STRATEGIES

Student's name ____________

General reading behavior (circle 1)

Rarely translates; guesses contextually	Translates; guesses noncontextually
Translates; guesses contextually	Translates; rarely guesses

Circle the strategies mentioned	Comments
1. Keeps meaning in mind.	____________
2. Skips unknown words (guesses contextually).	____________
3. Uses context in preceding and succeeding sentences and paragraphs.	____________
4. Identifies grammatical category of words.	____________
5. Evaluates guesses.	____________
6. Reads title (makes inferences).	____________
7. Continues if unsuccessful.	____________
8. Recognizes cognates.	____________
9. Uses knowledge of the world.	____________
10. Analyzes unknown words.	____________
11. Reads as though he or she expects the text to have meaning.	____________
12. Reads to identify meaning rather than words.	____________
13. Takes chances in order to identify meaning.	____________
14. Uses illustrations.	____________
15. Uses side-gloss.	____________
16. Uses glossary as last resort.	____________
17. Looks up words correctly.	____________
18. Skips unnecessary words.	____________
19. Follows through with proposed solutions.	____________
20. Uses a variety of types of context clues.	____________

Source: Adapted from Hosenfeld et al. (1981).

situation, and two levels of listening comprehension in class (getting the main idea and making inferences). Students are not required to perform the language task itself during the interview but are asked to consider how they typically do the task. This technique allows the learners to provide information in their own words about their learning strategies. Such interviews work well in small groups or with individuals, and lend themselves well to taping.

Semi-structured Interviews Semi-structured interviews are very useful for gathering information on your students' strategies. Here is one well-tested example by Anita Wenden. Some days before a semi-structured interview, students are given a list of broad questions outlining the main areas to be covered. They are asked to complete a grid of daily activities, on which they indicate the settings (e.g., TV watching, social conversation) in which they ordinarily find themselves during the week and what learning activities they employ in those settings. Students list only those settings in which they use the target language. During the interview, the learners answer broad questions, using information they have written down on their grid [8].

Think-Aloud Procedures Used Without Interviewing Just as you can interview students without using the think-aloud procedure, you can also use the think-aloud procedure without interviewing (that is, without any prompts or questions by the teacher or researcher). Betty Leaver has had success taping the conversations of a small group of adult Russian learners as they tried to figure out the meaning of taped listening comprehension dialogues. She also recorded the reactions of two children who were asked to figure out the meaning of taped dialogues. Tapes were transcribed and analyzed to determine the approach and strategies used by the students [9].

With this procedure, you must develop a way to categorize or make sense of the data. You can develop the scheme before the think-aloud data are analyzed or afterward, using the think-aloud material you have collected as a basis for defining categories. However, open-ended data collection like this requires skillful interpretation.

Like observations, interviews, and think-aloud procedures, note-taking can provide valuable information on students' strategy use.

Note-Taking

Note-taking is a self-report technique that can be extended to any language task. It is especially valuable when paired with interviewing. Here are three note-taking techniques for strategy assessment. First, a group of students is asked to note down their learning difficulties when performing a language task and to use these notes in an interview. A second use of note-taking involves a daily grid and occurs prior to the semistructured interview, already mentioned. A third technique asks students to take notes on a grid, describing the strategies they employ; then they rate those strategies in terms of frequency of use, enjoyment, usefulness, and efficiency [10]. As you can see, these note-taking schemes impose a bit of useful structure on students as they keep track of their strategy use. Another way for students to focus on how they use strategies is to write in a diary or journal.

Diaries or Journals

Diaries or journals are forms of self-report which allow learners to record their thoughts, feelings, achievements, and problems, as well as their impressions of teachers, fellow students, and native speakers. Diarists become "participant observers" in their own personal, ethnographic research [11]. You have already seen in Chapters 4 and 5 that keeping a diary or journal is a very useful learning strategy in itself, and this strategy can be used to help learners become aware of their whole range of strategies.

Most diaries tend to be subjective and free-form, without constraints on style or content, but some teachers find it helpful to provide guidelines. If you give your students some guidance as to subject matter or style for their diaries, these diaries are likely to be less personal, but the writers might object less to sharing their writing with you. You can ask students to use their diaries to focus specifically on language learning strategies. In some cases, learners need suggestions on how to report their strategy use and may need to take notes so as not to forget which strategies they used. If you are planning to read your students' diaries, you should, of course, tell students in advance, since diaries are frequently considered private.

Though learners are often asked to share their diaries with the teacher, students can also share their diaries among themselves. In addition, some teachers have used diaries as a stimulus to class discussions of strategy use. Some teachers set aside class time once a week to allow students to discuss their diaries.

The final strategy assessment procedure is self-report surveys, discussed next.

Self-Report Surveys

Self-report surveys are instruments used to gather systematic, written data on language learning strategy use. These surveys can vary from less structured to more structured.

Less-Structured Surveys Less-structured self-report surveys, also called subjective surveys, do not provide much organization for students in terms of the responses elicited. Such surveys contain open-ended questions designed to get the learner to describe his or her language learning strategies freely and openly in writing. The advantage is that learners can say what they want, and a lot of interesting information is generated. However, the results may be difficult to summarize across students. One survey first asks learners what kinds of strategies they generally use for certain learning tasks, and then asks them to reflect on their strategies in writing after completing a learning task [12].

More-Structured Surveys More-structured surveys, also called objective surveys, usually ask multiple-choice questions which can be objectively scored and analyzed. Because more-structured surveys use standardized categories for all respondents, such surveys make it easier to summarize results for a group and objectively diagnose problems of individual students. However, these surveys might miss the richness and spontaneity of less-structured formats [13].

The Strategy Inventory for Language Learning (SILL), in Versions 5.1 and 7.0, is a structured survey based on the strategy system used in this book. Earlier versions have been extensively field-tested, demonstrated to be highly valid and reliable, and used for both research and classroom practice. New, shorter versions (see Appendices B and C) are being field-tested and analyzed [14]. In various versions, the SILL has been used in many parts of the world with learners of many different languages, including Chinese, English, French, German, Italian, Japanese, Korean, Russian, Spanish, Thai, and Turkish.

Version 5.1 contains 80 items assessing the frequency of strategy use and takes about 30 minutes to complete. This form is shorter than many previous versions, is easier to self-score, and is keyed to the language learning strategies used throughout this book. Appendix B contains the SILL directions and items, the worksheet for answering and scoring, and the student profile of results. This version is for native English speakers.

SILL Version 7.0, containing 50 items, is geared to students of English as a second or foreign language (see Appendix C) and takes about 30 minutes to complete, depending on the skill level of the students. The language is very simplified, but this version operates similarly to Version 5.1 in most other respects.

The SILL's 5-point scale (for all versions) ranges from "never or almost never" to "always or almost always." The overall average indicates how often the learner tends to use learning strategies in general, while averages for each part of the SILL indicate which strategy groups the learner tends to use most frequently.

How to Choose a Technique for Checking Your Students' Strategies

All of the techniques described here are valuable for checking your students' use of language learning strategies. How do you know which one(s) you should use? To make a decision, think about why you want to discover your students' strategies: because of personal interest on your part, for use in orienting your teaching practices, for providing feedback to your students on their strategy use, or as a prelude to strategy training? Also, consider the kind of information you want to obtain, the amount of time you and your students have to devote to strategy assessment, the amount of detail you need, and the relative ease or difficulty of administration and analysis. These considerations, and Activity 6.1 below, will help you select the assessment techniques that will suit your needs the best.

How to Use Strategy Assessment Results

One of the soundest reasons to assess your students' learning strategies is so you can provide training on how to improve those strategies. It is always best to provide your students with the results of your assessment. No one likes to be treated like a guinea pig. Besides, they will be curious and eager to know something new about themselves. Interpretive feedback can be woven into the training itself, or it can be presented separately, depending on how you structure your training. You might like to divide your students into small groups by ethnic/national/cultural background to discuss their strategy assessment results. Students from similar backgrounds often find that they use strategies in similar ways. Then provide training so they can learn new strategies.

STRATEGY TRAINING

Once you know how students are currently learning, you can help them to learn more effectively. This section will help you plan and carry out training in language learning strategies.

Training of language learning strategies is called many things: "strategy training," "learner training," "learning-to-learn training," "learner methodology training," and "methodological initiation for learners." This book uses the term *strategy training*, because it is both descriptive and general enough to serve our needs.

The Scope of Strategy Training

The best strategy training not only teaches language learning strategies but also deals with feelings and beliefs about taking on more responsibility and about the role change implied by the use of learning strategies. Unless learners alter some of their old beliefs about learning, they will not be able to take advantage of the strategies they acquire in strategy training [15]. In addition, strategy training can cover more general aspects of language learning, such as the kinds of language functions used inside and outside the classroom, significance of group work and individual efforts in language learning, trade-offs between accuracy and fluency, fear of mistakes, learning versus acquisition, and ways in which language learning differs from learning other subjects [16].

The Need for Strategy Training

Learners need to learn how to learn, and teachers need to learn how to facilitate the process. Although learning is certainly part of the human condition, *conscious* skill in self-directed learning and in strategy use must be sharpened through training [17]. Strategy training is especially necessary in the area of second and foreign languages. Language learning requires active self-direction on the part of learners; they cannot be spoon-fed if they desire and expect to reach an acceptable level of communicative competence.

Many language teachers advocate *explicit* training of language learners in the "how to" of language study. The general goals of such training are to help make language learning more meaningful, to encourage a collaborative spirit between learner and teacher, to learn about options for language learning, and to learn and practice strategies that facilitate self-reliance [18]. Strategy training should not be abstract and theoretical but should be highly practical and useful for students.

No one knows everything about how people learn languages, but there is strong support for sharing, through strategy training, what we *do* know. Research shows us that learners who receive strategy training generally learn better than those who do not, and that certain techniques for such training are more beneficial than others.

How to Prepare Yourself to Conduct Strategy Training

Two issues should be considered as you prepare yourself for conducting strategy training: your knowledge of language learning strategies and your attitudes about role changes.

Expanded Knowledge of Language Learning Strategies The more you know about language learning strategies, the better trainer you will be. There is a great deal you can do to expand your knowledge in this area, beginning with a review of the parts of this book that are of greatest interest to you. Read other books and articles on the topic; see the reference list in this book for abundant suggestions. Attend language learning strategy sessions at professional conferences. Find or create in-service training activities that stress language learning strategies. Get your institution to sponsor such training for language teachers. Find out all you can!

But you do not have to wait until you become an expert on strategies before you can provide effective training for your students. If you follow the guidelines in this chapter and use what you know about learning strategies, you will be able to make a difference in your students' ability to learn languages.

Reconsider Your Attitudes About Roles Think through your assumptions about the roles of students and teachers, because these roles often undergo change when learners start to take more responsibility for their success in the language classroom. Having read thus far, you probably do not need intensive restructuring of your beliefs about learner and teacher roles. You are probably open-minded and may have already experimented with classroom activities allowing you to be more a facilitator than a director. Or perhaps you are interested in experimenting with such activities but do not know exactly where to begin. Talk with other teachers, particularly those who are open to new ideas about roles. Look for games, simulations, and structured exercises in which you and your students can experiment with new teacher and learner roles in class.

Three Types of Strategy Training

Language learning strategies can be taught in at least three different ways: awareness training, one-time strategy training, and long-term strategy training.

Awareness Training Awareness training is also known as consciousness-raising or familiarization training. In this situation, participants become aware of and familiar with the general idea of language learning strategies and the way such strategies can help them accomplish various language tasks. In awareness training, however, participants do not have to use the strategies in actual, on-the-spot language tasks.

Awareness training is very important, because it is often the individual's introduction to the concept of learning strategies. It should be fun and motivating, so that participants will be encouraged to expand their knowledge of strategies at a later time. For this reason, it is best not to use the lecture format for awareness training. Participants can be teachers, students, and anyone else interested in language learning processes; no special background in learning theory or strategies need be assumed. Two examples of exercises for awareness training are found at the end of Chapter 1: the Embedded Strategies Game and the Strategy Search Game.

One-Time Strategy Training One-time strategy training involves learning and practicing one or more strategies with actual language tasks, usually those found in the regular language learning program. This kind of training gives the learner information on the value of the strategy, when it can be used, how to use it, and how to evaluate the success of the strategy. However, one-time training is not connected to a long-term sequence of strategy training. One-time training is appropriate for learners who have a need for particular, identifiable, and very targeted strategies that can be taught in one or just a few session(s). An example is in the teaching of certain memory strategies without integrating them into a more prolonged strategy training approach. In general, one-time training is not as valuable as long-term training.

Long-Term Strategy Training Long-term strategy training, like one-time strategy training, involves learning and practicing strategies with actual language tasks. Again, students learn the significance of particular strategies, when and how to use them, and how to monitor and evaluate their own performance. Like one-time training, long-term training should be tied to the tasks and objectives of the language program. However, long-term training is more prolonged and covers a greater number of strategies. It is likely to be more effective than one-time training.

A Model for Strategy Training

The following eight-step model for strategy training, summarized in Table 6.2, assumes that you have already assessed your students' current learning strategies using one or more of the techniques described earlier.

This model focuses on the teaching of learning strategies themselves, rather than on the broader aspects of language learning. It is especially useful for long-term strategy training, usually closely tied to regular language learning, but can be adapted for one-time training by selecting specific units. Of course, you do not need to use this model if you are concerned only with awareness training at this point. The steps might not always have to be done in this order; some can be performed at the same time, or in a slightly different order [19].

The first five are planning and preparation steps, while the last three

Table 6.2 STEPS IN THE STRATEGY TRAINING MODEL

1. Determine the learners' needs and the time available.
2. Select strategies well.
3. Consider integration of strategy training.
4. Consider motivational issues.
5. Prepare materials and activities.
6. Conduct "completely informed training."
7. Evaluate the strategy training.
8. Revise the strategy training.

Source: Original.

involve conducting, evaluating, and revising the training. As you proceed through the design steps (1–5), try to get feedback from other people if possible. It always helps to get useful comments and suggestions. Better yet, work with a training partner, such as another teacher, throughout the whole sequence.

Step 1: Determine the Learners' Needs and the Time Available The initial step in your training program is to consider the needs of the learners and determine the amount of time you have for the activity. Consider first who the learners are and what they need. Are they children? Adolescents? College students? Graduate students? Adults in continuing education? Refugees or immigrants? Are they advanced language students? Intermediates? Beginners? What is their verbal ability [20]? What are their strengths and weaknesses? What learning strategies have your students been using, according to the strategy assessment results? Which strategies do you think they need to learn? Is there a wide gap between the strategies they have been using and those you think they need to learn? If so, do cultural factors play a role? How do these students view their roles as language learners? Do they take responsibility, or will you need to help them change their attitudes about learning? Have you given the learners a chance to express their desires about strategies they might like to learn? If so, what kinds of strategies were they interested in?

Consider how much time you and your students have available for strategy training, and when you might do it. Are you pressed for time, or can you work strategy training in with no trouble? Can you relate strategy training to the language tasks already under way, so that the strategies become immediately applied and learners can understand and practice them?

Step 2: Select Strategies Well First, select strategies which are related to the needs and characteristics of your learners. Note especially whether there are strong cultural or other biases in favor of (or against) a particular type of strategy, as shown by the strategy assessment you have conducted earlier. If strong biases exist, you might need to choose strategies that do not completely contradict what the learners are already doing, or if you do choose to train strategies which are counter to what learners now prefer, you might need to introduce the new strategies gradually while building on what the learners prefer.

Second, choose more than one kind of strategy to teach (by deciding the kinds of compatible, mutually supporting strategies that are important for your students). Third, choose strategies that are generally useful for most learners and transferable to a variety of language situations and tasks. Fourth, choose some strategies that are very easy to learn, and some strategies that are very valuable but might require a bit more effort. In other words, do not include all easy strategies or all difficult strategies.

Think of this training process as more than just teaching metacognitive and cognitive strategies, the usual fare of strategy training. Other kinds of strategies—memory, compensation, affective, and social—are also very important for strategy training.

The following sequence describes an example of a *broad focus* in strategy training, combining four groups of strategies: affective, compensation, social, and metacognitive. Learners initially try to listen to a target language passage that contains many words they do not know. They discuss their feelings (an affective self-assessment strategy) about trying to understand such a difficult passage. Then they learn and practice guessing strategies (a form of compensation strategy) in pairs or small groups, thus using social strategies. Next, learners evaluate the success of their guessing strategies (via the metacognitive strategies of self-monitoring and self-evaluating), and, finally, they discuss how they feel about themselves and about these strategies (another use of affective self-assessment). This sequence allows the interweaving of many different categories of strategies. It is not necessary to use this many different kinds of strategies in the same training exercise, but it is certainly feasible. This broad focus, including multiple strategy types, trains learners in large segments of the whole strategy classification system, shows students how strategies interact, and may give students a new understanding of the language learning process. However, this broad focus does not allow precise assessment of training effectiveness in reference to any specific strategy.

On the other hand, it is also possible to use a *narrow focus*, centering on the training of just one or two learning strategies rather than an integrated set of many strategies. The narrow focus leads to less overall training time, reduces the possibility of overloading the learner with diverse strategies, and allows more precise assessment of the effectiveness of the strategy training, but it does *not* allow for multiple strategies to interact to maximize learning potential. Note that the narrow focus is not necessarily the same as one-time strategy training, which concerns the amount of time spent. It is possible to do strategy training with a narrow focus over a long period of time, just as broad-focus training can be long-term.

A *combination* approach to training might be as follows: The trainer presents many strategies and strategy groups (*broad focus*), and learners are asked to rate subjectively the use of different strategies or strategy groups. Then, given these ratings, specific strategies are selected for more focused training and assessment (*narrow focus*) [21]. This is an excellent way to approach strategy training. It gives learners the "big picture" at first, then moves into specific strategies which the learners have chosen themselves. The element of learner choice in structuring training is very important, since learning strategies are the epitome of learner choice and self-direction.

Step 3: Consider Integration of Strategy Training In general, as hinted above, it is most helpful to integrate strategy training with the tasks, objectives, and materials used in the regular language training program. Attempts to provide relatively detached, content-independent strategy training have been at best only moderately successful. Learners sometimes rebel against strategy training that is not sufficiently linked with their own language training [22].

When strategy training is closely integrated with language learning, learners better understand how the strategies can be used in a significant, meaningful context [23]. Needless to say, meaningfulness makes it easier to remember the strategies. However, it is also necessary to show learners how to transfer the strategies to new tasks, outside of the immediate ones.

It is also possible to provide detached, nonintegrated strategy training (for instance, a short course on strategies unconnected with current language learning activities), followed by integrated, course-related strategy training. One way to do this is to provide short, well-planned programs of detached training on selected strategies, followed by unobtrusive "prompting" of learning strategies integrated into actual language instruction. The prompts or cues to use certain strategies are gradually faded during regular instruction, so that responsibility for initiation of appropriate learning strategies is eventually transferred from the teacher (or the materials) to the student [24].

Step 4: Consider Motivational Issues Consider the kind of motivation you will build into your training program. Decide whether to give grades or partial course credit for attainment of new strategies, or whether to assume that learners will be motivated to learn strategies purely in order to become more effective learners. Possibly a combination of both motivations will work. Of course, if learners have gone through a strategy assessment phase, their interest in strategies is likely to be heightened, and if you explain how using good strategies can make language learning easier, students will be even more interested in participating in strategy training. Another way to increase motivation is to let learners have some say in selecting the language activities or tasks they will use, or to let them choose the strategies they will learn.

A different type of motivational issue, already hinted at, relates to preexisting cultural (or other) preferences for certain types of strategies. If learners are brought up all their lives to prefer particular learning strategies, like analyzing grammar or memorizing word lists, they may not be highly motivated to drop these preferences and instantly learn a whole new set of strategies. Or they might become confused. You need to be sensitive to learners' original strategy preferences and the motivation that propels these preferences. Being sensitive to this issue does not mean, however, that you should avoid introducing new strategies! It means that you might need to phase in very new strategies gently and gradually, without whisking away students' "security blankets," no matter how dysfunctional you might consider those old strategies to be.

Step 5: Prepare Materials and Activities The materials you are using for language instruction will double well for strategy training materials. In addition, you might develop some handouts on when and how to use the strategies you want to focus on. You might even develop a handbook for learners to use at home and in class, especially if you are planning long-term strategy training. Better yet, get the learners to develop a strategy handbook themselves! They can contribute to it incrementally, as they learn new strategies that prove successful for them. In any case, choose language activities and materials that are likely to be interesting to the learners—or have the students select their own language activities and materials, as mentioned under Step 4.

Step 6: Conduct "Completely Informed Training" As you conduct strategy training, make a special point to inform the learners as completely as possible about why the strategies are important and how they can be used in new situations. Provide practice with strategies in several language tasks, and point out how transfer of strategies is possible from task to task. Give learners the explicit opportunity to evaluate the success of their new strategies, exploring the reasons why these strategies might have helped. Research shows that strategy training which fully informs the learner (by indicating why the strategy is useful, how it can be transferred to different tasks, and how learners can evaluate the success of the strategy) is more successful than training that does not [25].

The following sequence might be useful in presenting a new strategy: First, students try a language task *without* any training in the target strategy, and they comment on the strategies they spontaneously used to do the task. Second, you explain and demonstrate the new strategy. As you do so, build on what the learners said they were doing in the first step and show how they might either improve use of their current strategies or employ an entirely new strategy. Third, learners apply the new strategy to the same language task as before, or a similar one. Depending on the nature of the strategy, it is possible to get pairs of learners to work together to practice the strategy, with one student using the strategy and the other prompting; then they change roles [26].

Of course, completely informed training is undoubtedly the best and most effective training technique. However, in the *very rare* instances when this technique proves impossible, more subtle training techniques might be necessary. For example, when learners are, through cultural influences, adamantly opposed to new learning strategies, you might need to camouflage the new strategies, or introduce them very gradually, paired with strategies the learners already know and prefer [27].

Step 7: Evaluate the Strategy Training Learners' own comments about their strategy use are part of the training itself. These self-assessments provide practice with the strategies of self-monitoring and self-evaluating, and they offer useful data for you. Your own observations, during and after the training and following, are useful for evaluating the success of strategy training. Possible criteria for evaluating training are task improvement, general skill improvement, maintenance of the new strategy over time, transfer of strategy to other relevant tasks, and improvement in learner attitudes [28].

Step 8: Revise the Strategy Training As in any training effort, the evaluation (Step 7) will suggest possible revisions for your materials. This leads right back to Step 1, a reconsideration of the characteristics and needs of the learners in light of the cycle of strategy training that has just occurred. Of course, many of the steps will pass much more quickly after the first cycle. It is not necessary to start from scratch with each step after one cycle has been completed.

Concrete Examples of Strategy Training

A general curricular sequence developed for promoting good reading strategies for language learners, an example of informed training, involves three main procedures: (a) diagnosing the strategies learners already use via a think-aloud procedure, (b) setting the class climate by giving learners a few learning tasks and asking them to explain the strategies they use, and (c) introducing the new strategies and providing plenty of practice [29].

In addition to promoting the use of guessing strategies (a form of compensation strategy), this training sequence also encourages learners to express openly, in a group, their feelings about the effectiveness of the guessing strategies. This kind of evaluative discussion brings in organizational strategies (e.g., self-evaluating), affective strategies (e.g., discussing your feelings with someone else), and social strategies (cooperating with peers, becoming aware of others' thoughts and feelings).

This training sequence illustrates the teaching of strategies for improving target language reading skill, but it can be used for other language skills as well. In addition, any kind of language learning strategies can be taught with this kind of sequence.

Another example of a strategy training sequence, this time focused specifically on English as a second language [30], is similar to the sequence above in informing learners of the value of the strategies and in encouraging the mutually supportive use of different kinds of learning strategies. This sequence suggests encouraging ESL students to practice the new strategies outside of class and asking them to report on their extracurricular use of strategies. It also recommends reminding learners to use the new strategies in other tasks and checking with learners to make sure they are using the new strategies.

In addition to these two strategy training sequences, Chapter 7, on networking, describes many more examples of strategy training modes. The information already presented here and the examples to be presented in the next chapter will help you as you design your own strategy training sequence.

SUMMARY

This chapter has presented tips on assessing your students' strategies and conducting strategy training. The concrete techniques in this chapter will be very valuable in the assessment and training process.

ACTIVITIES FOR READERS

Activity 6.1. Think of Reasons for Assessing Strategy Use

Brainstorm all the reasons you can think of for assessing the kinds of language learning strategies people use. Make a list, then categorize the results.

Activity 6.2. Consider the Strategy Assessment Options

Which types of strategy assessment seem the most relevant to your students? Which could you apply in your own role as teacher? To answer these questions, complete Table 6.3.

Table 6.3 ACTIVITY ON STRATEGY ASSESSMENT OPTIONS

Strategy assessment technique	Purpose	Kind of information gained	Amount of detail (too much, too little, just right?)	Amount of time needed	Ease of adminis- tration and analysis
Observations					
Interviews					
Think-aloud procedures					
Note-taking					
Diaries					
Less-structured surveys					
More-structured surveys					
Combination (specify: ________ ________ ________)					

Source: Original.

Activity 6.3. Assess Your Own Strategies

Choose a technique of strategy assessment described in this chapter. Assess your own language learning strategies. When you have done this, consider what you may have learned about yourself that you did not know before. What implications does this new information have for you as a teacher?

Activity 6.4. Go Fishing

An ancient proverb says, "Give a man a fish and he eats for a day. Teach him how to fish and he eats for a lifetime" [31]. Explain what this saying means to you in the area of language learning and teaching. Give examples from your own experience, or give examples of the way you *wish* your own experience had been.

Now consider Tyacke and Mendelsohn's (1986, p. 178) response to this proverb: "But just as there are many different kinds of rods, different kinds of bait and different fishing locations, all of which offer a variety of choices and experiences, there are different ways of learning language." What does this rejoinder mean to you? How does it affect what you think of the proverb as applied to strategy training? What are the pros and cons of conducting strategy training, from your perspective?

Activity 6.5. Design a Strategy Training Sequence

This chapter offered tips for conducting strategy training. An eight-step system for planning and conducting strategy training was presented, as well as some concrete examples of strategy training designs. Consider these ideas, as well as the examples of real strategy training projects described in Chapter 7. Keeping these recommendations in mind, *design a strategy training sequence for a specific group of learners*.

If you are currently teaching, choose a class that could benefit from strategy training, and focus on designing a training sequence to meet their needs. Alternatively, think of a class you have taught in the past, or describe a hypothetical group of students who have certain characteristics (which you define).

Be as specific as possible in terms of the language activities and materials involved, as well as the strategies to be taught. Go through the first five planning and preparation steps in the training model presented in this chapter. Get feedback from others on your planning and preparation. Then explain in detail how you would handle the next three steps (conducting, evaluating, and revising the training).

EXERCISES TO USE WITH YOUR STUDENTS

Exercise 6.1. Assess Your Students' Strategies

Assess your students' language learning strategies using *at least two* of the techniques described in this chapter. Provide feedback to your students on their strategy use. Discuss which of the assessment techniques seemed to provide the most accurate information.

Exercise 6.2. Implement Strategy Training

Now that you have designed a strategy training program (Activity 6.5), implement it with your students. To do this, use Steps 6, 7, and 8 of the strategy training model. Make your own observations about the most effective and least effective aspects of the training, and ask for feedback from students, too. Consider ways to improve the strategy training.

Exercise 6.3. Develop a "Successful Strategies" Handbook

Ask your students to start contributing to a "Successful Strategies" handbook. It can contain tips on strategies the students find most useful, examples of strategies applied to specific kinds of tasks or materials, comments made during strategy training, selections from learners' diaries about strategies, or any other strategy-related information. Develop the handbook throughout the language course, with students adding to it and using it as a way to share strategy ideas. A loose-leaf notebook will allow easiest access and expansion.

Exercise 6.4. Discuss Diaries

Hold "diary discussions" once a week, perhaps every Friday, as a means of sharing ideas and impressions among students, based on use of strategies with their usual language learning tasks. If you want, provide short amounts of class time periodically for students to write in their diaries. Use of diaries can thus become part of a regular, ongoing strategy assessment and training effort, integrated with normal language activities.

Chapter 7

Networking at Home and Abroad

Example is better than precept.
LATIN PROVERB

PREVIEW QUESTIONS

1. How have language learning strategies been used in diverse settings and programs around the world?
2. What practical differences exist between explicit and implicit encouragement of strategy use?
3. Where can I find resources concerning language learning strategies?

INTRODUCTION TO NETWORKING

As you put language learning strategies into action, you might want to make connections with other people who are interested in strategies and active learning. You are not alone in your interests; other people can help you, and you can help them. You can develop a support network starting at home and reaching around the world. This chapter presents examples of language learning strategies in action in many countries. These resources will provide you with lots of good ideas, as well as people or institutions to contact for more information. The examples are in two general groups: *explicit encouragement of language learning strategies* and *active but implicit stimulation of language learning strategies*. Language learners involved in these examples include tourists, refugees, immigrants, government workers, businesspeople, military personnel, Peace Corps volunteers, and students of all ages enrolled in primary, secondary, and university language programs. They include children, teens, adults, and senior citizens. These examples suggest a wide range of options for using language learning strategies.

EXPLICIT ENCOURAGEMENT OF LANGUAGE LEARNING STRATEGIES

This group includes 11 examples of explicit learning strategy use from the United States, France, the Philippines, England, Denmark, and Israel. Learning strategies are a consistent focus but are handled differently in each of these examples.

The Language Learning Disc: A Videodisk for Training Language Learning Strategies (USA)

Joan Rubin, a founder of the research area of language learning strategies, has produced an exciting instructional tool known as the "Language Learning Disc" [1]. The disk, designed for adults (high school and above), is a two-sided (1-hour) interactive videodisk with five acompanying diskettes providing an average of 8 hours of instruction. This level 3 disk is programmed to run on a Pioneer LDV-1000 player, a Sony PVM 1271Q monitor, and an IBM PC with a Microkey 1000 interface card. With a Microkey 1125 card, other equipment can be substituted. The disk is currently being converted to run on the Sony View system as well.

Intended for use before beginning an introductory-level foreign language course, the disk is designed to help students take charge of their progress by learning how to learn a language. Says Rubin, disk users can expect to

1. Gain insights into their own approach to learning.
2. Learn to choose strategies appropriate to a task and learning purpose.
3. Learn to use these strategies in a classroom, self-study, or job situation.
4. Learn to use strategies specific to reading, listening, and conversation.
5. Be able to define strategies for improving memory for language learning.
6. Learn how to effectively transfer knowledge about language and communication from one language to another.
7. Learn to use resources wisely.
8. Be able to deal more effectively with errors.

Learners can accomplish these purposes using a wide range of topics, including reading an instructional manual to connect a videocassette recorder, watching a spy story, comparing elements of cross-cultural communication, reading a scuba text for new words, or comparing elements used in borrowing money to recognize speech variation. Students can work with 20 languages in this instructional program, thus gaining experience in the process of language learning. The disk includes 13 major dramatic scenarios, 48 locations, and some 60 actors. The four major characters—a military attaché assigned to Korea, a plant manager assigned to Argentina, a Russian translator who will be working on Russian texts and broadcasts, and a Japanese sales manager who will promote Japanese pharmaceuticals in the United States—all provide authentic role models.

Materials are presented in an integrated fashion so that students are exposed to the same strategy in several different lessons. If they don't grasp a strategy in one presentation, they can get it in another. Throughout the material, students can choose the language, the topic, and the level of difficulty. Coaching is provided throughout via inductive inferencing; that is, learners are given clues as to the most appropriate response. As a result of using this instructional material, learners focus on the *process of learning* in order to improve their learning of a foreign language.

The disk uses video in three ways: first, to model natural foreign language communication so that students can observe foreign language speakers using their native language; second, to enable students to participate and get feedback on their choices in a foreign language; and third, to model cognitive approaches to problem solving in foreign language situations. The disk is divided into three main sections: An Introduction; General Language Learning Strategies; and Strategies Related to Reading, Active Listening or Conversation [2]. Field testing of the materials with learners at the Defense Language Institute and at a large international corporation helped to refine the instructions and provide an evaluation of the disk. Responses were very positive.

The disk offers an appealing array of strategies and authentic situations. The technical quality of the presentation and the use of qualified native speakers makes the disk especially valuable. The disk holds promise for a range of language learners in secondary schools, universities, and other institutions. For more information, contact Joan Rubin, P.O. Box 143, Pinole, CA 94564, USA.

CALLA: A Model of Content-Based Language Learning Which Includes Training in Strategies (USA)

The Cognitive Academic Language Learning Approach (CALLA) has been designed by two of the most prolific contributors to the learning strategy area, Anna Uhl Chamot and J. Michael O'Malley. This model [3] embeds training in learning strategies within activities for developing both language skills and content area skills. CALLA provides transitional instruction for upper elementary and secondary students at intermediate and advanced levels of English as a second language. This model also teaches students to use relevant learning strategies to bolster both their language skills and their skills in various content areas. CALLA's purpose is to help learners use English, their new language, to learn through the integration of language and content. The model has three components:

1. The *content component* of the CALLA model represents declarative knowledge, e.g., concepts, facts, and skills for science, mathematics, and social studies, or (in the language area) grammatical, rhetorical, or literary knowledge.
2. The *English language development component* of CALLA aims to teach procedural knowledge that students need to use language as a tool for learning. Students are given practice using language in academic contexts so their language skills become automatic.
3. The *learning strategies instruction component* of the CALLA model suggests ways in which teachers can foster autonomy in their students [4].

Chamot and O'Malley rightly feel that strategies for learning languages and for learning other subjects are often the same, and that learning strategies can give limited English proficient learners a boost as these students prepare to make a transition or move into mainstream classes. The learning strategy instruction component of CALLA therefore shows students how to apply the strategies, suggests a variety of strategies for different tasks, provides examples throughout the curriculum to enhance transfer, and shows how teachers' prompting of strategies can gradually be reduced. Learning strategies are embedded in sample lesson plans in the areas of science, mathematics, and social studies [5]. In addition, the CALLA model includes a generalized lesson plan, divided into five phases: Preparation, Presentation, Practice, Evaluation, and Follow-Up Expansion.

Programs using CALLA are now being implemented in several school districts, and the model is continuing to be refined. The model is valuable for four reasons. First, the linkage between language and content skills using the CALLA model is fruitful. Second, the structured nature of the CALLA lesson plan helps teachers to include the right elements, such as learning strategies, language development, content skills, and ways to assess all three. Third, the model suggests cooperation between language teachers and mainstream content area teachers. While this kind of cooperation is often logistically difficult, it is truly necessary if limited English-proficient learners are to get the best education possible. Fourth, the CALLA model awakens teachers and learners to the possibilities of using learning strategies for both language development and content area skill development.

More information on the model is available from Anna Uhl Chamot, P.O. Box 40937, Washington, DC 20016, USA; or J. Michael O'Malley,

Evaluation Assistance Center-East, Georgetown University, 1916 Wilson Boulevard, Suite 302, Arlington, VA 22201, USA.

The CRAPEL Model of Self-Directed Language Learning (France)

CRAPEL, the Centre de Recherches et d'Applications Pédagogiques en Langues, is part of the Université de Nancy II in France. Since 1974 CRAPEL has been the hub of European research and experimentation on self-directed language learning [6]. CRAPEL provides self-directed language learning opportunities for a variety of learners, such as university students, outside students, and employees in local organizations desiring on-site courses [7]. A variety of course structures is offered, all of which allow some degree of learner autonomy—the ultimate goal.

Learners who choose immediate autonomy are assigned to a "helper," who is a native or competent speaker of English experienced in assisting autonomous learners. The helper consciously avoids the role of tutor or teacher and instead aids the learner in learning how to learn [8]. The helper assists learners at any stage of the learning process, acts as an objective observer, is open to discussion, and gives advice when asked. In addition, the helper provides opportunities for the learner to receive feedback in authentic situations, helps match the learner with peers and with appropriate tasks, offers materials when needed, helps the learner use strategies, keeps detailed notes on the learner, shows sincere caring, and prepares the learner psychologically and environmentally for the task of learning [9].

The learner's role is to take major responsibility for defining needs, goals, priorities; furnishing or selecting materials; organizing learning experiences; determining the pace and time of study; diagnosing his or her own learning difficulties; developing adequate learning techniques; self-monitoring; evaluating progress; and, in general, guiding and planning his or her own learning process. All of these are metacognitive strategies. The learner is also expected to maintain a high level of motivation, which would of course involve affective strategies [10].

The institution must provide a flexible structure allowing for self-direction, rapid availability and reproduction of materials, equipment when needed, contacts with native speakers, and logistical and financial management [11].

The individualized learner–helper design is not the only structure available. In 1977–1978 CRAPEL introduced a group self-tuition structure for senior citizens and others with available free time. In this structure, the group (10 to 15 people) has responsibility for organizing its own learning, after participating in five consecutive half-day sessions on how to do it. Each group defines its objectives, schedules, procedures, and materials.

Helpers take no part in the groups unless called upon, but they and various native speakers are available when needed.

Ongoing research and development occurs constantly at CRAPEL. For more information on CRAPEL and its programs, write Henri Holec, CRAPEL, Université de Nancy II, Nancy, France.

Training in Language Learning Strategies for Peace Corps Language Instructors and Volunteers (Philippines)

In the tropical heat of the Philippines an experiment was undertaken to improve the language learning strategies of students by (a) providing learning strategy materials and (b) influencing the teaching strategies of instructors. The project was a joint effort designed and led by Anne Lomperis, formerly of the Refugee Service Center (Manila Office) of the Center for Applied Linguistics, Washington, DC, USA, and Bibbet Palo, Language Specialist of the Peace Corps/Philippines. These project leaders saw a need for training both instructors and learners in strategies for communicative language teaching and learning as part of a larger training effort.

The language learners were Peace Corps Volunteers (PCVs) learning a variety of languages spoken in the Philippines in preparation for taking on their 2-year assignments in that country. Their language instructors and coordinators were native speakers from the Philippines, who were expected to provide 180 to 190 hours of language instruction to each of the PCVs. They previously had little or no intensive instruction in communicative language teaching strategies or student self-direction.

To help language instructors, coordinators, and PCVs, the Washington staff developed a language learning strategy handbook known as *Improving Your Language Learning: Strategies for Peace Corps Volunteers* [12]. This handbook is simple, direct, and geared toward the specific needs of the Peace Corps in Southeast Asia. The whole range of language learning strategies is included. Using this handbook and other training materials, the project leaders conducted teacher-training sessions on communicative language instruction. Response to the training was very positive. "The [strategy-related] materials . . . were useful and exciting to all; [the language instructors and coordinators] especially were fascinated by the concepts," said one of the leaders [13].

Language instructors and coordinators wanted more information on how learning strategies could be promoted by specific teaching activities. Inspired by the training, one language coordinator created a booklet of teaching activities matched with selected language learning strategies, to be shared with other instructional personnel. The training process had a "spillover effect" throughout the Southeast Asian region. Learning strategy materials were shared with other Peace Corps language staffers at a regional training session in Chieng Mai, Thailand.

In addition to teacher training, diagnosis of strategies was also an important part of the project. Using a short form of the Strategy Inventory for Language Learning (SILL), included in this volume, the project leaders gathered data about language learning strategies typically used by PCVs. For more information, contact Allene Grognet, Center for Applied Linguistics, 1118 - 22nd Street NW, Washington, DC 20037, USA.

A Eurocentre Experiment in Autonomy (England)

As described by Henri Holec, the Eurocentre language training institute in Bournemouth (UK) caters mainly to students who want to be able to live in the country of the target language, and who are less concerned with professional or vocational language requirements. An experiment in autonomous language learning was conducted at the Eurocentre language training institute [14]. This experiment involved continuous self-assessment of oral communicative skills. Even though teachers maintained their traditional, rather directive roles, it was possible to introduce some elements of learner autonomy by using self-assessment strategies. Self-assessment served two purposes: (a) aiding learners to discover and use assessment criteria, and (b) helping them evaluate their own progress in order to plan future activities.

In this project self-assessment was done by means of five diverse activities, ranging from more structured to less structured. Learners were taught to compare their self-assessments with those of others, although this technique had the danger of implying the existence of a single correct judgment. Furthermore, the assessment tools were mostly of the academic type and might not have been greatly relevant to extracurricular situations [15]. However, this was still an interesting and useful experiment in encouraging one important set of learning strategies in a traditional language learning environment. For further information, contact Bournemouth Eurocentre, Bournemouth, Dorset, England.

GRASP: An In-Service Teacher Training Project Involving Self-Direction for Teachers and Learners (England)

Project GRASP (Getting Results and Solving Problems) is a multiyear British project jointly funded by the Department of Trade and Industry; the Comino Foundation, a private educational trust; and Dudley Local Education Authority. This project is coordinated by Anna Smith and Peter

Revill of the Dudley L.E.A. in the English Midlands [16]. The project is concerned with the entire teaching-learning process. It focuses on providing in-service training to teachers, with the objective of encouraging active learning, self-direction, and problem solving for both teachers and students. The expectation is that the effort will lead to better results in the education system as a whole. Project leaders feel that the best way to encourage active learning in students is to train teachers in *teaching strategies* which will facilitate appropriate *learning strategies*. Teacher training must involve active learning and self-responsibility on the part of the teachers themselves, if the ultimate goal is to get students to become active learners [17].

The project involves 12 schools: four comprehensive secondary schools and eight primary schools. Eighty teachers are involved in the project at the moment, but this number will probably grow. Project teachers have responsibility for children aged 8 to 14. Five of the 12 schools are multiethnic and multicultural. Therefore, many project teachers—especially at the primary level—have become, of necessity, teachers of English as a second language as part of their instructional duties. The teaching and learning strategies fostered by this project are designed to have repercussions in all curriculum areas, including language.

To date the in-service has taken the following forms: (a) two 2-day residential conferences for project teachers, (b) one 2-day residential conference for school coordinators, (c) in-house in-service training in each of the schools, and (d) 2-day residential training for each school on team-building strategies. In-service conferences and sessions include active learning for teachers in the form of games, simulations, and other experiential exercises. For active learning purposes, traditional lectures are avoided, though they are not seen as inherently "wrong" in all circumstances. Through a variety of active exercises, teachers experientially learn a curriculum development sequence that consists of designing clear objectives, thinking of as many solutions as possible for achieving each objective (divergent thinking), selecting the best solution or solutions, putting the solution(s) into action, and reviewing the success of the solution(s). Teachers are learning how to make their own teaching strategies more open and more responsive to learners' characteristics. They are encouraged to use these new strategies in their classes and share their experiences with each other.

In this project the teachers are learning new roles and beliefs. They are consciously moving from the role of "fount of all knowledge" to "facilitator of learning," and from the belief of "I'm here to tell you the way" to "I'm here to help you." These changes involve some movement of responsibility to the children and a greater concern for learning strategies. For more details, contact Mrs. A. Smith, Project Deputy, GRASP Project, Dudley Teachers' Centre, Laburnum Road, Kingswinford, West Midlands, DY6 8EH, England.

Strategy Training in Primary School Classes Involving English as a Foreign Language (Denmark)

"The Flower Model" is the evocative name of Leni Dam's approach to primary school language instruction in Denmark [18]. The model assumes learner responsibility from the start and has been used with full classes in the range of 20 to 30 students. The children are in their first year of English and have 4 hours per week of English. In this model, students work out their own needs and interests, arrange their own syllabuses, make decisions, and form contracts with the teacher.

The model of language education is represented as a series of petals on a flower, as shown in Figure 7.1. In the center of the flower is the word NEGOTIATION. The petals include Objectives, Activities, Outcomes, Evaluation, Pupils' Contributions, and Materials. On each of the petals its concept is broken down into components; for example, the concept Pupils' Contributions is divided into emotions, attitudes, values, background, abilities, strategies, needs, interests, knowledge, and skills. There are arrows from the central part, NEGOTIATION, to each of the petals, and each of the petals is linked with all the other petals through a network of arrows. The Teacher's Contributions/Role is shown at the bottom of the flower in a rectangle.

At the beginning of the course learners are asked why they are learning English and what they want to do with the language. This helps learners decide on their own language needs. In the initial period, no text is used, and learning is based on materials the learners bring in themselves: stickers, stamps, children's books, jokes, magazines. Grammar is not taught explicitly, but children work out structure inductively and then make grammar wall-posters with the help of their teacher. Children are given interesting activities from which to choose. The teacher introduces a completed worksheet, and later students learn to do their own worksheets, gradually taking increased responsibility for choosing topics, deciding on what to achieve, specifying objectives, and evaluating progress. Specifying objectives is often very difficult for the students, who need a lot of help from the teacher at first but who gradually learn to do it. Regular self-evaluation is also part of the process. Learners' self-evaluations are generally very positive, both toward their language progress and toward their ability to make decisions about their own learning.

In this ambitious scheme, primary-school language learners are motivated by a variety of materials and activities, a range of possible strategies, and the chance to make decisions for themselves. Dam's own students are typically from working-class backgrounds and are *not* college-bound. That the model could work for such children makes the possibility of transfer to many other settings even greater. For information, write Leni Dam, Paedagogisk Central, Hundige Boulevard 11, 2670 Greve Strand, Denmark.

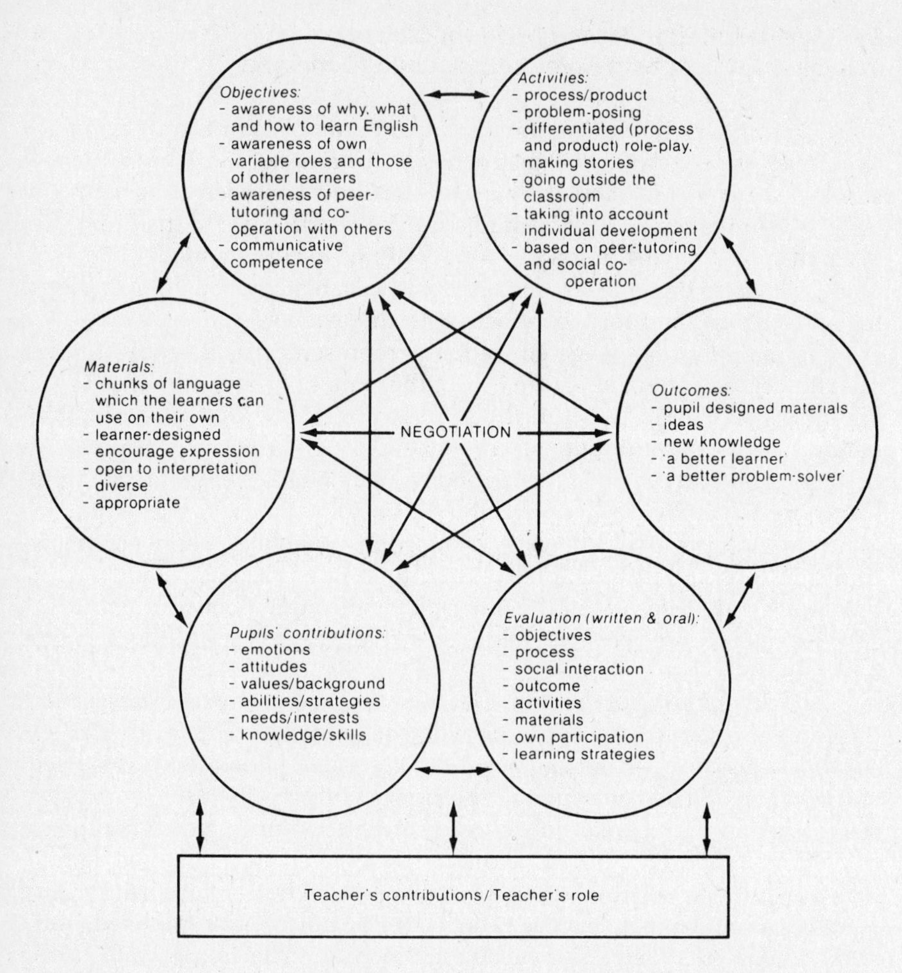

Figure 7.1 The Flower Model. (*Source*: Dam, cited in Dickinson (1987, p. 62).)

Exploring Language Learning in a University Language Institute (USA)

In a project at the intensive American Language Program of Columbia University, Anita Wenden explored a variety of language learning aspects, one of which was learning strategies [19]. She developed materials to be used with two multiethnic groups of very advanced learners of English. Wenden told the students that 2 of the class hours ordinarily devoted to developing conversational fluency would focus on the topic of language learning. According to Wenden, the goal was to sharpen and expand student awareness of various aspects of their language learning experience, including the following:

1. Strategies they utilized.
2. Aspects of language they attended to.
3. Their evaluation of their language proficiency (i.e., performance and competence as the outcome of their learning endeavors).
4. Criteria used for judging the usefulness of various learning contexts and strategies.
5. Their objectives.
6. Themselves as facilitating or inhibiting language learning (e.g., feelings, language aptitude, personality).
7. Their beliefs about how best to learn a language.

Each of these aspects formed the basis of a module, with modules reflecting "informed training" (see Chapter 6). As described by Wenden, materials comprised minilectures and readings about language learning, research findings on learning strategies, and student accounts of their learning. She provided training tasks, such as comprehension exercises, class discussions based on the reading or listening passages, outside language practice, and writing diaries.

As explained by Wenden, one class mutinied against the training program and dropped out, except for a small cadre of learners who met after school; the other class cooperated in a purely mechanical fashion. She traced the problem to the lack of integration of the learner training materials with the language training tasks and objectives. After she revised the materials to integrate them more closely with the language tasks and objectives, students became much more interested, thus underscoring the power of integrated rather than detached strategy training (see Chapter 6). It might also have helped to give the learners a choice about the nature of the training and to make sure that the materials were geared directly to the needs of these very advanced students. A less dedicated individual than Wenden might have given up in frustration, but she wisely persevered—with much more successful results after the revision. For complete details, contact Anita Wenden, 97-37 63rd Road, 15E, Forest Hills North, NY 11374.

"Language Therapy" in a Multiage Setting (Israel)

Andrew Cohen, a well-known researcher and teacher from the Hebrew University of Jerusalem, has become an unofficial "language therapist" for students of many ages at Ulpan Akiva in South Netanya, Israel [20]. Ulpan Akiva was founded 30 years ago by Shulamith Katznelson, who is still the director. Katznelson won the Israeli Knesset Education Prize for her outstanding work in bringing together peoples of different races, religions, ethnic backgrounds, and nations for "more than just language learning," as Cohen puts it. Striving to create peace, the Ulpan serves a variety of students—Jewish immigrants trying to improve their Hebrew, West Bank and Gaza Arabs sent by their employers to study Hebrew, other resident non-Jews such as diplomats, and tourists wanting to learn Hebrew. Ages range from teens to 80s.

Cohen's work at Ulpan Akiva started when he went there 8 years ago to study Arabic. As soon as he arrived as a student, the Ulpan put him to work as a lecturer because of his language instruction background. He has been going there once a month ever since, each time giving two formal, hour-long talks to the current students, usually about 40 to 50 students per talk. One of the sessions is in English and the other in Hebrew (for more advanced students). The talks concern various aspects of strategy use and self-direction. Themes vary—for instance, strategies for paying attention, for vocabulary learning, and for developing speaking, writing, and reading skill. When discussing strategies for speaking and writing, Cohen stresses that the payoff of error correction depends on when and how the correction is offered and how the learner relates to it. The talks are spontaneous and lively, trying to awaken students from their apathy. Cohen's particular challenge is coaching senior citizens learning Hebrew; he calls it "the old dog/new tricks syndrome." No empirical research exists on the effects of the talks, but Cohen receives feedback—sometimes ebullient—from students who try new strategies.

During his monthly visits, Cohen not only gives the two talks described above, but he also leads two informal rap sessions, each an hour long, one in Hebrew and the other in English. The title of the rap sessions is "Everything you ever wanted to know about language learning but were afraid to ask." Says Cohen, "And the students really do ask! In many ways I have become a language therapist at Ulpan Akiva."

Cohen is a rare combination of hard-nosed researcher and empathetic human being, with the knack of applying learning strategy research to practical language learning situations. At the Ulpan he provides awareness training (see Chapter 6), which gives encouragement as well as basic information about a variety of strategies. Because he visits the Ulpan only once a month, he cannot conduct continuous, integrated strategy training from day to day. Instead, he inspires learners to try better strategies on their own through his mixture of new information, humor, and friendly cajoling. For further information, contact Andrew Cohen, School of Education, Hebrew University, 91905 Jerusalem, Israel.

Strategy Training in a Typical University Spanish Class (USA)

Roberta Lavine, coordinator of teaching assistants and professor of Spanish at the University of Maryland, applied the concepts in this book to explore the use of strategies with a class of 22 second-semester Spanish students [21]. She initially used formal presentations about strategies but soon found that students' strategies improved most when strategy training was integrated into regular classroom activities in an informal, natural way rather than remaining abstract and disconnected from ongoing classroom work.

During the strategy training process she used a range of communicative classroom activities, some suggested by this book and some self-created, each time making specific suggestions to her students about the kinds of learning strategies they might employ with these activities. Students responded positively to these efforts and began to examine their strategies for the first time. Lavine successfully changed the classroom climate by introducing affective strategies to reduce anxiety. She also stressed that it was all right to make mistakes or ask friends for help in class—new ideas to most of the students.

Through diaries, classroom discussions, and peer sharing, the students periodically evaluated their old and new learning strategies, identifying the ones that worked best. Students liked sharing their strategies and coaching each other on how to learn more effectively. Of the newly introduced strategies, some of the most useful were metacognitive strategies, especially purposeful listening and planning for language tasks; social strategies, such as cooperating with peers and asking questions; compensation strategies, like guessing meanings and "talking around" an unknown word; and affective strategies, including the use of laughter and deep breathing. Before the training began, the students were unaware that they were already using a fairly extensive range of memory strategies, especially those involving imagery. Strategy training helped them become conscious of their ordinary use of these strategies. During the training they greatly increased their use of association and other memory strategies.

After the training, Lavine stated, "The difference is mindblowing. The great majority of the students show an openness and willingness to try things. Before it was just fear. . . . What my students gained was an awareness of an attitude for life, for learning in general, not just for learning Spanish. The most beneficial, long-lasting effect wasn't learning any particular strategy; it was a general awareness of how to learn, listen, speak, and better themselves. . . . This means willingness to assume responsibility." In regard to learners, here is the most telling comment of all: "Students are now saying, 'I never knew before that you could *use* this language!'"

Strategy training had an effect on Lavine's teaching. "It was really exciting for me. It helped me realize that I had to write on the board more, had to provide more visual clues, had to explain some things in English and not just in the target language. Before this, the frustration level was so high . . . and some students tuned out. Now I am changing my own teaching habits."

Other teachers have expressed keen interest in finding out about the learning strategies, so Lavine has started organizing in-service training sessions for them. She is continuing to work with strategy training and assessment in her own classes and is now analyzing data from studies of learners' diaries. For additional information, contact Roberta Z. Lavine, 4120 Alfalfa Terrace, Olney, MD 20832, USA.

Strategy Training with Adult Refugees (Denmark)

Will Sutter, an Australian-born language teacher and administrator in the Danish Refugee Council and the North Jutland Department of Adult Education in Aalborg, Denmark, conducted strategy training with approximately 100 students of Danish as a second language (DSL) in 12 classes [22]. The classes, which were chosen to include a variety of nationalities, ages, proficiency levels, and amounts of DSL-learning experience, were taught by Sutter and other teachers at the language training school of the Danish Refugee Council. Participating teachers used the strategy training exercises presented in this book for 2 months in any way they desired, with no restrictions on how or how often. According to Sutter, the most effective teachers were those who intentionally incorporated strategy training exercises into regular classroom activities, treated learning strategies as a means of enhancing the progress students were already making, and showed a consistent desire to enable students to take more responsibility for their own learning. Less successful teachers had very different characteristics. They did not try to integrate strategy training with normal classroom activities, they used the exercises in an obviously remedial, last-ditch effort to help demoralized students, or they viewed strategy training as a "vacation" from language teaching.

Three-fourths of the students found the strategy training exercises highly useful. According to Sutter, even more students would have profited from the exercises if strategy training had been made an integral part of the language course from the start. Particular students, notably those culturally accustomed to obeying authority without question, gave up their old strategies without understanding why, just because their teachers presented new strategies. These students could have used special help in learning to assess the value of various strategies.

In describing the most positive aspects of the training, Sutter said, "The students felt it was fun exploring new strategies and discovering their already existing learning processes. Certainly the more entertaining brain-teaser activities were very popular and students caught on quickly. Catching on made the exercises even more appealing. Many of the strategy training exercises (particularly those with communicative undertones) are already embodied in the teaching materials used daily; however, regarding them as strategy exercises had some surprisingly positive effects. I was also pleasantly surprised by how *teachers* became eager to make use of the exercises as their own personal 'think-aloud' tests of their students," said Sutter.

Students especially liked memory strategies, such as grouping and labeling, and enjoyed exercises which had humor or intellectual challenge, like Inventions (see Chapter 3), which they practiced repeatedly in their own free time. Metacognitive strategies were also well accepted. Students' willingness to participate in group learning activities blossomed with their increased awareness of the benefits of social strategies and with their realization that these activities made learning more fun. One class used the affective strategy of diary-keeping as the basis for a weekly discussion.

According to Sutter, language teachers specifically require two things: first, to be helped "out of the pit of 'approach-consciousness'—that is, a focus on particular instructional methods—so that they can pay more attention to learning strategies; and second, to be equipped to use more formalized strategy training practices." Sutter concluded, "It's very important to teach students how to transfer strategies and apply them to new language tasks. It's also important to work on the attitudes of teachers, so that they believe in learning strategies and want to integrate them into the regular language program." More information on Sutter's work with learning strategies (and his research on learning styles) is available by writing to Will Sutter, Terpetvej 160, 9830 Taars, Denmark.

The previous examples have described explicit strategy training in settings around the world. However, strategies can be implicitly encouraged even without overt strategy training, as you will see next.

ACTIVE BUT IMPLICIT SIMULATION OF LANGUAGE LEARNING STRATEGIES

The following examples—two from the United States, one worldwide, and one from Hungary—are outstanding cases of experiential language learning, in which the learners become highly motivated to use a wide range of learning strategies. These examples do not point out to the learners the specific language learning strategies they are using, why those strategies are good, and how they might be transferred to other settings or tasks. These excellent illustrations of active language learning might be even more powerful if strategy training were overtly included.

Language Learning Strategies in High-Technology Simulations (USA)

Language learning strategy use is fostered by imaginative and innovative high-technology simulations developed at the Massachusetts Institute of Technology. The Athena Language Learning Project, directed by Janet Murray at the Massachusetts Institute of Technology and sponsored by the Annenberg/CPB Project, is now producing high-technology prototypes for Spanish, French, German, Russian, Japanese, and English as a second language. Described here are two of these prototypes, both simulations combining a communicative approach to language learning with technological capabilities in an interactive videodisk [23].

NO RECUERDO ("I Don't Remember") is an interactive videodisk project now in development with Douglas Morgenstern as the instructional director. The language learner types in the original input in Spanish; the output consists of various combinations of still photos, film and video segments, audio, text, and graphics. This is a highly contextualized, long-term simulation using real-world data—principally based on explorations of Bogota, Colombia—combined with a fictional story containing elements of romance, intrigue, and science fiction. The learner "communicates" with two protagonists and often sees scenes from their conflicting memories. The result is a system of "multiple realities" with which the learner must deal.

DIRECTION PARIS, instructionally directed by Gilberte Furstenberg, is a sequence of activities based on three half-hour videodisks. One of these is a narrative, *A la rencontre de Philippe*, which focuses on Philippe, who asks the student to help him find an apartment in Paris. The student travels around the city, visiting numerous apartments. In Philippe's current apartment the student uses the telephone and the answering machine and finds clues to other apartments to rent. The student must make quick decisions about which apartments to see and whether to relay information from one character to another. Instead of helping Philippe find an apartment, the student may choose to make a guidebook to Paris by using a second videodisk, a documentary providing an incomplete guidebook; or the student may explore the neighborhood of St. Gervais by using the third videodisk, a documentary called *A la découverte d'un quartier*.

In these high-technology simulations, learners are entertained and motivated by interaction with various characters and exploration of diverse locales. In addition, the nature of the material challenges learners to rely on themselves and especially to call upon their own cognitive, metacognitive, affective, compensation, and memory strategies. If these simulations were adapted for use with small groups, social strategies would also be involved. Thus, the best computer-assisted language learning, especially when enhanced by interactive videodisk capabilities, can be an exciting, strategy-rich means of language learning. For more details on Project

Athena, contact Janet H. Murray, 20B-231, Massachusetts Institute of Technology, Cambridge, MA 02139, USA.

Language Learning Strategies in Low-Technology Simulations for Learning Spanish (USA)

A number of low-technology, classroom-based simulations not requiring computer or videodisk were designed by Douglas Morgenstern [24] for students of Spanish, but they could easily be adapted to other languages and other cultural settings. These simulations have been successfully run at Stanford University, Harvard University Extension (adult classes), and Massachusetts Institute of Technology as a regular part of the curriculum.

One of these simulations is called NEW IDENTITY, which lasts from 1 to 2 hours and can be spread over several classes. Each participant receives a handout sheet to complete as an assignment or else at the beginning of the in-class activity. Each person is to take on a new identity as a Hispanic residing in an unspecified Latin American city. Participants are given a choice of four Hispanic surnames and four places of work (restaurant, clinic, store, or bank). They are asked to form new family groups and workplace groups by a process of negotiation and information exchange.

After this preparatory work, semi-improvised scenes are presented, first by family groups and then by workplace groups. An interesting audience–performer relationship is created, because members of the audience are referred to and can later react when it is their time to perform. Debriefing occurs after scenes are presented. The facilitator gives observations on linguistic and cultural appropriateness of the performers' behavior, and a lively discussion often ensues.

This is just one of the simulations created by Morgenstern. All are different in tone and format, but each simulation encourages use of a wide array of language learning strategies—sometimes even more than do high-technology simulations. Unaided by fancy computers, low-technology simulations like NEW IDENTITY generally promote greater use of social strategies and authentic communication among learners. For more information contact Douglas Morgenstern, Foreign Languages and Literatures, Massachusetts Institute of Technology, Cambridge, MA 02139, USA.

Strategies in a Multilingual, International Simulation Using Telecommunications (Worldwide)

Another simulation, known as ICONS (International COmmunication and Negotiation Simulation), encourages the use of diverse language learning strategies in a worldwide, computer-networked telecommunications effort involving multiple teams and many languages [25]. ICONS was developed by Jonathan Wilkenfeld and Richard Brecht at the University of Maryland, and is based on POLIS, pioneered by Robert Noel at the University of California at Santa Barbara. European coordination of ICONS is traditionally provided by David Crookall in France, and South American coordination by Leopoldo Schapira in Argentina.

ICONS currently involves about 20 university teams and seven languages: English, French, German, Hebrew, Japanese, Russian, and Spanish. Each university team represents a different country in an international political scenario. Some of the teams represent their own countries, e.g., Argentina, Brazil, Chile, Canada, England, France, Israel, Japan, and the United States. Other countries are represented by nonnatives; for example, American teams currently represent the Soviet Union and China. Month-long simulation sessions occur twice a year. Throughout the simulation, an electronic newspaper, *The Diplomat*, inserts new data into the simulation and also plays the role of an ordinary newspaper. A range of international policy issues is explored: superpower relations, European integration, Middle-East conflicts, North–South relations, world economic policies, human rights, the Gulf War, NATO, OECD, and international trade, for example.

Communications between country-teams occur through a variety of computer technologies, which allow the simulation to run in "real time." Local microcomputers are equipped with word processors, telecommunications software, and modems. The microcomputers are linked via international telecommunications data networks—i.e., national packet switching systems connected by satellite—into a central computer (situated at the University of Maryland and equipped with sophisticated and easy-to-use software). While electronic mail is the primary mode, occasional "real-time" teleconferences are held in which participants throughout the world gather at their computer terminals for simultaneous discussions or negotiations on particular issues.

Many metacognitive, cognitive, compensation, and social strategies are implicitly encouraged by ICONS. Two broad types of foreign language skills are involved, translation and reading. In ICONS, a foreign language is no longer an abstract system devoid of meaning or consequence; it becomes a purposeful, authentic, and communicative activity, because the state of the world depends upon a full understanding of foreign language messages. Typically more than 3,000 messages, many over a page in length, are exchanged during a month-long exercise. For more information, contact Jonathan Wilkenfeld, Department of Government and Politics, Lefrak Hall, University of Maryland, College Park, MD 20742, USA.

Learning Strategies Encouraged by Games for Students of English as a Foreign Language (Hungary)

Maria Matheidesz and her colleagues are using a series of games for students of English as a foreign language in Budapest, Hungary. These games call forth the use of learning strategies in many of the same ways as did the simulations described above [26]. In a 2-year project funded by the Soros Foundation, Matheidesz is working with English language teachers at four Hungarian secondary schools. The skilled and enthusiastic project teachers have decided to concentrate on the age range of 15- to 16-year-olds, i.e., Form 2. This project involves just one selected class per teacher (generally 15 to 20 students per class). Thus, four groups/classes of students are included in the project. Project teachers are working together to make games more popular among other teachers, who receive demonstration classes and seminars about language games.

The English teaching-learning situation in Budapest is typical of foreign language teaching and learning in many other places. Class exposure is limited to 3 to 5 hours per week. Access to English-language materials (newspapers, magazines, and films) and native English speakers is severely limited. Although plenty of English pop music is available, it provides only listening practice, not speaking practice. In this relatively impoverished English-language situation, teachers must seek out interesting, communicative classroom activities so their students can develop the English-language skills they desire. The Hungarian government and the school each provide a syllabus or set of instructional guidelines for English-language teachers, but teachers are also allowed to improvise to a certain extent.

Matheidesz is working with the teachers in her project to use a set of low-technology games which she personally developed. Teachers are encouraged to fit the games, which last from 10 to 45 minutes, into their normal classroom activities whenever they can. Some of these games have been commercially published under the name "96," also known as SPEAKING FACES [27]. SPEAKING FACES games deal with packs of 96 cards, each card containing a professional-quality photograph of a face. Many kinds of faces are included: young, old, plain, attractive, sad, happy, tired, animated, multiethnic. The learners' self-generated descriptions of the people represented by these faces form the basis of many SPEAKING FACES games. All communication takes place using English as a foreign language. Not all 96 cards are used for every activity.

The many games available through SPEAKING FACES demonstrate six principles. First, faces of people are endlessly interesting, providing many clues about emotions, occupations, ages, education levels, experiences, and family relationships. Second, imagery is a powerful motivator as well as a useful learning strategy. Third, students can communicate using the same set of materials over and over in different ways—without ever getting bored or frustrated. Fourth, any teacher, just like Matheidesz, can think creatively and come up with interesting materials for communicative language learning. Fifth, low technology can work as well as high technology in encouraging students to learn. Sixth, good materials foster the use of an extensive array of language learning strategies [28].

Informal observations show that learners become very involved in the games. Students communicate with each other more naturally and use a wider variety of cognitive, metacognitive, affective, compensation, and social strategies in the games than in traditional classroom activities. Formal questionnaires so far indicate that students and teachers feel very positive about the games. Later on, Matheidesz will videotape each group to analyze in more detail the language learning strategies used during game playing [29]. Contact Maria Matheidesz, Budapest XII, Borbala 3, 1121 Hungary, for more information.

SUMMARY

This chapter has presented examples of language learning strategies in action around the world. The first group of examples includes explicit training or discussion of strategies. The second group of examples demonstrates how active learning techniques implicitly stimulate the use of language learning strategies.

It would be good to bring together the two modes—that is, to wed the explicit strategy focus with the focus on general active learning principles and techniques. This aim could be accomplished in two ways. First, make sure that active learning techniques and a degree of participant choice are the basis of all training—of learners and teachers alike—which focuses on language learning strategies. Second, add to active language learning experiences an explicit element of strategy training.

ACTIVITIES FOR READERS

Activity 7.1. Assess the Relevance of Examples for Your Own Setting

Review the examples given here. On the basis of the descriptions in this chapter, which examples provide the most useful ideas for your own setting? Why? How could you use the ideas presented in these examples? Be as specific as possible.

Activity 7.2. Follow Up on Your Three Favorite Examples

Write or call the contact people listed for at least three of the examples. Ask for information. When you receive the information, determine what is useful to you and how you can apply it.

Activity 7.3. Take a Closer Look at Explicit Training Examples

Answer the following questions, either alone or with others. Use brainstorming techniques where appropriate.

1. How were the needs of the learners taken into consideration by the 11 examples of explicit strategy encouragement?
2. Which of these examples used active, experiential learning principles?
3. Which seemed to most clearly embody self-direction and autonomy for learners in the way the activities or materials were structured?
4. Which were examples of informed training, in which the value and significance of the strategies were made clear?
5. In which of the examples did you find complete integration between strategy training and language instruction? a moderate level of integration? no integration?

Activity 7.4. Take a Closer Look at Implicit Strategy Encouragement

Answer the following questions, either alone or with others. Use brainstorming techniques when appropriate.

1. Look at each of the four examples of implicit strategy encouragement. In what way could strategy use be made more explicit in each of these examples? What would be the effect?
2. What do all these examples have in common? List as many characteristics as you can think of.
3. What makes these examples so exciting and effective in a language learning situation?
4. What other examples of active, experiential language learning do you know about? Have you used some of these? How successful were they, and why? How did they implicitly or explicitly involve language learning strategies?

EXERCISES TO USE WITH YOUR STUDENTS

Exercise 7.1. Experiment!

After contacting some of the resource people mentioned in this chapter, try out their programs, activities, games, or simulations with your students.

Exercise 7.2. Find Out Which Strategies Are Used

In conducting the experiment in Exercise 7.1, observe the strategies of your students, or better yet, do think-aloud interviews to find out what strategies your students are using. Ask your students if they are learning any differently as a result of the new activities, and allow them to discuss this among themselves.

Epilogue

Where to Go from Here

The best is yet to be.
ROBERT BROWNING

You have been on a journey with this book. Your travels began as you examined language learning strategies in general terms in the first chapter. Next you discovered direct strategies—memory, cognitive, and compensation—and applied them to the four language skills. Then you explored indirect strategies—metacognitive, affective, and social—and learned how they could enhance all the language skills. Traveling on, you considered techniques for assessing and teaching language learning strategies. Finally, you found a number of resources for strategic networking, some relatively close to home and some in distant countries. In the course of these travels, you encountered a wealth of practical activities to do yourself and exercises to use with your students.

Now you have reached the epilogue, a milestone in your travels. However, your journey does not end here; in a real sense it has just begun. Do not put this book on the shelf and say, "That's nice, but I'm too busy to do anything with language learning strategies." Use what you have learned here to help your students become better language learners, able to use their new language communicatively both now and when you are no longer there to help them. Language skills and self-reliance *can* and *must* develop together. You can assist this process by helping your students use appropriate strategies.

If you have not already begun to work with learning strategies, quickly review the first five chapters to make sure you understand the principles and applications. Then assess your students' strategies and begin to conduct strategy training using the eight-step model (see Chapter 6), as well as the student exercises found throughout this book. If you need help, start creating a support network for yourself by calling or writing some of the experienced individuals mentioned in the book, especially those in Chapter 7. Find other sources of ideas using the reference list. Your understanding of strategies will grow by leaps and bounds once you begin putting strategies into practice.

Maybe you have been fostering good language learning strategies in your students for a long time. Even if you are already a promoter of strategies or a veteran strategy expert, you might use this book as a springboard to deeper explorations of strategies in all four language skill areas. Adapt this book's exercises, activities, and training and assessment procedures to your own needs, and expand your existing network of strategy colleagues.

Of course, this book is not the final word on language learning strategies. Much more remains to be discovered about how people learn languages and exactly how conscious use of learning strategies aids the process. Although some technical mysteries still exist, research and practice both indicate that strategies can increase learners' language proficiency, self-confidence, and motivation. Continue your explorations, and help your students tap the power of language learning strategies.

Notes

CHAPTER 1

1. This book has a very practical slant and is directed mainly toward teachers of second or foreign languages. Other very different but helpful kinds of resources might include edited books, each containing a variety of viewpoints (e.g., O'Neil, 1978; Weinstein, Goetz, & Alexander, 1988; Wenden & Rubin, 1987), books presenting hints for language learners (e.g., Rubin & Thompson, 1982), books on self-directed language learning (e.g., Holec, 1980, 1981; Dickinson, 1987), books on communication strategies (e.g., Faerch & Kasper, 1983b), and books addressing both learners and teachers simultaneously (e.g., Cohen, in press). For research findings, see notes below.
2. Krashen (1982).
3. Littlewood (1984).
4. These include Campbell and Wales (1970), Canale and Swain (1980), Hymes (1972), and Omaggio (1986).
5. See, e.g., H. D. Brown (1984).
6. Littlewood (1984) explains in greater depth the differences between foreign and second language learning.
7. Lobuts and Pennewill (1989, p. 177).
8. See Savignon (1983).
9. Other concepts related to communicative competence are *proficiency* and *achievement*. Proficiency is the degree of skill measured without reference to a particular curriculum, and achievement is the degree of skill measured with reference to a particular curriculum. Proficiency and achievement each have two parts: *competence*, i.e., what the learner knows, and *performance*, which reflects competence and is observable/measurable (Savignon, 1972). Chomsky (1965) proposed yet another distinction between competence and performance. Canale (1983) stated that the distinction between competence and performance is not well understood, and he circumvented the issue by avoiding the term *performance* (i.e., using the term *actual communication* instead of, for example, *communicative performance*). For further information on issues related to perfor-

mance or competence, see Bachman (forthcoming), Clark (1972), Munby (1978), Omaggio (1986), Rivera (1984), and Wesche (1983).

10. For instance, see Faerch and Kasper (1983a).

11. This well-known model is by Canale and Swain (1980), further developed by Canale (1983).

12. The concepts of coherence and cohesion were originally described by Widdowson (1978).

13. A specific example of this is the statement "Tactics is the art of using troops in battle; strategy is the art of using battles to win wars" (Von Clausewitz, cited in James, 1984, p. 15).

14. The *adversarial, competitive* aspect of strategy use has prevailed for centuries. The concept of strategy has spread outside the bounds of physical warfare into a variety of other conflict or threat situations, such as business, politics, games, and even conversations—all of which have been viewed by some as battles of will or wits. However, recent examples exist of the *nonadversarial, cooperative* use of strategies to reach a goal or complete an action. For instance, strategies are used by depressed people to escape from their mental prisons (Rowe, 1983), by spiders to spin webs (Koestler, 1964), by gamers to cooperate rather than to compete with each other (Colman, 1982; Hart & Simon, 1988; Oppenheimer & Winer, 1988), by speakers to communicate (Faerch & Kasper, 1983b; Littlewood, 1984), and by language learners to operate a computer simulation (Diadori, 1987). Riley (1985) explicitly calls for linguists to formally recognize the collaborative aspect of strategies.

15. Alternative terms which have been used (appropriately or not) for learning strategies include *tactics, techniques, potentially conscious plans, consciously employed operations, learning skills, functional skills, cognitive abilities, processing strategies, problem-solving procedures,* and *basic skills* (Wenden, 1987). Learning strategies have also been called *thinking skills, thinking frames, reasoning skills, basic reasoning skills,* and *learning-to-learn skills*. Most, but not all, of these terms focus on the rational, cognitive aspects of learning strategies, ignoring—at our own peril and that of our students—the emotional and social aspects.

16. See Rigney (1978) and Dansereau (1985).

17. These features are distilled from many sources. See the lists of features of language learning strategies in Chamot (1987), Wenden (1987), Oxford (1985a, 1986f), Oxford, Lavine, and Crookall (1989), and other sources in the reference list.

18. See Oxford, Lavine, and Crookall (1989) for more details on the communicative approach and language learning strategies.

19. Two terms, *learner self-direction* and *learner autonomy*, are often applied in relation to language learning strategies. These terms have been used in various ways. For instance, Dickinson (1987) used *self-direction* to refer to the learner's attitude of responsibility, and he used *autonomy* to refer to the learning mode, situation,

or techniques associated with the responsible attitude. Holec (1980, 1981) used the same two terms in reverse, with *self-direction* referring to the learning mode, situation, or techniques and *autonomy* referring to the learner's attitude.

20. See Knowles (1976).

21. See Wenden (1987).

22. These two quotations are by Gibson (1973, p. 72) and Harmer (1983, p. 203). Other interesting comments on teachers' roles are found in T. Wright's (1987) chapter, "Teaching Tasks and Strategies."

23. See Wenden (1985a) for more details on teachers' expanded role.

24. See Holec (1981).

25. For instance, Chamot (1987) says, "Learning strategies are intentional on the part of the learner."

26. A very different example of unconscious use of learning strategies occurs when the lesson itself encourages the learner to use certain strategies. For example, lesson-controlled preview questions, comprehension questions, and metaphor-based explanation techniques all encourage learners to use certain strategies, although learners might not be aware of doing so. Learning in this way can be very efficient. However, if learners become *aware* of the strategies they are using in these instances and how such strategies work, they will find it easier to transfer them to new situations or other kinds of materials.

27. This book rejects the unnecessary distinction between training and education, in which trainers sometimes view educators as impractical, grandiose, and insufficiently grounded, and educators occasionally see trainers as superficial, mechanistic, and representative of stimulus-response behaviorism.

28. See Oxford (1989) for a complete review of these factors.

29. Leaning toward caution, this book avoids the term *taxonomy*, which implies a clear set of hierarchical relationships. None of the strategy classification systems currently available should be called a taxonomy, despite earlier usage of the term (see Oxford, 1985a, 1986f). The strategy classification system in this book owes a great deal to the excellent work of Chamot, O'Malley, Dansereau, and Rubin, but the present author takes responsibility for the categories and definitions used here.

30. For the most detailed discussion of problems in defining and classifying language learning strategies, see Oxford, Cohen, and Sutter (in press). See also O'Malley, Chamot, Stewner-Manzanares, Küpper, and Russo (1985).

31. Holec (1981, p. 3).

32. The Embedded Strategies Game is original. However, in another context Bob Burbridge of the UN Language School also thought of the idea of giving funny names to language learning strategies. He cleverly devised such strategy names as Samuel Pepys, Mona Lisa, Fortunetelling, Freebies, and Dental Work. Figure those out!

CHAPTER 2

1. This is called the "loci" or "places" technique. For a wonderful explanation of oral memory strategies, see Ong (1987).

2. The precise physical workings of memory are much more complex and less well understood than these simple memory principles. Memory is still the "black hole in the center of neurobiology" (Begley, Springen, Katz, Hager, & Jones, 1986a, p. 48). See human neurobiology texts for information on brain processes, including memory; see also Begley et al., 1986a, 1986b, for a simplified discussion of memory-related brain structures and of electrochemical and biochemical changes caused by memory formation. The traditional belief is that the left hemisphere of the brain is for storage of speech and language, while the right is for spatial, pictorial, and other nonverbal stimuli. However, new evidence (Goleman, 1986; Van Lancker, 1987) suggests that this distinction may not be totally accurate. Researchers have made progress in understanding the physical aspects of short-term and long-term memory, such as protein synthesis and modification (Leaver, 1984). Short-term and long-term memory appear to be differently constructed systems. Moreover, there are different kinds of long-term memory (Baddeley, 1986; Tulving, 1985) and even different kinds of short-term memory. Howard (1983) provides a succinct and interesting discussion of network theories of long-term memory, including episodic and semantic memory.

3. Thompson (1987) raises questions about whether memory strategies lead the learner *away* from meaning. However, the correct use of memory strategies to learn languages necessarily involves meaning. After all, that is what semantic memory is all about!

4. Lord, quoted in Hague (1987, p. 221).

5. Cognitive psychologists such as Anderson (1976, 1983, 1985) have identified two major kinds of knowledge: *declarative knowledge* (facts, definitions, rules, images, and sequences) and *procedural knowledge* (skills, such as applying and using rules). Both knowledge types are helpful in language learning, especially for adolescents and adults. Declarative and procedural knowledge are stored differently in memory. Anderson assumes that declarative knowledge is stored as nodes, associated by links of various types, while procedural knowledge is stored via "production systems" (if-then systems involving conditions and actions) in three stages, ranging from conscious to automatic. For details on how this theory relates to language learning, see O'Malley, Chamot, and Walker (1987). A simplified explanation of the assumptions and tenets of Anderson's theory is found in Howard (1983).

6. Forgetting the language is a serious problem after formal language training is over, when the learner no longer has the support of a teacher, or of classmates and structured lessons. A new research field called "language skill attrition" or "language loss" has been identified to investigate this problem (see Lambert & Freed, 1982; Oxford, 1982a, 1982b; Weltens, 1986).

7. For details on visual imagery as used for memory, see Nyikos (1987), Miller (1956), Shephard (1967), Bower (1970), Higbee (1979), and Goleman (1986).

8. For information on language learning style preferences relating to sensory modalities, see Reid (1987) and Rossi-Le (1988).

9. The frequency of use of memory strategies is under debate. Some research (e.g., Nyikos & Oxford, 1987; Reiss, 1985) has found that university students report using memory strategies infrequently. On the other hand, other studies using different research methods (for example, Cohen & Aphek, 1981; Nyikos, personal communication, February 8, 1987) revealed that memory strategies were indeed widely used, and that these strategies made vocabulary learning easier and more effective over the long term. The utility of memory strategies for vocabulary learning was reconfirmed by McDonough and McNerney (reported in Tyacke & Mendelsohn, 1986). Successful students in a foreign language writing study used memory strategies (Amber, as reported by Tyacke & Mendelsohn, 1986). However, use of memory strategies can sometimes make initial learning slower, although more effective (Cohen & Aphek, 1981).

10. A. Wright (1987, p. 53).

11. Semantic mapping is not just a good memory strategy, but it is also useful as a prelistening or prereading strategy for aiding comprehension. It can also be the basis of an entire reading or listening lesson (see Hague, 1987). Semantic mapping is discussed at length by Hague (1987) and Oxford (1988). This technique has been used for many years under a variety of labels. This technique was employed by Novak and Gowin (1984) under the name of Conceptual Mapping as the basis of an entire "learning how to learn" system. This technique is also known as a Semantic Network (Halff, 1986), used as a basis for artificial intelligence by computer; a Concept Tree (Brown-Azarowicz, Stannard, & Goldin, 1986), used for memorizing foreign language vocabulary; and Note Mapping (A. Wright, 1987), used for taking notes on reading. All of these usages can be related to psychological concepts about how knowledge is stored as a network, as discussed in Note 5 above. For details, see Oxford (1988). In a different vein, some sociolinguistic experts might have questions about whether semantic mapping might isolate or decontextualize a concept or set of words; these experts might prefer to talk in terms of "frames," "schemes," and "scripts" (Haru Yamada, personal communication, June 11, 1988). The counterargument is that semantic mapping is actually a way of contextualizing a word or concept in an expanding network of related words or concepts, and that such a strategy helps learners make important linkages that carry over into more richly contextualized communication situations.

12. Unlike many memory techniques for foreign and second languages, the keyword has benefited from a good deal of research, all of which shows that it is remarkably successful for vocabulary learning (see the research summaries in Oxford, 1985b, 1986f). One caution with the keyword is that some of the auditory links may not be perfect. That is, the new word in the target language may not sound exactly like the familiar word in one's own language. The

keyword strategy, under the name of Link Word, has been used as the foundation of a whole language learning system, the Link Word Language System, which includes not only vocabulary but grammar points as well (Gruneberg, 1987a, 1987b). This system currently has instructional books available in Spanish, Italian, French, and German. For more information, write Corgi Books, Transworld Publishers, 61–63 Uxbridge Road, Ealing, London W5 5SA, England (also published in Australia and New Zealand by Transworld). The Link System of Lorayne and Lucas (1974) involves keywords (a combination of sound and image) in a sequential and interactive chain—a task not usually necessary for language learning. A different memory strategy, called the pegword (or the memory hook), is also used to remember a string of words in a certain order; see Lorayne and Lucas (1974) and A. Wright (1987) for information on the pegword strategy.

13. From Lorayne and Lucas (1974).

14. Memory for verbal information in one's own language is influenced by time factors, such as primacy, recency, duration, spacing, pacing, and crowding of stimuli; things that are stored together tend to be recovered together (Stevick, 1976). This suggests that scheduling is very important, and the memory strategy of structured reviewing is therefore crucial. Structured reviewing, which encourages spaced review intervals, is related to other strategies: (a) the cognitive strategy of repeating and (b) the metacognitive strategy of organizing. Repeating is a broad strategy that involves both imitating native speakers and repeating target language material. Organizing involves, among other things, scheduling one's learning but does not suggest any particular intervals for reviewing.

15. Asher's (1966a, 1966b) language instructional practice called Total Physical Response involves this memory strategy.

16. Cognitive strategies are often defined as including memory strategies and guessing strategies. Memory strategies are given their own niche in this book because of their specialized function, helping learners store and retrieve new information. Guessing strategies are placed among compensation strategies, because they compensate for missing knowledge in listening and reading.

17. O'Malley et al. (1985a, 1985b) and Chamot, O'Malley, Küpper, and Impink-Hernandez (1987) found that high school ESL students and university foreign language students used considerably more cognitive strategies than metacognitive strategies; however, Chamot et al. (1987) discovered that the use of metacognitive strategies increased somewhat as learners progressed to higher levels of language learning. Russo and Stewner-Manzanares (1985) found that U.S. Army soldiers studying ESL reported using cognitive strategies with simpler tasks and metacognitive strategies with more complex tasks. Many other studies have examined the use of cognitive strategies, among other types of strategies. See, for example, Grandage (in Tyacke & Mendelsohn, 1986), Nyikos and Oxford (1987), Papalia and Zampogna (1977), and Reiss (1985).

18. See Oxford and Rhodes (1988) for estimates of the amount of time to reach proficiency in various languages.

19. The importance of practice—especially naturalistic practice involving communication—has been demonstrated repeatedly; see, for instance, Rubin (1975), Bialystok (1981), and Ramirez (1986).

20. Read Leaver (forthcoming) for interesting data on the use of analytic and reasoning strategies and commentary on whether or not this use is related to age.

21. See Selinker (1972, 1981), the originator of the term *interlanguage*.

22. For example, see Hosenfeld (1977).

23. Amazingly enough, guessing strategies—which compensate for a limited language repertoire in listening and reading—have never before been linked in any way with compensation strategies for speaking or writing, despite the obvious similarity in compensatory function. Guessing strategies are used for listening comprehension (Grandage in Tyacke & Mendelsohn, 1986; Henner-Stanchina, 1986), reading comprehension (Papalia & Zampogna, 1977; Ramirez, 1986), and vocabulary learning (McDonough & McNerney in Tyacke & Mendelsohn, 1986). Note that Ellis (1986) uses the term "compensatory strategies" (coined independently from the term "compensation strategies" as used here) to refer only to production-oriented strategies which compensate for missing knowledge—a far narrower scope than that of "compensation strategies" as described in this book.

24. MacBride (1980, p. 28).

25. Researchers have used the term *communication strategies* in a very restricted sense, referring to strategies which compensate for missing knowledge only during conversational speech production. Tarone's (1977, 1980, 1983) list of communication strategies includes paraphrasing (approximating, word coinage, and circumlocution), borrowing (literal translation, language switch, appeal for assistance, and mime), and avoidance (topic avoidance and message abandonment). As Tarone uses it, the term *communication strategies* refers only to the speaking situation, and this usage might seem to imply that communication does not occur when the learner is engaged in the other three skills, listening, reading, and writing—certainly an erroneous implication. Another difficulty with the term *communication strategies* is that some researchers feel these strategies cannot simultaneously be learning strategies, on the assumption that the purpose is communication, not learning (Chamot, personal communication, July 4, 1987). The argument that communication strategies cannot also be learning strategies is inaccurate. It is often impossible to determine whether the learner intends to use a given strategy to communicate or to learn; often the motivations are mixed, and besides, learning often results even if communication is the main goal (Tarone, 1983; Rubin, 1987a). Simply put, "Learning takes place *through* communication" (Faerch & Kasper, 1983a, p. xvii). "Communication, learning, and instruction interact and influence each other" (Candlin, 1983, p. x). To paraphrase Howatt, learners can either "learn to use the language" or "use the language to learn it" (Howatt, 1984). To avoid the false split between communication strategies and learning strategies, as well as the overly narrow (one-skill) interpretation of communication embodied in most uses of the term *communication strategies*, this book refers instead to *compensation strategies*.

26. Littlewood (1984) explains the uses of these kinds of strategies for learning, not just communicating.

27. Mendelsohn (1984) distinguishes among linguistic, paralinguistic, and extralinguistic clues for guessing. Somewhat similarly, Bialystok (1978) lists three sources of information for guessing: explicit linguistic knowledge, implicit linguistic knowledge, and general knowledge of the world.

CHAPTER 3

1. People do use all four skills, though in different amounts or to varying degrees. Adults spend 40 to 50% of their communication time listening, 25 to 30% speaking, 11 to 16% reading, and 9% writing, according to Rivers (1981). However, the need for concerted effort to develop each of the four skills might be a novel idea to some people. For instance, Krashen and colleagues (1984, pp. 263 and 273) have suggested that the development of the two production skills, speaking and writing, does not require any special effort, on the assumption that these skills cannot be taught but will "emerge" simply through sufficient exposure to listening and speaking. Conversely, other people have neglected listening on the grounds that it is a passive skill or merely a means of teaching speaking (see Morley, 1984; Mendelsohn, 1984; Brown, 1984, for criticisms of such a viewpoint). However, *there is no evidence to support the concept that any one of the language skills will simply "emerge" solely through practicing other skills, or that one skill is just a means of teaching another skill. The neglect of any of the four skills is likely to restrict the degree of proficiency a student can attain.* Each skill deserves attentive instruction and practice, and many exercises exist for instruction and practice in all four skills.

2. The examples in this chapter come from the following sources. Original (created by the author): Norberto, Jennie, Lucien, Stephanie, Mike, Corazon, Benjamin, Glennys, Katya, Keith, Adel, Quang, Helen, Jeff, Mariette, Jill, Brian, Alice, Howard, Jeremy, Yolande, Rollande, Rudy, Kelley, Gerard, Kiri, Misha, Akram, Jack, Milton, Lyle, Lori, Yacoub, Marian and Heidi, Adrienne and Giovanni, Steve, Maya, Elisabeth, Haruko, Parker, Lisha, Sam, Rosine, Ferenc, Natalya, Jean-Claude, Monica, Rowena and Jim, Pascual, Rusty, Sandrine, Susan, Pablo, Marc, Akira, Ellen, Louisa, Julio, Roberta, Marcie, Marianne, Lugo, Marcello, Martina, Lloyd, Marijane, Stanley, Nora, Luis, Rita, John, Reba, Lillian, Billie, Herb, Lauren, Elton, Amado, Martha, Dwight, Erwin, Mildred, Jana, Monte, Eli, Gilberto, Frank, Sally, Vivian, Broderick, Molly, Andrew, Miguel, Millicent, Hilde, Robert, Norman, Terry, Kirsten, Jaime, Marcelle, Vanya, Nina, Nubia, Stavros, Domenico, and Siu. Grucz and McKee (1986) provided the following examples: Donny, Bud, and Lih. The Antonio example is from A. Wright (1987). Stewner-Manzanares, Chamot, Kupper, and Russo (1984) offered the examples of Carlos and Rashid. Leni's example is from Ur (1984), while Michel's is from Lorayne and Lucas (1974). Gruneberg (1987c) provided examples of Bernie, Julianne, and Mathilde. Examples of Josef, Gabriele, Leslie, June, Henri, Clive and Hector, Edna, Constanze, and Heinrich are from Tarone, Cohen, and Dumas (1983). Littlewood (1984) offered the

examples of Miki, Cesar, Mario, Fritz (adapted), Trudy, Aviva, Laura, Gottfried, Lucille, Omar, and Renato. Andrey, Wladislaw, Simone, Ismael, and Lisette are from Mendelsohn (1984). Tarone (1983) contributed the examples Geraldo, Tonio, Carmelita, Franny, Zoltan, and Osmin. Examples of Nicki and Liz are from Bialystok (1983). My colleagues also contributed examples from their own personal experience or that of their friends. The example of David is from David Crookall. Haru Yamada offered the examples of Brooke and Ron, and Richard's example is from MaryAnn Zima. Roger Rexroth contributed the example of cross-dialect transfer in note 26.

3. This is called a *tax haven* in British English.

4. See Howard (1983) for formal structures proposed by network theories of long-term memory to describe how people make associations and remember information. These structures are maps or networks, related in a very loose way to the semantic maps spontaneously generated by language learners. See also Hague (1987) and Oxford (1988).

5. See Asher (1966a, 1966b).

6. Such a complicated acronym must work rapidly when the learner needs to retrieve the target language information. Therefore, the learner must know the acronym very well, to the point of automaticity. It is necessary to expend some initial energy learning the particular memory device, in this case an acronym. This process might seem to slow learners down, but the longer-term retention caused by using such devices often makes the initial effort worthwhile. See Cohen and Aphek (1981) for a discussion of speed and effectiveness of memory strategies.

7. Repeating words (orally or in writing) that are *not* understood prevents students from accessing background knowledge or setting the new words in an understandable context.

8. Of course the "tell 'em" and "lead paragraph" rules do not fit well into the discourse styles of some languages, which require less direct, more oblique modes of expression.

9. See Brown (1987, p. 30).

10. Ur (1984) provides a number of exercises for formally practicing with sounds. See also Wong (1987).

11. Listening *comprehension* exercises, as opposed to listening *perception* exercises, benefit from having live speech.

12. It is usually pronounced *ee*, as in *famille* and *gentille*, but it is sometimes pronounced *eel*, as in *ville* and *Lille*, or pronounced *iye*, as in *paille*.

13. See Leaver (1984) and Brown-Azarowicz et al. (1986), for detailed suggestions about how to practice new writing systems.

14. Authentic speech contains many ungrammatical, reduced, and incomplete forms, as well as hesitations, false starts, repetitions, fillers, and pauses (up to 30–50% of the conversation!). Moreover, the topic often shifts rapidly. Learners

need to become used to these features as they occur in the target language. Geddes and White (1978) distinguish between two kinds of "authentic speech": (a) unmodified authentic discourse produced for nonteaching purposes, and (b) simulated authentic discourse produced for teaching purposes but having many features that are likely to occur in genuine communication. Omaggio (1986), like many others, calls the second kind of authentic speech "teacher talk" or "caretaker talk," which is typically slower and simpler than the first kind of authentic speech but still contains redundancies, hesitations, backtracking, and so on. The second kind of authentic speech is often better for classroom activities, especially in the early stages of language learning.

15. Language learners need as much realistic listening comprehension practice as possible. However, many classroom listening comprehension exercises do not reflect real-world listening, in which we listen with a purpose; are often required to respond; can usually see the speaker; have the benefit of environmental cues; deal with rapid, short, redundant chunks of speech; and are interested in what is being said (Ur, 1984; Mendelsohn, 1984; Meyer, 1984). Because many listening exercises lack these characteristics, they are boring, childish, and meaningless. Many language teaching specialists—such as Ur (1984), Omaggio (1986), Geddes and White (1978), Mendelsohn (1984), Morley (1984), and Meyer (1984)—have shown how listening exercises can be planned to be more effective. See especially Ur (1984) for a wide variety of useful and relevant listening comprehension exercises.

16. Radio stations often broadcast in foreign languages; the BBC, for instance, broadcasts in some 35 languages. Listening to target language songs on the radio often provides an interesting, nonthreatening way to catch accents and intonations. Listening to radio gives the flavor of the language as spoken at its normal speed and with all its subtle cues to meaning. Some radio stations also broadcast lessons for learners (foreign and native) who want to improve their language skills; for instance, Radio Moscow carries Russian lessons, and the BBC broadcasts the excellent and well-known "English by Radio" series (see Norbrook, 1984). For further information on shortwave broadcasting, see Crookall (1983c, 1984b), or purchase a recent, detailed description of international shortwave broadcasting known as *Passport to World Band Radio* (available from the BBC World Shop, Bush House, London, England). You can use these radio resources in class, and you can give your students sheets describing the radio resources they can use at home.

17. Problems exist with the videocassette, such as finding sources of prerecorded tapes or of material to record oneself. Prerecorded tapes in other languages are not typically found in video shops and clubs, but there are services which specialize in foreign language films (for instance, Facets Video Rental-by-Mail, Facets Cinemathèque, 1517 West Fullerton Avenue, Chicago, IL 60614, USA; Films Incorporated, 1213 Willmette Avenue, Willmette, IL 60091, USA). It is possible to ask one's friends who live abroad to record programs from their TV sets, but this raises technical problems with compatibility of standards. There are three main video/TV standards in the world: NSTC is used in the United States, SECAM in France, and PAL in the UK, in most of Europe, and

in many other countries. Overcoming compatibility problems may involve use of multistandard equipment (for information contact Cartridge King, 825 West End Avenue, New York, NY 10025, USA) or copying and conversion services. One further source of listening material is DBS. For example, in Europe many programs in different languages from neighboring countries can be accessed via DBS using a dish antenna. In the United States dish antennae can pick up programs by DBS from the Soviet Union and other countries, and many of these are being transformed (for example, by the Defense Language Institute in Monterey, California) by means of computers into a means for interactive listening practice. Legal and practical constraints must, of course, be considered. See also Krashen et al. (1984, p. 273) for further information on listening materials using sound only or sound plus image.

18. Aston (1987) provides an excellent discussion of the "comity" (friendship) aspects of learning a new language.

19. See the following writing texts, which might be of use in your foreign or second language classroom: Hamp-Lyons and Heasley (1987), McKee (1981), Hartfiel, Hughey, Wormuth, and Jacobs (1985), Cramer (1985), Blanchard and Root (1984), Raimes (1983), Oshima and Hogue (1985, 1988), Clark (1985). Houpt (1984) provides specific ideas about using conversation as a prewriting stimulus to composition in the new language. Also watch the language teaching journals for reviews of good books on writing.

20. See Jones (1985) for RADIO COVINGHAM; see Crookall (1985) for NEWSIM.

21. For more information on dialogue journals, see Staton (1980, 1987), and Staton, Shuy, and Kreeft (1982). A different kind of written student–teacher exchange is called the "working journal" (Spack & Sadow, 1983). Like dialogue journals, working journals are ungraded, uncorrected, and nonthreatening. However, working journals differ from dialogue journals in two ways. First, the topic of working journals is somewhat less free-ranging and is specifically focused on the learners' description of, and feelings about, the writing process (but it is easy to see how this topic could be extended to the language learning process more generally). This slant is intended to give students a flavor of writing for an audience on a focused topic. Second, the teacher regularly writes journals to the entire class on the same subject and includes in those journals selected student journal entries. Working journals, like dialogue journals, have produced excellent results with language learners at various proficiency levels.

22. Cummins (1986) describes microcomputer communication networks for social and cultural exchange.

23. See Cummins (1986) for details on the Newswire, and Crookall and Wilkenfeld (1985) for information on ICONS.

24. For information on sending students' short stories to the BBC World Service, see Crookall (1986).

25. Sentence diagramming is a familiar form of analyzing expressions. This technique, which has lost much of its appeal in recent years, can help many learners

understand sentence structure. The danger with such techniques is that teachers sometimes focus on them to the exclusion of face-to-face communicative activities.

26. Transferring inappropriately can even occur across different dialects of the same language. For instance, in the United States, it is entirely possible to talk about the lovely embroidered *napkins* on the table, but you should not do so in Australia, where the correct term is *serviettes* and where the term *napkins* has a very restricted usage and is not typically mentioned in polite conversation.

27. The term *raw notes* is used in a different way from that used by Hamp-Lyons (1983), who says that the shopping list and the T-list (i.e., T-formation) can both be used at the raw note stage. I feel that the shopping list and the T-list are one step up from raw notes, which are often chaotic and completely unorganized.

28. See Hamp-Lyons (1983) for another example of the tree diagram for taking notes.

29. Clarke and Nation (1980) have shown how to use linguistic clues to guess meanings in a reading passage.

30. Many of these clues come from what sociolinguists might call frames or scripts.

31. O'Malley, reported in Chamot (1987).

32. Mendelsohn (1984) suggested these examples: (a) On the one hand he was right, but on the other hand . . . (students complete); (b) The dying king called for a priest to . . . (students complete); (c) The man dropped his shopping bag and everything spilled out. He went up to a young girl watching and . . . (students complete).

33. The definition of adjusting or abandoning is from Littlewood (1984).

34. References for the quotations in Activity 3.1 are found in Appendix D.

CHAPTER 4

1. See Rubin (1975), Amber in Tyacke and Mendelsohn (1986), and Oskarsson (1984). For information on self-awareness of language learners, see Wenden (1986b). For comments on self-monitoring in writing, see Bialystok (1981).

2. See, for instance, O'Malley et al., (1985a); Chamot et al., (1987).

3. Nyikos and Oxford (1987), Oxford (1986d), and Oxford and Nyikos (1989). McGroarty (1987) found that even when language learners were surrounded by practice opportunities in the community, they did not necessarily take advantage of those chances to practice.

4. This learning strategy is related to the instructional strategy called *advance organizers*. Advance organizers have been in existence as a formal instructional strategy since the early 1900s, but they were more recently popularized by

Ausubel (1963), who defined them in the specific sense of *overviews* used for simultaneously (a) previewing concepts in detailed written material, (b) reviewing concepts already in the learner's mind, and (c) linking both sets of concepts. See Barnes and Clawson (1975) for an excellent review of research on this instructional strategy.

5. Many language theorists (e.g., Dulay, Burt, & Krashen, 1982) have espoused the "silent period" as a necessary precursor to oral production, and some have called for it to be part of the curriculum. During this period, learners are said to comprehend the language but are unable to speak it. The period might last for only a few hours for adults but could take from 1 to 6 months for children (Krashen & Terrell, 1983). However, in an article reviewing numerous studies of the silent period, Gibbons (1985) disputed the nature of the silent period, stating that (a) this period probably begins as a period of *silent incomprehension* rather than *silent comprehension*; (b) if prolonged, the silent period may represent psychological withdrawal rather than language acquisition; and (c) consequently, initial silence in the target language is not necessarily desirable.

6. Brown (1987, p. 99).

7. The classification of certain learner variables—for example, anxiety, risk taking, inhibition, tolerance for ambiguity, empathy, and culture shock—as either cognitive, affective, or social is often a matter of judgment or taste. Each of these learner variables contains cognitive, affective, and social elements in differing degrees. Three specific classifications might be questioned by some readers. *Tolerance for ambiguity* could have been classified as an aspect of overall cognitive style (Brown, 1987; Shipman & Shipman, 1985) or sociocultural adjustment (Ruben, 1987), but it is included here as an affective factor because it often manifests itself in emotional reactions. *Culture shock*, while sometimes listed as a sociocultural aspect of language learning (e.g., by Brown, 1987), is reflected so strongly and often so negatively in the emotions of the learner that it must be discussed among the affective factors. In addition, *empathy* is sometimes included as an affective trait (Brown, 1987), but because empathy is so socially loaded (Ruben, 1987), it is included here as a social variable. These classifications are not as important as an understanding of the basic concepts.

8. Naiman, Fröhlich, and Todesco (1975). See also Wenden (1986b), who describes how learners analyze their own feelings and attitudes.

9. See White (1959). Global self-esteem emerges about mental age 8 and is based on one's self-perceived success or competence in various broad areas—such as academic competence, athletic competence, social competence, social acceptance, physical appearance, and behavior/conduct—combined with one's judgments of how important these areas are (McCombs, 1987). Global self-esteem can be altered by helping students succeed better in these broad areas, or alternatively by helping students discount the importance of the areas where they are unsuccessful but which they think are extremely important (Harter, 1986). Learners with high self-esteem maintain positive evaluations of themselves through perceiving the world in a rosy, not necessarily accurate way (Tesser & Campbell, 1982, in McCombs, 1987). High self-esteem students often

exaggerate their competence or adequacy, whereas low self-esteem students frequently judge themselves harshly (Harter, 1985). Amber (in Tyacke & Mendelsohn, 1986) found that unsuccessful language learners had lower self-esteem than successful language learners.

10. Over the last 30 years, language learning motivation has been viewed in terms of two primary orientations: instrumental and integrative (see Gardner, 1985). Some studies (e.g., Gardner & Lambert, 1972; Spolsky, 1969) indicate that integrative motivation is a more significant influence on language proficiency than is instrumental motivation, but other studies (e.g., Lukmani, 1972) show that instrumental motivation sometimes results in better language learning than does integrative motivation. Many factors influence the relative importance of these two motivational orientations on language proficiency: the environment where the language is being learned, perceived target community support, and learner attitudes toward the target community. Moreover, there may not be as great a difference between instrumental and integrative motivation as once thought, since they correlate with each other statistically; and other motivations besides instrumental and integrative may also operate in learning a new language.

11. See Gardner (1985).

12. Results on global language proficiency come from research by Clément, Major, Gardner, and Smythe (1977), Clément, Gardner, and Smythe (1980), Gardner and Lambert (1959), Gardner and Smythe (1975a, 1975b) and Gardner (1985). Results on specific components of language proficiency come from Tucker, Hamayan, and Genesee (1976) and Genesee (1978).

13. Gardner, Lalonde, Moorcroft, and Evers (1985).

14. For an effective and comprehensive training system for improving learner motivation, see especially McCombs and Dobrovolny (1982), and read McCombs (1987, 1988) for background information. Various components of McCombs's training system include all three sets of affective strategies listed in this chapter (under different names), combined with metacognitive strategies such as goal setting and social strategies such as cooperation.

15. See Littlewood's (1984) description of typical language classrooms and their effects.

16. "Culture shock . . . is . . . a form of anxiety that results from the loss of commonly perceived and understood signs and symbols of social intercourse" (Adler, 1987, p. 25). While not all language learning involves the identity crisis of culture shock, language learners living in the target culture frequently experience it (see Blair, 1983). Culture-shocked learners may experience regression, panic, anger, self-pity, indecision, sadness, alienation, "reduced personality," and physical illness. However, if handled effectively, culture shock can become a cross-cultural learning experience involving increased cultural awareness, increased self-awareness, and reintegration of personality (Adler, 1987).

17. Adler & Vogel (1986).

18. Beebe (1983).

19. Stevick (1976).

20. Alcohol and tranquilizers might help lower inhibitions (see experiments described in Brown, 1987), but few language teachers would recommend these to their students! Some recent teaching practices, such as Community Language Learning, the Silent Way, and Suggestopedia, all focus on lowering inhibitions.

21. Naiman, Fröhlich, Stern, and Todesco (1978).

22. Chapelle (1983).

23. Ehrman and Oxford (1989) and Oxford and Ehrman (1989).

24. See, for instance, Chamot et al. (1987).

25. Another affective element influencing language learning is extraversion-introversion, i.e., the degree to which the person is energized by other people or by the inner world of ideas. For information on this dimension, see Brown (1987), Ehrman and Oxford (1989), and Oxford and Ehrman (1989).

26. Jacob and Mattson (1987) and Slavin (1983).

27. Kagan (1986) and Kohn (1987).

28. Kohn (1987) and Dansereau (1983, 1988).

29. In addition, research on cooperative learning outside of the language area indicates the following. Such learning succeeds best when students are not just grouped into small units, such as pairs or triads, but are also trained in the kinds of strategies to use in their small groups. When students in a cooperative group are *similar in learning style*, they do better. However, students of *different ability levels* help each other more than students whose ability levels are the same. Cooperative groups do not benefit from competing against other groups. Cooperation does not always mean agreement. Finally, the optimal size for a cooperative group appears to be two or three, except for complex tasks that demand up to six. See References for citations on this topic.

30. See, for example, Sharan et al. (1985), Bejarano (1987), Gunderson and Johnson (1980), Bassano and Christison (1988), Wong Fillmore (1985), Gaies (1985), and Seliger (1983). Cooperation is at the heart of many current language instruction practices, such as Community Language Learning, derived from Counseling-Learning. This model encourages students to value each other and cooperate in developing a supportive learning community.

31. Reid (1987) and O'Malley et al. (1985a). However, this might differ by sex, since females show a more cooperative social orientation than do males (Maccoby & Jacklin, 1974; Gilligan, 1982; Bardwick, 1971). See Oxford, Nyikos, and Ehrman (1988) for sex differences in language learning strategies.

32. Kohn (1987).

33. See Bailey's (1983) review of diary studies for information on competitiveness

in language learning. See also Lobuts and Pennewill (1989) for an analysis of destructive competition.

CHAPTER 5

1. Prewriting exercises like nonstop writing (McKee, 1981) help learners overview the content of the next writing task and link it with what they already know. In nonstop writing, students write for 10 minutes without censoring their ideas or expression in any way. If they can't think of a word, they can write, "I can't think of it," and just proceed. This can be done in one's native language or, better yet, in the target language, then shared in a small group to get feedback and expansion of the thoughts.
2. See Houpt (1984) for ideas about prewriting debates and discussions.
3. See Gibbons (1985).
4. Two relatively recent, easy-to-read, helpful books are *How to Be a More Successful Language Learner* (Rubin & Thompson, 1982) and *Yes! You Can Learn a Foreign Language* (Brown-Azarowicz et al., 1986). Wenden (1986a) lists some other helpful resources, some a bit dated and some more recent: Cornelius (1955), Crawford and Leitzell (1980), Hall (1973), Kraft and Kraft (1966), Moulton (1966), Nida (1957), Pei (1966), Pimsleur (1980), and Politzer (1965). See Wenden (1986a) for still other books of guidance for language learners. Ambitious students able to deal with technical details might value Wenden and Rubin (1987), Stern (1983), Rivers (1981), and Omaggio (1986), even though these books are geared more toward researchers and teachers than toward students.
5. Crookall (1983a) provides excellent ideas for such discussions.
6. For information on the nature and purpose of various speech forms, see Byrnes (1984). For details on the importance of spontaneous free speech, as in friendly conversations, read Aston (1987). A fascinating discussion of differences between orality and literacy is given by Ong (1987).
7. See Grellet (1981) for details.
8. See Omaggio (1981) for information on how to use error analysis to determine the source of errors.
9. O'Malley (reported in Chamot, 1987).
10. The examples of Hans and Alberto are from Littlewood (1984). All the other examples in this chapter which bear the names of learners (e.g., Ricky, Anh) are original.
11. See discussion in Semke (1984).
12. See, for example, the useful diagnostic profile for writing provided by Hartfiel et al. (1985).
13. Oskarsson (1984).

14. Quoted in Spack and Sadow (1983, p. 586).
15. Information on laughter therapy is found in Long (1987).
16. See various applications of diaries in Rubin (1981) and Bailey (1983).

CHAPTER 6

1. A number of strategy observation scales have been published and are readily available. One useful scale is the Observation Schedule of Language Learners (Rubin, 1981). The Class Observation Guide (O'Malley et al., 1985b, pp. 563–564) includes information on the source of a given language learning strategy, the activity in which it is used, the setting, the materials involved, and the approach of the teacher and the students during strategy use.
2. See Cohen and Hosenfeld (1981) for complete details.
3. Self-observation that takes place immediately is called *introspection*. Self-observation that occurs later is called *retrospection*, and it introduces the forgetting factor.
4. Recent revisions of this model (Cohen, 1987b) include three categories: self-report (the frequently used mode in which learners tell what they *usually* do or think, not what they are doing in a particular learning event); self-observation (introspection and retrospection); and self-revelation (thinking aloud and talking aloud, the latter occurring when thoughts are already in verbal form in the learner's mind).
5. See Hosenfeld, Arnold, Kirchofer, Laciura, and Wilson (1981). A few minor criticisms can be mentioned concerning the content of the Interviewer Guide, such as the confusing sequence of strategies, but in general the guide is useful for gathering information on strategies which cannot be observed.
6. A more intensive think-aloud procedure was developed by Chamot and her colleagues (1987) for a longitudinal study of learning strategies. In this study, learners of Russian and Spanish described the strategies they used while working on various language tasks. Students received training and practice in thinking aloud, as well as a warm-up and other preparation before being assessed. Data collection in this study took about 1 to1½ hours per student, much longer than Hosenfeld's procedure for think-aloud interviews described earlier in Chapter 6. During the actual think-aloud assessment, interviewers asked questions like "What are you thinking?" or "How did you figure that out?" Other questions were tied to specific tasks, e.g., "Are you listening word by word, or to groups of words, or to whole sentences?" for the listening tasks. When certain nonverbal behaviors occurred, such as staring, long silences, or looking back over the word, interviewers asked about those behaviors. Painstaking analysis, recently completed, determined how the effective learners and the ineffective learners differed in the strategies they reported. This excellent adaptation of the think-aloud procedure produced interesting information for the entire lan-

guage field. For most teachers, this use of the procedure is too complex for classroom use, but researchers of language learning strategies will find it valuable.

7. For a copy of this guide, see O'Malley et al. (1985b).

8. See Wenden (1986a, 1986b) for more details.

9. See Leaver (forthcoming) for complete information on the procedure used.

10. The three techniques are described, respectively, in Cohen, Glasman, Rosenbaum-Cohen, Ferrara, and Fine (1979), Wenden (1986a, 1986b) and Allwright (1980).

11. See Long (1979) for the participant-observer concept of diaries. For diary studies focusing on psychological and social themes, see, for example, Jones (1977) and Schumann and Schumann (1977). Bailey's article (1983) discusses competitiveness and anxiety as expressed in language learning strategies. Bailey and Ochsner (1983) suggested ways to shape diaries to make them suitable as research documents. Rubin (1981) provides information on guided and unguided diary-keeping. Spack and Sadow (1983) discuss "working journals," which students use to describe their efforts to develop language skills and their feelings about the process. "Dialogue journals" (see Staton, 1980, 1983, 1987; Staton et al., 1982) are useful for describing thoughts and feelings of any kind. For working journals and dialogue journals, the teacher responds in writing.

12. Martha Nyikos of Indiana University developed this technique. An example is shown in her survey called "Assuming Responsibility for Learning: Study Strategy Worksheet" (Nyikos, n.d).

13. Some examples of relevant self-report surveys include the following: **Strategy Questionnaire:** An unnamed but published strategy questionnaire was used by Politzer (1983). This 51-item survey includes strategies explicitly categorized into three scales: general behaviors, classroom behaviors, and interaction with others outside of class. This survey uses a 5-point Likert-type scale ranging from 0 to 4. **Behavior Questionnaire:** This published survey was used in the Politzer and McGroarty study (1985). It contains 66 items, divided into three scales: classroom behavior, learning behavior during individual study, and interacting with others outside the classroom. Learners are to respond either yes or no to each item. Politzer and McGroarty described the survey in their article (p. 107): "The behaviors included in the three parts of the questionnaire do not correspond to any unified psychological construct. They represent a collection of ideas put together from intuition and existing suggestions," i.e., suggestions from the work of Rubin (1981) and Naiman et al. (1978). The authors stated that internal consistency of each of the three scales was low, but it improved to a moderate level (.51, .61, .63) when problematic items were removed. **Language Learning Strategy Student Questionnaire:** This is another example of an objective survey. The 56-item survey was developed by McGroarty (1987) and was based on work by Politzer and McGroarty. This survey uses a 7-point Likert-type scale ranging from 0 (not applicable) to 6 (always) in reference to the frequency of use of the various learning strategies.

Again, the items are divided into three distinct scales: strategies used in the classroom, interacting with others outside the class, and individual study. **Learning Strategies Inventory:** This is a 48-item questionnaire describing various things a student might do when learning a foreign language. It is divided into five sections: listening to the language in class, speaking the language in class, listening and speaking outside the class, writing the language, and reading the language. The items relate to different ways of applying a total of 16 strategies. The survey asks students to respond (on a 4-point scale) that the statement is almost always true of them, usually true, sometimes true, or almost never true. This survey was used in the series of three studies conducted by Chamot and her colleagues (Chamot et al., 1987).

14. The SILL was originally developed for the Language Skill Change Project, which periodically assesses the amount of change found in language skills after the learner's foreign language training has been completed. This longitudinal study is jointly sponsored by the Defense Language Institute Foreign Language Center, Monterey, California, and the Army Research Institute for the Behavioral and Social Sciences, Alexandria, Virginia. Versions of the SILL have been used with groups of foreign language learners in high schools and universities around the world, as well as at the Defense Language Institute, the Foreign Service Institute, and the Peace Corps/Philippines. Adults learning English as a second language and English as a foreign language in several countries have also used the SILL. It is now being translated into several languages, such as Chinese, Japanese, and Spanish. Items in various forms of the SILL were based on the author's strategy system, and additional items were adapted from early surveys and strategy lists by O'Malley, Chamot, and Rubin. Version 5.1 in Appendix B has 80 items, and Version 7.0 in Appendix C has 50 items. Reliability and validity data are now being assessed for these two versions.

    A slightly earlier, 121-item version of the SILL has been most extensively studied from a psychometric viewpoint. Internal consistency reliability of the 121-item form using Cronbach's alpha is .96 for a 1,200-person university sample (Nyikos & Oxford, 1987; Oxford & Nyikos, 1987; Oxford, Nyikos, & Crookall, 1987) and .95 for a 483-person military sample (Oxford, 1986a, 1986b, 1986c). Reliability of 9 of 10 factors (obtained from a factor analysis) found in the military sample is moderate to high, ranging from .60 to .86, while the 10th factor is lower (.31) (Oxford, 1986a, 1986b, 1986c). Content validity is .95, based on classificatory agreement between two independent raters, who "blindly" matched each of the SILL items with the strategies in the comprehensive list shown elsewhere (Oxford, 1986a, 1986b, 1986c). Concurrent validity of the 121-item form is found in strong, statistically significant relationships between SILL results and self-ratings of target language proficiency and motivation in the 1,200-person university sample (Nyikos & Oxford, 1987; Oxford & Nyikos 1987; Oxford et al., 1987). Learners who were more proficient and more motivated consistently reported on the SILL that they used a wider range of strategies, and used them more frequently, than did learners who were less proficient and less motivated. Another piece of evidence for concurrent validity comes from a Foreign Service Institute study (Ehrman & Oxford, 1989; Oxford & Ehrman, 1989). In that study of approximately 80 adults, the more highly skilled linguists reported more intense and wide-ranging strategy use than less-skilled linguists. Interestingly, females have consistently reported greater strategy use than males on the SILL. Social desirability response bias—the tendency to falsify responses in order to make a good impression (give responses that are thought to be desirable)—was empirically monitored with three samples: 23 clinical trial subjects in the Washington, DC, area in 1985, 483 field test subjects at DLI in 1985, and the 1,200 university students in 1986. Both statistical and ethnographic data were checked. No evidence of social desirability response bias appeared for the three samples.

15. See Wenden (1987).

16. Crookall (1983a) provides details on training that covers these topics.

17. Holec (1981), Riley (1982), Crookall (1983a), and Prowse (1983) eloquently explain the need for strategy training.

18. See Crookall (1983a), Oxford (1986f), and Rodgers (1978) for aims of such training.

19. The author has never seen any detailed, comprehensive, step-by-step guidelines on how to structure language learning strategy training. However, a number of sources provide good ideas about various pieces or aspects of strategy training. See, for example, Wenden's (1986a) criteria for strategy training; and research on strategy training by Brown, Campione, and Day (1980a, 1980b), Dansereau (1985), Derry and Murphy (1986), Stewner-Manzanares et al. (1985), and Weinstein and Underwood (1985).

20. Strategy training is often most successful with those who are in the middle range of verbal ability, rather than at the very top or the very bottom, according to Dansereau (1985). But *all* learners can benefit from strategy training, no matter what their ability level.

21. Dansereau (1985) describes the broad, narrow, and combination approaches.

22. However, Wenden (1986a) notes that in some instances, strategy training which is relatively unintegrated with language training may actually be preferable. For example, some adult learners who have very limited time and need to work autonomously might prefer a separate strategy training course, not closely integrated with language training. By and large, however, greater integration with language training is usually more effective.

23. Dansereau (1985) recommends using integrated strategy training (he calls it content-dependent), starting with more general strategies and moving to more specific ones. Integration of learning strategies with standard subject matter is the approach successfully used in the Chicago Mastery Learning Reading Program with Learning Strategies, or CMLR/LS (Jones, 1983; Jones, Aniran, & Katias, 1985). Another approach that successfully integrates strategy training with content training is found in the Cognitive Academic Language Learning Approach, or CALLA (Chamot & O'Malley, 1986, 1987), which is described in Chapter 7.

24. This compromise is suggested by Derry and Murphy (1986), based on Rigney (1980).

25. Informed training is much more useful than uninformed training. Four levels of information are possible in strategy training. Level A consists of *encouragement of strategy use in general without special training*. In Level A, stimulating activities promote an unfocused, unselected, wide range of strategies without providing any kind of special training or information about these strategies. Because of the interesting activities, learners are stimulated to use whatever strategies suit their fancy. The problem at Level A is that learners, although encouraged in general, might not focus on the most appropriate strategies. They will not know how to assess the value of particular strategies or how and when to transfer strategies to new tasks. Level B is called *blind training*. At this level the tasks or materials themselves call for the use of *particular* strategies, which are often unconsciously used by the learner and are thus called "hidden strategies." No information is given about the significance of those strategies. "Blind training leaves the trainees in the dark about the importance of the activities (strategies) they are being induced to use" (Wenden, 1986a, p. 316). Blind training results in improved performance in the immediate task, but learners generally do not continue to use the strategy, nor do they transfer the strategy to other relevant situations (Brown et al., 1980a, 1980b; Brown, Bransford, Ferrara, & Campione, 1983; Rigney, 1978). Bright students are exceptions to this rule; they sometimes, without any help, figure out the strategy and how to use it in other settings. Examples of blind training are preview questions, advance organizers, inserted questions, comprehension questions at the end, explanation techniques based on metaphor or analogy, and material already blocked into categories for the learner. Of course, the moment these examples are openly discussed with the learner in terms of their function and value, they are no longer "hidden strategies," and there has been a move to the next level. Level C is *informed training*. At this level some, but not complete, information is given about the significance of the strategies being trained. Informed training tells the learner that a particular strategy can be helpful and explains why. In informed training the learner is both induced to use a particular strategy and given some information concerning the significance of that strategy (Brown et al., 1980a, 1980b). For example, learners might be taught to rehearse and be given feedback about their improved performance, or they might be taught to rehearse a task in multiple contexts so they can see the utility of the strategy. Informed training results in (a) improved performance on the task, (b) maintenance of the strategy across time, and (c) some degree of transfer of the strategy to other similar tasks (Brown et al., 1980a, 1980b). Thus, informed strategy training is more effective than blind strategy training. Level D consists of *completely informed training* (*strategy-plus-control training* or *self-control training*). At this level, complete information is given about the strategy and how to use, control, and transfer it. This is an even more explicit mode of strategy training. In this mode, the learner "is not only instructed in the use of strategy, but is also explicitly instructed in how to employ, monitor, check and evaluate that strategy" (Brown et al. 1980a, p. 5). Most learners perform best with completely informed training (Brown et al., 1980a).

26. Some of these ideas came from Dansereau (1985).

27. Thanks to Will Sutter for his suggestions regarding initial camouflaging of strategies which are new and very different from what particular learners prefer.

28. See Wenden (1986a) for suggestions concerning these evaluation criteria. More technical evaluation of strategy training, involving statistical analysis, is discussed in Dansereau (1985) and Weinstein and Underwood (1985).
29. Hosenfeld et al. (1981) developed this sequence.
30. This sequence was developed by Stewner-Manzanares et al. (1985).
31. Quoted from Wenden (1985b, p. 1).

CHAPTER 7

1. See, for example, Rubin (1985; 1987b, p. 275); also read more detailed reports by Rubin (1986, 1989). The description in this chapter comes directly from these sources and from Joan Rubin (personal communication, February 24, 1988).
2. Current price at the time of this writing is $995 for a 1-hour disk, five diskettes, and an instruction manual. Price subject to change; check with Dr. Rubin.
3. See Chamot and O'Malley (1986, 1987) and O'Malley and Chamot (1989).
4. These principles appear to be largely based on John Anderson's theory of declarative and procedural knowledge (1976), Jim Cummins's view of contextualized language and task complexity (1982, 1983), and Bernard Mohan's concepts of content-based language learning (1986).
5. See Chamot and O'Malley (1986).
6. This description is summarized from explanations given by Henner-Stanchina (1976), Henner-Stanchina and Holec (1977), Holec (1981), and Dickinson (1987, pp. 44–46). For more information, see reports by Abé, Henner-Stanchina, and Smith (1975), Moulden (1978, 1980), and Wenden (1986a).
7. Dickinson (1987).
8. Dickinson (1987).
9. Henner-Stanchina (1976).
10. Henner-Stanchina and Holec (1977).
11. Henner-Stanchina (1976).
12. This handbook, based on earlier strategy work by Shleppegrell and Oxford, is by Grala, Oxford, and Schleppegrell (1987). A later version designed for the whole Peace Corps organization, not just for the Peace Corps/Philippines, is by Schleppegrell and Oxford (1988).
13. Anne Lomperis (personal communication, September 3, 1987).
14. See Holec (1981).
15. These cautions are from Holec (1981).

16. This information is based on an interview conducted with Mrs. Smith at a recent international conference of the Society for the Advancement of Games and Simulations in Education and Training (SAGSET), Cardiff, Wales.

17. As Keeler (1982, p. 259) stated, "In their training courses teachers must be given the opportunity to experience the methodology and to put it into practice themselves. Training courses should be 'do'-courses."

18. Described by Dickinson (1987).

19. Wenden describes the project (1986a, pp. 130–131).

20. Summarized from Andrew Cohen (personal communication, December 13, 1987).

21. Information obtained from Roberta Lavine (personal communication, May 6, 1988).

22. Details provided by Will Sutter (personal communication, May 15, 1988).

23. See Morgenstern (1987) and Murray, Morgenstern, and Furstenberg (1989).

24. See Morgenstern (1987).

25. Information on ICONS comes from a variety of sources: personal observation of ICONS sessions at the University of Toulon, France; a national ICONS training workshop at the University of Maryland, USA; discussions with developers and coordinators of ICONS; and various publications about ICONS (especially Crookall & Wilkenfeld, 1985, 1987; Noel, Crookall, Wilkenfeld, & Schapira, 1987; Crookall, Oxford, Saunders, & Lavine, 1989).

26. The information here comes from my own observations, a personal interview with Matheidesz at an international conference (Society for the Advancement of Games and Simulations in Education and Training, Cardiff, Wales), written communications, and published articles and games (Matheidesz, 1987a, 1987b, 1988a, 1988b).

27. Matheidesz (1987a).

28. In addition to games using the 96 faces, Matheidesz is also training the teachers to use a board game involving "gift giving" to stimulate classroom communication in English and to train learners in certain sociolinguistic skills, such as taking turns. Another game, RUNNING ERRANDS (Matheidesz, 1987b), is also included in the project.

29. Matheidesz has also worked with language teachers and programmers to produce a series of computer-assisted language games, all available in English and some available in Spanish, German, and Russian. These computer games, like the other games, encourage a large range of strategies. In addition to these efforts, Matheidesz has completed the Teletext English Language Scheme, a full year's program which is now on Hungarian TV each day.

References

Abé, D., Henner-Stanchina, C., & Smith, P. (1975). New approaches to autonomy: Two experiments in self-directed learning. *Mélanges Pedagogiques.*

Adler, B., & Vogel, M. (1986). True or false? Test anxiety is potent and common. *Washington Post,* May 29, p. B-5.

Adler, R. S. (1987). Culture shock and the cross-cultural learning experience. In L. F. Luce & E. C. Smith (Eds.), *Towards internationalism: Readings in cross-cultural communication* (2nd ed., pp. 24–35). New York: Newbury House.

Allwright, R. L. (1980). *What do we want teaching materials for?* Paper presented at the annual meeting of TESOL.

Anderson, J. R. (1976). *Language, memory, and thought.* Hillsdale, NJ: Erlbaum.

Anderson, J. R. (1983). *The architecture of cognition.* Cambridge, MA: Harvard University Press.

Anderson, J. R. (1985). *Cognitive psychology and its implications* (2nd ed.). New York: W. H. Freeman.

Asher, J. J. (1966a). The learning strategy of the total physical response: A review. *Modern Language Journal, 50,* 3–17.

Asher, J. J. (1966b). The strategy of the total physical response: An application to learning Russian. *International Review of Applied Linguistics, 3,* 291–300.

Aston, G. (1987). Casual chat and the teaching of language as comity. *Lingua e Nuova Didattica (LEND), 16*(1), 26–41.

Ausubel, D. A. (1963). *The psychology of meaningful verbal learning: An introduction to school learning.* New York: Grune & Stratton.

Bachman, L. F. (in press). *Fundamental considerations in language testing.* Reading, MA: Addison-Wesley.

Baddeley, A. (1986). *Your memory: A user's guide.* Harmondsworth: Penguin.

Bailey, K. N. (1983). Competitiveness and anxiety in adult second language learning: Looking at and through the diary studies. In H. W. Seliger & M. H. Long (Eds.), *Classroom-oriented research in second language acquisition* (pp. 67–103). Rowley, MA: Newbury House.

Bailey, K. N., & Ochsner, R. (1983). A methodological review of the diary studies: Windmill tilting or social science. In K. N. Bailey, M. H. Long, & S. Peck (Eds.), *Second language acquisition studies* (pp. 188–198). Rowley, MA: Newbury House.

Bardwick, J. (1971). *Psychology of women: A study of biocultural conflicts.* New York: Harper & Row.

Barnes, D. R., & Clawson, E. U. (1975). Do advance organizers facilitate learning? Recommendations for further research based on analysis of 32 studies. *Review of Educational Research, 45*(4), 637–659.

Bassano, S., & Christison, M. A. (1988). Cooperative learning in the ESL classroom. *TESOL Newsletter, 22*(2), 1, 8–9.

Beebe, L. M. (1983). Risk-taking and the language learner. In H. W. Seliger & M. H. Long (Eds.), *Classroom-oriented research in second language acquisition* (pp. 39–66). Rowley, MA: Newbury House.

Begley, S., Springen, K., Katz, S., Hager, M., & Jones, E. (1986a). Memory: Science achieves important new insights into the mother of the Muses. *Newsweek,* September 29, pp. 48–54.

Begley, S., Springen, K., Katz, S., Hager, M., & Jones, E. (1986b). The maze of memory. *Newsweek on Health,* Winter, pp. 16–20.

Bejarano, Y. (1987). A cooperative small-group methodology in the language classroom. *TESOL Quarterly, 21*(3), 483–504.

Bialystok, E. (1978). A theoretical model of second language learning. *Language Learning, 28,* 69–83.

Bialystok, E. (1981). The role of conscious strategies in second language proficiency. *Modern Language Journal, 65,* 24–35.

Bialystok, E. (1983). Some factors in the selection and implementation of communication strategies. In C. Faerch & G. Kasper (Eds.), *Strategies in interlanguage communication* (pp. 100–118). London: Longman.

Blair, K. (1983). *Cubal analysis: A post sexist model of the psyche.* Weston, CT: Magic Circle Press.

Blanchard, K., & Root, C. (1984). *Ready to write.* New York: Longman.

Bower, G. W. (1970). Analysis of a mnemonic device. *American Scientist, 50,* 495–510.

Brown, A. L., Bransford, J. D., Ferrara, R., & Campione, J. C. (1983). Learning, remembering, and understanding. In J. N. Flavell & E. M. Markham (Eds.), *Carmichael's manual of child psychology* (Vol. 1). New York: Wiley.

Brown, A. L., Campione, J. C., & Day, J. D. (1980a). Learning to learn: On training students to learn from texts. *Educational Researcher, 10,* 14–21.

Brown, A. L., Campione, J. C., & Day, J. D. (1980b). *Learning to learn: On training students to learn from texts.* Manuscript, Center for the Study of Reading, University of Illinois.

Brown, H. D. (1984). The consensus: Another view. *Foreign Language Annals, 17*(4), 277–280.

Brown, H. D. (1987). *Principles of language learning and teaching* (2nd ed.). Englewood Cliffs, NJ: Prentice-Hall.

Brown-Azarowicz, M., Stannard, C., & Goldin, M. (1986). *Yes! You can learn a foreign language.* Lincolnwood, IL: Passport Books.

Burgess, A. (1963). *A clockwork orange.* New York: Mouton.

Byrnes, H. (1984). The role of listening comprehension: A theoretical base. *Foreign Language Annals, 17*(4), 317–329.

Campbell, R., & Wales, R. (1970). The study of language acquisition. In J. Lyons (Ed.), *New horizons in linguistics.* Harmondsworth: Penguin.

Canale, M. (1983). From communicative competence to communicative language pedagogy. In J. Richards & R. Schmidt (Eds.), *Language and communication.* London: Longman.

Canale, M., & Swain, M. (1980). Theoretical bases of communicative approaches to second language teaching and testing. *Applied Linguistics, 1,* 1–47.

Candlin, C. (1983). Preface. In C. Faerch & G. Kasper (Eds.), *Strategies in interlanguage communication* (pp. ix–xiv). London: Longman.

Carver, D. (1984). Plans, learner strategies, and self-direction in language learning. *System, 12*(2), 123–131.

Chamot, A. U. (1987). The power of learning strategies. *Ohio Bilingual-Multicultural Update,* March, 4, 6–11.

Chamot, A. U., & O'Malley, J. M. (1986). *Cognitive Academic Language Learning Approach: An ESL content-based curriculum.* Rosslyn, VA: National Clearinghouse for Bilingual Education, and InterAmerica Research Associates.

Chamot, A. U., & O'Malley, J. M. (1987). The Cognitive Academic Language Learning Approach: A bridge to the mainstream. *TESOL Quarterly, 21*(2), 227–249.

Chamot, A. U., O'Malley, J. M., Kupper, L., & Impink-Hernandez, M. V. (1987). *A study of learning strategies in foreign language instruction: First year report.* Washington, DC: InterAmerica Research Associates.

Chapelle, C. A. (1983). *The relationship between ambiguity tolerance and success in acquiring English as a second language in adult learners.* Unpublished doctoral dissertation, University of Illinois.

Chomsky, N. (1965). *Aspects of theory of syntax.* Cambridge, MA: M.I.T. Press.

Clark, B. L. (1985). *Talking about writing: A guide for tutor and teacher conferences.* Ann Arbor: University of Michigan Press.

Clark, J. L. D. (1972). *Foreign language testing: Theory and practice.* Philadelphia: Center for Curriculum Development.

Clarke, D. F., & Nation, J. S. R. (1980). Guessing the meaning of words from context: Strategy and techniques. *System, 8*(3), 211–220.

Clément, R., Gardner, R. C., & Smythe, P. C. (1980). Social and individual factors in second language acquisition. *Canadian Journal of Behavioural Science, 12,* 293–302.

Clément, R., Major, L., Gardner, R. C., & Smythe, P. C. (1977). Attitudes and motivation in second language acquisition: An investigation of Ontario francophones. *Working Papers on Bilingualism, 12,* 1–20.

Cohen, A. D. (1987a). Recent uses of mentalistic data in reading strategy research. *D.E.L.T.A., 3*(1), 57–84. (Depto. de Língüistica, Pontifícia Universidade Católica de São Paulo).

Cohen, A. D. (1987b). Studying learner strategies: How we get the information. In A. Wenden & J. Rubin (Eds.), *Learner strategies in language learning* (pp. 31–40). Englewood Cliffs, NJ: Prentice-Hall.

Cohen, A. D. (in press). *Second language learning: Insights for learners, teachers, and researchers.* New York: Newbury House/Harper & Row.

Cohen, A. D., & Aphek, E. (1981). Easifying second language learning. *Studies in Second Language Acquisition, 3*(2), 221–236.

Cohen, A. D., Glasman, H., Rosenbaum-Cohen, P. R., Ferrara, J., & Fine, J. (1979). Reading English for specialized purposes: Discourse analysis and the use of student informants. *TESOL Quarterly, 13*(4), 551–564.

Cohen, A. D., & Hosenfeld, C. (1981). Some uses of mentalistic data in second language research. *Language Learning, 31*(2), 285–313.

Colman, A. (1982). *Game theory and experimental games: The study of strategic interaction.* Oxford: Pergamon.

Cornelius, E. J., Jr. (1955). *How to learn a foreign language*. New York: Thomas Crowell.

Cramer, N. A. (1985). *The writing process: 20 projects for group work*. Rowley, MA: Newbury House.

Crawford, C., & Leitzell, E. M. (1980). *Learning a new language*. Los Angeles: University of Southern California.

Crookall, D. (1979). Variations on the theme of "Alibi." *Modern English Teacher, 7*(1), 12–13. Reprinted in S. Holden (Ed.), (1983), *Second selections from Modern English Teacher*. Harlow: Longman.

Crookall, D. (1983a). Learner training: A neglected strategy—Parts 1 and 2. *Modern English Teacher, 11*(1), 31–33; *11*(2), 41–42.

Crookall, D. (1983b). Picture stories. *Modern English Teacher, 10*(4), 16–19.

Crookall, D. (1983c). Voices out of the air: World Communications Year, international broadcasting and foreign language learning. *System, 11*(3), 295–302.

Crookall, D. (1984a). Comparing facts and figures. *Practical English Teaching, 4*(3), 24–25.

Crookall, D. (1984b). Rigs and posts: Radio reception technology for FLL. *System, 12*(2), 151–167.

Crookall, D. (1985). Media gaming and NEWSIM: A computer-assisted, "real news" simulation. *System, 13*(3), 259–268.

Crookall, D. (1986). Writing short stories for the BBC World Service. *System, 14*(3), 295–300.

Crookall, D., Oxford, R., Saunders, D., & Lavine, R. (1989). Our multicultural global village: Foreign languages, simulations and network gaming. In D.Crookall & D. Saunders (Eds.), *Communication and simulation: From two fields to one theme*. (pp. 91–106) Clevedon, Avon: Multilingual Matters.

Crookall, D. & Watson, D. R. (1985). Some applied and theoretical perspectives on a jigsaw reading exercise. *ITL Review of Applied Linguistics, 69*, 43–79.

Crookall, D., & Wilkenfeld, J. (1985). ICONS: Communications technologies and international relations. *System, 13*(3), 253–258.

Crookall, D., & Wilkenfeld, J. (1987). Information technology in the service of worldwide multi-institutional simulation. In J. Moonen & T. Plomp (Eds.), *Developments in educational software and courseware* (pp. 157–162). Oxford: Pergamon.

Culhane, T. (1986). *Russian language and people*. London: BBC Books.

Cummins, J. (1982, February). Tests, achievement, and bilingual students. *Focus*, No. 9. Wheaton, MD: National Clearinghouse for Bilingual Education.

Cummins, J. (1983). Conceptual and linguistic foundations of language assessment. In S. S. Seidner (Ed.), *Issues of language assessment: Language assessment and curriculum planning* (Vol. 2, pp. 7–16). Wheaton, MD: National Clearinghouse for Bilingual Education.

Cummins, J. (1986). Cultures in contact: Using classroom microcomputers for cultural interchange and reinforcement. *TESL Canada Journal, 3*(2), 13–31.

Dansereau, D. F. (1983). *Cooperative learning: Impact on acquisition of knowledge and skills* (Technical Report No. 586). Alexandria, VA: Army Research Institute for the Behavioral and Social Sciences.

Dansereau, D. F. (1985). Learning strategy research. In J. W. Segal, S. F. Chipman, & R. Glaser (Eds.), *Thinking and learning skills: Relating learning to basic research* (pp. 209–240). Hillsdale, NJ: Erlbaum.

Dansereau, D. F. (1988). Cooperative learning strategies. In C. E. Weinstein, E. T. Goetz, & P. A. Alexander (Eds.), *Learning and study strategies: Issues in assessment, instruction, and evaluation.* New York: Academic Press.

Derry, S. J., & Murphy, D. A. (1986). Designing systems that train learning ability: From theory to practice. *Review of Educational Research, 56*(1), 1–39.

Diadori, R. (1987). Simulation strategy and communicative approach in CALL. In D. Crookall, C. S. Greenblat, A. Coote, J. H. G. Klabbers, & D. R. Watson (Eds.), *Simulation-gaming in the late 1980s* (pp. 111–115). Oxford: Pergamon.

Dickinson, L. (1987). *Self-instruction in language learning.* Cambridge: Cambridge University Press.

Dulay, H. C., Burt, M. K., & Krashen, S. (1982). *Language two.* New York: Oxford University Press.

Ehrman, M., & Oxford, R. (1989). Effects of sex differences, career choice, and psychological type on adult language learning strategies. *Modern Language Journal, 73*(1), 1–13.

Ellis, R. (1986). *Understanding second language acquisition.* Oxford: Oxford University Press.

Faerch, C., & Kasper, S. (1983a). On identifying communication strategies in interlanguage production. In C. Faerch & G. Kasper (Eds.), *Strategies in interlanguage communication* (pp. 210–238). London: Longman.

Faerch, C., & Kasper, S. (1983b). Plans and strategies in foreign language communication. In C. Faerch & G. Kasper (Eds.), *Strategies in interlanguage communication* (pp. 20–60). London: Longman.

Frank, C., & Rinvolucri, M. (1983). *Grammar in action: Awareness activities for language learning.* Oxford: Pergamon.

Gaies, S. J. (1985). *Peer involvement in language learning.* New York: Harcourt Brace Jovanovich.

Gardner, R. C. (1985). *Social psychology and second language learning: The role of attitudes and motivation.* London, Ontario: Edward Arnold.

Gardner, R. C., & Lambert, W. E. (1959). Motivational variables in second language acquisition. *Canadian Journal of Psychology, 13,* 266–272.

Gardner, R. C., & Lambert, W. E. (1972). *Attitudes and motivation in second language learning.* Rowley, MA: Newbury House.

Gardner, R. C., Lalonde, R. H., Moorcroft, R., & Evers, F. T. (1985). *Second language attrition: The role of motivation and use* (Research Bulletin 638). London, Ontario: University of Western Ontario.

Gardner, R. C., & Smythe, R. C. (1975a). *Second language acquisition: A social psychological approach* (Research Bulletin No. 322). London, Ontario: Department of Psychology, University of Western Ontario.

Gardner, R. C., & Smythe, R. C. (1975b). Motivation and second language acquisition. *Canadian Modern Language Review, 31,* 218–238.

Geddes, M., & White, R. (1978). The use of semi-scripted simulated authentic speech in listening comprehension. *Audiovisual Language Journal, 16*(3), 137–145.

Genesee, F. (1978). Second language learning and language attitudes. *Working Papers on Bilingualism, 16,* 19–42.

Gibbons, J. (1985). The silent period: An examination. *Language Learning, 26,* 267–280.

Gibson, J. (1973). Teachers talking. Quoted in S. Delamont, *Interaction in the classroom* (2nd ed.). London: Methuen.

Gilligan, C. (1982). *In a different voice: Psychological theory and women's development*. Cambridge, MA: Harvard University Press.

Goleman, D. (1986). Mental images: New research helps clarify their role. *New York Times*, August 12, C1, C6.

Grala, M., Oxford, R., & Schleppegrell, M. (1987). *Improving your language learning: Strategies for Peace Corps volunteers*. Washington, DC: Center for Applied Linguistics.

Grellet, F. (1981). *Developing reading skills*. Cambridge: Cambridge University Press.

Grucz, M. M., & McKee, E. (1986). Mnemonic devices: Pegs on which to hang your students' memory. *AATF National Bulletin*, *11*(3), 8–11.

Gruneberg, M. M. (1987a). *The Link Word language system: French*. London: Corgi.

Gruneberg, M. M. (1987b). *The Link Word language system: German*. London: Corgi.

Gruneberg, M. M. (1987c). *The Link Word language system: Italian*. London: Corgi.

Gruneberg, M. M. (1987d). *The Link Word language system: Spanish*. London: Corgi.

Gunderson, B., & Johnson, D. (1980). Building positive attitudes by using cooperative learning groups. *Foreign Language Annals*, *13*(1), 39–43.

Hague, S. A. (1986a). Bridging the gap between learning to read and reading to learn: A remedy that works. *Northeast Conference Newsletter*, *19*, 46–47.

Hague, S. A. (1986b). Learning to read and reading to learn: Bridging the gap in second language acquisition. *Hispania*, *69*(2), 400–402.

Hague, S. A. (1987). Vocabulary instruction: What L2 can learn from L1. *Foreign Language Annals*, *20*(3), 217–225.

Halff, H. M. (1986). Instructional applications of artificial intelligence. *Educational Leadership*, March, 24–31.

Hall, R., Jr. (1973). *New ways to learn a foreign language*. Ithaca, NY: Spoken Language Services.

Hamp-Lyons, L. (1983). Review of *Survey of materials for teaching advanced listening and note-taking*. *TESOL Quarterly*, *17*(1), 109–121.

Hamp-Lyons, L., & Heasley, B. (1987). *Study writing: A course in written English for academic and professional purposes*. Cambridge: Cambridge University Press.

Harmer, J. (1983). *The practice of English language teaching*. Harlow: Longman.

Hart, J., & Simon, N. (1988). Iterative Prisoner's Dilemma: A program for instructional and experimental use. In D. Crookall (Ed.), *Simulation/gaming and the new technolgies*. Special issue of *Simulation/Games for Learning*, *18*(1).

Harter, S. (1986). Feeling good about yourself isn't enough. *Today*, *8*(2), 2–3.

Hartfiel, V. F., Hughey, J. B., Wormuth, D. R., & Jacobs, H. (1985). *Learning ESL composition*. Rowley, MA: Newbury House.

Henner-Stanchina, C. (1976). Two years of autonomy: Practise and outlook. *Mélanges Pedagogiques*.

Henner-Stanchina, C. (1986). *Teaching strategies for listening comprehension*. Paper presented at the Fourth Annual Conference on Learning Strategies, LaGuardia (NY) Community College.

Henner-Stanchina, C., & Holec, H. (1977). Evaluation of an autonomous learning scheme. *Mélanges Pedagogiques*.

Higbee, K. L. (1979). Recent research on visual mnemonics: Historical roots and educational fruits. *Review of Educational Research*, *49*(4), 611–629.

Holec, H. (1980). Learner training: Meeting the needs of self-directed learning. In H. B. Altman & C. V. James (Eds.), *Foreign language teaching: Meeting individual needs*. Oxford: Pergamon.

Holec, H. (1981). *Autonomy and foreign language learning*. Oxford: Pergamon.

Hosenfeld, C. (1977). *A learning-teaching view of second-language instruction: The learning strategies of second language learners with reading-grammar tasks*. Unpublished doctoral dissertation, Ohio State University.

Hosenfeld, C., Arnold, V., Kirchofer, J., Laciura, J., & Wilson, L. (1981). Second language reading: A curricular sequence for teaching reading strategies. *Foreign Language Annals, 14*(5), 415–422.

Houpt, S. (1984). Inspiring creative writing through conversation. *Foreign Language Annals, 3*(17), 185–189.

Howard, D. V. (1983). *Cognitive psychology: Memory, language, and thought*. New York: Macmillan.

Howatt, A. P. R. (1984). *A history of English language teaching*. Oxford: Oxford University Press.

Hymes, D. (1972). On communicative competence. In J. B. Pride & D. Hymes (Eds.), *Sociolinguistics*. Harmondsworth: Penguin.

Jacob, E., & Mattson, B. (1987). *Using cooperative learning with language minority students: A report from the field*. Washington, DC: Center for Language Education and Research, Center for Applied Linguistics.

James, B. G. (1984). *Business wargames*. Harmondsworth: Penguin.

Jones, B. F., Aniran, M., & Katias, M. (1985). Teaching cognitive strategies and text structures within language arts programs. In J. W. Segal, S. F. Chipman, & R. Glaser (Eds.), *Thinking and learning skills* (Vol. 1, pp. 259–297). Hillsdale, NJ: Erlbaum.

Jones, K. (1985). *Graded Simulations 1: SURVIVAL, FRONT PAGE, RADIO COVINGHAM*. Oxford: Basil Blackwell.

Jones, L. (1983). *Eight simulations: For upper-intermediate and more advanced students of English*. Cambridge: Cambridge University Press.

Jones, L., & Kimbrough, V. (1987). *Great ideas: Listening and speaking activities for students of American English*. Cambridge: Cambridge University Press.

Jones, R. A. (1977). *Psychological, social and personal factors in second language acquisition*. Unpublished master's thesis, English Department (ESL Section), University of California at Los Angeles.

Kagan, S. (1986). Cooperative learning and sociocultural factors in schooling. In *Beyond language: Social and cultural factors in schooling language minority students* (pp. 231–290). Bilingual Education Office, California State Department of Education.

Keeler, S. (1982). Practising what we preach: Teaching teachers about self-directed learning through the integrated use of self-access environments in the teacher training course. *System, 10*(3), 258–268.

Kinder Monatszeitschrift. (1986). *VIII*(3).

Kinder Monatszeitschrift. (1986). *VIII*(6).

Knowles, M. (1975). *Self-directed learning: A guide for learners and teachers*. Chicago: Association Press.

Koestler, A. (1964). *The art of creation*. London: Hutchinson.

Kohn, A. (1987). It's hard to get out of a pair—Profile: David and Roger Johnson. *Psychology Today*, October, pp. 53–57.

Kraft, C. H., & Kraft, M. E. (1966). *Where do I go from here? A handbook for continuing language study in the field*. United States Peace Corps.

Krashen, S. D. (1982). *Principles and practice in second language acquisition*. Oxford: Pergamon.

Krashen, S. D., & Terrell, T. D. (1983). *The natural approach to language acquisition in the classroom*. Oxford/San Francisco: Pergamon/Alemany.

Krashen, S. D., Terrell, T. D., Ehrman, M. E., & Herzog, M. (1984). A theoretical basis for teaching the receptive skills. *Foreign Language Annals*, *4*(17), 261–275.

Lambert, R. D., & Freed, B. F. (Eds.). (1982). *The loss of language skills*. Rowley, MA: Newbury House.

Leaver, B. L. (1984). Twenty minutes to mastery of the Cyrillic alphabet. *Foreign Language Annals*, *17*(1), 215–220.

Leaver, B. L. (forthcoming). *The acquisition/learning dichotomy: Another look*. Submitted for publication.

Littlewood, W. (1984). *Foreign and second language learning: Language acquisition research and its implications for the classroom*. Cambridge: Cambridge University Press.

Lobuts, J. F., & Pennewill, C. L. (1989). Individual and organizational communication and destructive competition. In D. Crookall & D. Saunders (Eds.), *Communication and simulation: From two fields to one theme* (pp. 177–187). Clevedon, Avon, UK: Multilingual Matters.

Long, M. (1979). *Inside the "black box": Methodological issues in research on teaching*. Paper presented at the annual meeting of TESOL, Boston, MA.

Long, P. (1987). Laugh and be well? *Psychology Today*, 28–29.

Lorayne, H., & Lucas, J. (1974). *The memory book*. New York: Ballantine.

Lukmani, Y. (1972). Motivation to learn and language proficiency. *Language Learning*, *22*(2), 261–273.

MacBride, S., et al. (1980). *Many voices, one world*. London: Kogan Page, UNESCO.

Maccoby, E. E., & Jacklin, C. (1974). *The psychology of sex differences*. Stanford, CA: Stanford University Press.

Manzo, A. (1969). The ReQuest procedure. *Journal of Reading*, *13*, 123–126.

Matheidesz, M. (1987a). *96 (SPEAKING FACES)*. Budapest: Babilon.

Matheidesz, M. (1987b). Running errands: A communication board game. *Simulation/Games for Learning*, *17*(3), 120–126.

Matheidesz, M. (1988a). Games for language learning. In D. Saunders, A. Coote, & D. Crookall, (Eds.), *Learning from experience through games and simulation*. Loughborough, Leics, UK: Society for the Advancement of Games and Simulations in Education and Training.

Matheidesz, M. (1988b). Self-access language practice through CALL games. In D. Crookall, (Ed.), *Simulation/gaming and the new technologies*. Special issue of *Simulation/Games for Learning*, *18*(1).

McCombs, B. L. (1987). *The role of affective variables in autonomous learning*. Paper presented at the annual meeting of AERA, Washington, DC.

McCombs, B. L. (1988). Motivational skills training: Combining metacognitive, cognitive, and affective learning strategies. In C. E. Weinstein, E. T. Goetz, & P. A. Alexander (Eds.), *Learning and study strategies: Issues in assessment, instruction, and evaluation*. New York: Academic Press.

McCombs, B. L., & Dobrovolny, J. L. (1982). *Student motivational skill training package: Evaluation for air force technical training* (Technical Report No. AFHRL-TR-82-31). Air Force Human Resources Laboratory, Air Force Systems Command, Brooks Air Force Base, Texas; Logistics and Technical Training Division, Technical Training Branch, Lowry Air Force Base, Colorado.

McGroarty, M. (1987). *Patterns of persistent second language learners: Elementary Spanish*. Paper presented at the annual meeting of TESOL, Miami, Florida.

McKee, E. (1981). Teaching writing in the second language composition/conversation class at the college level. *Foreign Language Annals, 14*(4–5), 273–278.

Mendelsohn, D. J. (1984). There ARE strategies for listening. *TEAL Occasional Papers, 8*, 63–76.

Meyer, R. (1984). "Listen my children, and you shall hear . . ." *Foreign Language Annals, 17*(4), 343–344.

Miller, G. A. (1956). The magical number seven, plus or minus two: Some limits on our capacity for processing information. *Psychological Review, 63*, 81–90.

Mohan, B. A. (1986). *Language and content*. Reading, MA: Addison-Wesley.

Moran, P. R. (1984). *Lexicarry: An illustrated vocabulary-builder for second languages*. Brattleboro: ProLingua.

Morgenstern, D. (1987). Artifice vs. real-world data. In D. Crookall, C. S. Greenblat, A. Coote, J. H. G. Klabbers, & D. R. Watson (Eds.), *Simulation-gaming in the later 1980s* (pp. 101–109). Oxford: Pergamon.

Morley, J. (1984). *Listening and language learning in English as a second language: Developing a self-study activities for listening comprehension*. Orlando: Harcourt Brace Jovanovich/Center for Applied Linguistics.

Moulden, H. (1978). Extending self-directed learning of English in an engineering college: Experiment year one. *Mélanges Pedagogiques*, 81–102.

Moulden, H. (1980). Extending self-directed learning of English in an engineering college. Experiment two. *Mélanges Pedagogigues*, 83–116.

Moulton, W. G. (1966). *A linguistic guide to language learning*. New York: Modern Language Association to America.

Munby, J. (1978). *Communicative syllabus design*. Cambridge: Cambridge University Press.

Murray, J. M., Morgenstern, D., & Furstenberg, G. (1989). In W. F. Smith (Ed.), *Modern technology in foreign language education* (pp. 97–118). Lincolnwood, IL: National Textbook Company.

Naiman, N., Fröhlich, M., & Todesco, A. (1975). The good second language learner. *TESL Talk, 6*(1), 58–75.

Naiman, N., Fröhlich, M., Stern, H. H., & Todesco, A. (1978). *The good language learner*. Research in Education Series, 7. Toronto: Ontario Institute for Studies in Education.

Nida, E. (1957). *Learning a foreign language: A handbook prepared especially for missionaries*. Friendship Press for the National Council of Churches in the USA.

Noel, R. C., Crookall, D., Wilkenfeld, J., & Schapira, L. (1987). Network gaming: A vehicle for international communication. In D. Crookall, C. S. Greenblat, A. Coote, J. H. G. Klabbers, & D. R. Watson (Eds.), *Simulation-gaming in the late 1980s* (pp. 5–21). Oxford: Pergamon Press.

Norbrook, H. (1984). Extensive listening: How can radio aid comprehension? (Parts 1 and 2). *Modern English Teacher*, 12.

Novak, D., & Gowin, D. B. (1984). *Learning how to learn.* Cambridge: Cambridge University Press.

Nyikos, M. (1987). *The effect of color and imagery as mnemonic strategies on learning and retention of lexical items in German.* Unpublished doctoral dissertation, Purdue University.

Nyikos, M. (n.d.). *Assuming responsibility for learning: Study strategy worksheet.* West Lafayette, IN: Purdue University.

Nyikos, M., & Oxford, R. (1987). *Strategies for foreign language learning and second language acquisition.* Paper presented at the Conference on Second Language Acquisition and Foreign Language Learning, University of Illinois, Champaign-Urbana.

Omaggio, A. C. (1981). *Helping learners succeed: Activities for the foreign language classroom.* Washington, DC: Center for Applied Linguistics.

Omaggio, A. C. (1986). *Teaching language in context: Proficiency-oriented instruction.* Boston: Heinle & Heinle.

O'Malley, J. M., & Chamot, A. U. (1989). *Learning strategies in second language acquisition.* Cambridge: Cambridge University Press.

O'Malley, J. M., Chamot, A. U., Stewner-Manzanares, G., Küpper, L., & Russo, R. (1985a). Learning strategies used by beginning and intermediate ESL students. *Language Learning, 35*(1), 21–46.

O'Malley, J. M., Chamot, A. U., Stewner-Manzanares, G., Russo, R., & Küpper, L. (1985b). Learning strategy applications with students of English as a second language. *TESOL Quarterly, 19*(3), 557–584.

O'Malley, J. M., Chamot, A. U., & Walker, C. (1987). Some applications of cognitive theory in second language acquisition. *Studies in Second Language Acquisition, 9*(3).

O'Neil, H. F., Jr. (Ed.). (1978). *Learning strategies.* New York: Academic Press.

Ong, W. J. (1987). *Orality and literacy: The technologizing of the word.* London: Methuen.

Oppenheimer, J., & Winer, M. (1988). Using and creating a simulation authoring system: Cooperation and conflict. In D. Crookall (Ed.), *Computerized simulation in the social sciences: Issues and practices,* Special Issue of *Social Science Computer Review, 6*(1).

Oshima, A., & Hogue, A., (1983). *Writing academic English.* Reading, MA: Addison-Wesley.

Oshima, A., & Hogue, A. (1988). *Introduction to academic writing.* Reading, MA: Addison-Wesley.

Oskarsson, M. (1984). *Self-assessment of foreign language skills: A survey of research and development work.* Strasbourg, France: Council of Europe, Council for Cultural Cooperation.

Oxford, R. (1982a). Research on language loss: A review with implications for foreign language teaching. *Modern Language Journal, 66*(2), 168–169.

Oxford, R. (1982b). Technical issues in designing and conducting research on language skill attrition. In R. Lambert & B. F. Freed (Eds.), *The loss of language skills.* Rowley, MA: Newbury House, pp. 119–137.

Oxford, R. (1985a). *A new taxonomy of second language learning strategies.* Washington, DC: ERIC Clearinghouse on Languages and Linguistics.

Oxford, R. (1985b). Second language learning strategies: What the research has to say. *ERIC/CLL News Bulletin, 9,* 3–5.

Oxford, R. (1986a). *Development and psychometric testing of the Strategy Inventory for Language Learning (SILL)* (ARI Technical Report 728). Alexandria, VA: Training Research Laboratory, US Army Research Institute for Behavioral and Social Sciences.

Oxford, R. (1986b). *Development of a new survey and taxonomy for second language learning.* Paper presented at the Fourth Annual Conference on Learning Strategies, LaGuardia (NY) Community College.

Oxford, R. (1986c). *Development of the Strategy Inventory for Language Learning.* Paper presented at the Language Testing Research Colloquium, Monterey, CA.

Oxford, R. (1986d). Research on the successful language learner. *Minibib.* Washington, DC: ERIC Clearinghouse on Languages and Linguistics.

Oxford, R. (1986e). *Researching and assessing strategies for learning a second language.* Paper presented at the annual meeting of AERA, San Francisco.

Oxford, R. (1986f). *Second language learning strategies: Current research and implications for practice.* Los Angeles: Center for Language Education and Research, University of California at Los Angeles.

Oxford, R. (1988). *Problems and solutions in foreign/second language vocabulary learning: The potential role of semantic mapping.* Reston, VA: Advanced Technology.

Oxford, R. (1989). Use of language learning strategies: A synthesis of studies with implications for strategy training. *System, 17*(2).

Oxford, R., Cohen, A., & Sutter, W. (in press). Language learning strategies: Evolution of a concept.

Oxford, R., & Crookall, D. (1988). Learning strategies. In J. Berko-Gleason (Ed.), *You CAN take it with you: Helping students maintain second language skills* (pp. 23–49). Englewood Cliffs, NJ: Prentice-Hall.

Oxford, R., & Ehrman, M. (1989). Psychological type and adult language learning strategies: A pilot study. *Journal of Psychological Type, 16,* 22–32.

Oxford, R., Lavine, R., & Crookall, D. (1989). Language learning strategies, the communicative approach, and their classroom implications. *Foreign Language Annals, 22*(1), 29–39.

Oxford, R., & Nyikos, M. (1987). *Second language learning strategies: New research findings.* Paper presented at the Symposium on Second Language Learning Styles and Strategies, Center for Applied Linguistics, Washington, DC.

Oxford, R., & Nyikos, M. (1989). Variables affecting choice of language learning strategies by university students. *Modern Language Journal, 73*(2).

Oxford, R., Nyikos, M., & Crookall, D. (1987). *Learning strategies of university foreign language students: A large-scale study.* Paper presented at the annual meeting of TESOL, Miami, FL.

Oxford, R., Nyikos, M., & Ehrman, M. (1988). Vive la différence? Reflections on sex differences in use of language learning strategies. *Foreign Language Annals, 21*(4), 321–329.

Oxford, R., & Rhodes, N. C. (1988). U.S. foreign language instruction: Assessing needs and creating an action plan. *ERIC/CLL News Bulletin, 11*(2), 1, 6–7.

Papalia, A., & Zampogna, J. (1977). Strategies used by foreign language students in deriving meaning from a written text and in learning vocabulary. *Language Association Bulletin,* 7–8.

Pei, N. (1966). *How to learn languages and what languages to learn.* New York: Harper & Row.

Phillips, J. K. (1984). Practical implications of recent research in reading. *Foreign Language Annals, 17*(4), 285–296.

Pimsleur, P. (1980). *How to learn a foreign language.* Boston: Heinle & Heinle.

Politzer, R. L. (1965). *Foreign language learning: A linguistic introduction.* Englewood Cliffs, NJ: Prentice-Hall.

Politzer, R. L. (1983). An exploratory study of self-reported language learning behaviors and their relation to achievement. *Studies in Second Language Acquisition, 6*(1), 54–65.

Politzer, R. L., & McGroarty, M. (1985). *An exploratory study of learning behaviors and their relation to gains in linguistic and communicative competence.* Unpublished manuscript, Stanford University.

Private Eye. (1979). *Bumper book of boobs.* London: Private Eye/Deutsch.

Prowse, R. (1983). Talking about learning. *TESOL-France News, 3*(2), 18–19.

Raimes, A. (1983). *Techniques in teaching writing.* Oxford: Oxford University Press.

Ramirez, A. G. (1986). Language learning strategies used by adolescents studying French in New York schools. *Foreign Language Annals, 19*(2), 131–141.

Reid, J. M. (1987). The learning style preferences of ESL students. *TESOL Quarterly, 21,* 87–111.

Reiss, M-A. (1985). The good language learner: Another look. *Canadian Language Review/La Revue Canadienne des Langues Vivantes, 41*(3), 511–523.

Rigney, J. W. (1978). Learning strategies: A theoretical perspective. In H. F. O'Neil, Jr. (Ed.), *Learning strategies* (pp. 165–205). New York: Academic Press.

Rigney, J. W. (1980). Cognitive learning strategies and dualities in information processing. In R. E. Snow, R. Federico, & W. E. Montague (Eds.), *Aptitude, learning and instruction* (Vol. 1, pp. 315–343). Hillsdale, NJ: Erlbaum.

Riley, P. (1982). Topics in communicative methodology: Including a preliminary and selective bibliography on the communicative approach. *Mélanges Pedagogiques,* 93–132.

Riley, P. (1985). "Strategy": Conflict or collaboration. *Mélanges Pedagogiques,* 91–116.

Rivera, C. (Ed.). (1984). *Language proficiency and academic achievement.* Clevedon, UK: Multilingual Matters.

Rivers, W. N. (1981). *Teaching foreign language skills* (2nd ed.). Chicago: University of Chicago Press.

Rodgers, T. S. (1978). Towards a model of learner variation in autonomous foreign language learning. *Studies in Second Language Acquisition, 2*(1), 73–97.

Rossi-Le, L. (1988). *The perceptual learning differences and the relationship to language learning strategies in adult students for English as a second language.* Unpublished dissertation proposal, Drake University.

Rowe, D. (1983). *Depression: The way out of the prison.* London: Routledge & Kegan Paul.

Ruben, B. D. (1987). Guidelines for cross-cultural communication effectiveness. In L. F. Luce & E. C. Smith (Eds.), *Towards internationalism: Readings in cross-cultural communication* (2nd ed., pp. 36–48). New York: Newbury House.

Rubin, J. (1975). What the "good language learner" can teach us. *TESOL Quarterly, 9*(1), 41–51.

Rubin, J. (1981). Study of cognitive processes in second language learning. *Applied Linguistics, 11*(2), 118–131.
Rubin, J. (1985). *The Language Learning Disc.* Descriptive pamphlet, Joan Rubin Associates, Berkeley, CA.
Rubin, J. (1986). *The Language Learning Disc.* Paper presented at SALT conference.
Rubin, J. (1987a). Learner strategies: Theoretical assumptions, research, history, and typology. In A. Wenden & J. Rubin (Eds.), *Learner strategies in language learning* (pp. 15–30). Englewood Cliffs, NJ: Prentice-Hall.
Rubin, J. (1987b). Videodisc teaches language learning skills. FL News, *Foreign Language Annals, 20*(3), 275.
Rubin, J. (1989). The Language Learning Disc. In W. F. Smith (Ed.), *Modern technology in foreign language education* (pp. 269–275). Lincolnwood, IL: National Textbook.
Rubin, J., & Thompson, I. (1982). *How to be a more successful language learner.* Boston: Heinle & Heinle.
Russo, R. P., & Stewner-Manzanares, G. (1985). *The training and use of learning strategies for English as a second language in a military context.* Rosslyn, VA: InterAmerica Research Associates.
Savignon, S. J. (1972). *Communicative competence: An experiment in foreign language teaching.* Philadelphia: Center for Curriculum Development.
Savignon, S. J. (1983). *Communicative competence: Theory and practice.* Reading, MA: Addison-Wesley.
Schleppegrell, M., & Oxford, R. (1988). *Language learning strategies for Peace Corps volunteers.* Washington, DC: Center for Applied Linguistics.
Schumann, F. E., and Schumann, J. N. (1977). Diary of a language learner: An introspective study of second language learning. In H. D. Brown, C. A. Yorio, & R. Crymes (Eds.), *On TESOL '77: Teaching and learning ESL.* Washington, DC: TESOL.
Seliger, H. W. (1983). Learner interaction in the classroom and its effect on language acquisition. In H. W. Seliger & M. H. Long (Eds.), *Classroom-oriented research in second language acquisition.* Rowley, MA: Newbury House.
Selinker, L. (1972). Interlanguage. *International Review of Applied Linguistics, 10*(3), 201–231.
Selinker, L. (1981). Updating the interlanguage hypothesis. *Studies in Language Acquisition, 3*(2), 201–228.
Semke, H. D. (1984). Effects of the red pen. *Foreign Language Annals, 17*(3), 195–202.
Sharan, S., Kussell, R., Hertz-Lazarowitz, R., Bejarano, Y., Raviv, S., & Sharan, Y. (1985). Cooperative learning effects on ethnic relations and achievement on Israeli junior-high-school classrooms. In R. Slavin, S. Sharan, S. Kagan, R. Hertz-Lazarowitz, C. Webb, & R. Schmuck (Eds.), *Learning to cooperate, cooperating to learn* (pp. 313–343). New York: Plenum.
Shephard, R. N. (1967). Recognition memory for words, sentences, and pictures. *Journal of Verbal Learning and Verbal Behavior, 6,* 156–163.
Shipman, S., & Shipman, V. C. (1985). Cognitive styles: Some conceptual, methodological, and applied issues. *Review of Research in Education* (Vol. 12, pp. 229–291). Washington, DC: American Educational Research Association.
Slavin, R. (1983). *Cooperative learning.* New York: Longman.

Spack, R., & Sadow, C. (1983). Student-teacher working journals in ESL freshman composition. *TESOL Quarterly, 17*(4), 575–594.

Spolsky, B. (1969). Attitudinal aspects of learning. *Language Learning, 19*, 271–283.

Staton, J. (1980). Writing and counseling: Using a dialogue journal. *Language Arts, 57*(5), 514–518.

Staton, J. (1983). Dialogue journals: A new tool for teaching communication. *ERIC/CLL News Bulletin, 6*, 1–2, 6.

Staton, J. (1987). New research on dialogue journals. *Dialogue, IV*(1), 1–24.

Staton, J., Shuy, R., & Kreeft, J. (1982). *Analysis of dialogue journal writing as a communicative event* (Vol. 1) (Final report to the National Institute of Education). Washington, DC: Center for Applied Linguistics.

Stern, H. W. (1983). *Fundamental concepts in language teaching*. Oxford: Oxford University Press.

Stevick, E. W. (1976). *Memory, meaning, and method: Some psychological perspectives on language learning*. Rowley, MA: Newbury House.

Stewner-Manzanares, G., Chamot, A. U., Küpper, L., & Russo, R. P. (1984). *A teacher's guide for using learning strategies in English as a second language instruction*. Rosslyn, VA: InterAmerica Research Associates.

Stewner-Manzanares, G., Chamot, A. U., O'Malley, J. M., Küpper, L., & Russo, R. P. (1985). *Learning strategies in English as a second language instruction: A teacher's guide*. Rosslyn, VA: InterAmerica Research Associates.

Strasheim, L. A. (1988). *Getting around in a German-speaking city: Testing the Indiana level one listening competence*. Indianapolis: Center for School Improvement and Performance.

Tarone, E. (1977). Conscious communication strategies in interlanguage: A progress report. In H. D. Brown, C. A. Yorio, & R. Crymes (Eds.), *On TESOL '77: Teaching and learning ESL* (pp. 194–203). Washington, DC: TESOL.

Tarone, E. (1980). Communication strategies, foreigner talk, and repair in interlanguage. *Language Learning, 30*(2), 417–31.

Tarone, E. (1983). Some thoughts on the notion of "communication strategy." In C. Faerch & G. Kasper (Eds.), *Strategies in interlanguage communication* (pp. 61–74). London: Longman.

Tarone, E., Cohen, A. D., & Dumas, G. (1983). A closer look at some interlanguage terminology: A framework for communication strategies. In C. Faerch & G. Kasper (Eds.) *Strategies in interlanguage communication*. London: Longman.

Tesser, A., & Campbell, J. (1982). *Self-evaluation maintenance processes and individual differences in self-esteem*. Paper presented at the annual meeting of the American Psychological Association, Washington, DC.

Thompson, J. (1987). Memory in language learning. In A. Wenden & J. Rubin (Eds.), *Learner strategies in language learning* (pp. 43–56). Englewood Cliffs, NJ: Prentice-Hall.

Tucker, G. R., Hamayan, E., & Genesee, F. H. (1976). Affective, cognitive, and social factors in second language acquisition. *Canadian Modern Language Review/La Revue Canadienne des Langues Vivantes, 32*, 214–226.

Tulving, E. (1985). How many memory systems are there? *American Psychologist, 40*(4), 385–398.

Tyacke, M., & Mendelsohn, D. (1986). Student needs: Cognitive as well as communicative. *TESOL Canada Journal*, Special Issue 1, 171–183.

Ur, P. (1984). *Teaching listening comprehension.* Cambridge: Cambridge University Press.

URSS: Le plus ancien des "refuseniks" Vladimir Slepak a quitté Moscou pour Israel. *Le Monde*, Octobre 27, 1987, p. 48.

Van Lancker, D. (1987). Old familiar voices. *Psychology Today, 21*(11), 12–13.

Weinstein, C. E., Goetz, E. T., & Alexander, P. A. (Eds.) (1988). *Learning and study strategies: Issues in assessment, instruction, and evaluation.* New York: Academic Press.

Weinstein, C. E., & Underwood, V. L. (1985). Learning strategies: The how of learning. In J. Segal, S. Chipman, & R. Glaser (Eds.), *Relating instruction to basic research* (pp. 241–259). Hillsdale, NJ: Erlbaum.

Weltens, B. (1986). The attrition of foreign-language skills: A literature review. *Applied Linguistics, 8*(1), 22–36.

Wenden, A. L. (1985a). Facilitating learning competence: Perspectives on an expanded role for second-language teachers. *Canadian Modern Language Review/ La Revue Canadienne des Langues Vivantes, 41*(16), 981–990.

Wenden, A. L. (1985b). Learner strategies. *TESOL Newsletter, 19*(5), 1–7.

Wenden, A. L. (1986a). Helping language learners think about learning. *ELT Journal, 40*(1), 3–12.

Wenden, A. L. (1986b). What do second-language learners know about their language learning? A second look at retrospective accounts. *Applied Linguistics, 7*(2), 186–205.

Wenden, A. L. (1987). Conceptual background and utility. In A. Wenden & J. Rubin (Eds.), *Learner strategies in language learning* (pp. 3–13). Englewood Cliffs, NJ: Prentice-Hall.

Wenden, A. L., & Rubin, J. (Eds.). (1987). *Learner strategies in language learning.* Englewood Cliffs, NJ: Prentice-Hall.

Wesche, M. B. (1983). Communicative testing in a second language. *Modern Language Journal, 67*(1), 43–55.

White, R. H. (1959). Motivation reconsidered. *Psychology Review, 66*(5), 297–333.

Widdowson, H. G. (1978). *Teaching language as communication.* Oxford: Oxford University Press.

Withrow, J. (1987). *Effective writing: Writing skills for intermediate students of American English.* Cambridge: Cambridge University Press.

Wong, R. (1987). *Teaching pronunciation: Focus on English rhythm and intonation.* Englewood Cliffs, NJ: Prentice-Hall.

Wong Fillmore, L. W. (1985). Second language learning in children: A proposed model. *Issues in English language development.* Rosslyn, VA: National Clearinghouse on Bilingual Education.

Wright, A. (1987). *How to improve your mind.* Cambridge: Cambridge University Press.

Wright, T. (1987). *Roles of teachers and learners.* Oxford: Oxford University Press.

Appendix A

General Instructions to Administrators of the Strategy Inventory for Language Learning (SILL)

Important—Please Read Carefully

List and Explanation of Student Materials

1. Each student will receive:
   a. Directions and Items.
   b. Worksheet for Scoring and Administering the SILL (1 sheet). For the convenience of the students, do not staple the Worksheet directly to the Directions and Items; keep it as a separate page. However, give the Worksheet to students at the same time as Directions and Items.
   c. Profile of Results on the SILL. *The Profile should not be given to students until they have completed the Worksheet! This is very important.* If students receive the Profile at the same time as they receive Directions, Items, and Worksheet, bias can be introduced into the results. Students might be tempted to respond in what they think is a "socially desirable" way, given the descriptions on the Profile. To avoid this situation, simply distribute the Profile sheets when it appears that most students have completed their Worksheets.
   d. Background Questionnaire (Optional). See below.
2. Be sure to read carefully all the student materials listed above, so that you will be familiar with them and be able to answer any questions students might have.

Time Requirements

1. Allow approximately 30 minutes for students to complete the SILL (longer for beginning ESL or EFL students), plus about 15–20 minutes for them to

fill out the Worksheet and the Profile. Times will vary with the students' age, maturity, and familiarity with completing questionnaires.

2. If your class periods are an hour long, you might want to use one period for students to complete the Worksheet and the Profile, and part or all of another class period for a discussion of the Profiles and of language learning strategies in general.

Advance Preparation

1. It is helpful to give students a little advance notice, perhaps 1 to 3 days ahead, that they will be taking the SILL on a certain day. Explain (in your own words) that the SILL is designed to help students understand better how they learn a new language and that the information helps them become better learners.
2. In addition, you might stimulate interest by asking students to be thinking about and noticing the things they do to learn a new language; this is not required but might be useful.
3. Make the needed copies of student materials.
4. Gather a few extra pens or pencils.
5. (Optional) Gather a few hand calculators to speed up the scoring when students use their Worksheets. However, the calculations are fairly simple; most students can easily do them without calculators, as previous administrations of the SILL have demonstrated.

The Confidentiality/Anonymity Question

1. In most SILL research in the past, we have asked students to complete the SILL using their own names, i.e., not anonymously. This method is simple and allows you to use the results to help individual students improve their strategies. Assure students that the *results for each student will not be publicly posted or shared with other students, will not be compared with the results of any other individual student, will not be used for grading or for any negative purpose, and will be used only to help them become better learners*; then you are likely to have no problems.
2. However, if you feel that your students might require anonymity in order to be candid, you can assign each student a code number to be used in place of the name. They will need to use the *same code number consistently on the Worksheet and the Profile* (and on the optional Background Questionnaire, if used).

What to Do When Administering the SILL

1. Just before handing out the SILL Directions, Items, and Worksheet, make sure that everyone has a pen or pencil. Then provide the following general overview aloud, preferably in your own words:

The Strategy Inventory for Language Learning (SILL) is designed to assess how you go about learning a language. Most students who have taken the SILL have found it interesting and fun. Each item represents a particular kind of language learning behavior. The results will help you know more about yourself as a language learner, and it will help me [or, "your teacher"] to help you learn more effectively.

So that you will get your SILL results quickly, you will score your own SILL and complete your own Profile. Taking the SILL will probably raise a number of interesting issues for you about language learning. We will have plenty of time to discuss these issues after you have completed the SILL.

Respond to the items in terms of what you typically do to learn the language you are now studying [or if not studying a language now, what you did to learn the language you most recently studied]. Remember there are no right or wrong answers. Your SILL results will be kept in complete confidence and will not affect your grade or anyone's opinion about you.

2. Now distribute the Directions, Items, and Worksheet.
3. Tell students to write their own name (or a code number) at the top of the Worksheet. See confidentiality/anonymity discussion above. Remind students to use the same name or number on the Profile, which they will receive later (and on the Background Questionnaire, if used).
4. Ask students to read the Directions sheet silently and then raise their hands if they have any questions about the Directions. ESL students might need some help with understanding, depending on their level of proficiency.
5. As students take the SILL, they write down their answers on the Worksheet. Then they calculate their averages on the same Worksheet following the detailed directions given there. You may allow use of hand calculators to speed up the arithmetic, although they are in no way essential (as noted earlier).
6. When it appears that most students have finished the Worksheet, it is time to distribute the Profile. (Do not distribute the Profile earlier; see above.) The Profile is self-explanatory in terms of how it should be completed. Students should complete the Profile as soon as they have finished the Worksheet.
7. (Optional) Have students graph their results if desired. Many students like to see their results in a graphic form, in which comparisons of frequencies of strategy types are easy to understand.
8. (Optional) If you do not have time to discuss the Profiles in the same class period when the SILL is administered, it might be advantageous to take up the Profiles, along with all the rest of the SILL materials, so that nothing gets lost.

Discussing the Results

1. Make sure each student has his or her own completed Profile. This is essential.
2. Remind students that there are no right or wrong answers.
3. Discuss in general the meaning of each of the categories of language learning behaviors (strategies). Rather than going through the categories one by one

in a boring way, it is best if you *ask students to suggest their favorite categories and describe which strategies they like to use in those categories.* Encourage students to ask questions about categories or specific strategies they do not fully understand.

4. Explain that the higher a student's *average for a given SILL category,* the more frequently the student uses that particular category of language learning strategies. The higher a student's *overall SILL average across all categories,* the more frequently the student uses language learning strategies in general.
5. To get a good discussion going, you might want to raise three or four of the following questions. (Or make up your own!)
   a. *Which language strategies do you think people use the most and why?*
   b. *Which kinds of strategies do you think are the most effective in general for most people?*
   c. *Which kinds of language learning strategies might help you personally become a better language learner?*
   d. *Are there some new language learning strategies in the SILL which you have not considered before and which you might like to try in the next few weeks or months?*
   e. *How do you think your own motivation for language learning might be related to the kinds of language learning strategies you choose?*
   f. *Which kinds of language learning strategies do you think are useful for different kinds of people (e.g., younger, older; in school, out of school; in a new country, in their own country; people who learn best by hearing, by sight, or by touch/movement; people who like to analyze vs. people who like to get an overall impression; impulsive vs. reflective people)?*
   g. *Is it possible that males and females have contrasting patterns of using language learning strategies? What might those patterns be?*
   h. *How might people from various nationalities or cultural backgrounds use different kinds of language learning strategies?*
   i. *In what ways would people who have different reasons for language learning (e.g., travel, job, academic advancement, pleasure) use contrasting strategies for learning a new language?*
   j. *How might different languages affect the choice of learning strategies?*

   During the discussion, do not overwhelm students with research findings; in the discussion, students should be encouraged to provide most of the input and come to their own conclusions as much as possible. *Use research information as background for yourself—or bring it up from time to time as part of the discussion only if students are interested.*
6. Remind students that *people learn languages differently, and no single formula is right for everybody.* BUT: *There may be some strategies that are generally useful in most circumstances,* such as actively seeking practice opportunities, practicing the language in authentic situations, using all possible clues to guess meanings, asking questions, paying attention. It is best to let the students themselves identify any generally useful strategies as part of the discussion.
7. Do not compare one student's results with another student's results in front of the whole group. If students want to compare results with each other on their own or if they volunteer their findings, that's OK, as long as they

refrain from judging their results on the basis of those of others. (You might want to divide students into small groups to compare their results. These groups might be based on ethnicity or cultural background.)

8. (Optional) You might want to collect the Profiles temporarily so as to figure out class averages for each of the categories and for the overall SILL. This can be helpful information for planning any strategy training. If you share the class averages with the students, *be careful how you handle this information*. Some students might feel that if they do not fit the class averages they are doing something wrong, and this might not be the case at all!
9. (Optional but very useful) You might use the discussion of SILL results as a bridge to actual strategy training. It's usually best to integrate strategy training with regular language learning activities. Design strategy training based on what you know from the SILL about the learning strategies the students are already using (or not using).

(Optional) Using the Background Questionnaire

1. The Background Questionnaire (see below) is included as an optional feature. It has been used in SILL research studies to provide additional inforation on student characteristics. This information helps teachers and students better understand the SILL results in context.
2. You might revise the Background Questionnaire or invent one of your own. If you already know the answers to some of the questions—i.e., if age or mother tongue are the same for all your students—then delete such questions as irrelevant. The wording might need to be simplified for ESL students.
3. The Background Questionnaire takes about 10 minutes and can be administered just before the SILL or at another time. It is preferable not to administer it just after the SILL.

BACKGROUND QUESTIONNAIRE

1. Name ____________________ 2. Date ____________________
3. Age ______ 4. Sex ______ 5. Mother tongue ____________________
6. Language(s) you speak at home ____________________
7. Language you are now learning (or have most recently learned) List one language only

   ____
8. How long have you been studying the language listed in #7?

   ____
9. How do you rate your overall proficiency in the language listed in #7 as compared with the proficiency of *other students in your class*? (Circle one)

   Excellent Good Fair Poor
10. How do you rate your overall proficiency in the language listed in #7 as compared with the proficiency of *native speakers of the language*? (Circle one)

    Excellent Good Fair Poor
11. How important is it for you to become proficient in the language listed in #7? (Circle one)

    Very important Important Not so important
12. Why do you want to learn the language listed in #7? (Check all that apply)

    ______ interested in the language

    ______ interested in the culture

    ______ have friends who speak the language

    ______ required to take a language course to graduate

    ______ need it for my future career

    ______ need it for travel

    ______ other (list): ____

    ____
13. Do you enjoy language learning? (Circle one) Yes No
14. What other languages have you studied?

    ____
15. What has been your favorite experience in language learning?

    ____

    ____

    ____

Appendix **B**

Strategy Inventory for Language Learning (SILL)

Version for English Speakers Learning a New Language

Strategy Inventory for Language Learning (SILL)

Version 5.1

Directions

The STRATEGY INVENTORY FOR LANGUAGE LEARNING (SILL) is designed to gather information about how you, as a student of a foreign or second language, go about learning that language. On the following pages, you will find statements related to learning a new language. Please read each statement. On the separate answer sheet, mark the response (1, 2, 3, 4, or 5) that tells how true the statement is in terms of what you actually do when you are learning the new language.

1. Never or almost never true of me
2. Generally not true of me
3. Somewhat true of me
4. Generally true of me
5. Always or almost always true of me

Never or almost never true of me means that the statement is very rarely true of you ; that is, you do the behavior which is described in the statement only in very rare instances.
Generally not true of me means that the statement is usually not true of you; that is, you do the behavior which is described in the statement less than half the time, but more than in very rare instances.
Somewhat true of me means that the statement is true of you about half the time; that is, sometimes you do the behavior which is described in the statement, and sometimes you don't, and these instances tend to occur with about equal frequency.
Generally true of me means that the statement is usually true of you; that is, you do the behavior which is described in the statement more than half the time.
Almost or never true of me means that the statement is true of you in almost all circumstances; that is, you almost always do the behavior which is described in the statement.

Use the separate Worksheet for recording your answers and for scoring. Answer in terms of how well the statement describes you, not in terms of what you think you should do, or what other people do. Answer in reference to the language you are now learning (or the language you most recently learned). There are no right or wrong responses to these statements. Work carefully but quickly. You will score the SILL yourself using the attached Worksheet. On the Worksheet, write your name, the date, and the language learned.

EXAMPLE

1. Never or almost never true of me
2. Generally not true of me
3. Somewhat true of me
4. Generally true of me
5. Always or almost always true of me

Read the item, and choose a response (1 through 5 as above), and write it in the space after the item.

I actively seek out opportunities to talk with native speakers of the new language. __________

You have just completed the example item. Answer the rest of the items on the Worksheet.

Strategy Inventory for Language Learning

Version 5.1

1. Never or almost never true of me
2. Generally not true of me
3. Somewhat true of me
4. Generally true of me
5. Always or almost always true of me

(Write answers on Worksheet)

Part A

When learning a new word . . .

1. I create associations between new material and what I already know.
2. I put the new word in a sentence so I can remember it.
3. I place the new word in a group with other words that are similar in some way (for example, words related to clothing, or feminine nouns).
4. I associate the sound of the new word with the sound of a familiar word.
5. I use rhyming to remember it.
6. I remember the word by making a clear mental image of it or by drawing a picture.
7. I visualize the spelling of the new word in my mind.
8. I use a combination of sounds and images to remember the new word.
9. I list all the other words I know that are related to the new word and draw lines to show relationships.
10. I remember where the new word is located on the page, or where I first saw or heard it.
11. I use flashcards with the new word on one side and the definition or other information on the other.
12. I physically act out the new word.

When learning new material . . .

13. I review often.

14. I schedule my reviewing so that the review sessions are initially close together in time and gradually become more widely spread apart.

15. I go back to refresh my memory of things I learned much earlier.

1. Never or almost never true of me
2. Generally not true of me
3. Somewhat true of me
4. Generally true of me
5. Always or almost always true of me

(Write answers on Worksheet)

Part B

16. I say or write new expressions repeatedly to practice them.

17. I imitate the way native speakers talk.

18. I read a story or dialogue several times until I can understand it.

19. I revise what I write in the new language to improve my writing.

20. I practice the sounds or alphabet of the new language.

21. I use idioms or other routines in the new language.

22. I use familiar words in different combinations to make new sentences.

23. I initiate conversations in the new language.

24. I watch TV shows or movies or listen to the radio in the new language.

25. I try to think in the new language.

26. I attend and participate in out-of-class events where the new language is spoken.

27. I read for pleasure in the new language.

28. I write personal notes, messages, letters, or reports in the new language.

29. I skim the reading passage first to get the main idea, then I go back and read it more carefully.

30. I seek specific details in what I hear or read.

31. I use reference materials such as glossaries or dictionaries to help me use the new language.

32. I take notes in class in the new language.

33. I make summaries of new language material.

34. I apply general rules to new situations when using the language.

35. I find the meaning of a word by dividing the word into parts which I understand.

36. I look for similarities and contrasts between the new language and my own.

37. I try to understand what I have heard or read without translating it word-for-word into my own language.

38. I am cautious about transferring words or concepts directly from my language to the new language.

39. I look for patterns in the new language.

1. Never or almost never true of me
2. Generally not true of me
3. Somewhat true of me
4. Generally true of me
5. Always or almost always true of me

(Write answers on Worksheet)

40. I develop my own understanding of how the language works, even if sometimes I have to revise my understanding based on new information.

Part C

41. When I do not understand all the words I read or hear, I guess the general meaning by using any clue I can find, for example, clues from the context or situation.
42. I read without looking up every unfamiliar word.
43. In a conversation I anticipate what the other person is going to say based on what has been said so far.
44. If I am speaking and cannot think of the right expression, I use gestures or switch back to my own language momentarily.
45. I ask the other person to tell me the right word if I cannot think of it in a conversation.
46. When I cannot think of the correct expression to say or write, I find a different way to express the idea; for example, I use a synonym or describe the idea.
47. I make up new words if I do not know the right ones.
48. I direct the conversation to a topic for which I know the words.

Part D

49. I preview the language lesson to get a general idea of what it is about, how it is organized, and how it relates to what I already know.
50. When someone is speaking the new language, I try to concentrate on what the person is saying and put unrelated topics out of my mind.
51. I decide in advance to pay special attention to specific language aspects; for example, I focus the way native speakers pronounce certain sounds.
52. I try to find out all I can about how to be a better language learner by reading books or articles, or by talking with others about how to learn.
53. I arrange my schedule to study and practice the new language consistently, not just when there is the pressure of a test.
54. I arrange my physical environment to promote learning; for instance, I find a quiet, comfortable place to review.
55. I organize my language notebook to record important language information.
56. I plan my goals for language learning, for instance, how proficient I want to become or how I might want to use the language in the long run.

1. Never or almost never true of me
2. Generally not true of me
3. Somewhat true of me
4. Generally true of me
5. Always or almost always true of me

(Write answers on Worksheet)

57. I plan what I am going to accomplish in language learning each day or each week.

58. I prepare for an upcoming language task (such as giving a talk in the new language) by by considering the nature of the task, what I have to know, and my current language skills.

59. I clearly identify the purpose of the language activity; for instance, in a listening task I might need to listen for the general idea or for specific facts.

60. I take responsibility for finding opportunities to practice the new language.

61. I actively look for people with whom I can speak the new language.

62. I try to notice my language errors and find out the reasons for them.

63. I learn from my mistakes in using the new language.

64. I evaluate the general progress I have made in learning the language.

Part E

65. I try to relax whenever I feel anxious about using the new language.

66. I make encouraging statements to myself so that I will continue to try hard and do my best in language learning.

67. I actively encourage myself to take wise risks in language learning, such as guessing meanings or trying to speak, even though I might make some mistakes.

68. I give myself a tangible reward when I have done something well in my language learning.

69. I pay attention to physical signs of stress that might affect my language learning.

70. I keep a private diary or journal where I write my feelings about language learning.

71. I talk to someone I trust about my attitudes and feelings concerning the language learning process.

Part F

72. If I do not understand, I ask the speaker to slow down, repeat, or clarify what was said.

73. I ask other people to verify that I have understood or said something correctly.

74. I ask other people to correct my pronunciation.

75. I work with other language learners to practice, review, or share information.

76. I have a regular language learning partner.

1. Never or almost never true of me
2. Generally not true of me
3. Somewhat true of me
4. Generally true of me
5. Always or almost always true of me

(Write answers on Worksheet)

77. When I am talking with a native speaker, I try to let him or her know when I need help.

78. In conversation with others in the new language, I ask questions in order to be as involved as possible and to show I am interested.

79. I try to learn about the culture of the place where the new language is spoken.

80. I pay close attention to the thoughts and feelings of other people with whom I interact in the new language.

Your Name ______________________________ Date ______________

Language Learned Now or Most Recently ______________________________

Worksheet for Answering and Scoring

the Strategy Inventory for Language Learning (SILL)

Version 5.1 (c) R. Oxford, 1989

1. Write your response to each item (that is, write 1, 2, 3, 4, or 5) in each of the blanks, which are numbered to correspond to each item on the SILL.

2. Total each column and put the result on the line marked "SUM".

3. Divide by the number under "SUM" to provide an average for each column. Round this average off to the nearest tenth, as in 3.4. Because the only possible response for a SILL item is 1, 2, 3, 4, or 5, your average across items for each part of the SILL should be between 1.0 and 5.0. You can make sure your fiiguring is correct by checking whether your average for each part is within the range of 1.0 to 5.0.

4. Calculate your overall average. To do this, add up all the SUMS for the different parts of the SILL. This will give you the total raw score. Divide by 80, the number of items on the SILL. This will give you the overall average, which should be within the range of 1.0 and 5.0.

5. When you have completed this Worksheet, your teacher will give you the Profile of results on the Strategy Inventory for Language Learning (SILL). Transfer your averages (for each part and for the whole SILL) from the Worksheet to the Profile in order to obtain an interpretation of your SILL results.

SILL Worksheet (continued)

Version 5.1

Part A	Part B	Part C	Part D	Part E	Part F	Whole SILL
1. ____	16. ____	41. ____	49. ____	65. ____	72. ____	SUM Part A ____
2. ____	17. ____	42. ____	50. ____	66. ____	73. ____	SUM Part B ____
3. ____	18. ____	43. ____	51. ____	67. ____	74. ____	SUM Part C ____
4. ____	19. ____	44. ____	52. ____	68. ____	75. ____	SUM Part D ____
5. ____	20. ____	45. ____	53. ____	69. ____	76. ____	SUM Part E ____
6. ____	21. ____	46. ____	54. ____	70. ____	77. ____	SUM Part F ____
7. ____	22. ____	47. ____	55. ____	71. ____	78. ____	
8. ____	23. ____	48. ____	56. ____		79. ____	
9. ____	24. ____		57. ____		80. ____	
10. ____	25. ____		58. ____			
11. ____	26. ____		59. ____			
12. ____	27. ____		60. ____			
13. ____	28. ____		61. ____			
14. ____	29. ____		62. ____			
15. ____	30. ____		63. ____			
	31. ____		64. ____			
	32. ____					
	33. ____					
	34. ____					
	35. ____					
	36. ____					
	37. ____					
	38. ____					
	39. ____					
	40. ____					
SUM ____	SUM ____	SUM ____	SUM ____	SUM ____	SUM ____	SUM ____
÷ 15 = ____	÷ 25 = ____	÷ 8 = ____	÷ 16 = ____	÷ 7 = ____	÷ 9 = ____	÷ 80 = ____ (OVERALL AVERAGE)

Your Name ____________________ Date ______________

Language Learned Now or Most Recently ______________________

Profile of Results on the Strategy Inventory for Language Learning (SILL)

Version 5.1

You will be given this Profile after you have completed the Worksheet for Answering and Scoring the Strategy Inventory for Language Learning (SILL). This Profile will summarize your results on SILL and show the kinds of strategies you use in learning a new language. Please note that there are no right or wrong answers and no "best" average scores for each part, since people learn languages differently.

To complete this Profile, transfer your averages for each part of the SILL, and for the whole SILL, from the Worksheet.

Part	What Strategies Are Covered	Your Average on This Part
A.	Remembering More Effectively: Grouping; making associations; placing new words into a context to remember them; using imagery, sounds, sound-and-image combinations, actions, etc. in order to remember new expressions; reviewing in a structured way; going back to review earlier material.	______
B.	Using Your Mental Processes: Repeating; practicing with sounds and writing systems; using formulas and patterns; recombining familiar items in new ways; practicing the new language in a variety of authentic situations involving the four skills (listening, reading, speaking, and writing); skimming and scanning to get the idea quickly; using reference resources; taking notes; summarizing; reasoning deductively (applying general rules); analyzing expressions; analyzing contrastively via comparisons with another language; being cautious about word-for-word translating and direct transfers from another language; looking for language patterns; adjusting your understanding according to new information.	______
C.	Compensating for Missing Knowledge: Using all possible clues to guess the meaning of what is heard or read in the new language; trying to understand the overall meaning and not necessarily every single word; finding ways to get the message across in speaking or writing despite limited knowledge of the new language; for instance, using gestures, switching to your own language momentarily, using a synonym or description, coining new words.	______
D.	Organizing and Evaluating Your Learning: Overviewing and linking with material you already know; deciding in general to pay attention; deciding to pay attention to specific details; finding out how language learning works; arranging to learn (schedule, environment, notebook); setting goals and objectives; identifying the purpose of a language task; planning for a language task; finding practice opportunities; noticing and learning from your errors; evaluating your progress.	______
E.	Managing Your Emotions: Lowering your anxiety; encouraging yourself through positive statements; taking risks wisely; rewarding yourself; noting physical stress; keeping a language learning diary; talking with someone about your feelings/attitudes.	______
F.	Learning with Others: Asking questions for clarification or verification; asking for correction; cooperating with peers; cooperating with proficient users of the new language; developing cultural awareness; becoming aware of others' thoughts and feelings.	______

YOUR OVERALL AVERAGE ______

Version 5.1

Key to Understanding Your Averages

High	Always or almost always used	4.5 to 5.0
	Generally used	3.5 to 4.4
Medium	Sometimes used	2.5 to 3.4
Low	Generally not used	1.5 to 2.4
	Never or almost never used	1.0 to 1.4

Graph Your Averages Here

If you want, you can make a graph of your SILL averages. What does this graph tell you? Are you very high or very low on any part?

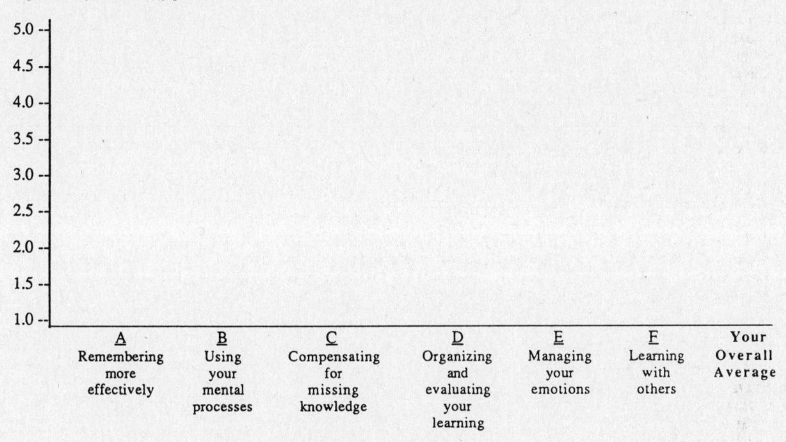

What These Averages Mean to You

The overall average indicates how frequently you use language learning strategies in general. The averages for each part of the SILL show which groups of strategies you tend to use the most in learning a new language. You might find that the averages for each part of the SILL are more useful than your overall average.

Optimal use of language learning strategies depends on your age, personality, stage of language learning, purpose for learning the language, previous experience, and other factors. Nevertheless, there may be some language learning strategies that you are not yet using which might be beneficial to you. Ask your teacher for more information on language learning strategies.

Appendix C

Strategy Inventory for Language Learning (SILL)

Version for Speakers of Other Languages Learning English

Strategy Inventory for Language Learning (SILL)

Version 7.0 (ESL/EFL)
(c) R. Oxford, 1989

Directions

This form of the STRATEGY INVENTORY FOR LANGUAGE LEARNING (SILL) is for students of English as a second or foreign language. You will find statements about learning English. Please read each statement. On the separate Worksheet, write the response (1, 2, 3, 4, or 5) that tells HOW TRUE OF YOU THE STATEMENT IS.

1. Never or almost never true of me
2. Usually not true of me
3. Somewhat true of me
4. Usually true of me
5. Always or almost always true of me

NEVER OR ALMOST NEVER TRUE OF ME means that the statement is very rarely true of you.

USUALLY NOT TRUE OF ME means that the statement is true less than half the time.

SOMEWHAT TRUE OF ME means that the statement is true of you about half the time.

USUALLY TRUE OF ME means that the statement is true more than half the time.

ALWAYS OR ALMOST ALWAYS TRUE OF ME means that the statement is true of you almost always.

Answer in terms of how well the statement describes you. Do not answer how you think you should be, or what other people do. There are no right or wrong answers to these statements. Put your answers on the separate Worksheet. Please make no marks on the items. Work as quickly as you can without being careless. This usually takes about 20-30 minutes to complete. If you have any questions, let the teacher know immediately.

EXAMPLE

1. Never or almost never true of me
2. Usually not true of me
3. Somewhat true of me
4. Usually true of me
5. Always or almost always true of me

Read the item, and choose a response (1 through 5 as above), and write it in the space after the item.

I actively seek out opportunities to talk with native speakers of English. ________

You have just completed the example item. Answer the rest of the items on the Worksheet.

Strategy Inventory for Language Learning

Version 7.0 (ESL/EFL)

(c) R. Oxford, 1989

1. Never or almost never true of me
2. Usually not true of me
3. Somewhat true of me
4. Usually true of me
5. Always or almost always true of me

(Write answers on Worksheet)

<u>Part A</u>

1. I think of relationships between what I already know and new things I learn in English.
2. I use new English words in a sentence so I can remember them.
3. I connect the sound of a new English word and an image or picture of the word to help me remember the word.
4. I remember a new English word by making a mental picture of a situation in which the word might be used.
5. I use rhymes to remember new English words.
6. I use flashcards to remember new English words.
7. I physically act out new English words.
8. I review English lessons often.
9. I remember new English words or phrases by remembering their location on the page, on the board, or on a street sign.

Part B

10. I say or write new English words several times.
11. I try to talk like native English speakers.
12. I practice the sounds of English.
13. I use the English words I know in different ways.
14. I start conversations in English.
15. I watch English language TV shows spoken in English or go to movies spoken in English.
16. I read for pleasure in English.
17. I write notes, messages, letters, or reports in English.
18. I first skim an English passage (read over the passage quickly) then go back and read carefully.

1. Never or almost never true of me
2. Usually not true of me
3. Somewhat true of me
4. Usually true of me
5. Always or almost always true of me

(Write answers on Worksheet)

19. I look for words in my own language that are similar to new words in English.
20. I try to find patterns in English.
21. I find the meaning of an English word by dividing it into parts that I understand.
22. I try not to translate word-for-word.
23. I make summaries of information that I hear or read in English.

Part C

24. To understand unfamiliar English words, I make guesses.
25. When I can't think of a word during a conversation in English, I use gestures.
26. I make up new words if I do not know the right ones in English.
27. I read English without looking up every new word.
28. I try to guess what the other person will say next in English.
29. If I can't think of an English word, I use a word or phrase that means the same thing.

Part D

30. I try to find as many ways as I can to use my English.
31. I notice my English mistakes and use that information to help me do better.
32. I pay attention when someone is speaking English.
33. I try to find out how to be a better learner of English.

34. I plan my schedule so I will have enough time to study English.

35. I look for people I can talk to in English.

36. I look for opportunities to read as much as possible in English.

37. I have clear goals for improving my English skills.

38. I think about my progress in learning English.

1. Never or almost never true of me
2. Usually not true of me
3. Somewhat true of me
4. Usually true of me
5. Always or almost always true of me

(Write answers on Worksheet)

Part E

39. I try to relax whenever I feel afraid of using English.

40. I encourage myself to speak English even when I am afraid of making a mistake.

41. I give myself a reward or treat when I do well in English.

42. I notice if I am tense or nervous when I am studying or using English.

43. I write down my feelings in a language learning diary.

44. I talk to someone else about how I feel when I am learning English.

Part F

45. If I do not understand something in English, I ask the other person to slow down or say it again.

46. I ask English speakers to correct me when I talk.

47. I practice English with other students.

48. I ask for help from English speakers.

49. I ask questions in English.

50. I try to learn about the culture of English speakers.

Your Name ______________________________ Date ______________

<u>Worksheet for Answering and Scoring</u>

<u>the Strategy Inventory for Language Learning (SILL)</u>

Version 7.0 (ESL/EFL)

1. The blanks (______) are numbered for each item on the SILL.

2. Write your response to each item (that is, write 1, 2, 3, 4, or 5) in each of the blanks.

3. Add up each column. Put the result on the line marked SUM.

4. Divide by the number under SUM to get the average for each column. Round this average off to the nearest tenth, as in 3.4.

5. Figure out your overall average. To do this, add up all the SUMS for the different parts of the SILL. Then divide by 50.

6. When you have finished, your teacher will give you the Profile of Results. Copy your averages (for each part and for the whole SILL) from the Worksheet to the Profile.

SILL Worksheet (continued)

Version 7.0 (ESL/EFL)

Part A	Part B	Part C	Part D	Part E	Part F	Whole SILL
1. _____	10. _____	24. _____	30. _____	39. _____	45. _____	SUM Part A _____
2. _____	11. _____	25. _____	31. _____	40. _____	46. _____	SUM Part B _____
3. _____	12. _____	26. _____	32. _____	41. _____	47. _____	SUM Part C _____
4. _____	13. _____	27. _____	33. _____	42. _____	48. _____	SUM Part D _____
5. _____	14. _____	28. _____	34. _____	43. _____	49. _____	SUM Part E _____
6. _____	15. _____	29. _____	35. _____	44. _____	50. _____	SUM Part F _____
7. _____	16. _____		36. _____			
8. _____	17. _____		37. _____			
9. _____	18. _____		38. _____			
	19. _____					
	20. _____					
	21. _____					
	22. _____					
	23. _____					
SUM _____	SUM _____	SUM _____	SUM _____	SUM _____	SUM _____	SUM _____
÷ 9 = _____	÷ 14 = _____	÷ 6 = _____	÷ 9 = _____	÷ 6 = _____	÷ 6 = _____	÷ 50 = _____ (OVERALL AVERAGE)

Your Name ________________________________ Date ________________

Profile of Results on the Strategy Inventory for Language Learning (SILL)

Version 7.0

You will receive this Profile after you have completed the Worksheet. This Profile will show your SILL results. These results will tell you the kinds of strategies you use in learning English. There are no right or wrong answers.

To complete this profile, transfer your averages for each part of the SILL, and your overall average for the whole SILL. These averages are found on the Worksheet.

Part	What Strategies Are Covered	Your Average on This Part
A.	Remembering more effectively	________
B.	Using all your mental processes	________
C.	Compensating for missing knowledge	________
D.	Organizing and evaluating your learning	________
E.	Managing your emotions	________
F.	Learning with others	________
YOUR OVERALL AVERAGE		________

SILL Profile of Results (continued)

Version 7.0

Key to Understanding Your Averages

High	Always or almost always used	4.5 to 5.0
	Usually used	3.5.to 4.4
Medium	Sometimes used	2.5 to 3.4
Low	Generally not used	1.5 to 2.4
	Never or almost never used	1.0 to 1.4

Graph Your Averages Here

If you want, you can make a graph of your SILL averages. What does this graph tell you? Are you very high or very low on any part?

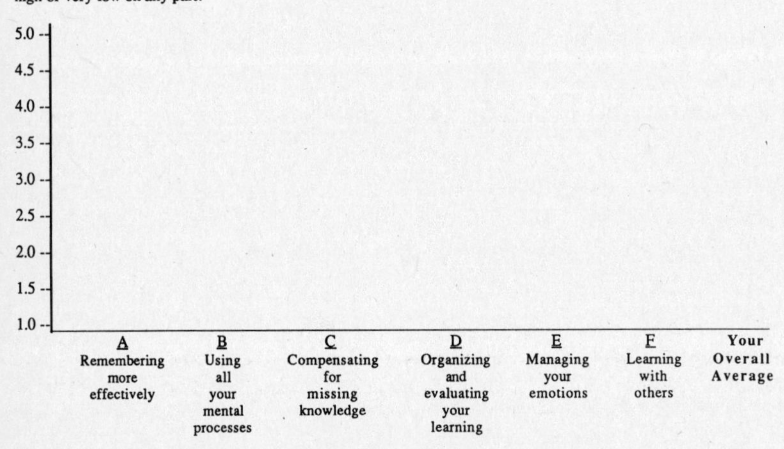

What These Averages Mean to You

The overall average tells how often you use strategies for learning English. Each part of the SILL represents a group of learning strategies. The averages for each part of the SILL show which groups of strategies you use the most for learning English.

The best use of strategies depends on your age, personality, and purpose for learning. If you have a very low average on one or more parts of the SILL, there may be some new strategies in these groups that you might want to use. Ask your teacher about these.

Appendix D

Sources of Quotations

Preface

John L. Taylor's speech at SIMULTEC '87, Geneva, Switzerland, September 1987, suggested three lines of this verse; I added the other two (a more receptive ear, a more fluent tongue).

Chapter 1

Strevens, P. (1982). In P. S. Green, Review of H. B. Altman and C. W. James (Eds.). (1980), *Foreign language teaching: Meeting individual needs* (Oxford: Pergamon). *System 10*(3), 291.

Chapter 2

Eliot, T. S. (1970). East Coker, *Four quartets* (pp. 30–31). London: Faber & Faber.
DeQuincey, T. (1955). *Confessions of an English opium-eater*, Pt. I. In D. C. Brownling, (Ed.), *Everyman's dictionary of quotations and proverbs* (p. 93). London: Readers' Union, J. M. Dent.
Shakespeare, W. (1987). *Hamlet*, I, v, 137. In S. Wells & G. Taylor, (Eds.), *The complete Oxford Shakespeare, Vol. III: The tragedies*. London: Guild Publishing.
16th-century proverb, in Brownling, p. 487; also Bloomsbury, p. 280.

Chapter 3

Russian proverb, *Newsweek*, June 6, 1988, p. 17.
Eliot, T. S. (1970). Little Gidding, *Four quartets* (pp. 55). London: Faber & Faber.
John 1:1. (1987). *Holy Bible: New International Version*. London: Hodder & Stoughton.
Sullivan, A. Speech, July 1894. In Bloomsbury, p. 339.

Activity 3.1 in Chapter 3

Carroll, L. *Through the Looking-Glass* (chap. 4). In Bloomsbury, p. 93.

Burke, E. (1984). *Letters*. In N. Ewart, *The writer and the reader: A book of literary quotations* (p. 17). Poole, Dorset, England: Blandford.

Stevenson, R. L. (1882). *Talk and talkers*. In R. T. Tripp (Ed.). (1979), *The international thesaurus of quotations* (p. 608). Harmondsworth, Middlesex, England: Penguin.

Prick up your ears. Movie title. From J. Lahr (1987), *Prick up your ears: A biography of Joe Orton*. Harmondsworth, Middlesex, England: Penguin.

Pope, A. *Essay on criticism*. In Brownling, p. 242.

Phillips, J. (1986, September 17). Foreign language reading: Process, practice, and proficiency. Talk at the Foreign Service Institute, Arlington, VA.

Shakespeare, W. *Julius Caesar*, III, ii, 74. In Wells & Taylor.

Tennyson, A., Lord. (1967). Morte d'Arthur. In G. B. Harrison, *A book of English poetry* (p. 371). Harmondsworth, Middlesex, England: Penguin.

Shakespeare, W. *Hamlet*, II, ii, 193–194. In Wells & Taylor.

Edison, T. A. Newspaper interview. In Brownling, p. 108.

Allen, W. (1987). Quoted in A. Wright, *How to improve your mind* (p. x). Cambridge: Cambridge University Press.

Byron, G. G., Lord. *Hints from Horace*. In Ewart, p. 32.

Whitehorn, K. Attrib. In Bloomsbury, p. 375.

Maugham, S. (1978). In W. A. Auden & L. Kronenberger, *The Faber book of aphorisms* (p. 277). London: Faber & Faber.

Chapter 4

Adams, H. (1907). *The education of Henry Adams*, p. 21. In Tripp, p. 347.

Pope, A. *An essay on man*, Epistle i, 1. In Brownling, p. 245.

Milton, J. (1951). *Paradise Lost*, Book I. In A. M. Witherspoon, (Ed.). *The college survey of English literature* (shorter ed., rev., p. 387). New York: Harcourt Brace & World.

Botkin, J. W., et al. (1979). *No limits to learning*. Oxford: Pergamon. In R. M. Smith (1985), *Learning how to learn: Applied theory for adults* (p. 106). Milton Keynes: Open University Press.

Chapter 5

Buck, P. S. (1967). *To my daughters with love*. In Tripp, p. 449.

Aesop, "Hercules and the waggoner," *Fables*. In Bloomsbury, p. 3.

Lord Chesterfield (1979). In Tripp, p. 177.

Dumas, A. (1952). *The three musketeers* (trans. Lord Sudley). Harmondsworth, Middlesex, England: Penguin.

Chapter 6

Rogers, C. R. (1969). *Freedom to learn: A view of what education might become.* Columbus, OH: C. E. Merrill.

Epilogue

Browning, R. (1967). Rabbi Ben Ezra. In Harrison, p. 380.

Appendix E

How to Find Activities for Readers

Each chapter contains activities for you, the reader, to do by yourself or with others. This table provides information which will help you find the readers' activities most relevant for your needs and circumstances. Note that the activities are numbered according to the chapter. For instance, activities in Chapter 1 are numbered 1.1, 1.2, and so on.

NUMBER	NAME	PURPOSE	PAGES
1.1	Brainstorm the Features of Learning Strategies	Obtain an overview of key features.	22
1.2	Place Strategies on the Learning-Acquisition Continuum	Discover how the six strategy groups relate to learning and acquisition.	23
1.3	Consider Degrees of Learner Responsibility	Check your own values on how much responsibility learners should have.	23
1.4	Discuss Teacher Roles	Assess the possible roles teachers might take; again, a values activity.	23–24
1.5	Consider Your Own Strategy Use	Describe your own past use of strategies for learning.	24
2.1	Check Your Attitudes Toward Memory Strategies	Assess your beliefs about mnemonics.	51

NUMBER	NAME	PURPOSE	PAGES
2.2	Examine Memory Strategies in Different Settings	Discover how memory strategies can be used in learning and acquisition.	51
2.3	Think About Language Loss	Consider how memory strategies might have prevented language loss.	51
2.4	Consider the Nature of Practicing	Compare more realistic vs. less realistic practicing.	52
2.5	Work with Skimming and Scanning	Assess your own use of two important reading strategies, skimming and scanning.	52
2.6	Find Resources	List possible student resources.	52
2.7	List the Pros and Cons of Analyzing/ Reasoning	Assess ways that analyzing/reasoning can aid or hinder proficiency.	52
2.8	Consider the Need for Structure	List typical uses of structuring strategies in daily life and in language learning.	52
2.9	Notice Students' Compensatory Speaking Strategies	List students' use of compensation strategies in speech and prioritize by frequency.	52–53
2.10	Consider Learning and Communication	Explain your feelings about how learning might take place through communication.	53

NUMBER	NAME	PURPOSE	PAGES
3.1	You Can Quote Me on That!	List skills and strategies related to a series of quotations; an entertaining way to understand direct strategies.	98–99
3.2	Remark on Remembering	Give examples of functions of memory strategies related to four language skills.	100
3.3	Cogitate About Cognitive Strategies	List observed cognitive strategies and identify skills.	100
3.4	Accentuate the Positive	Brainstorm the utility of compensation strategies.	100
3.5	Stalk the Strategies	Study the students' exercises and indicate the strategies involved.	100
4.1	Consider a Difficult Subject	Consider your own metacognitive and affective control over a difficult subject.	148
4.2	Experiment with Metacognitive and Affective Strategies	Try out new strategies for yourself and see the results.	148
4.3	Ask Questions	Consider your own questioning style.	148–149
4.4	Judge Your Empathy	Assess your degree of empathy and how it affects your language ability.	149
4.5	Weigh Competitiveness and Cooperation	Study your own tendencies toward competitiveness and cooperation.	149

NUMBER	NAME	PURPOSE	PAGES
5.1	Examine Indirect Strategies in the Four Skills	List indirect strategies and determine how they relate to the four language skills.	174, including Table 5.1
5.2	Consider Your Use of the Indirect Strategies	Rate your use of these strategies when you were a language student.	174
5.3	Ponder the Purposes of Writing and Speaking	List writing and speaking formats and determine the purposes.	175
6.1	Think of Reasons for Assessing Strategy Use	Brainstorm reasons for strategy assessment.	209–210
6.2	Consider the Strategy Assessment Options	Complete a table about strategy assessment possibilities.	210, including Table 6.3
6.3	Assess Your Own Strategies	Use an assessment technique from the chapter to check your own strategy use.	210
6.4	Go Fishing	Consider two contrasting positions on strategy training.	211
6.5	Design a Strategy Training Sequence	Use the chapter to design a strategy training sequence for your students.	211
7.1	Assess the Relevance of Examples for Your Own Setting	Consider the real-life strategy use examples in the chapter and their utility to you.	232
7.2	Follow Up on Your Three Favorite Examples	Contact three strategy experts.	232

NUMBER	NAME	PURPOSE	PAGES
7.3	Take a Closer Look at Explicit Training Examples	Answer questions about explicit strategy training techniques.	233
7.4	Take a Closer Look at Implicit Strategy Encouragement	Answer questions about implicit strategy encouragement without explicit training.	233

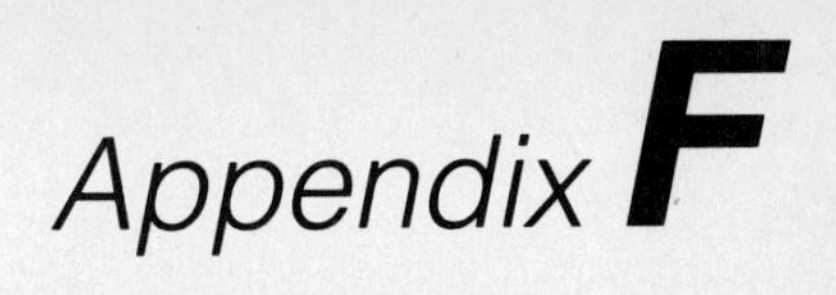

How to Find Exercises to Use with Your Students

Each chapter contains exercises for you to use with your students. The number and type of exercises are geared to the content of each chapter. Some chapters, notably the ones which focus on applications of strategies (such as Chapters 3 and 5), contain a great number of exercises; other chapters intentionally have fewer exercises.

This table provides information which will help you find the exercises most relevant for your students' needs and circumstances. Note that the exercises are numbered according to the chapter. For instance, exercises in Chapter 1 are numbered 1.1, 1.2, and so on.

NUMBER	NAME	PURPOSE	PAGES
1.1	Embedded Strategies Game	Become acquainted with language learning strategies and see how they are embedded in certain activities.	24–30
1.2	Strategy Search Game	Determine how strategies relate to a set of sometimes complex language learning or acquisition tasks/ situations.	30–35
2.1	Ask Students to Identify Their Memory Strategies	Consider kinds of memory strategies used and keep a running list.	53
2.2	Get the Message	Practice a variety of strategies for understanding an oral message using film, cartoon, or program.	53–54

NUMBER	NAME	PURPOSE	PAGES
2.3	Play Twenty Questions	Practice guessing using a familiar game.	54–55
2.4	Hold a Conversation	Consider kinds of strategies used in a conversation.	55
3.1	Memory Practice	Distribute or space memory practice using several memory strategies.	101
3.2	Grouping and Labeling	Discover the value of grouping and labeling while learning vocabulary.	101–103
3.3	Make Your Own Groups	Create new word groups and determine criteria for these groups.	103–104
3.4	Find the Odd Word	Extend grouping exercises by finding the word that does not fit.	104–105
3.5	Yes/No Game	Improve sound perception and discrimination.	105–106
3.6	Finding Your Way	Mark a map route according to spoken directions using combined strategies.	106–107, Fig. 3.12 on 107, Fig. 3.13 on 108
3.7	Physical Response	Listen and physically move.	107–109
3.8	Jigsaw Listening	Listen to different extracts and then, with other people, collate them to understand the whole situation.	109–110, Table 3.1 on 109
3.9	Guessing the Meaning of a Reading Passage	Guess meaning and explain how the guesses were made.	110–112

NUMBER	NAME	PURPOSE	PAGES
3.10	Guessing with Pictures	Guess meaning via pictures.	112, Fig. 3.14 on 113
3.11	Scanning a Reading Passage for Personal Facts	Scan for particular information.	112, 114
3.12	Skimming a Reading Passage for the Main Idea	Skim a passage to locate the central theme.	114–115
3.13	Inventions	Practice naturalistically and use information to complete a diagram.	115–117, Fig. 3.15 on 116
3.14	Jigsaw Reading	Put together pieces of a written text using guessing strategies and other strategies.	117–121, Fig. 3.16 on 119, Fig. 3.17 on 120
3.15	Alibi	Use strategies in a suspenseful, communicative situation.	121–122
3.16	What We Have in Common	Communicate about personally important information using strategies.	123
3.17	What's My Line?	Guess and practice naturalistically in an entertaining format.	123–124
3.18	Picture Stories	Create stories using pictures and a variety of memory strategies and compensation strategies.	124–126
3.19	Crystal Ball	Develop prediction/ guessing skills using reading.	126–127
3.20	Protest	Make guesses from context and write meaningfully about an incident.	127–129

NUMBER	NAME	PURPOSE	PAGES
3.21	Interviews	Use a range of strategies in classroom interviews and in a subsequent write-up.	129–130
3.22	Sending a Telegram	Use cognitive and compensation strategies in a meaningful situation.	130–132, Fig. 3.18 on 131
3.23	Doctor Appointment	Use metacognitive, comprehension, and other strategies to plan for and carry out a multiskill task.	132–133
4.1	Listen to Self-Talk	List positive and negative statements students make about themselves as language learners.	149
4.2	Let Students Consider Cooperation and Competition	Use a cooperative learning activity as a springboard to student discussion of cooperation and competition.	150
4.3	Try Out Indirect Strategies	Experiment with a range of indirect strategies and assess results.	150
5.1	Make a Weekly Schedule	Produce a general schedule useful for each week.	175–177, including Table 5.2 on 176
5.2	Create a Language Learning Notebook	Create a notebook that contains sections for different aspects of language learning.	177–178
5.3	Set Your Goals and Objectives	Establish aims for language learning.	178–180, including Table 5.3 on 179–180

NUMBER	NAME	PURPOSE	PAGES
5.4	Opportunity Knocks!	Consider possibilities for practicing the new language.	180–181, including Table 5.4 on 181
5.5	Gauge Your Skill Progress	Assess progress in language learning skill by skill.	182–183, including Table 5.5 on 182–183
5.6	Relaxing	Use relaxation strategies in order to deal with language learning.	183–184
5.7	Calm Down Through Meditation and Music	Use these two strategies to relax for better language learning.	185
5.8	Praise Be!	Praise yourself for good work using affirmations.	185–187
5.9	Assess Your Emotions	Use an emotional checklist for language learning.	187–189, including Table 5.6 on 188–189
5.10	Stress Check	Use a stress checklist, consider causes of stress, and try to reduce unnecessary stress.	189–190, including Table 5.7 on 190
5.11	Keep a Diary	Record feelings about language learning.	190–191
6.1	Assess Your Students' Strategies	Assess students' strategies using at least two techniques.	211–212
6.3	Implement Strategy Training	Implement a strategy training sequence or program.	212
6.4	Develop a "Successful Strategies" Handbook	Develop a student handbook of the most successful strategies.	212
6.5	Discuss Diaries	Hold regular diary discussions about language learning.	212

Appendix G

Strategy Applications Listed According to Each of the Four Language Skills

This table helps you locate definitions and explanations of strategies useful for each of the four skills. The activities and exercises in this book give a wide variety of strategy applications for you to explore after you have read the definitions and explanations indexed below. You may also discover additional strategies that help develop proficiency in the four language skills.

STRATEGIES USEFUL FOR LISTENING

STRATEGY GROUP	STRATEGY SET	STRATEGY	PAGE
Memory	Creating mental linkages	Grouping	40, 58–60
Memory	Creating mental linkages	Associating/ elaborating	41, 60
Memory	Creating mental linkages	Placing new words into a context	41, 60–61, 68
Memory	Applying images and sounds	Using imagery	41, 61
Memory	Applying images and sounds	Semantic mapping	41, 61–62, Fig. 3.3 on 63, Fig. 3.4 on 64, Fig. 3.5 on 65
Memory	Applying images and sounds	Using keywords	41–42, 62–63, 68
Memory	Applying images and sounds	Representing sounds in memory	42, 63–64

STRATEGY GROUP	STRATEGY SET	STRATEGY	PAGE
Memory	Reviewing well	Structured reviewing	42, 66, Fig. 3.6 on 67
Memory	Employing action	Using physical response or sensation	43, 66
Memory	Employing action	Using mechanical techniques	43, 68
Cognitive	Practicing	Repeating	45, 70–71
Cognitive	Practicing	Formally practicing with sounds and writing systems	45, 71–72
Cognitive	Practicing	Recognizing and using formulas and patterns	45, 72–74
Cognitive	Praticing	Practicing naturalistically	45, 74–79
Cognitive	Receiving and sending messages	Getting the idea quickly	46, 80–81
Cognitive	Receiving and sending messages	Using resources for receiving and sending messages	46, 81–82
Cognitive	Analyzing and reasoning	Reasoning deductively	46, 82–83
Cognitive	Analyzing and reasoning	Analyzing expressions	46, 83
Cognitive	Analyzing and reasoning	Analyzing contrastively (across languages)	46, 83–84
Cognitive	Analyzing and reasoning	Translating	46, 84–85
Cognitive	Analyzing and reasoning	Transferring	47, 85–86
Cognitive	Creating structure for input and output	Taking notes	47, 86–88, Fig. 3.9 on 88, Fig. 3.10 on 89
Cognitive	Creating structure for input and output	Summarizing	47, 88–89

STRATEGY GROUP	STRATEGY SET	STRATEGY	PAGE
Cognitive	Creating structure for input and output	Highlighting	47, 89–90
Compensation	Guessing intelligently	Using linguistic clues	49, 90–91
Compensation	Guessing intelligently	Using other clues	49, 92–94
Metacognitive	Centering your learning	Overviewing and linking with already known material	138, 152–154
Metacognitive	Centering your learning	Paying attention	138, 154–155
Metacognitive	Centering your learning	Delaying speech production to focus on listening	138, 155–156
Metacognitive	Arranging and planning your learning	Finding out about language learning	139, 156
Metacognitive	Arranging and planning your learning	Organizing	139, 156
Metacognitive	Arranging and planning your learning	Setting goals and objectives	139, 157–158
Metacognitive	Arranging and planning your learning	Identifying the purpose of a language task	139, 158–159
Metacognitive	Arranging and planning your learning	Planning for a language task	139, 159–160
Metacognitive	Arranging and planning your learning	Seeking practice opportunities	139, 160
Metacognitive	Evaluating your learning	Self-monitoring	140, 161–162
Metacognitive	Evaluating your learning	Self-evaluating	140, 162–163
Affective	Lowering your anxiety	Using progressive relaxation, deep breathing, or meditation	143, 164

STRATEGY GROUP	STRATEGY SET	STRATEGY	PAGE
Affective	Lowering your anxiety	Using music	143, 164
Affective	Lowering your anxiety	Using laughter	143, 164–165
Affective	Encouraging yourself	Making positive statements	143, 165–166
Affective	Encouraging yourself	Taking risks wisely	144, 166
Affective	Encouraging yourself	Rewarding yourself	144, 166
Affective	Taking your emotional temperature	Listening to your body	144, 167
Affective	Taking your emotional temperature	Using a checklist	144, 167
Affective	Taking your emotional temperature	Writing a language learning diary	144, 167–168
Affective	Taking your emotional temperature	Discussing your feelings with someone else	144, 168
Social	Asking questions	Asking for clarification and verification	146–147, 169–170
Social	Cooperating with others	Cooperating with peers	147, 171
Social	Cooperating with others	Cooperating with proficient users of the new language	147, 171–172
Social	Empathizing with others	Developing cultural understanding	147, 172–173
Social	Empathizing with others	Becoming aware of others' thoughts and feelings	147, 173

STRATEGIES USEFUL FOR READING

STRATEGY GROUP	STRATEGY SET	STRATEGY	PAGE
Memory	Creating mental linkages	Grouping	40, 58–60
Memory	Creating mental linkages	Associating/ elaborating	41, 60
Memory	Creating mental linkages	Placing new words into a context	41, 60–61
Memory	Applying images and sounds	Using imagery	41, 61
Memory	Applying images and sounds	Semantic mapping	41, 61, 62, Fig. 3.3 on 63, Fig. 3.4 on 64, Fig. 3.5 on 65
Memory	Applying images and sounds	Using keywords	41–42, 62–63
Memory	Applying images and sounds	Representing sounds in memory	42, 63–64
Memory	Reviewing well	Structured reviewing	42, 66, Fig. 3.6 on 67
Memory	Employing action	Using physical response or sensation	43, 66
Memory	Employing action	Using mechanical techniques	43, 68
Cognitive	Practicing	Repeating	45, 70–71
Cognitive	Practicing	Recognizing and using formulas and patterns	45, 72–74
Cognitive	Practicing	Practicing naturalistically	45, 74–79
Cognitive	Receiving and sending messages	Getting the idea quickly	46, 80–81
Cognitive	Receiving and sending messages	Using resources for receiving and sending messages	46, 81–82
Cognitive	Analyzing and reasoning	Reasoning deductively	46, 82–83

STRATEGY GROUP	STRATEGY SET	STRATEGY	PAGE
Cognitive	Analyzing and reasoning	Analyzing expressions	46, 83
Cognitive	Analyzing and reasoning	Analyzing contrastively (across languages)	46, 83–84
Cognitive	Analyzing and reasoning	Translating	47, 84–85
Cognitive	Analyzing and reasoning	Transferring	47, 85–86
Cognitive	Creating structure for input and output	Taking notes	47, 86–88, Fig. 3.9 on 88, Fig. 3.10 on 89
Cognitive	Creating structure for input and output	Summarizing	47, 88–89
Cognitive	Creating structure for input and output	Highlighting	47, 89–90
Compensation	Guessing intelligently	Using linguistic clues	49, 90–91
Compensation	Guessing intelligently	Using other clues	49, 92–94
Metacognitive	Centering your learning	Overviewing and linking with already known material	138, 152–154
Metacognitive	Centering your learning	Paying attention	138, 154–155
Metacognitive	Arranging and planning your learning	Finding out about language learning	139, 156
Metacognitive	Arranging and planning your learning	Organizing	139, 156
Metacognitive	Arranging and planning your learning	Setting goals and objectives	139, 157–158
Metacognitive	Arranging and planning your learning	Identifying the purpose of a language task	139, 158–159

STRATEGY GROUP	STRATEGY SET	STRATEGY	PAGE
Metacognitive	Arranging and planning your learning	Planning for a language task	139, 159–160
Metacognitive	Arranging and planning your learning	Seeking practice opportunities	139, 160
Metacognitive	Evaluating your learning	Self-monitoring	140, 161–162
Metacognitive	Evaluating your learning	Self-evaluating	140, 162–163
Affective	Lowering your anxiety	Using progressive relaxation, deep breathing, or meditation	143, 164
Affective	Lowering your anxiety	Using music	143, 164
Affective	Lowering your anxiety	Using laughter	143, 164–165
Affective	Encouraging yourself	Making positive statements	143, 165–166
Affective	Encouraging yourself	Taking risks wisely	144, 166
Affective	Encouraging yourself	Rewarding yourself	144, 166
Affective	Taking your emotional temperature	Listening to your body	144, 167
Affective	Taking your emotional temperature	Using a checklist	144, 167
Affective	Taking your emotional temperature	Writing a language learning diary	144, 167–168
Affective	Taking your emotional temperature	Discussing your feelings with someone else	144, 168
Social	Asking questions	Asking for clarification and verification	146–147, 169–170
Social	Cooperating with others	Cooperating with peers	147, 171

STRATEGY GROUP	STRATEGY SET	STRATEGY	PAGE
Social	Cooperating with others	Cooperating with proficient users of the new language	147, 171–172
Social	Empathizing with others	Developing cultural understanding	147, 172–173
Social	Empathizing with others	Becoming aware of others' thoughts and feelings	147, 173

STRATEGIES USEFUL FOR SPEAKING

STRATEGY GROUP	STRATEGY SET	STRATEGY	PAGE
Memory	Creating mental linkages	Placing new words into a context	41, 60–61, 68
Memory	Applying images and sounds	Representing sounds in memory	42, 63–64
Memory	Reviewing well	Structured reviewing	42, 66, Fig. 3.6 on 67
Cognitive	Practicing	Repeating	45, 70–71
Cognitive	Practicing	Formally practicing with sounds and writing systems	45, 71–72
Cognitive	Practicing	Recognizing and using formulas and patterns	45, 72–74
Cognitive	Practicing	Recombining	45, 74
Cognitive	Practicing	Practicing naturalistically	45, 74–79
Cognitive	Receiving and sending messages	Using resources for receiving and sending messages	46, 81–82
Cognitive	Analyzing and reasoning	Reasoning deductively	46, 82–83

STRATEGY GROUP	STRATEGY SET	STRATEGY	PAGE
Cognitive	Analyzing and reasoning	Translating	46, 84–85
Cognitive	Analyzing and reasoning	Transferring	47, 85–86
Compensation	Overcoming limitations in speaking and writing	Switching to the mother tongue	50, 94–95
Compensation	Overcoming limitations in speaking and writing	Getting help	50, 95
Compensation	Overcoming limitations in speaking and writing	Using mime or gesture	50, 95
Compensation	Overcoming limitations in speaking and writing	Avoiding communication partially or totally	50, 95–96
Compensation	Overcoming limitations in speaking and writing	Selecting the topic	50, 96
Compensation	Overcoming limitations in speaking and writing	Adjusting or approximating the message	50, 96–97
Compensation	Overcoming limitations in speaking and writing	Coining words	50, 97
Compensation	Overcoming limitations in speaking and writing	Using a circumlocution or synonym	51, 97
Metacognitive	Centering your learning	Overviewing and linking with already known material	138, 152–154
Metacognitive	Centering your learning	Paying attention	138, 154–155

STRATEGY GROUP	STRATEGY SET	STRATEGY	PAGE
Metacognitive	Centering your learning	Delaying speech production to focus on listening	138, 155–156
Metacognitive	Arranging and planning your learning	Finding out about language learning	139, 156
Metacognitive	Arranging and planning your learning	Organizing	139, 156
Metacognitive	Arranging and planning your learning	Setting goals and objectives	139, 157–158
Metacognitive	Arranging and planning your learning	Identifying the purpose of a language task	139, 158–159
Metacognitive	Arranging and planning your learning	Planning for a language task	139, 159–160
Metacognitive	Arranging and planning your learning	Seeking practive opportunities	139, 160
Metacognitive	Evaluating your learning	Self-monitoring	140, 161–162
Metacognitive	Evaluating your learning	Self-evaluating	140, 162–163
Affective	Lowering your anxiety	Using progressive relaxation, deep breathing, or meditation	143, 164
Affective	Lowering your anxiety	Using music	143, 164
Affective	Lowering your anxiety	Using laughter	143, 164–165
Affective	Encouraging yourself	Making positive statements	143, 165–166
Affective	Encouraging yourself	Taking risks wisely	144, 166
Affective	Encouraging yourself	Rewarding yourself	144, 166
Affective	Taking your emotional temperature	Listening to your body	144, 167

STRATEGY GROUP	STRATEGY SET	STRATEGY	PAGE
Affective	Taking your emotional temperature	Using a checklist	144, 167
Affective	Taking your emotional temperature	Writing a language learning diary	144, 167–168
Affective	Taking your emotional temperature	Discussing your feelings with someone else	144, 168
Social	Asking questions	Asking for correction	147, 170
Social	Cooperating with others	Cooperating with peers	147, 171
Social	Cooperating with others	Cooperating with proficient users of the new language	147, 171–172
Social	Empathizing with others	Developing cultural understanding	147, 172–173
Social	Empathizing with others	Becoming aware of others' thoughts and feelings	147, 173

STRATEGIES USEFUL FOR WRITING

STRATEGY GROUP	STRATEGY SET	STRATEGY	PAGE
Memory	Creating mental linkages	Placing new words into a context	41, 60–61, 68
Memory	Applying images and sounds	Using keywords	41–42, 68*
Memory	Reviewing well	Structured reviewing	42, 66, Fig. 3.6 on 67
Memory	Employing action	Using mechanical techniques	43, 68

*NOTE: This strategy is mainly for getting information that has been heard or read into the memory. However, p. 68 demonstrates how it can be employed to retrieve the information to use in writing. It can likewise be employed for retrieval in a speaking situation.

STRATEGY GROUP	STRATEGY SET	STRATEGY	PAGE
Cognitive	Practicing	Repeating	45, 70–71
Cognitive	Practicing	Formally practicing with sounds and writing systems	45, 71–72
Cognitive	Practicing	Recognizing and using formulas and patterns	45, 72–74
Cognitive	Practicing	Recombining	45, 74
Cognitive	Practicing	Practicing naturalistically	45, 74–79
Cognitive	Receiving and sending messages	Using resources for receiving and sending messages	46, 81–82
Cognitive	Analyzing and reasoning	Reasoning deductively	46, 82–83
Cognitive	Analyzing and reasoning	Translating	46, 84–85
Cognitive	Analyzing and reasoning	Transferring	47, 85–86
Cognitive	Creating structure for input and output	Taking notes	47, 86–88, Fig. 3.9 on 88, Fig. 3.10 on 89
Cognitive	Creating structure for input and output	Summarizing	47, 88–89
Cognitive	Creating structure for input and output	Highlighting	47, 89–90
Compensation	Overcoming limitations in speaking and writing	Selecting the topic	50, 96
Compensation	Overcoming limitations in speaking and writing	Adjusting or approximating the message	50, 96–97
Compensation	Overcoming limitations in speaking and writing	Coining words	50, 97

STRATEGY GROUP	STRATEGY SET	STRATEGY	PAGE
Compensation	Overcoming limitations in speaking and writing	Using a circumlocution or synonym	51, 97
Metacognitive	Centering your learning	Overviewing and linking with already known material	138, 152–154
Metacognitive	Centering your learning	Paying attention	138, 154–155
Metacognitive	Arranging and planning your learning	Finding out about language learning	139, 156
Metacognitive	Arranging and planning your learning	Organizing	139, 156
Metacognitive	Arranging and planning your learning	Setting goals and objectives	139, 157–158
Metacognitive	Arranging and planning your learning	Identifying the purpose of a language task	139, 158–159
Metacognitive	Arranging and planning your learning	Planning for a language task	139, 159–160
Metacognitive	Arraning and planning your learning	Seeking practice opportunities	139, 160
Metacognitive	Evaluating your learning	Self-monitoring	140, 161–162
Metacognitive	Evaluating your learning	Self-evaluating	140, 162–163
Affective	Lowering your anxiety	Using progressive relaxation, deep breathing, or meditation	143, 164
Affective	Lowering your anxiety	Using music	143, 164
Affective	Lowering your anxiety	Using laughter	143, 164–165
Affective	Encouraging yourself	Making positive statements	143, 165–166

STRATEGY GROUP	STRATEGY SET	STRATEGY	PAGE
Affective	Encouraging yourself	Taking risks wisely	144, 166
Affective	Encouraging yourself	Rewarding yourself	144, 166
Affective	Taking your emotional temperature	Listening to your body	144, 167
Affective	Taking your emotional temperature	Using a checklist	144, 167
Affective	Taking your emotional temperature	Writing a language learning diary	144, 167–168
Affective	Taking your emotional temperature	Discussing your feelings with someone else	144, 168
Social	Asking questions	Asking for correction	147, 170
Social	Cooperating with others	Cooperating with peers	147, 171
Social	Cooperating with others	Cooperating with proficient users of the new language	147, 171–172
Social	Empathizing with others	Developing cultural understanding	147, 172–173
Social	Empathizing with others	Becoming aware of others' thoughts and feelings	147, 173

Index

This index is divided into two parts. The first of these is the Subject Index, which covers the main topics in the book, as well as many important details. Specific games are noted here in capital letters (e.g., TWENTY QUESTIONS, INVENTIONS). In the interest of conserving space, the Subject Index does not list separately every strategy that is mentioned in the book. In the Subject Index only the main *strategy groups* (memory, cognitive, compensation, metacognitive, affective, and social) and the two *strategy classes* (direct and indirect) are shown. When a particular strategy, such as guessing, is brought up in the text, it is clustered with other related strategies under the broad classifications of group (in this case, compensation strategies) and class (in this instance, direct). See Appendix G for a complete cross-indexing of separate strategies (e.g., translating, writing a language learning diary) applied to each of the four language skills.

The second part of this index is the Index of Authors, Researchers, and Teachers. It lists many people whose ideas have helped strengthen the language learning field and who have been cited in this book.

Subject Index

Index of Authors, Researchers, and Teachers Mentioned in This Book

Credits

Activity 1.4: Adaptation from *Roles of Teachers and Learners*, 1987, pp. 52–53, Tony Wright; Oxford University Press, Walton Street, Oxford OX2 6DP, England. **Exercise 3.4:** From *Helping Learners Succeed: Activities for the Foreign Language Classroom*, 1981, p. 27, Alice Omaggio; Center for Applied Linguistics, 118 22nd St. NW, Washington, DC 20008 USA. **Exercise 3.8:** Adapation from *Teaching Listening Comprehension*, 1984, pp. 152–154, Penny Ur; Cambridge University Press, 32 East 57th Street, New York, NY 10022 USA. © Cambridge University Press 1984. Reprinted with the permission of Cambridge University Press. **Exercises 3.11, 3.12:** From "Practical Implications of Recent Research in Reading," *Foreign Language Annals*, 17 (4), 1984, pp. 290–291, June K. Phillips; c/o ACTFL, 6 Executive Blvd., Upper Level, Yonkers, NY 10701 USA. **Exercise 3.13:** From "Comparing Facts and Figures," *Practical English Teaching*, 1984, p. 25, David Crookall; Scholastic Inc., P.O. Box 644, Lyndhurst, NY 07071-0655 USA; Mary Glasgow Publications, Avenue House, 131–133 Holland Park Ave., London W11 4UT, England. **Exercise 3.16:** From *Grammar in Action*, 1983, p. 17, Christine Frank and Mario Rinvolucri; Simon & Schuster, 66 Wood Lane End, Hemel Hempstead, Hertfordshire HP2 4RG. England (for Pergamon Press). **Exercise 3.19:** From "Bridging the Gap Between Learning to Read and Reading to Learn," *Northeast Conference Newsletter*, 20, 1986, pp. 46–47, Sally Hague; Original ReQuest procedure designed by A. Manzo; Northeast Conference on the Teaching of Foreign Languages, P.O. Box 623, Middlebury, VT 05753-0623 USA. **Exercise 3.20:** From *Great Ideas: Listening and Speaking Activities for Students of American English*, 1987, pp. 60–61, L. Jones and V. Kimbrough; Cambridge University Press, 32 East 57th Street, New York, NY 10022 USA. © 1984 Cambridge University Press. Reprinted with the permission of Cambridge University Press. **Exercise 3.22:** *Russian Language and People*, 1986, p. 120, Terry Culhane; BBC Publications, 35 Marlebone High St., London W1M 4AA, England; EMC Publishing, 300 York Ave., St. Paul, MN 55010 USA. **Exercise 3.23:** From *Learning Strategies in ESL Instruction: A Teacher's Guide*, 1985, p. 33, Gloria Stewner-Manzanares, Anna Uhl Chamot, Lisa Kupper, and Rocco Russo; InterAmerica Research Associates, Inc., 7926 Jones Branch Drive, Suite 1100, McLean, VA 22102.

Table 3.1: From: *Teaching Listening Comprehension*, 1984, p. 153, Penny Ur; Cambridge University Press, 32 East 57th Street, New York, NY 10022 USA. © 1984 Cambridge University Press. Reprinted with the permission of Cambridge University Press. **Figure 3.3:** From "Vocabulary Instruction: What L2 Can Learn

From L1," *Foreign Language Annals*, 20 (3), 1987, p. 222, Sally Hague; c/o ACTFL, 6 Executive Blvd., Upper Level, Yonkers, NY 10701 USA. **Figures 3.4, 3.5:** From: *Yes! You Can Learn a Foreign Language*, 1986, pp. 32–33, M. Brown-Azarowicz, C. Stannard, & M. Goldin; NTC Publishing Group, 4255 Touhy Ave., Lincolnwood, IL 60646-1975 USA. **Figures 3.8, 3.9:** From "Review Article: Survey of Materials for Teaching Advanced Listening and Note-taking," by Liz Hamp-Lyons, 1983, *TESOL Quarterly 17* (1) pp. 112, 118. Copyright 1982 by Teachers of English to Speakers of Other Languages. Reprinted by permission. c/o TESOL, 1118-22nd St. NW, Washington, DC 20037 USA. **Figure 3.12:** From *Teaching Listening Comprehension*, 1984, p. 61, Penny Ur; Cambridge University Press, 32 East 57th Street, New York, NY 10022 USA. © Cambridge University Press 1984. Reprinted with the permission of Cambridge University Press. **Figure 3.13:** From "Getting Around in a German-Speaking City: Testing the Indiana Level One Competence," 1988, Lorraine A. Strasheim, Coord. for School Foreign Language Programs, Office of School Programs, Ed. 253, Indiana University, Bloomington, IN 47405, USA. **Figure 3.14:** From *Lexicarry: An Illustrated Vocabulary-Builder for Second Languages*, 1984, rev. 1989, Patrick R. Moran; Pro Lingua Associates, 15 Elm St., Brattleboro, VT 05301 USA. **Figure 3.15:** Adaptation from "Comparing Facts and Figures," *Practical English Teaching*, 1984, p. 25, David Crookall; Scholastic Inc., P.O. Box 644, Lyndhurst, NY 07071-0655 USA; Mary Glasgow Publications, Avenue House, 131–133 Holland Park Ave., London W11 4UT, England. **Figures 3.16, 3.17:** From *Kinder Monatszeitschrift* VIII (3), 1986 and VIII (6) 1986, c/o European Language Institute, P.O. Box 6, 62019 Recanati, Italy. **Figure 3.18:** From *Russian Language and People*, 1986, p. 120, Terry Culhane; BBC Publications, 35 Marlebone High St., London W1M 4AA, England; EMC Publishing, 300 York Ave., St. Paul, MN 55010 USA. **Table 6.1:** Adaptation from "Second Language Reading; A Curricular Sequence for Teaching Reading Strategies," *Foreign Language Annals*, 14 (5), 1981, pp. 415–422, C. Hosenfeld, V. Arnold, J. Kirchofer, J. Laciura, and L. Wilson; c/o ACTFL, 6 Executive Blvd., Upper Level, Yonkers, NY 10701 USA. **Figure 7.1:** From *Self-Instruction in Language Learning*, 1987, p. 62, Leslie Dickinson (author); Leni Dam (model designer); Cambridge University Press, 32 East 57th Street, New York, NY, 10022 USA. © Leslie Dickinson 1987. Reprinted with the permission of Cambridge University Press.

About the Author

Rebecca L. Oxford is currently Associate Professor of language instructional methodology and Russian at the University of Alabama. She is experienced in foreign languages, English as a second language, and bilingual education. She has taught at both secondary and university levels, has directed an intensive English program for international students at the Pennsylvania State University, and has led teacher training workshops throughout the United States and in Europe and Southeast Asia. She has written widely on language learning styles and strategies for professional journals such as *Modern Language Journal*, *Foreign Language Annals*, and *The Journal of Psychological Type* and has written chapters on these topics for a number of books. With David Crookall she co-edited *Language Learning Through Simulation/Gaming*, which will be published by Newbury House. She holds two degrees in Russian (Vanderbilt University and Yale University) and two in educational psychology (Boston University and the University of North Carolina).